THE SPANISH
MISSIONS OF
LA FLORIDA

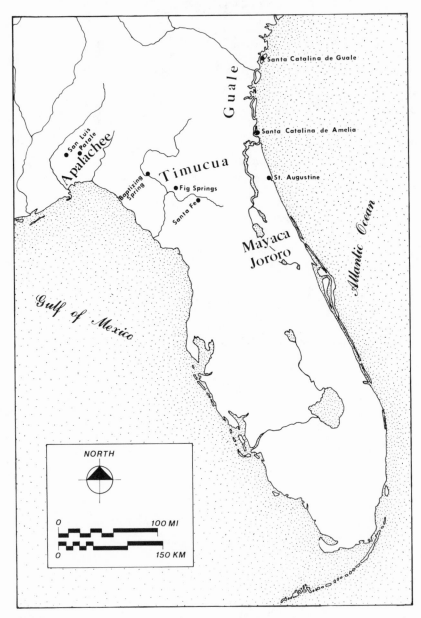

Map of Spanish Florida showing locations of cultural groups, towns, and missions discussed in text.

THE SPANISH
MISSIONS OF
LA FLORIDA

EDITED BY

Bonnie G. McEwan

University Press of Florida

Gainesville · Tallahassee · Tampa · Boca Raton

Pensacola · Orlando · Miami · Jacksonville

Publication of this volume was made possible in part by the Program for Cultural Cooperation between Spain's Ministry of Culture and United States' Universities.

Columbus Quincentenary Series

Library of Congress Cataloging-in-Publication Data

The Spanish missions of La Florida / edited by Bonnie G. McEwan.
p.   cm.
Includes bibliographical references and index.
ISBN 0–8130–1231–7. — ISBN 0–8130–1232–5 (pbk.)
1. Spanish mission buildings—Florida.   2. Florida—Antiquities.
3. Excavations (Archaeology)—Florida.   4. Florida—History—Spanish
colony, 1565–1763.   5. Missions, Spanish—Florida—History.
6. Indians of North America—Florida—Missions.   I. McEwan, Bonnie
G. (Bonnie Gain), 1954–   .
F312.S67   1993   93–7937
975.9′03—dc20   CIP

This book was originally published by the Florida Anthropological Society in its journal *The Florida Anthropologist* 44, 2–4 (1991), as a special issue.

The University Press of Florida is the scholarly publishing agency for the State University System of Florida, comprised of Florida A & M University, Florida Atlantic University, Florida International University, Florida State University, University of Central Florida, University of Florida, University of North Florida, University of South Florida, and University of West Florida.

University Press of Florida
15 Northwest 15th Street
Gainesville, FL 32611

To John W. Griffin,
who has inspired us in countless ways

NOV 1993

CONTENTS

✪

CONTENTS

FIGURES

✪

TABLES

❖

FOREWORD

✷

We are but a mere decade from the three hundredth anniversary of the
end of the Spanish mission system in Florida, yet we are only now beginning to reach a detailed understanding of the century or more of
Spanish and Native American interaction in the mission settlements before their destruction by outside forces. While some scattered studies of
both an archaeological and a documentary nature date back a half century, it is only in the period since 1980 that there has been a pronounced expansion of archaeological research and interpretation by an
active group of scholars, most of whom are represented by the chapters
in this book.

The mission provinces of Apalachee, Timucua, and Guale are treated
herein. These were the areas through which the L-shaped chain of mission
settlements stretched westward and northward from the presidio of St.
Augustine. The time frame involved is basically the seventeenth century,
the period of maximum development and activity. At its height in the
mid-seventeenth century there were 40 missions manned by 70 friars
serving 26,000 Christianized Indians. All of this collapsed, partially
through disastrous introduced diseases and finally through the agency of
neighboring British colonists and their Indian allies.

Most of the chapters in this book are the direct results of field research on mission sites. The authors are grappling with complex problems of the settlement pattern(s) of the mission villages and the search for
the pattern(s) of the church complex within the village. They are concerned with evidences of acculturation and of ethnic, social, and gender
variables as they may be revealed in the archaeological record. They are
examining changes through time in both the European approach to the
Native American and the reactions of the natives to the interlopers. Other
chapters are concerned with the contributions of bioarchaeology, zooarchaeology, and ethnobotany to the developing picture of the subsistence
base and the health of the inhabitants. The breadth and depth of prob-

lems being addressed and the collaboration of specialists in the disciplines just named, as well as the continued excellent cooperation of historians, bode well for the development of our knowledge.

We are finally beginning to understand something about the site plan and architecture of the church complex at the missions, including the fact that at least in much of the time period in question burials were beneath the floor of the churches, not, as originally thought, in cemeteries outside the church. Each excavation yields a little more data on the appearance of the structures of the church complex, which were built of wood and other perishable materials. Only painstaking fieldwork can provide the information even for graphic reconstructions, but the accumulating evidence suggests that substantial carpentry was involved in some of the buildings, in agreement with documentary sources.

Perhaps it is just as well that we in Florida have been denied the highly visible masonry or adobe missions of the western borderlands, because this denial has spared us the often faulty or fanciful restorations and reconstructions of other areas. It is sometimes impossible to separate fact from fiction in the fabric of some of these restored structures, and the records of what was done are often incomplete or lacking. Here in Spanish Florida such errors have only been committed to paper, such as in the often reproduced Spanish mission on the endpapers of Lanning's *Spanish Missions of Georgia*, which was based on the erroneous mission attribution to the ruins of a nineteenth-century sugar mill. One shudders to think of the result had this romantic reconstruction been turned into bricks and mortar. Should actual reconstruction come to our Florida missions, archaeology as presented in these pages will keep it honest.

This book also speaks to the strength of the programs in historical archaeology, and anthropology in general, at the University of Florida and Florida State University. With only a few exceptions, and these mostly in specialized subfields or allied disciplines, the authors are products of one or both of these institutions in the programs established by Hale G. Smith and Charles H. Fairbanks, both pioneers in the development of the archaeology of historic sites.

Given the vast amount of recent work and the resulting expansion of our knowledge of the period, it is highly appropriate that these contributions be presented to a broad readership. If the present rate of research continues, the authors of this collection joined by other colleagues will be able to provide us with another volume by the time we reach the three hundredth anniversary of the destruction of the mission chain in the year 2004.

John W. Griffin
Research Associate
St. Augustine Historical Society

PREFACE

❂

"After the salvation of my soul, there is nothing I desire more than to be in Florida, to end my days saving souls."

Pedro Menéndez de Avilés, 7 September 1574

Motivated by the righteous cause that prevailed during the *Reconquista* of Spain, the spread of Christianity was a critical force in shaping Spanish New World colonization. In many areas of the Americas, missionaries were the cultural emissaries who established relations with native groups and founded far-ranging settlements that constituted the first step toward a Spanish foothold in the hinterlands. In this respect, the work of the church served the purposes of religious zealots, military leaders, and colonists alike by "taming" and converting the Indian element. However, missionization was also a source of dissension among competing factions within Spanish colonial communities, and even more so within native societies whose response to European religious indoctrination varied dramatically.

Shortly after Pedro Menéndez de Avilés founded St. Augustine in 1565, Jesuit missionaries began their attempt to missionize the Indians of *La Florida*. The first decades of Spanish-Indian interaction were generally hostile, and the threat to traditional aboriginal lifeways posed by the missionaries, among other factors, led to the murder of a number of Jesuits by natives. This prompted the Jesuit authorities in Spain to terminate activities in Florida in 1572.

The first Franciscans arrived the following year. However, their missionization efforts did not begin in earnest until 1587, at which time they gradually established missions among the coastal Timucua and Guale Indians. By 1606 the Franciscans began expanding their presence into western Timucua, and by 1633 missions were firmly established across much of north Florida and into Apalachee Province. Missions to the interior were unique in that leading chiefs requested Franciscans during the first decade of the seventeenth century and their religious conversion appears to have been voluntary.

The Florida missions were structured hierarchically and all were eventually brought under the labor *repartimiento*. Prominent mission villages (*doctrinas*) often had a resident friar and a number of satellite villages (*visitas*) under their jurisdiction. Other missions, such as Santa Catalina de Guale on St. Catherines Island and San Luis de Talimali in Apalachee, served as northern and western subcenters of Spanish authority and appear to have been prosperous communities with religious, military, and probably civilian components. It was from these provincial capitals that labor and supplies were usually commandeered for St. Augustine. Thus while the missions served a number of functions, including centers for religious conversion and military activities, their most important role was that of a support system imperative to the maintenance of the colony of *La Florida*.

The mission era of Spanish Florida ended abruptly between 1702 and 1704 after a series of military strikes by the British and their Creek allies. During these devastating raids virtually all of the missions except those confined to the immediate vicinity of St. Augustine were abandoned or destroyed.

This collection of papers originated as a special edition of *The Florida Anthropologist* in order to provide an overview of current mission research. From Guale to Timucua to Apalachee, the papers are organized in a roughly chronological and geographical sequence, with the earliest missions extending northward from St. Augustine and the later ones radiating westward into the Florida panhandle and southward into central Florida (see frontispiece). Of the first eleven papers, all but two are site-specific studies that present detailed data on various aspects of mission complexes. Hann and Deagan have each contributed synthetic treatments of the missions and their impact among the Jororo and Mayaca, and on the town of St. Augustine, respectively. The final five papers are biological and material analyses with implications for mission studies as a whole. They detail patterns of Spanish-Indian interaction through skeletal remains (see also Hoshower and Milanich), subsistence practices, and the manufacture and use of particular artifacts.

These contributions explore the impact of missionization on various native populations, the nature of interaction between different elements of Spanish and Indian society, forms of adaptation and accommodation made by both cultures, and variability within and between mission settlements. Equally important is the ongoing attempt to determine and refine archaeological and historical techniques that effectively address these issues. Taken together, the collection provides an accurate reflection of current trends in mission research in Spanish Florida.

When Mark F. Boyd, Hale G. Smith, and John W. Griffin wrote their seminal treatise *Here They Once Stood: The Tragic End of the Apalachee Missions* more than forty years ago, it synthesized much of what was known about the missions at that time and posed as many provocative questions as it answered. This collection summarizes much of what has been accomplished in mission research in the intervening years and underscores how much we still have to learn.

Acknowledgments

Many individuals and institutions deserve special thanks for making this publication possible. The Florida Anthropological Society initially contacted me about editing a volume on the Florida missions. Louis Tesar and Art Lee of FAS were particularly helpful in seeing the first phase of the project through to completion.

James J. Miller (Florida Bureau of Archaeological Research), Jerald T. Milanich (Florida Museum of Natural History), and Michael V. Gannon (Institute for Early Contact Period Studies, University of Florida) provided a great deal of guidance and institutional support toward the completion of this book. I am also grateful to John H. Hann, Clark Spencer Larsen, and Jeffrey M. Mitchem, who helped with the manuscript in many ways and to Charles B. Poe, who drafted many of the figures. And many thanks to my indefatigable assistant, Jean S. Wilson, who handled much of the word processing—including the arduous task of setting up tables and standardizing references.

Kathleen Deagan was kind enough to make Jill Loucks's manuscript available for publication, and Jerry Milanich provided several footnotes to bring Jill's article up to date in light of additional research at Baptizing Spring.

Finally, I would like to thank all of the contributors whose work on the missions of Spanish Florida has made this area of inquiry extremely productive and rewarding.

Bonnie G. McEwan
San Luis Archaeological and Historic Site

INTRODUCTION

✿

The past decade has witnessed a remarkable flowering of Spanish Florida mission archaeology. In the old domains of *La Florida*, from St. Catherines Island in the north to St. Augustine in the south, from Amelia Island in the east to Tallahassee in the west, historical archaeologists, with historians at their elbows, have been retrieving the remains of a mission system that dotted Florida's shore and hinterland like strands of rosary beads nearly two centuries before the better-known missions of California.

This efflorescence of mission period study did not begin de novo, as a sudden new idea and enterprise. Rather, it took shape in the fullness of time as a natural consequence of the foundations laid long ago by John W. Griffin, Hale G. Smith, John Goggin, Ripley Bullen, B. Calvin Jones, and others. The close working partnership of archaeology and history, which characterizes every one of the recent and current excavations, follows the exemplar established by Griffin and Smith with historian Mark F. Boyd at missions San Francisco de Oconee and San Luis de Talimali in the late 1940s. One remembers the prescient statement made in the very first sentence of their jointly authored book, *Here They Once Stood: The Tragic End of the Apalachee Missions* (Gainesville: University of Florida Press, 1951): "Although history and archaeology are often considered as distinct and unrelated disciplines, they are in fact but different techniques of approaching historical problems."

This present collection brings together most of the principals in the expansion and intensification period of mission studies. David Hurst Thomas reports on his 15-year project at Santa Catalina de Guale (where in 1965 John Griffin, whose name appears frequently in these articles, was the first to establish a search for the mission site as having "the highest priority") and describes the church, yard, cemetery, friary, and kitchen that have been found. Of special interest is Thomas's use of newly available remote sensing technology that not only provides efficient assessment of the archaeological record but is also nondestructive of that record. Rebecca Saunders has worked at the relocated Santa Catalina de Guale and Santa María de Yamassee, missions founded at different periods and for different populations at the Harrison Homestead site on Amelia Island. The site has yielded a large number of human remains, which are under analysis by Clark Spencer Larsen.

Motherhouse for the Franciscan effort in Florida was the Convento de San Francisco in St. Augustine. Kathleen Hoffman traces the several friaries that stood on the site and discusses the artifacts that have yielded to the archaeologist's trowel, noting and explaining the marked absence of sacred objects. Kathleen Deagan, who was the first to investigate the *convento* site, writes here about St. Augustine the town and its relationship to the missions in the frontier. Her interests include competition for Indian trade goods between friars in the hinterland and entrepreneurs at St. Augustine, the use of mission Indians as *cargadores* and as labor in the town, and the rapid decline of Indian populations in the period 1703–1763.

Florida mission historians have never been numerous: in the past 25 years one may name only Robert Matter, David J. Weber, Amy Bushnell, Fred Lamar Pearson, Jr., John Hann, and this writer. Certainly John Hann has made the most original and prolific contributions in recent years, and in this collection he reminds us how far below St. Augustine seventeenth-century mission activity extended, with a careful discussion of the documentary record for missions to the Mayaca and Jororo. The site of Santa Fé de Toloca, long sought by John Goggin, was located and tested in the Robinson Sinks area of northwestern Alachua County by Kenneth W. Johnson, who describes the structures and artifacts he has unearthed at the mission complex. Another area investigated by Goggin is Ichetucknee Springs State Park, where Brent R. Weisman has identified the so-called Fig Springs mission site, which he believes to have been San Martín de Timucua. This well-preserved complex—church, *convento*, cemetery, plaza, and village—has been thoroughly studied thanks to assistance from the Florida Department of Natural Resources, Division of Recreation and Parks. In a separate article Lisa M. Hoshower and Jerald T. Milanich report on osteological and bioanthropological analysis that they conducted in the high-density burial area at Fig Springs.

The late L. Jill Loucks wrote in 1983 about her work at Baptizing Spring in Suwannee County (possibly San Agustín de Urica), and her article, appropriately included here, interprets the information recovered from four probable aboriginal structures and two wattle-and-daub Spanish buildings. The Apalachee site of San Pedro y San Pablo de Patale was first excavated by B. Calvin Jones in 1971. During the period 1984–1992 Rochelle A. Marrinan subjected the site to intensive testing, and she presents here a comprehensive report on the findings of eight field seasons. In her conclusion she explores the fact that, contrary to the regularity of Franciscan designs and structures in the American Southwest, the Florida mission model presents no predictive consistency.

Bonnie G. McEwan, into whose capable hands has come the San Luis de Talimali site in Tallahassee following the untimely death of Gary Shapiro, addresses the unique features of that mission cum garrison which was, during its brief life, the most important Spanish frontier community in the east-west chain. The fact that not only friars and soldiers but also lay civilians inhabited the site provides McEwan with an opportunity to interpret Hispanic frontier life along several demographic lines. In a companion article Jeffrey M. Mitchem reports on the analysis of beads and pendants found at the San Luis site. The number and quality of imported adornment articles from Europe suggests to Mitchem an unanticipated degree of affluence at this part of the frontier that was lacking in St. Augustine itself. According to analyses by Richard Vernon and Ann S. Cordell, colono-ware recovered from San Luis helps explicate the Spanish-Apalachee relationships at the site. Most of these ceramics were locally made, presumably for use by Spaniards.

Mission bioarchaeology, which Clark Spencer Larsen has practiced on mortuary remains at numerous mission sites, has led to some surprising discoveries about the effects on Native American survivorship and health of long-term contact with Europeans and their agricultural-intensive lifeways and diet. Those students of mission culture who thought that settled agricultural life was a good thing for the mission populations, and the more agriculture the better, will be dismayed by Larsen's findings, particularly in Guale. Mission agriculture in Apalachee is the subject of C. Margaret Scarry's contribution to this collection. Plant data from both late prehistoric and postcontact sites constitute her archaeobotanical evidence, which she interpets in the framework of changing life-styles and foodways. Similarly, Elizabeth J. Reitz addresses faunal remains in the mission sites, where animal use differed according to region. Her enumeration of the different meats eaten in the various villages and provinces and her discussion of the relative importance of animal use in the seventeenth century provide valuable new information for the Florida mission data bank.

Certainly this collection of interpretive essays carries Florida mission studies to another level. As an earlier generation of scholars leaned on the pioneer work of Griffin-Smith-Boyd, not forgetting the pioneer historian of the missions, Maynard Geiger, O.F.M., so the work of these contributors establishes a new foundation for the future. I incur no risk whatever in predicting that this collection will be cited well into the next century.

Michael V. Gannon, director
Institute for Early Contact Period Studies
University of Florida

❂ 1 ❂

The Archaeology of Mission Santa Catalina de Guale: Our First 15 Years

DAVID HURST THOMAS

In 1977 the American Museum of Natural History began searching for Mission Santa Catalina de Guale, located somewhere on St. Catherines Island (Georgia). Four years later we found that site and have been excavating the sixteenth- and seventeenth-century archaeological remains ever since. Here we review how we located Santa Catalina, summarize the findings to date, and set out the research framework for additional work. We have learned much, but we caution the reader that despite our 15 years of archaeological investigations, the human story played out at Mission Santa Catalina remains very much a work in progress (see Thomas 1987, 1988a, 1988b).[1]

Ethnohistorical Background

The Guale Indians living at Santa Catalina and elsewhere along the Georgia coast were among the first indigenous peoples met by Europeans exploring north of Mexico (Jones 1978; Larson 1978; Sturtevant 1962; Swanton 1922:81, 1946:603; Thomas 1990). In 1526 the Spanish made brief contact with this Muskhogean-speaking group and the French encountered them in 1562–1563. Then, beginning in 1566, the Guale were exposed to a long, intensive period of Spanish colonization. By 1684 the gradual withdrawal of the Spanish to the south and the correlative southward expansion of the Carolina colony prompted relocation and reorganization of the vastly reduced Guale population.

St. Catherines Island may (or may not) have been an important settlement during the earliest phase of European contact, but there is no doubt that an important Guale town existed there by at least 1576 (Jones 1978:203). Spanish mission efforts were minimal at this point; the year 1584 found only four Franciscan friars stationed throughout all of *La Florida*, and they spent their time ministering to Spanish needs at St. Augustine and Santa Elena, with little time for missionizing the Guale and Timucua.

The Spanish named the Guale Indians for the chiefdom centered at the principal town on St. Catherines Island; the associated Franciscan mission eventually became known as Santa Catalina de Guale. By 1597, a decade after the abandonment of Santa Elena, 14 friars were stationed in *La Florida* and several of these served in Guale (Geiger 1940). That year, the Indians of Guale staged a major revolt partly played out on St. Catherines Island—an uprising with distinctly nativistic overtones (Sturtevant 1962:58).

For a time the missions were abandoned, but after their resettlement in the early seventeenth century (Ross 1926), Spanish hegemony remained unchallenged until 1670, when the English established Charles Town, South Carolina. Spanish missions on the barrier islands of coastal Georgia became the first victims in the so-called conflict over the "debatable land" (Bolton and Ross 1925). After the Spanish launched an unsuccessful expedition to attack and destroy Charles Town, the southernmost British settlement, the British retaliated in force, steadily pushing down the coast and across the interior toward the Mississippi.

In 1680 the British forces attacked the fortified mission at Santa Catalina, which was defended by a small and hastily organized band of Spaniards and Guale Indians (Bolton and Ross 1925:36). Although the Guale successfully held off the invaders, they were horrified by the attack and St. Catherines Island was soon abandoned. British travelers in 1687 and 1738 described the ruins of Santa Catalina (Dunlop 1929:131; Hvidt 1980:39), but the mission site was "lost" soon thereafter.

Previous Attempts to Find Santa Catalina

We were hardly the first to look for Santa Catalina de Guale. Historians and ethnographers have debated the whereabouts of the site of Santa Catalina for decades. Swanton (1922:50–55) thought that the principal town of Guale and its associated mission were initially established on St. Catherines Island in the spring of 1566. A member of our research team, Grant Jones (1978:203), has argued that prior to 1575 the town of Guale was *not* on St. Catherines Island but rather to the north, either near Skidaway Island or on Ossabaw. There was no question, however, that by 1587 both the Guale chiefdom and the associated Franciscan mission existed somewhere on St. Catherines Island (Bolton and Ross 1925; Gannon 1965:39; Jones 1978:204; Lyon 1976:154; Ross 1926).

Such conjecture was then supplemented by hands-on archaeology in the 1950s and 1960s (fig. 1.1). As part of the Georgia Historical Commission search for sixteenth-/seventeenth-century Spanish mission sites along the Georgia coast, Lewis Larson visited St. Catherines Island in 1952. Among the "good candidates for the location of a mission," Larson (1952:2) listed "Wamassee Head on St. Catherines as the location of Santa Catherina de Guale," but he cautioned that "no final and conclusive identification of a mission site can be made until adequate excavation . . . has been undertaken."

Larson returned to excavate at Wamassee Creek six years later. The recovered sherd sample consisted primarily of aboriginal wares dating to the Spanish period, and majolica was found comparable to that from Spanish mission sites in Florida. But no structural evidence of Santa Catalina emerged in these limited tests.

In the mid-1950s the general location of Santa Catalina was "rediscovered" by John W. Bonner and Carrol Hart, who had been retained by Edward John Noble to prepare a historical overview of St. Catherines Island. Apparently unaware of Larson's earlier work, Hart and Bonner used the 1687 account (Dunlop 1929) to look for Santa Catalina. Before long, Bonner and Gaffney Blalock photographed several olive jar and majolica sherds eroding from the creek bed, correctly pinpointing Wamassee Creek as the probable location of Santa Catalina de Guale.

In April 1965 John W. Griffin (then staff archaeologist, National Park Service) visited St. Catherines Island to gather information regarding the

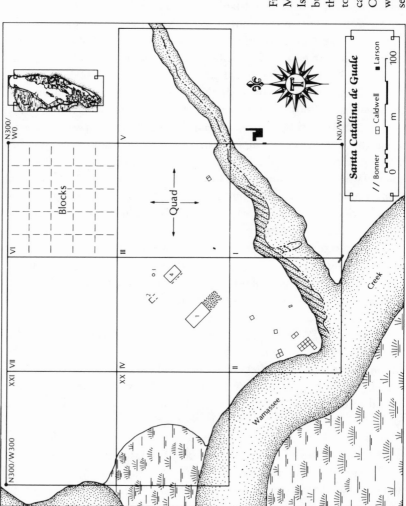

Figure 1.1. Map showing the location of Mission Santa Catalina on St. Catherines Island, Georgia. The numbered mission buildings in Quad IV were excavated by the American Museum of Natural History (1981–1990). Previous archaeological investigations by Larson, Bonner, and Caldwell are also indicated. Reproduced with the permission of the American Museum of Natural History.

eligibility of the site of Santa Catalina mission as a Registered National Historic Landmark. Although he subsequently reported that "further work on the site of Santa Catalina mission is in some respects of the highest priority" (Griffin 1965a:10–11), Griffin also warned that given "the perishable nature of the structures themselves—they were of poles and thatch, not masonry—it can readily be seen that extensive archaeological work would be needed to pinpoint individual buildings of the settlement" (Griffin 1965b:5–7).

Joseph R. Caldwell and students from the University of Georgia conducted three seasons of archaeological fieldwork on St. Catherines Island in 1969–1971. Although they excavated mostly in mounds elsewhere on the island (see Larsen and Thomas 1982:271–342), they sank several test pits in the Wamassee Creek area. In unpublished field notes Caldwell concluded: "There is no reason to believe, at present, that this is not the site of the mission of Santa Catalina. So far, however, our excavations have yielded little structural detail" (J. R. Caldwell n.d.).

Such was the state of knowledge regarding the location of Mission Santa Catalina when the American Museum of Natural History started working on St. Catherines Island in 1974. The combined French, English, and Spanish historic documentation available in the late 1970s supplied little more than general geographic clues. The limited archaeological evidence suggested only that *if* any mission structures remained intact they were likely to be buried somewhere near the southwestern marsh on St. Catherines Island.

Discovering Mission Santa Catalina: 1977–1981

We began our own search for Santa Catalina with an extensive program of reconnaissance and site evaluation for all of St. Catherines Island; here we briefly summarize that research (see Thomas 1987, 1988a).

THE REGIONAL RANDOM SAMPLE

We initially employed a research design deliberately patterned after our earlier work at Pleistocene Lake Tonopah, Nevada. This survey generated a 20 percent sample of the island, obtained in a series of 31 east-west transects, each 100 m wide. We found 135 archaeological sites, ranging from massive shell heaps to small, isolated shell scatters; each "site" was explored with two or more 1-m-square test units; more than 400 such test pits were dug in this phase of excavation. We are presently completing a book-length treatment of these survey findings (Thomas n.d.; see also Thomas 1989:228–230).

In addition to providing extensive data on the settlement pattern and cultural ecology of St. Catherines Island during the precontact period, the survey sampling also clearly demonstrated that sixteenth-/seventeenth-century Spanish period remains occurred at only a handful of the 135 archaeological sites investigated. Significantly, relevant mission period materials showed up only around Wamassee Creek (as earlier investigators had correctly surmised).

Abortive Efforts at Randomized Test Pitting

This regional approach confirmed and complemented earlier archaeological investigations by Larson, Bonner, Griffin, and Caldwell: Mission Santa Catalina almost certainly was in a 10-ha tract near Wamassee Creek. But the nature of the mission ruins remained unknown. Did Santa Catalina survive merely as sixteenth- and seventeenth-century garbage middens, or was structural evidence buried somewhere nearby?

In 1980 the research focus shifted from systematic regional to intrasite sampling. Where in these 10 ha should we begin digging? Although we tried randomized test pitting, such blind testing was slow, tedious, and rather unproductive. Roughly 200 person-days were invested in the randomized test pit procedures at Santa Catalina, but we soon recognized that to understand the structure of this site, a huge sampling fraction would be required. We dug up plenty of intriguing material—mostly from the Spanish period—but these excavations lacked any sense of context because of the relatively small "window" provided by each 1-m test pit. At Santa Catalina, randomized test pitting told us little more than where not to dig.

Auger Sampling

Looking around for better ways to find the needle hidden somewhere in this haystack, we were inspired by Kathleen Deagan's successful search for sixteenth-century St. Augustine. Following her example, we initiated a systematic auger test survey throughout the high-probability area at Wamassee Creek (Deagan 1981; see also Shapiro 1987).

Auger testing quickly generated the data we needed. Once field testing was complete (by mid-1981), we plotted the distribution of Spanish
period materials in a series of simple dot-density maps. Sherd density
varied considerably across the 10 ha sampled, with the central and western zones containing extremely high densities of Spanish period aboriginal sherds and Hispanic ceramics. Accepting the conventional wisdom
that Hispanic/aboriginal sherd ratios reflect social status (e.g., Deagan
1983:114–116; South 1977:172–175), a single 100-m-by-100-m tract
emerged as the most probable location for the central mission complex
(fig. 1.1).

This area, termed Quad IV, was a totally unremarkable piece of real
estate, covered by the same scrub palmetto/live oak forest typical of the
western margin of St. Catherines. The only evidence of any human occupation was a little-used field road for island research vehicles. Although
shell midden scatters were evident here and there, Quad IV contained
absolutely no surface evidence distinguishing it from its surroundings. In
effect, the simple and expedient auger testing had narrowed the focus
from 10 ha to 1 ha.

Significantly, Quad IV contained relatively little shell midden compared with surrounding areas. After all, if this was a "sacred" precinct,
then it should have been (and apparently was) kept fairly clear of everyday (secular) garbage. Ironically, had we followed the conventional search
strategy (find the largest shell midden and center punch it), we would
certainly have missed the mission church, cemetery, and associated *convento* complex.

A SUCCESSFUL APPEAL TO REMOTE SENSING TECHNOLOGY

At this point we shifted methods once again—from relatively destructive subsurface testing to more noninvasive, nondestructive remote
sensing. We followed three specific objectives in this phase of our work at
Santa Catalina: (1) to locate and define the mission complex, (2) to
determine the general size and configuration of buried features and structures before they were excavated, and (3) to build a baseline library of
geophysical signatures to be projected against the independent evidence
of future archaeological excavation.

The initial instrument prospection at Santa Catalina was a proton
magnetometer survey, conducted in May 1981 by Ervan G. Garrison and

James Tribble; subsequent surveys took place over the next two years. Although several computer graphic techniques helped filter and refine the magnetic survey data (see Garrison, Baker, and Thomas 1985; Thomas 1987:47–161), such remote sensing paid off significantly even before the computer plots were available.

We explored three major magnetic anomalies in the few remaining days of our May 1981 field season. The first such anomaly, located near an auger hole that had previously produced daub, turned out to be the well-preserved Franciscan church (*iglesia*), which we identified as Structure 1. The second anomaly was the mission kitchen (*cocina*), now denoted as Structure 2. The third magnetic anomaly was a mission period barrel well.

Although the magnetometer survey yielded accurate indications of daub wall segments, subsequent soil resistivity studies provided a better way to define the configuration and extent of the unexcavated buildings. In the spring of 1982, Gary Shapiro and Mark Williams conducted a pilot study to determine the potential and feasibility of large-scale resistivity prospection at Santa Catalina (Thomas 1987:47–161, 1989:238–241; see also Shapiro 1984). Not only did soil resistivity provide a general projection of site structure across the central mission precinct, but it also gave us excellent structure-by-structure resolution, defining the shape, orientation, and extent of several unexcavated buildings at Santa Catalina. This soil resistivity survey also disclosed the presence of a previously unknown building, the mission *convento* (Structure 4). These projections were then tested against independent data generated from ground-penetrating radar studies across Quad IV, conducted in 1984.

We believe that today's remote sensing technology provides archaeologists with powerful, cost-effective means of generating noninvasive, nondestructive assessments of the archaeological record (Weymouth 1986:311), and we are at present expanding our remote sensing efforts at Santa Catalina (see below).

Excavating at Santa Catalina: 1981–1990

We have been digging at Santa Catalina for a decade, and our field investigations continue. Although future excavations and analysis will doubtless refine our interpretations, the basics of site structure are now quite apparent. The entire mission complex and the Guale pueblo that surrounded it followed a rigid grid system in which the long axis of the church was oriented 45° west of magnetic north (see Thomas 1987:47–161, 1988b). The central plaza was rectangular, measuring 23 m by approximately 40 m. The church (Structure 1) defined the western margin of the central plaza; the *cocina* and *convento(s)* defined the eastern margin (figs. 1.1 and 1.2).

THE CHURCHES OF SANTA CATALINA

The church at Santa Catalina has been completely exposed; except for the eastern wall, preserved as a witness section, the entire church deposit was excavated. We can recognize two sequential church structures. The late sixteenth-century *iglesia* was destroyed by fire, probably in September 1597. These ruins were personally inspected by Governor Gonzalo Méndez de Canzo, who had traveled north from St. Augustine to observe for himself the aftermath of the Guale rebellion (Geiger 1937:103–104). Unfortunately, later building episodes have largely obscured the appearance of the earlier church.

After a period of abandonment, Santa Catalina was resettled by the Spanish in 1604 and the mission church was reconstructed (apparently on the sixteenth-century site). Most of what we term Structure 1 at Santa Catalina is the primary seventeenth-century church, abandoned shortly after the British siege in 1680. This later church was constructed on a single nave plan, lacking both transept and chancel. The rectangular structure is 20 m long and 11 m wide. The facade, facing southeast, was the only one built strictly of wattlework; it was anchored to four round uprights set into shell-lined postholes. Either a pointed gable was elevated to support a steep thatch roof (as in Manucy 1985:fig. 5), or the facade sported a false front projecting above the single-story construction of the nave.

The lateral church walls were constructed of both wattlework and pine planking. The nave portion of the church was 16 m long and decorated in places by figures sculpted in clay (as in fig. 1.3, top).

The symbolic separation between nave and sanctuary was emphasized by a composite construction technique. The sanctuary (northwestern) end of the church, constructed entirely of wooden planking, was apparently elevated above the lateral wattle-and-daub walls of the nave. Some evidence suggests that the interior of the sanctuary may have been decorated with a reredos, several ornamental metal panels that were apparently not removed before the church was abandoned.

Opposite: Figure 1.2. Low-level aerial photograph showing excavations in Quad IV at Santa Catalina de Guale (as of May 1984). The top of the photograph is magnetic north, and the white tick marks are spaced at 20-m intervals. Toward the bottom center is the church (Structure 1); the two dark linear daub concentrations (upper right) form the *convento/cocina* complex (see also structure placement in fig. 1.1). The light-colored vertical stripes are 4-m-wide shallow test trenches. Reproduced with the permission of the American Museum of Natural History (photograph by Dennis O'Brien).

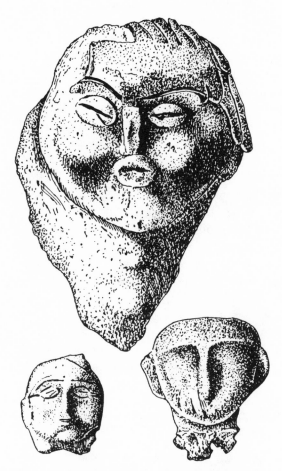

Figure 1.3. Selected Guale Indian human sculptures found at Mission Santa Catalina. Reproduced with the permission of the American Museum of Natural History.

Although we have relied heavily on the available historical documentation to date the various daub walls encountered at Mission Santa Catalina, independent and *strictly archaeological* evidence is also desirable. Ceramic evidence helps, but we were looking for something more precise. In consultation with Robert Dunnell (Department of Anthropology, University of Washington), we have conducted a pilot study of thermoluminescence dating of these wall daub deposits. The first step was to determine the chemical composition of daub at Santa Catalina by X-ray fluorescence analysis; Dunnell's analysis indicates that the daub was almost certainly obtained from nearby marsh mud sources. Several dosimeters were buried over two-year intervals around the site to monitor the degree of contemporary thermoluminescent activity. Numerous archaeological samples, which were then taken from the collapsed walls of the *iglesia, convento*, and *cocina*, are currently being processed in the thermoluminescence laboratory of the University of Washington.

A clearly demarcated sacristy, measuring 5 m wide by 3 m deep, was built on the Gospel side of the church (the left-hand side of the sanctuary as one faces the altar). This room was presumably used for storage of vestments, linens, candles, processional materials, and other ritual paraphernalia essential to celebration of the Mass (Bushnell 1990). Inside we found a cache of charred wheat, which was probably destined to be baked into the "host," the flat bread used in the Eucharist. Donna L. Ruhl (Department of Anthropology, University of Florida) is currently analyzing these materials as part of her more extensive analysis of paleobotanical remains recovered from Santa Catalina (see also Ruhl 1990).

Although wheat had never assumed great dietary importance to Spaniards living in *La Florida*, this inglorious cache inside the sacristy underscores the effectiveness of the Franciscan order in obtaining the supplies necessary for the proper conduct of church ritual—even on the most remote northern frontier of the Guale province. Amy Bushnell (research associate, American Museum of Natural History and Department of History, Johns Hopkins University) is pursuing this matter in detail, analyzing the documentary evidence of the economic support systems necessary to sustain Mission Santa Catalina (Bushnell 1992).

The Churchyard (*Atrio*)

Fronting the church at Santa Catalina is a square shell-covered subplaza, measuring about 15 m on a side. This *atrio* was probably a low-

walled enclosure demarcating the public entrance to the church. Ubiquitous features of New World religious architecture, such churchyards not
only served as decorous entryways into the church but also functioned as
outdoor chapels, areas to contain overflow congregations, and sometimes
as cemeteries (Kubler 1940:73–75; Montgomery, Smith, and Brew
1949:54).

The churchyard at Santa Catalina was constructed of water-rolled
marine shell, available from naturally occurring deposits scattered along
the intracoastal waterway; today these massive shell bars, accessible only
by watercraft, continue to provide building aggregate to an island lacking
local stone.

The Cemetery (*Campo Santo*)

The only known cemetery at Santa Catalina was found inside the
church, where we encountered a minimum of 431 individuals buried
beneath the floor of the nave and sanctuary. Clark Spencer Larsen (research associate, American Museum of Natural History, and professor of
anthropology, University of North Carolina) supervised the complete excavation of this cemetery between 1982 and 1986; the extensive biocultural evidence from Santa Catalina has been discussed elsewhere (see
Larsen 1990:8–10; Larsen et al. 1990; and Larsen, this volume).[2]

The *campo santo* at Santa Catalina also contained a truly astounding
array of associated grave goods, including nearly three dozen crosses (fig.
1.4), medallions (fig. 1.5), small medals (fig. 1.6), so-called Jesuit finger
rings (with unique sculpted Sacred Heart castings), and a cast figurine
depicting the infant Jesus holding a cross in one hand and raising the
other in a gesture of blessing. The material, form, and iconography of
nearly three dozen Catholic religious items have been analyzed by Richard E. Ahlborn (curator, National Museum of American History,
Smithsonian Institution).

Additional grave goods in the *campo santo* include four complete
majolica vessels, several projectile points, a chunkey stone, a rattlesnake
shell gorget in the "Tellico" style, two complete glass cruets, two mirrors,
two hawk's bells, one rosary, eight shroud pins, two copper plaque fragments, and one large piece of shroud cloth. The cemetery also contained
literally tens of thousands of glass beads, which are currently being analyzed. Most were embroidery beads sewn onto clothing and sashes;
other beads were portions of jewelry and ornaments. Rosary beads were

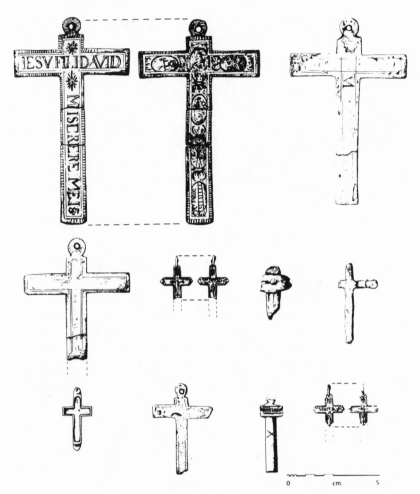

Figure 1.4. Selected crosses found in Christian Guale graves at Santa Catalina. Note the variety in means of manufacture, design, and size (particularly when compared to the uniformity of the small religious medals in fig. 1.6). Latin inscription on upper left cross translates "Jesus, son of David, have mercy on me." On the reverse side of this cross are six oval reserves with symbols and instruments of the Passion (suffering) of Jesus. *Left to right*: Crossed hammer and pliers; wounds of hands, feet, and side; three crossed nails; crown of thorns and stars (?); two dice, lance, and staff with vinegar in sponge; ladder and the six (?) pieces of silver to pay Judas (Ahlborn 1991). Reproduced with the permission of the American Museum of Natural History.

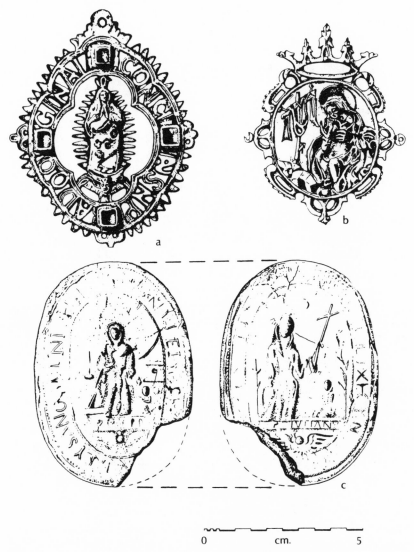

Figure 1.5. Three medallions recovered from the *campo santo* at Santa Catalina. Richard Ahlborn (1991) offers the following iconographic interpretations:

(a) Cast and glass enameled medallion with Spanish inscription that translates "Hail, Mary, conceived without original sin." High mercury content suggests that this medallion may have been gilded. The scene recalls the popular image of Our Lady of Guadalupe, which the Franciscan order had successfully established in Mexico after 1531 before the first friar reached Santa Catalina.

(b) Silver medallion with mercury gilding, found near the altar and associated with the phalanx of a 2-year-old, some copper links, and a textile fragment with three seed beads woven into it. It depicts the heavily robed and hooded "Sorrowing Mother" of Jesus, seated in grief on rocks at Golgotha. In the background is a cross with three

(*continued*)

commonly found accompanying burials. The remainder of the beads are aboriginal shell beads and lapidary beads.

THE FRIARY (*Convento*) COMPLEX

Eastward across the plaza stood the *convento* and *cocina* complex. The *convento* (usually translated as monastery, convent, or friary) comprised one or more subsidiary buildings in which friars and lay brothers lived cloistered lives according to the rules of their Franciscan order.

At least two superimposed *conventos* exist at Santa Catalina. The earlier structure was probably built in the late 1580s shortly after the Franciscans arrived. Second only in size to the church itself, it measured at least 10 m by 20 m, the long axis running roughly northwest-southeast (at an angle of 310°). Construction was entirely of rough wattle and daub (considerably coarser than that employed in building the church). This early building was supported by relatively large posts set in holes with clean sand fill. It appears to have been divided into at least three rooms. The kitchen and refectory were probably housed inside the sixteenth-century *convento*; the other rooms were probably used for living quarters and storage. Kitchen debris and table scraps were tossed out the back door, where a fringe of shell midden accumulated against the rear wall— well out of sight from the church. A clearly incised drip line demonstrates that the sixteenth-century *convento* had eaves extending about a meter beyond the rear wall.

This building was probably burnt by rebellious Guale in the fall of 1597. When Fray Ruiz supervised the reconstruction in 1604, he appar-

---

nails and a shroud. Similar to *veneras* worn on clothing by fashionable women in seventeenth-century Spain (Muller 1972:124).

(c) Made of sandy micaceous clay, low fired, and cast from two molds, this medallion could have been used to impress wax seals. *Left side*: The lengthy circumferential and basal inscriptions, probably in Latin, have not yet been transcribed. A standing male in a hooded habit holds in one hand a thin, vertical device (a cross?) over a small kneeling figure; his lowered hand holds a chain. Below a basal inscription (perhaps abbreviated) is a winged angel's head. This scene recalls Jesuit and Franciscan missionaries martyred in the sixteenth century while evangelizing in Asia. *Right side*: This design is similar to the obverse, but the large figure has his cowl back and his head radiates light. He also raises a cross over the kneeling figure. To one side is a thin plant and above is a birdlike form; at the bottom, below an inscription, is a winged angel's head. Reproduced with the permission of the American Museum of Natural History.

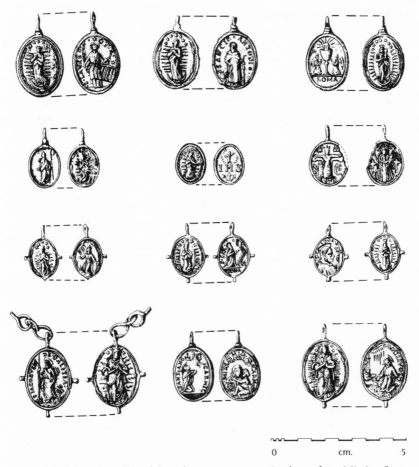

Figure 1.6. Selected small medals with cross-set suspension loops from Mission Santa Catalina de Guale. They contain various inscriptions referring to specific religious concepts or identities, generally involving a prayer for protection from a holy personage such as Jesus, his mother in several advocations, and various saints (Ahlborn 1991). Reproduced with the permission of the American Museum of Natural History.

ently separated sacred from secular, for a distinct *cocina* was erected 20 m to the north of the new *convento*. The detached kitchen was also a common feature within urban St. Augustine (Deagan 1983:247).

The southeastern wall of both sixteenth- and seventeenth-century *conventos* was built on the same location. But the later structure was somewhat smaller, measuring only about 10 m by 9 m. Moreover, the long axis of the seventeenth-century *convento* is 325°; the ± 15° difference in orientation greatly facilitated separating the two buildings during excavation.

The western wall was enclosed by a well-defined arcade, probably a colonnaded porch marking the eastern margin of the central plaza. At least three doorways faced the church to the west. This porch was exactly aligned with the western wall of the *cocina*. An addition of some sort, apparently not of wattle and daub, was appended to the southern wall.

The later friary consists of three well-defined and one less well preserved daub walls, accompanied in all cases by in situ wall posts. Set into the clay floor of the central room was a curious feature: a rectangular clay foundation, standing 25 cm above the floor, scooped out to receive an oval metallic receptacle. Although this floor font might have held holy water, it was more likely employed for personal hygiene, perhaps as a foot bath.[3]

Immediately outside the back of the *convento*, we found a concentration of nearly four dozen bronze bell fragments (other fragments have been found haphazardly scattered about Santa Catalina). Several pieces show punch and axe marks, indicating that the bells were deliberately destroyed; at least four different bells are represented. The mission bell always held a special significance, at times symbolizing the entire mission enterprise. Like all sacred vessels of the church, bells were consecrated and blessed, this status continuing even after the breaking of a bell; bell fragments were collected at missions San Miguel and San Luis Rey in Alta California and sent to Mexico, ultimately to be recast into new bells (Walsh 1934:32).

Elsewhere (Thomas 1988a:104) I have speculated that the fragments found behind the seventeenth-century *convento* were from bells broken by rebellious Guale during the uprising of 1597. Friars who returned to Santa Catalina some years later undoubtedly came upon some of these fragments, and the broken bells found behind the *convento* may be a deliberate cache of still-consecrated fragments, perhaps intended for recycling into new bells.

THE KITCHEN (*Cocina*)

The new friary was about 15 percent smaller than its predecessor, but this size differential was more than counterbalanced by the new *cocina* (kitchen) built 20 m to the northwest. The seventeenth-century kitchen, measuring 4.5 m by 6 m, was constructed of wattle and daub on three sides. These walls were supported by squared-off pine posts placed in pits. The southern end of the kitchen was apparently left open, presumably to facilitate both access and ventilation.

The cooking for the friars was probably shifted to this new structure early in the seventeenth century. Although most kitchen debris was discarded some distance away (probably outside the walled mission compound), some midden accumulated in pits near the *cocina*, and occasional smaller pieces of garbage were trampled underfoot, being thus incorporated in the kitchen floor. Elizabeth J. Reitz (Museum of Natural History, University of Georgia) and her students have completed the identification of the nonhuman bones from the *cocina* and elsewhere in the Mission Santa Catalina excavations; these results, when published, will enhance the already growing body of zooarchaeological data from the missions of *La Florida* (Reitz 1990 and this volume).

THE MISSION WELLS

Two wells were found on the eastern side of the plaza. The first, initially located by the magnetometer survey, was a simple barrel well consisting of seven decomposing iron rings above the well-preserved remains of an oak casing (item 3 in fig. 1.1). The construction pit was relatively small, perhaps 1.5 m in diameter, with the much smaller barrel well located inside. Relatively little was found in the construction pit and well fill (some olive jar and majolica sherds, plus a metal plate). This well obviously had a relatively short use-life, and we think it likely that it dates from the sixteenth century.

A second, much larger well was encountered later, directly between the *cocina* and the *convento* (fig. 1.7). When first recognized, the large circular construction pit was more than 4 m in diameter, with a dark, largely circular stain in the middle. As we excavated downward, the construction pit narrowed, with distinct "steps" on both sides; a seventeenth-century cave-in is recorded in the southern sidewall, where one of the sand steps apparently collapsed. Although the well and its contents are still being analyzed, some details are now available.

The well was originally much smaller, having been first constructed with standard barrels. It was subsequently renovated using a casement constructed of two U-shaped cypress logs that were lowered into the construction pit, then nailed together. This later, handmade well casing

Figure 1.7. Photograph of 1988 excavation of the primary well at Mission Santa Catalina.

was at least 2 m in diameter, considerably larger than any of the mission period wells encountered in Spanish Florida. This well clearly crosscuts surrounding features in the *convento/cocina* complex; it was one of the last features built at the mission and was probably in use until the final mission abandonment in the 1680s.

The well reached a depth of roughly 2.5 m. A fair amount of cultural and botanical remains were included in both the construction pit and well fill. A quantity of waterlogged items found at the base of the well includes a broken iron hatchet (with a partial wooden handle still intact, possibly broken during the carving of the casement), two wooden balls (roughly the size of pool balls), at least five reconstructible aboriginal vessels (two are unbroken, and one is painted on the interior and exterior), most of two olive jars, and many seeds and pits including grape, peach, and squash. At the bottom of the well were quantities of burnt cut wood, which may have been part of a superstructure that once covered the well.

Exploring the Guale Pueblo and Beyond

Although we have learned a great deal about the central mission compound at Santa Catalina, the surrounding Guale Indian pueblo remains a mystery—both because the Hispanic documents gloss over such mundane matters and because of limited archaeological exploration of the entire mission context.

Within the past year, we shifted the archaeological focus of attention at Santa Catalina from the Hispanic core to the Native American outskirts. We tested the surrounding Guale pueblo in several places, but our concern was primarily chronological—to be certain that this extensive habitation area surrounding the mission buildings was occupied during the sixteenth and seventeenth centuries.

Responding to our interest in establishing this broader context, the St. Catherines Island Foundation and the Edward John Noble Foundation have generously granted us three additional years of excavation and analysis designed specifically to learn more about the mission period Indians on St. Catherines Island. In this newest research phase, begun in January 1991, our primary goal is to define the nature and extent of the Guale pueblo at Mission Santa Catalina and to find out how Guale lifeways were modified by interactions with Europeans.

What Are We Looking For?

Reliable evidence regarding the appearance of either precontact or mission period Guale settlements is rare in the documentary sources. Perhaps the following account of the town of Orista in 1666 can be applied to most Guale towns: "The Ttowne is scituate on the side or rather in the skirts of a faire forrest, in which at several distances are diverse fields of maiz with many little houses straglingly amongst them for the habitations of the particular families" (Sandford 1911).

In a letter dated 22 September 1602, Governor Gonzalo Méndez de Canzo commented that in the Guale settlements "the natives that there are in these provinces do not have cities nor towns or organized villages [*pueblos avezindados*] amounting to anything more than that each cacique has a community house where the Indians came together to hold their dances and assemblies and to drink a brew [*brevage*] of casina, which cannot be done in any other place except in the said house of the said cacique and they are all scattered about with their little houses [*casillas*] at intervals on the edges of the woods" (Méndez de Canzo 1602). This account can probably be considered a credible description because it was written by a governor who was well acquainted with the coastal Guale villages, having destroyed a considerable number of them.

Both accounts suggest a "dispersed town" settlement pattern, with horticultural plots and residences scattered in the vicinity of the town center. The maize plots would have been located behind the town center itself. The households of the *mico*, or village chief, and other principal leaders were located near the center of the Guale towns (Jones 1978:198) and perhaps in the mission pueblos as well. Such towns also contained large plazas used for public activities including the ritual chunkey game, performed with poles and a disk-shaped stone and common to many southeastern aboriginal groups (Hudson 1976; Sandford 1911; San Miguel 1902). Such a playing field would certainly be expected in the precontact Guale town and perhaps at Guale missions as well.

We know that missionaries and other Spanish officials permitted the Apalachee neophytes to participate in their ritual ball game in the mission context (Bushnell 1978; Hann 1988). If the chunkey game was viewed in similar fashion in Guale territory, then we might expect to find a plaza/chunkey field in the pueblo at Santa Catalina. In fact, Governor

Rebolledo explicitly stipulated in his regulatory code for Apalachee that the ball game be permitted (Hann 1986:89).

Clearly the most remarkable feature of any Guale town was the large community building (*buhío*) in which periodic councils and intercommunity feasts were held. The council house, in mission times and well before, symbolized and enshrined critical sociopolitical bonds. Friars recognized the importance of the council house and sanctioned its construction on the mission grounds—encouraging local Indians to think of the mission as "their home."

Nobody knows what a Guale council house looked like. Ayllón's expedition of 1526 into Guale territory reported an abandoned, rectangular *buhío* (measuring about 4–8 m wide by at least 80 m long) constructed of lashed pine uprights and big enough to accommodate 300 men, but this description has been discounted by Swanton (1946:406), Jones (1978:199), and Shapiro and Hann (1990:515). Subsequent accounts consistently describe Guale council houses as round structures, varying in size from less than 25 m to more than 60 m in diameter (Jones 1978; Shapiro and Hann 1990). These would have been conspicuous features on the mission landscape, and evidence must have been preserved at the Guale missions.

The nature of aboriginal domestic dwellings along the Georgia coast is even more uncertain. Laudonnière (1975:43) described one Guale house with a lavish interior "decorated with tapestries of various colored feathers up to the height of a pike. The place where the king slept was covered with white coverlets embroidered with fine workmanship and fringed in scarlet." In 1595 Fray Andrés de San Miguel (1902) noted that Guale houses at Asao were constructed of wooden timbers and covered with palmettos. Jones (1978:199) suggests that the precontact Guale houses were circular, built on the same general principle as the *buhío*, only smaller.

Limited archaeological evidence suggests otherwise for Guale dwellings during the mission period. At the north end of Harris Neck, Larson (1980) encountered several squarish and overlapping Spanish period aboriginal structures aligned on a grid system approximately 10° west of north. Several wall trench outlines of Spanish period aboriginal domestic structures were also uncovered by S. K. Caldwell at Fort King George, near Darien (S. K. Caldwell 1953, 1954; see also Larson 1980; Thomas 1987:95–97). These seem to be wattle-and-daub structures built with shallow wall trenches and small round postholes and divided into several rooms. Incidentally, we are currently reanalyzing all mission period materials recovered by Caldwell from Fort King George, in the hope of defining more firmly the context of these important structures.

These skimpy data suggest that the pueblo at Santa Catalina probably consisted of rectangular buildings constructed of wattle and daub and/or wall trenches and perhaps separated by "streets." The Native American sector was probably built as an extension of the initial Spanish gridwork.

So How Do We Find These Things Archaeologically?

Virtually all we know about Santa Catalina comes from a decade of digging around the plaza in the central part of Santa Catalina—the church, *convento*, and *cocina* complex—an area of about 5000 m². If we are to address the pueblo periphery, the research frame must be expanded to *at least* 10 ha, and this is a very conservative estimate. Because our proposed pueblo project must cover at least twenty times the area investigated in our 1980–1990 research and because this work must be completed within just three years, a different archaeological strategy is clearly in order.

Once again we think that remote sensing provides part of the solution. In collaboration with John Weymouth (Department of Physics and Astronomy, University of Nebraska), we are at present developing a multivariate approach to geophysical prospection at Santa Catalina. We feel that the value of remote sensing studies has not been fully realized in modern archaeology and hope that the pueblo at Santa Catalina can serve as a case study to demonstrate the potential of such methods.

In our initial search for Santa Catalina 15 years ago, we employed three primary remote sensing techniques: proton precession magnetometry, soil resistivity, and ground-penetrating radar (Thomas 1987:47–161, 1989:chap. 7). In the ongoing work at the pueblo, we will continue to use these techniques but will also employ several others—not only to learn more about the pueblo but also to understand better the strengths and weaknesses of various geophysical currencies and approaches. Our most recent efforts (1990–1991) on the Santa Catalina pueblo have utilized paired proton precession magnetometry, gradiometry, high-speed soil resistivity, and soil conductivity; other techniques are being considered as well. We have every confidence that at least some of this technology will prove fruitful.

Preliminary testing also suggests that the pueblo contains huge samples of faunal remains. In continued collaboration with Elizabeth J. Reitz, we are expanding our investigation of vertebrate utilization during the late prehistoric and mission periods. We are particularly interested in exploring the nature of intrasite variability at Mission Santa Catalina. Relatively large zooarchaeological samples have already been studied from the *cocina* and other "central" mission contexts; the proposed 1991–1993 excavations should produce comparable samples from the Mission Santa Catalina pueblo.

We also think that important data lie outside the mission compound proper and even outside the pueblo. When Captain Dunlop visited the ruins of Santa Catalina in 1687, he reported "the ruins of severall houses which we were informed the Spaniards had deserted for ffear of the English about 3 years agoe; the Setlement was great, much clear ground in our view for 7 or 8 miles together" (Dunlop 1929:131). Even allowing for considerable exaggeration, this rare eyewitness account indicates that Mission Santa Catalina was surrounded by a huge agricultural field complex. But what did these fields look like? How were they organized? What crops were grown there?

Once again, we are required to shift the scale: the 5000 m² around the mission plaza covers only the religious precinct; the 10-ha area surrounding the plaza contains only the aboriginal pueblo. But in order to obtain a more complete view of Mission Santa Catalina as an economic entity, we must be willing to operate on the scale of several dozen hectares.

Large-scale patterning is one way to look for the potential residues left from mission period agriculture. Recent investigators using the techniques of landscape archaeology have enjoyed some success by analyzing the distribution of plant opal phytoliths; an example is Irwin Rovner's (1988) successful reconstruction of Thomas Jefferson's gardens and fodder fields at Monticello, Virginia. We would like to do the same at Santa Catalina.

But in these days of conservation-oriented archaeology, *no one* should contemplate digging several hectares (even if the resources and the sites were available). Instead, we should be seeking ways to monitor variability on a scale previously unattainable in archaeology. Our specific objective here is to reconstruct the distribution and configuration of the agricultural field systems surrounding Mission Santa Catalina. To do so, we are required to conduct considerable baseline studies of phytolith taxonomy and depositional processes. In collaboration with Irwin Rovner (North Carolina State University), we have begun a comprehensive study of plant phytoliths at Santa Catalina (and other contact period sites on St. Catherines Island).

Although this landscape approach is far-reaching indeed, we wish to expand the scope still further. In collaboration with Joseph Jimenez (City University of New York), we intend to explore the nature of socioeconomic change between the late prehistoric and the early contact periods. To complement our expanded studies at the Santa Catalina pueblo, we have selected five additional sites on St. Catherines Island for detailed investigation: three mission period sites plus two Irene period (late precontact) sites. We are at present using geophysical techniques at these sites, and they will be further mapped and tested in conjunction with our expanded work at the Santa Catalina pueblo.

We also continue our collaboration with Clark Spencer Larsen to further refine our previous biocultural findings. In 1991 Larsen returned to South End Mound, previously excavated by C. B. Moore and retested by the American Museum of Natural History (Larsen and Thomas 1986:1–46), in hopes of expanding the Irene period mortuary sample. We are simultaneously exploring several other late prehistoric and mission period St. Catherines Island sites in the search for additional mortuary evidence.

We hope that this expanded regional approach will enable us not only to determine the nature of precontact Guale adaptations but also to see whether the mission system was able to exert significant social and economic control beyond the confines of Mission Santa Catalina proper. We also believe that intensive investigations at these key sites will enable us to assess changing social relations between precontact and contact period villages, to trace intravillage changes through microanalysis of ceramic traits, to refine the late precontact and contact period ceramic chronologies, and to perfect archaeological indicators of seasonality.

Without question, our inquiry will not prove equally successful in all these potential directions. But we are confident that by extending our mission research far beyond the Hispanic hub, we can learn more about the lifeways of the majority of people living under the umbrella of Mission Santa Catalina de Guale.

Acknowledgments

I express my sincerest thanks to the trustees of the St. Catherines Island and Edward John Noble foundations for providing both the opportunity and the support to conduct the archaeological research described here. We are particularly grateful to Mr. and Mrs. Frank Y. Larkin for their truly extraordinary level of interest and benefaction. Additional funding for our excavations has been provided by the Richard K. Lounsbery Foundation, the National Science Foundation, the Georgia Endowment for the Humanities, Donald McClain, the James Ruel Smith Fund, the Geiger Lumber Company, the Sander and Ray Epstein Charitable Foundation, the General William Mayer Foundation, the Ogden Mills Fund, and Earthwatch.

I also thank Royce Hayes, superintendent of St. Catherines Island, who made our work both effective and pleasurable; we are also grateful to his able-bodied staff for always being willing to lend a hand. I am likewise grateful to the special people who helped supervise the excavations at Mission Santa Catalina de Guale: Stacy Goodman, Debra Guerrero, Joseph Jimenez, Clark Spencer Larsen, Deborah Mayer O'Brien, Dennis O'Brien, Lorann S. A. Pendleton, Donna Ruhl, William Sandy, and Rebecca Saunders. This manuscript benefited considerably from the editorial and substantive suggestions provided by Margot Dembo, Lorann Pendleton, and three anonymous reviewers. Nicholas Amorosi and Dennis O'Brien prepared the artwork for this article. We also thank Richard Ahlborn (National Museum of American History, Smithsonian Institution) for allowing us to draw upon his iconographic research on the Santa Catalina religious artifacts.

Notes

1. Some years ago we published an overview of the natural and cultural history of St. Catherines Island (Thomas et al. 1978:155–248), and that monograph serves as a backdrop for this discussion as well.

Although the archaeology of Mission Santa Catalina has consumed much of our research energies on St. Catherines Island, we have spent considerable effort looking at the precontact archaeological remains as well. We began our research on the island in 1974, by focusing on the Refuge and Deptford phase mortuary complex (Thomas and Larsen 1979:1–180). Larsen (1982:155–270) subsequently conducted a detailed examination of prehistoric biocultural adaptations on St. Catherines Island (see also Larsen, this volume). This program in mortuary archaeology continued in 1977 and 1978, when two St. Catherines period burial mounds (Johns and Marys Mounds) were also studied. Both mounds were initially excavated by Joseph Caldwell and his students at the University of Georgia, and we combined their results with our own (Larsen and Thomas 1982:271–342). More recently we reported on excavations at two additional prehistoric burial mounds (Larsen and Thomas 1986:1–46). South End Mound I, an Irene period mortuary site, had been initially excavated by C. B. Moore during the winter of 1896–1897. South End Mound II, a previously unrecorded St. Catherines/Savannah period burial mound, was discovered not far from Moore's excavations. Other related mortuary excavations are reported elsewhere (Thomas, South, and Larsen 1977:393–420).

2. We must emphasize the sensitivity required when excavating such mission period human remains (see Thomas 1987:147–148, 1988b:124–125). Because we could establish no biological descendants of those buried at Santa Catalina—the Guale people disappeared in the eighteenth century—we focused on working with those who maintained the closest cultural and religious affinity with the remains. From our earliest tests in the *campo santo*, it was clear that this was a Catholic cemetery, containing the remains of hundreds of Guale Indians who had explicitly opted for Christian burial.

Accordingly, we established contact with Father Raymond Lessard, bishop of Savannah. Bishop Lessard assured us that the Catholic church supported and encouraged our excavations. On 25 May 1984 Bishop Lessard returned to St. Catherines Island to conduct a service dedicated to "reblessing the ground and reburial of remains," and he has assisted in the on-site reburial of remains. Further, recognizing that two Franciscans had been martyred at Santa Catalina in 1597, the Franciscan order also sent a representative, Fr. Conrad Harkins, to participate in the excavations at the *iglesia* and *convento* (see Harkins 1990).

3. It remains possible, however, that this unusual feature was a brazier, designed to hold glowing embers to ward off the wintertime cold; but a more likely charcoal-filled "brazier" was discovered along the southern margin of the *convento*.

Bibliography

Ahlborn, Richard E.
1991　Religious Devices from Santa Catalina de Guale, Georgia: 1566–1686. Anthropological Papers of the American Museum of Natural History. New York. In preparation.

Bolton, Herbert E., and Mary Ross
1925　*The Debatable Land.* Berkeley: University of California Press.

Bushnell, Amy T.
1978   "That Demonic Game": The Campaign to Stop Indian *Pelota* Playing in Spanish Florida, 1675–1684. *The Americas* 35:1–19.

1990   The Sacramental Imperative: Catholic Ritual and Indian Sedentism in the Provinces of Florida. In *Columbian Consequences*. Vol. 2: *Archaeological and Historical Perspectives on the Spanish Borderlands East*, edited by David Hurst Thomas, 475–490. Washington, D.C.: Smithsonian Institution Press.

1992   *The Archaeology of Mission Santa Catalina de Guale: 3. The Support System of a Spanish Maritime Periphery*. Anthropological Papers of the American Museum of Natural History. New York. In press.

Caldwell, Joseph R.
n.d.   Unpublished field notes on file, Laboratory of Anthropology, St. Catherines Island, Georgia.

Caldwell, Sheila K.
1953   Excavations at a Spanish Mission Site in Georgia. *Southeastern Archaeological Conference Newsletter* 3(3):31–32.

1954   A Spanish Mission House near Darien. *Early Georgia* 1(3):13–17.

Deagan, Kathleen A.
1981   Downtown Survey: The Discovery of Sixteenth-Century St. Augustine in an Urban Area. *American Antiquity* 46(3):626–634.

1983   *Spanish St. Augustine: The Archaeology of a Colonial Creole Community*. New York: Academic Press.

Dunlop, Captain
1929   Journall Capt. Dunlop's Voyage to the Southward, 1687. *South Carolina Historical and Genealogical Magazine* 30(3):127–133.

Gannon, Michael V.
1965   *The Cross in the Sand: The Early Catholic Church in Florida, 1513–1870*. Gainesville: University of Florida Press.

Garrison, Ervan G., James G. Baker, and David Hurst Thomas
1985   Magnetic Prospection and the Discovery of Mission Santa Catalina de Guale. *Journal of Field Archaeology* 12:299–313.

Geiger, Maynard J., O.F.M.
1937   *The Franciscan Conquest of Florida, 1573–1618*. Studies in Hispanic-American History, vol. 1. Washington, D.C.: Catholic University of America.

1940   *Biographical Dictionary of the Franciscans in Spanish Florida and Cuba (1528–1841)*. Franciscan Studies, no. 21. Paterson, N.J.: St. Anthony's Guild Press.

Griffin, John W.

1965a Notes on the Archeology of St. Catherines Island, Georgia. Report to the Edward John Noble Foundation. Ms. on file, Department of Anthropology, American Museum of Natural History, New York.

1965b Santa Catalina Mission, Liberty County, Georgia. Documentation for Consideration as a Registered National Historic Landmark. Ms. on file, Department of Anthropology, American Museum of Natural History, New York.

Hann, John H.

1986 Translation of Governor Rebolledo's 1637 Visitation of Three Florida Provinces and Related Documents. In *Spanish Translations*, 81–145. Florida Archaeology no. 2. Tallahassee: Florida Bureau of Archaeological Research.

1988 *Apalachee: The Land between the Rivers*. Ripley P. Bullen Monographs in Anthropology and History, no. 7. Gainesville: University Presses of Florida.

Harkins, Conrad, O.F.M.

1990 On Franciscans, Archaeology, and Old Missions. In *Columbian Consequences*. Vol. 2: *Archaeological and Historical Perspectives on the Spanish Borderlands East*, edited by David Hurst Thomas, 459–474. Washington, D.C.: Smithsonian Institution Press.

Hudson, Charles

1976 *The Southeastern Indians*. Knoxville: University of Tennessee Press.

Hvidt, Kristian

1980 *Von Reck's Voyage: Drawings and Journal of Philip Georg Friedrich von Reck*. Savannah, Ga.: Beehive Press.

Jones, Grant

1978 The Ethnohistory of the Guale Coast through 1684. In *The Anthropology of St. CatherinesIsland:1. Natural and Cultural History*, by David Hurst Thomas, Grant D. Jones, Roger S. Durham, and Clark Spencer Larsen, 178–210. Anthropological Papers of the American Museum of Natural History, vol. 55, pt. 2. New York.

Kubler, George

1940 *The Religious Architecture of New Mexico in the Colonial Period and since the American Occupation*. Colorado Springs: Taylor Museum.

Larsen, Clark Spencer

1982 *The Anthropology of St. Catherines Island: 3. Prehistoric Human Biological Adaptation*. Anthropological Papers of the American Museum of Natural History, vol. 57, pt. 3. New York.

Larsen, Clark Spencer, ed.
1990   *The Archaeology of Mission Santa Catalina de Guale: 2. Biocultural Interpretations of a Population in Transition.* Anthropological Papers of the American Museum of Natural History, no. 68. New York.

Larsen, Clark Spencer, and David Hurst Thomas
1982   *The Anthropology of St. Catherines Island: 4. The St. Catherines Period Mortuary Complex.* Anthropological Papers of the American Museum of Natural History, vol. 57, pt. 4. New York.

1986   *The Archaeology of St. Catherines Island: 5. The South End Complex.* Anthropological Papers of the American Museum of Natural History, vol. 63, pt. 1. New York.

Larsen, Clark Spencer, Margaret J. Schoeninger, Dale L. Hutchinson, Katherine F. Russell, and Christopher B. Ruff
1990   Beyond Demographic Collapse: Biological Adaptation and Change in Native Populations of *La Florida.* In *Columbian Consequences.* Vol. 2: *Archaeological and Historical Perspectives on the Spanish Borderlands East,* edited by David Hurst Thomas, 409–428. Washington, D.C.: Smithsonian Institution Press.

Larson, Lewis H., Jr.
1952   1952 Season. Georgia Historical Commission, Archaeological Survey of the Georgia Coast. Ms. on file, University of Georgia, Athens.

1978   Historic Guale Indians of the Georgia Coast and the Impact of the Spanish Mission Effort. In *Tacachale: Essays on the Indians of Florida and Southeastern Georgia during the Historic Period,* edited by Jerald Milanich and Samuel Proctor, 120–140. Ripley P. Bullen Monographs in Anthropology and History, no. 1. Gainesville: University Presses of Florida.

1980   The Spanish on Sapelo. In *Sapelo Papers: Researches in the History and Prehistory of Sapelo Island, Georgia,* edited by D. P. Juengst, 77–87. West Georgia College Studies in the Social Sciences, no. 19. Carrollton.

Laudonnière, René
1975   *Three Voyages.* Translated by Charles E. Bennett. Gainesville: University Presses of Florida.

Lyon, Eugene
1976   *The Enterprise of Florida: Pedro Menéndez de Avilés and the Spanish Conquest of 1565–1568.* Gainesville: University Presses of Florida.

Manucy, Albert
1985   *The Houses of St. Augustine.* St. Augustine: St. Augustine Historical Society.

Méndez de Canzo, Gonzalo
1602 Letter to the King, St. Augustine, 22 September 1602. Archivo General de Indias, Santo Domingo 226, reel 2, Jeannette Thurber Connor Collection. P. K. Yonge Library of Florida History, University of Florida, Gainesville.

Montgomery, Ross Gordon, Watson Smith, and John Otis Brew
1949 *Franciscan Awatovi.* Papers of the Peabody Museum of American Archaeology and Ethnology, no. 36. Cambridge: Harvard University.

Muller, Priscilla E.
1972 *Jewels of Spain, 1500–1800.* New York: Hispanic Society of America.

Reitz, Elizabeth J.
1990 Zooarchaeological Evidence for Subsistence at *La Florida* Missions. In *Columbian Consequences.* Vol. 2: *Archaeological and Historical Perspectives on the Spanish Borderlands East,* edited by David Hurst Thomas, 543–554. Washington, D.C.: Smithsonian Institution Press.

Ross, Mary
1926 The Restoration of the Spanish Missions in Georgia, 1598–1606. *Georgia Historical Quarterly* 10(3):171–199.

Rovner, Irwin
1988 Macro- and Micro-ecological Reconstruction Using Plant Opal Phytolith Data from Archaeological Sediments. *Geoarchaeology* 3(2):155–163.

Ruhl, Donna L.
1990 Spanish Mission Paleoethnobotany and Culture Change: A Survey of the Archaeobotanical Data and Some Speculations on Aboriginal and Spanish Agrarian Interactions in *La Florida.* In *Columbian Consequences.* Vol. 2: *Archaeological and Historical Perspectives on the Spanish Borderlands East,* edited by David Hurst Thomas, 555–580. Washington, D.C.: Smithsonian Institution Press.

Sandford, R.
1911 A Relation of a Voyage on the Coast of the Province of Carolina [1666]. In *Original Narratives of Early American History,* vol. 15, edited by A. S. Salley, 82–108. New York: Charles Scribner's Sons.

San Miguel, Fray Andrés de
1902 Relación de las Trabajos que la Gente de una nao llamada Nra Señora de la Merced Padeció y de algunas Cosas que en Aquella Flota Sucedieron. In *Dos Antiguas Relaciones de la Florida,* edited by G. Garcia, 153–226. Mexico: J. Aguilar Vera y Compania.

Shapiro, Gary
1984 A Soil Resistivity Survey of Sixteenth-Century Puerto Real, Haiti. *Journal of Field Archaeology* 11(1):101–110.

1987 *Archaeology at San Luis: Broad-Scale Testing, 1984–1985.* Florida Archaeology no. 3. Tallahassee: Florida Bureau of Archaeological Research.

Shapiro, Gary N., and John H. Hann

1990 The Documentary Image of the Council Houses of Spanish Florida Tested by Excavations at the Mission of San Luis de Talimali. In *Columbian Consequences.* Vol. 2: *Archaeological and Historical Perspectives on the Spanish Borderlands East,* edited by David Hurst Thomas, 491–510. Washington, D.C.: Smithsonian Institution Press.

South, Stanley

1977 Method and Theory in Historical Archaeology. New York: Academic Press.

Sturtevant, William C.

1962 Spanish-Indian Relations in Southeastern North America. *Ethnohistory* 9(1):41–94.

Swanton, John R.

1922 *Early History of the Creek Indians and Their Neighbors.* Bureau of American Ethnology Bulletin no. 73. Washington, D.C.: Smithsonian Institution Press.

1946 *The Indians of the Southeastern United States.* Bureau of American Ethnology Bulletin no. 137. Washington, D.C.: Smithsonian Institution Press.

Thomas, David Hurst

1987 *The Archaeology of Mission Santa Catalina de Guale: 1. Search and Discovery.* Anthropological Papers of the American Museum of Natural History, vol. 63, pt. 2. New York.

1988a *St. Catherines: An Island in Time.* Atlanta: Georgia Endowment for the Humanities (Georgia History and Culture Series).

1988b Saints and Soldiers at Santa Catalina: Hispanic Designs for Colonial America. In *The Recovery of Meaning: Historical Archaeology in the Eastern United States,* edited by Mark P. Leone and Parker B. Potter, Jr., 73–140. Washington, D.C.: Smithsonian Institution Press.

1989 *Archaeology.* 2d ed. Fort Worth: Holt, Rinehart and Winston.

1990 The Spanish Missions of *La Florida*: An Overview. In *Columbian Consequences.* Vol. 2: *Archaeological and Historical Perspectives on the Spanish Borderlands East,* edited by David Hurst Thomas, 357–397. Washington, D.C.: Smithsonian Institution Press.

n.d. The Regional Archaeology of St. Catherines Island. In preparation.

Thomas, David Hurst, and Clark Spencer Larsen

1979 *The Anthropology of St. Catherines Island: 2. The Refuge-Deptford Mor-*

tuary Complex. Anthropological Papers of the American Museum of Natural History, vol. 56, pt. 1. New York.

Thomas, David Hurst, Stanley South, and Clark Spencer Larsen
1977   *Rich Man, Poor Men: Observations on Three Antebellum Burials from the Georgia Coast*. Anthropological Papers of the American Museum of Natural History, vol. 54, pt. 3. New York.

Thomas, David Hurst, Grant D. Jones, Roger S. Durham, and Clark Spencer Larsen
1978   *The Anthropology of St. Catherines Island: 1. The Natural and Cultural History*. Anthropological Papers of the American Museum of Natural History, vol. 55, pt. 2. New York.

Walsh, Marie T.
1934   *The Mission Bells of California*. San Francisco: Hart Wagner.

Weymouth, John W.
1986   Geophysical Methods of Archaeological Site Surveying. In *Advances in Archaeological Method and Theory*, vol. 9, edited by Michael B. Schiffer, 311–395. Orlando: Academic Press.

❂ 2 ❂

Architecture of the Missions
Santa María and
Santa Catalina de Amelia

REBECCA SAUNDERS

During the seventeenth century the Harrison Homestead site (8NA41; the northern three acres has been renamed the Dorion site, 8NA41d) was the location of two successive Spanish missions. Excavation of portions of both those missions has produced data on Spanish mission settlement location, settlement plans, and building design, construction, and function. Though most proveniences were disturbed by erosion or subsequent occupations, sufficient data remain to suggest that both Amelia Island missions deviated from the "ideal" to a significant degree.

A Brief History of the Mission Period on Amelia Island

The Harrison Homestead site housed the remains of two Spanish missions. One of these has been positively identified as the site of Santa Catalina de Guale by the recovery of the seal of Santa Catalina from the *convento*. Several other areas, including a cemetery, can be associated with Santa Catalina on the basis of alignment and proximity. A second cemetery and the substructural remains of an overlying church have been posited to be the earlier mission of Santa María de Yamassee.

As the name reflects, Santa María de Yamassee was occupied by

Yamassee Indians, peoples originally inhabiting the interior of Georgia. The Yamassee began filtering into Florida around 1650. The exact date of the foundation of Santa María is unknown. It was not listed among the missions extant during 1655 (Geiger 1940:125) but did appear in 1675 on Bishop Calderón's mission enumeration (Wenhold 1936). Later that same year Pedro de Arcos (Boyd 1948) noted no functioning missions on the island and described Santa María as a place with about 40 "infidels."

It may be that at the time of Arcos's visit the mission simply lacked a priest, for references continue to be made to Yamassee in the mission on Amelia until they departed in 1683 (Bushnell 1986:4–5). In that year, the Amelia Island Yamassee were to be relocated by the Spanish governor to St. Catherines Island off the northern Georgia coast. The mission on St. Catherines, once the administrative center for the province of Guale and a breadbasket for St. Augustine, had been completely abandoned after an attack by British-led Yamassee Indians in 1680 (Hann 1990:25). It is strange that the Spanish thought to reestablish the mission with other Yamassee Indians; the Amelia Yamassee apparently failed to appreciate the irony and, fearing that St. Catherines Island was too dangerous, "went north" to join their rebellious brethren (Bushnell 1986:5).

Meanwhile, the Guale population of the St. Catherines Island mission, along with other refugees from the northern and middle Georgia coast, had settled on Sapelo Island. In 1686 the St. Catherines Island Guale, along with the people of Satuache, were relocated to Amelia Island. The other groups on Sapelo abandoned the Spanish settlements for the interior. After 1686 there were no Spanish missions in operation north of the St. Marys River. Amelia Island thus became the northern frontier of Spanish holdings along the eastern seaboard and the *doctrina*, or administrative center, for the province of Guale. The name for the old administrative center of Guale, Santa Catalina, was transferred to the new settlement, a common Spanish practice. However, the name Santa María continued to be used to refer to the island. It was also used in both the 1696 Dickinson narrative (Andrews and Andrews 1945) and the 1695 visitation (Bushnell 1986:6) to refer to a town, suggesting the continuation of a local place-name despite the administrative title.

Santa Catalina on St. Catherines Island appears to have been a productive mission, and the Guale transferred to Amelia should have been cognizant of the expectations of the Spanish. The neophytes at Santa Catalina on Amelia, however, did not fulfill their "obligations." Documents from the 1695 visitation indicate that the Indians neglected to plant the two required communal fields (one for the support of the indigents and those "busied in His Majesty's service" and the other for the acquisition of church ornaments). Of greater concern to the Spanish official conducting the visitation was that the stockade planned in 1691 had not been completed. The Indians defended their inaction by complaining that wood had to be carried from too far away and that they had neither the manpower nor the food to support such an endeavor (Hann 1986). Other documents of the period also convey an impression of low mission populations and labor shortages exacerbated by the continual movement of individuals from one town (and one chief) to another (Boyd 1948; Bushnell 1986; Hann 1986). This indicates a breakdown of authority of both priests and Native American leaders.

In 1700 Zúñiga y Zerda reported fewer than 200 Indians on all of Amelia; the stockade still had not been completed (Bushnell 1986:10–11). There is no record indicating whether it was completed by 1702, when the island was the first to be burned in South Carolina Governor James Moore's strategic attack on St. Augustine. The documents do not detail precisely what was ultimately accomplished, though the narrative of the destruction of 1702 alluded to both a guardhouse with a thatch roof and an enclosed *convento* (Bushnell 1986). In an account of the attack, the lieutenant in charge of Santa Catalina provided a population estimate for the last days of the mission on Amelia. Captain Fuentes attributed this quote to the chiefs of the town: "*Señor teniente*, we cannot stay here and hold this enclosure with nine Indians (and five of them no good) and these children and women" (quoted in Bushnell 1986:11). The population of the settlement abandoned the mission just as the British arrived. No lives were lost (Arnade 1959:15), but the mission was burned. Santa Catalina de Guale would be reestablished again at Nombre de Dios near St. Augustine (Larson 1978:20). After 1702 no attempt was made to settle any missions along the Atlantic coast outside the purview of St. Augustine.

Previous Excavation

The Harrison Homestead site was first identified by Bullen and Griffin in their 1950 survey of Amelia Island. Their surface survey (Bullen and Griffin 1952:56) indicated that the site was spread over some 10 acres. They noted that except for the Oldtown site on the north end of the island, 8NA41 was the only site on the island to produce olive jar sherds.

The site remained untested until 1971, when Hemmings and Deagan (1973:4) dug three exploratory trenches approximately 800 feet south of the Santa Catalina mission compound. The area was determined to represent a mission period Indian village. At present, however, it is not known whether this village area was associated with the Santa María or the Santa Catalina mission (or both). An archaeologist for the state of Florida, B. Calvin Jones, also visited the site in the early 1970s (Hardin 1986; B. Calvin Jones, personal communication 1987).

More recent investigations were initiated in 1985 at the behest of the present landowners, George and Dottie Dorion. The Dorions were planning to build on the property when human skeletal remains were discovered in the roots of trees being cleared for their homesite. They contacted Kenneth Hardin of Piper Archaeological Research/Janus Research. Hardin (1986) has chronicled the evolution of the project from its inception until 1986, when stewardship of the site was transferred to the Florida Museum of Natural History. The final field season was in the summer of 1990 (see Larsen and Saunders 1987; Milanich and Saunders 1986; and Saunders 1987, 1988, 1990; a more detailed version of this report is on file at the Florida Division of Historical Resources).

During eight field seasons at the site, the Santa Catalina cemetery was completely excavated, the *convento* associated with the Santa Catalina mission was exposed, three activity areas (one of which may be the kitchen) were explored, and an aboriginal structure was located and excavated. In addition, another mission church, probably that of Santa María de Yamassee (Saunders 1987), and associated burials were excavated. The amount of data recovered is enormous, and the diversity of that data, from site layout to human skeletal remains to material culture, will be invaluable for addressing questions about transculturation between the Spanish and the southeastern Indians. This paper is limited to disclosing information pertaining to the architectural (in the broadest sense of the word) aspects of the site.

Site Location and Layout

It was no accident that Mission Santa María and Mission Santa Catalina were built only 40 m apart (fig. 2.1). The Harrison Homestead site was located on the lee side of Amelia Island in the only place that Harrison

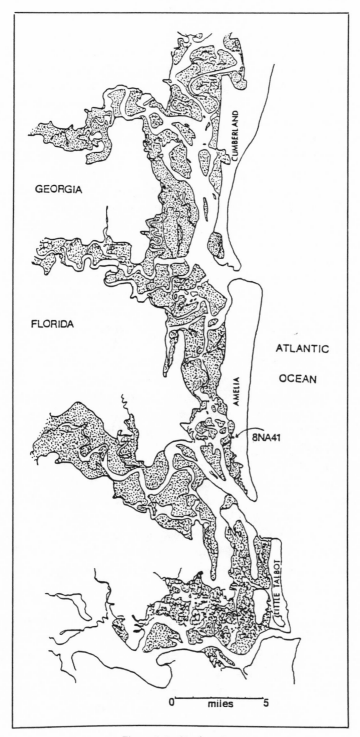

Figure 2.1. Site location.

Creek abutted the island (elsewhere salt marsh separates the two). Artesian fresh water was also present in the area. This environmental situation—a central location on a barrier island with access to the intracoastal waterway and fresh water—was common to several Atlantic coast missions established after 1606. Such a location has obvious advantages for both supply and defense.

The site base map with relevant mission period features associated with Santa María and Santa Catalina is presented in figure 2.2. These features were extracted from a bewildering array of post–mission period "disturbances"; all mission period components sustained a greater or lesser degree of disturbance from subsequent site use, which began when a British planter moved to the site in 1790 and continued to the present.

For Santa María, only the church is known. The layout of the mission compound is more complete for Santa Catalina. Architecturally speaking, the most complete building for the later mission is the *convento*. South of that building was a plaza with a series of features of unknown function. While lacking adequate architectural features allowing us to describe the building, the church is believed to have been over the cemetery. The mission kitchen may have been north and west of the *convento*. Another activity area was excavated east of the *convento*. Each of these blocks will be discussed below. In addition to those just cited, two other areas were intensively excavated. A portion of a possible palisade line was uncovered and an aboriginal structure was also located on the four acres examined during this project. These will not be discussed in detail here.

Few archaeologists are provided with primary documents picturing the layout of their sites. However, a map purporting to depict the mission of Santa Catalina on the island of Santa María (Amelia Island) in 1691 does indeed exist (fig. 2.3). In actuality, the map may have been the "plan" of the stockade cited in the 1695 visitation (see above). As such, it represents an idealized settlement layout for Spanish missions in the area (Saunders 1990; Thomas 1987:76, 1990). When the 1691 plan was scaled to the site base map (fig. 2.4), it became clear that there were some rather large discrepancies between the so-called ideal and our interpretation of the features of the site. First, we found no evidence for a moat, but a coastal location probably obviated the need for one. Second, we had no evidence for a garrison house on the tracts we investigated. The overlay suggested one possible reason: it may have eroded into Harrison Creek. It is more likely, however, that the inevitable competition and animosity between the military and the religious orders accounts for the fact that a

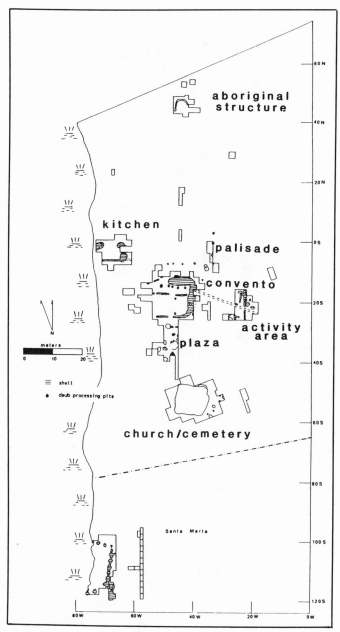

Figure 2.2. Base map showing excavation blocks with major mission period features.

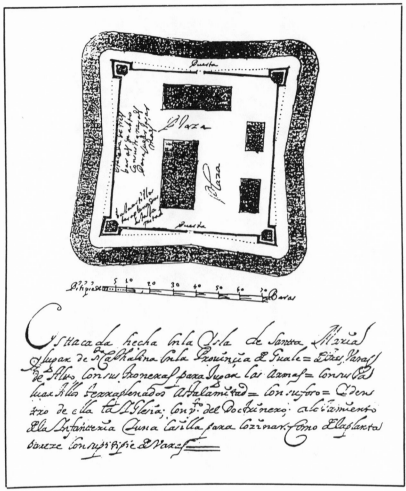

Figure 2.3. The 1691 plan.

garrison house has not been found in close proximity to other mission buildings anywhere in *La Florida* except at San Luis. The garrison house may have been uncovered by Robert Johnson (personal communication 1989) on property some 60 m north of the *convento*.

The buildings that were located were aligned with one another at 21° east of north. This orientation was unusual with respect to the orientation of missions in Apalachee, most of which lay between 45° and 81° east or west of north (Jones and Shapiro 1990:505). An orientation of 21° east of

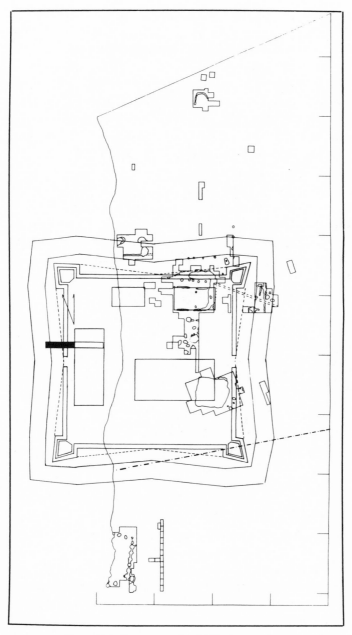

Figure 2.4. Base map with 1691 plan overlay.

north aligns the Spanish structures more or less with the modern orientation of the bluff line. Santa María was built with its long axis 30° east of
north, the present-day orientation of the bluff where it was constructed.
While more published data are needed on local topography for the sites
in question, it seems that after the Council of Trent, when east-west church
orientation was abandoned, structural orientation was determined principally by local physiography (see also Thomas 1988:108). The conformity
noted in Apalachee may be due to the directionality of the Tallahassee
Hills. Finally, the buildings of Santa Catalina de Guale on Amelia were not
arranged in a quadrangle pattern like that of Santa Catalina on St. Catherines Island, or even a right triangle like the plan modeled for Apalachee
(Jones and Shapiro 1990:504). If our functional attributions are correct,
the kitchen, *convento*, and church were arranged almost linearly.

Documentary and archaeological evidence (the latter most especially
from San Luis) indicate that the mission complex would have been situated on one end of a large town plaza; an aboriginal council house would
have been at the other end of the plaza, facing the church (e.g., Shapiro
1987). Though we found no archaeological evidence for a council house
either on- or off-site (in road cuts to the south and east), Jonathan Dickinson mentioned that one existed at "Santa María" in 1696 (Andrews and
Andrews 1945).

The *Convento*

The *convento* was a wattle-and-daub structure erected on surface
foundations (sleepers) of dense shell midden or scattered shell (fig. 2.5).
Major support posts were of pine; each had been squared, indicating the
presence of metal tools and the supervision of the Spanish in the construction. Both cane and what appeared to have been lathing were used to
create the wattle fabric of the building. Wrought nails and spikes were
common throughout the construction; 108 nails and 26 spikes were recovered.

Burned daub distribution indicated that only the interior portion of
the building was enclosed by wattle-and-daub walls; this area was floored
with clay as well. This walled portion of the structure measured about 7
m x 12 m. These dimensions were close to the 13.5-m-by-7.5-m *convento*
drawn on the 1695 plan.

There were doorways through both the north and south wattle-and-
daub walls. The north doorway was over the sleeper but a wooden sill

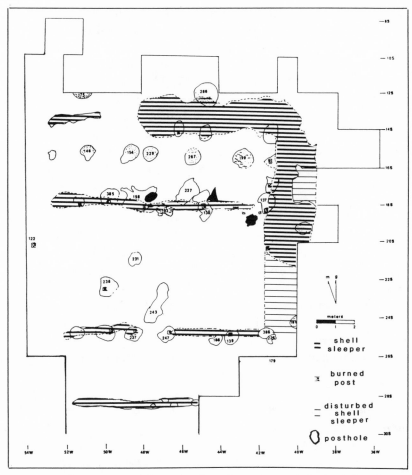

Figure 2.5. The *convento* of Santa Catalina. (Note: Post–mission period and some mission-period features not shown.)

was laid over the shell. Burned posts were found on either side of this sill, which was affixed to the posts with large wrought nails (this feature was removed as a block and is on display at the Amelia Island Museum of History). Directly opposite the sill, on the south side of the wattle-and-daub structure, the sleeper stopped, suggesting another doorway.

The doorways led out onto broad porches on the north and south sides of the building. The roof probably extended to the north side of the northernmost sleeper and either to or slightly beyond the southernmost sleeper. In any case, the covered portion of the structure appeared to have been about 16 m x 12 m. (Another row of postholes 4 m north of the north edge of the *convento* [fig. 2.2] appeared to be outside the building, but because these were exposed in a bulldozer cut, we cannot be sure.)

The sleepers took two forms (fig. 2.5). The north and south wattle-and-daub walls were elevated on thin sleepers (approximately 40 cm wide and 10 cm deep) composed of moderately dense shell. North and east of these sleepers, however, was a broad, 2-m-wide, 10-cm-deep shell "side-walk" composed of dense midden. On the north side, the "sidewalk" extended only a little more than half the width of the building, stopping just west of the north doorway. After a hiatus of about 3 m (another doorway?), shell continued west, but this deposit was composed of finely crushed shell in a very shallow deposit. A small brass hat badge, the only religious artifact recovered from the *convento* other than the seal of Santa Catalina, was discovered on the surface of this feature. The seal was found in the general mission period stratum within the wattle-and-daub portion of the building.

The fact that shell extended over the postholes (spaced approximately every 2 m) indicates that all sleepers were laid down after the posts were set. The northern "sidewalk" sleeper also overlay a large daub processing pit, indicating that the wattle-and-daub portion of the building was completed before the so-called sidewalk was put down. This evidence, coupled with the fact that the northern sleeper did not extend to the west side of the building, suggests that the wider sleepers represented an addition, one that perhaps was not completed.

The more elaborate treatment of the north side of the building (in the silled doorway and the "sidewalk") led me to consider it the front of the building, which would be expected to face the church across a small courtyard. However, in the absence of any evidence of a church to the north (and pits were put in where a church would have been either according to the 1691 plan or by analogy to the relationship of structures on St. Catherines Island, as well as other locations suggested by artifacts or artifact densities), the church must have been over the cemetery to the south (see below). The northernmost third of the *convento*, then, may have had a specialized function. Ongoing analysis into vessel forms and other data recovered from the excavation suggest that the function may have been storage. That might explain the "sidewalk" surrounding this portion of the building—it would have provided extra security against dampness. One would, however, expect walls around a storage area.

Another hypothesis, which would not necessarily preclude the storage function, is that the area served as a cloister.

The Plaza

In the 1691 plan, the area between the *convento* and the church was labeled a plaza area. How this area was traditionally used in *La Florida* is unknown, though in most archaeological reports the plaza is defined as relatively free of debris (e.g., Thomas 1987, fig. 27). Our data suggest that the plaza (fig. 2.6) was a heavily used activity area.

Several types of features were uncovered in the block. The most enigmatic was a square feature with gray sand fill bordered with burned wood

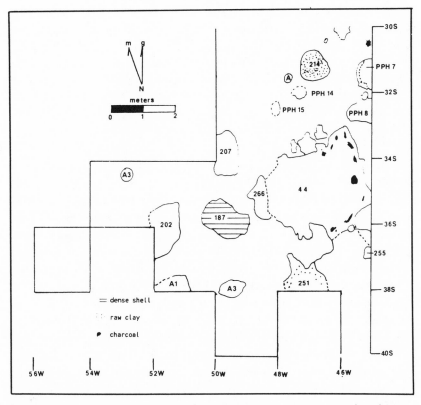

Figure 2.6. The plaza at Santa Catalina. (Note: Post–mission period and some mission-period features not shown.)

(Feature 44). This feature was not aligned with either the *convento* or the cemetery. Instead, it was oriented almost due north-south. A number of postholes were uncovered north of this feature, though whether they were associated with it is unknown. Feature function was not determined.

A series of pits was uncovered west and southwest of Feature 44. These pits shared a similar configuration: subrectangular, over 1.5 m long, and just under 1 m wide (Features 187, 202, 207, and 266). All of these features had a sandy fill with scattered shell except for Feature 187, which was midden-filled. One of these features, Feature 202, contained a possible colono-ware stemmed cup or goblet.

Our excavations shed little light on what specific activities might have taken place in the mission compound courtyard. Nevertheless, the concentration of mission period features and the fact that pottery was as abundant in this area as in most other areas indicate that it was heavily used. It may have functioned as a courtyard (*atrio*). In Mexico *atrios* were used for processions of religious brotherhoods (*cofradías*) and for religious instruction. The 11 wrought nails and 8 spikes recovered suggest some minor building activity, perhaps for stations of the cross or other small constructions. Burials also took place in the Mexican *atrio*; however, there were no human remains in the area we excavated.

The Kitchen

North and west of the *convento* was a set of features suggesting the presence of a kitchen (fig. 2.7). The area contained the only mission period midden and the highest frequency of mission period pottery on the site. Three large midden-filled pits were uncovered. These features were hypothesized to have been postholes; a fourth (for the southwest corner) probably eroded into the marsh. It would have completed a small rectangular structure. The southern posthole was intruded on by a midden-filled trench that followed the Spanish grid. There was some question, however, whether this trench was mission period. Similar features in the excavation block east of the *convento* were also suspect (see below).

Burned clay was scarce in the kitchen area; five wrought nails were the only iron hardware recovered. These data indicate that if a structure existed, it would have been an open shed, with members held together by lashings and perhaps with a thatch or palm roof (e.g., Manucy 1962, 1985). Such a light structure associated with a midden is consistent with a kitchen. However, the dimensions of this hypothetical structure, about 6

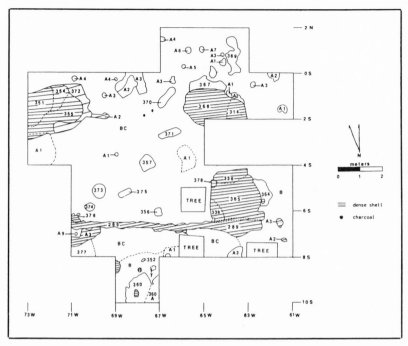

Figure 2.7. The possible kitchen of Santa Catalina. (Note: Post–mission period and some mission-period features not shown.)

m × 3 m, made the building considerably smaller than the 12-m-by-7-m kitchen drawn on the 1691 plan. Our excavations may not have uncovered the entire structure. Just south of the "structure" was a possible hearth that contained particulate charcoal, as well as charred wood and seeds (including sable palmetto, corn, bean, and grape; Donna Ruhl, personal communication 1991). There were also several inclusive deposits of shell and bone near this possible hearth, though none of these materials was burned.

While locating a kitchen on the bluff would have obvious advantages for fire control, the Laws of the Indies stated that the church, not the lowly kitchen, was the structure that should be seen from the water (see below).[1] An alternative hypothesis for this complex of features is that the pits were used for storage and then backfilled. This would not be inconsistent with the hypothesis that a kitchen was in this general location. Finally, if the row of postholes (mentioned above) located north of the *convento* was part of a fence or palisade enclosing the mission compound, our "kitchen" would have been outside the compound proper. Ovens appear to have been situated outside French forts (Le Moyne 1976:26), and the same may be true for Spanish mission kitchens. Alternatively, a lookout platform may have been established there.

ACTIVITY AREA

The area excavated east of the *convento* (figs. 2.2, 2.8) was originally believed to be the kitchen: if the 1691 plan were reversed, the location of this area relative to the *convento* was almost identical to that on the old map. However, there seemed to be too little organic material in this area to indicate a kitchen. A patchy shell midden with a maximum thickness of 20 cm overlay the features. This midden contained a mixture of plantation and mission period artifacts and was probably a plantation period

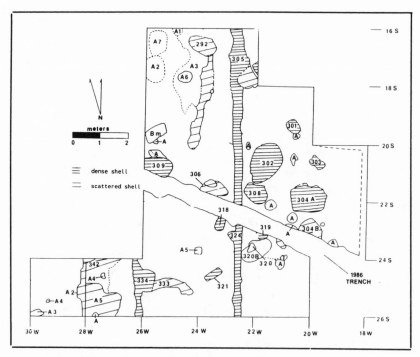

Figure 2.8. Activity area outside the mission compound. (Note: Post–mission period and some mission-period features not shown.)

deposit associated with the Harrison House. A small amount (relative to the *convento*) of daub and burned clay was recovered, but feature patterning did not suggest a structure. These data notwithstanding, this was an activity area of some sort. There was a 1-m-deep midden-filled feature at the western edge of the block. There were also five other, smaller and shallower mission period shell-filled pits, one of which held a cache of 23 wrought iron spikes or nails and a Spanish hoe blade. Other features included four narrow, shell-filled trenches like the one encountered in the kitchen area; these trenches appeared to have been associated with postholes. The similarity of these features to those identified by South (1983) at Santa Elena suggest that they may be vineyard ditches. Nevertheless, they could be attributable to either the mission period or the early plantation period.

This excavation block lay east of a line of postholes that may have been part of an eastern fence or palisade (fig. 2.2; these postholes corresponded with the eastern palisade line as depicted in the 1691 plan—fig. 2.4). If these postholes in fact represented the boundary of the mission compound, this activity area would have been outside the compound proper. Whatever specific activities occurred immediately outside the mission compound are still obscure, though activities related to horticulture are a possibility.

THE CHURCH/CEMETERY

Testing of the Santa Catalina cemetery (fig. 2.9) began under Piper Archaeology in 1985. Because it was necessary to determine quickly whether a mission cemetery was involved, and, if so, to convince the private landowner of the site's significance, a series of backhoe trenches was dug to define the limits of the cemetery. Once the boundaries were established, a bulldozer was used to remove the modern and plantation period deposits overlying the mission period stratum. While this strategy allowed for the efficient removal of almost 180 burials (see Larsen, this volume), the trenches and bulldozing may have destroyed evidence of a structure. However, it is more likely that the area was cleared of mission period surface debris by Samuel Harrison, who built a house over the western part of the cemetery in 1790.

What structural evidence remained was meager at best. Some burned clay and daub was recovered, as were 14 nails and 3 spikes. This is,

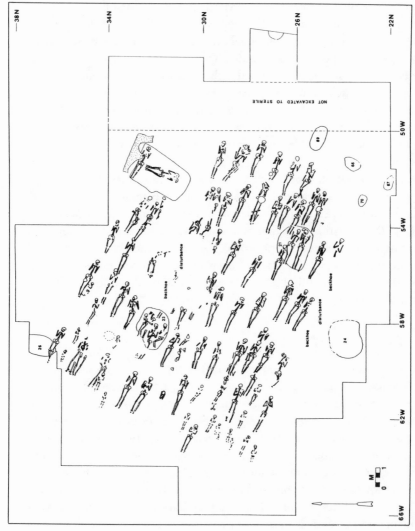

Figure 2.9. The church/cemetery of Santa Catalina. (Note: Post–mission-period and some mission-period features not shown.)

however, more construction material than was recovered from any other area on the site except the *convento*/plaza excavations. Postdepositional disturbances, both plantation period and modern (including archaeologists), made assessment difficult, but these data do suggest the presence of a structure.

The most convincing evidence that the interments were within a church is that most burial pits had raw clay in them. A small, angular patch of the same kind of clay overlay the top of the ossuary (see Larsen, this volume) in the northeast corner of the cemetery. These data suggest that burial pits were dug through the clay floor of a church, though it is not impossible that an outdoor area was surfaced with clay, particularly if it functioned as an *atrio*.

The most problematical aspect of the proposition that the church was over the cemetery is the lack of postholes around the edges of the cemetery. Several mission period postholes were uncovered along the eastern edge of the cemetery (fig. 2.9); however, these might be associated with the palisade or fence proposed earlier. Conversely, the church might have been built into the fence. Another, very deep mission period post was found several meters east of the projected palisade. This post might have been part of a facade, though the front of the church should have been on the western end of the church if the burials faced the altar. No other positively identifiable mission period postholes were exposed along the edges of the cemetery. No other features were as large or as deep as those along the eastern edge of the cemetery, nor did they have the clean sand fill characteristic of those postholes.

One argument against a structure over the cemetery is that the size of the burial area was much smaller than the average 11 m × 20 m of most mission churches in *La Florida* (Jones and Shapiro 1990). However, the aforementioned average includes structures identified as churches that did not contain burials. Evidence accruing from recent excavations suggests that all mission period churches contained burials and that those structures previously identified as churches with no burials may not have been churches (McEwan 1991; Marrinan 1990, 1991). The Santa Catalina cemetery was only 12 m × 10 m (or 13 m × 10 m if the length was measured to the eastern postholes), and the area was more nearly square than rectangular—a highly irregular configuration for a single-nave church. The long axis of the burials corresponded to the long axis of the hypothetical structure, as do all burials located within known churches.

Santa María

The Laws of the Indies stated that coastal churches should be built so that they might be seen by sailors putting out to sea. The location of the church of Santa María de Yamassee (fig. 2.10) conforms more exactly to this decree than does the hypothetical church of Santa Catalina. Its placement on the bluff has been detrimental to its preservation, however; a substantial portion of the western half of the structure, and the burials interred within, have eroded into Harrison Creek. Except for this erosion, disturbances to the church have been minimal. A modern privy, constructed of green-painted planks and galvanized wire nails, was the only major intrusion (see also Saunders 1988).

The earlier mission of Santa María shared some of the architectural peculiarities of Santa Catalina in that it was at least partially built on shell sleepers. This occurred despite the fact that the two missions did not have personnel in common (Geiger 1940). However, it is likely that the remains of the Santa María mission were still visible when Santa Catalina was established. The Santa Catalinans may have appreciated and adopted the innovation.

As figure 2.10 illustrates, a shell sleeper ran under the east wall; large postholes and a sleeper defined the south wall. The north wall, however, had no sleeper; the reasons for these differences are unknown.

Shell midden was used for other purposes besides the sleepers. All the postholes for the north, east, and south walls were backfilled with shell. Because there was no midden overlying the church, this shell must have been brought in from elsewhere. Presumably the midden would hold a post more firmly than sand; the sweetened soil may have preserved posts longer than did the more acid sand matrix.

The two posts exposed on the bluff line and the two postholes just east of them were much deeper than the others excavated. This suggested that these four postholes held central support posts (and also indicated that up to half of the structure had eroded away). The total area of the church was projected to be about 18 m to 20 m long and 12 m wide.

Several pieces of evidence argue for the entrance at the south end of the church and the altar to the north. First, the large postholes on the south wall may have supported posts of a more elaborate facade than the shallower postholes on the north wall. In addition, burial density was lower in the northern one-third of the building, reinforcing notions of

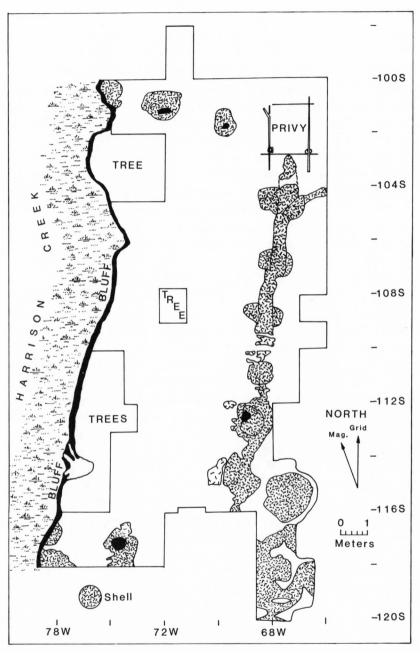

Figure 2.10. Santa María.

status differences in spatial location of burials within Catholic churches (Thomas 1988:113). Tradition dictated that burials usually faced the altar; the altar would be on the north wall if that were the case for the burials at Santa María. Finally, while there was a great deal of raw clay both in the matrix and in the burial pits of those individuals interred in the southern half of the building, there was relatively little clay in the northern half. This indicates that the (relatively shallow) nave was floored with clay and the sanctuary had a different floor, perhaps wood.

There was little evidence with which to construe the fabric of the church walls. We found no evidence of daub processing pits; however, no proveniences exterior to the church were excavated to sterile. Raw clay walls would surely have eroded away through time, but one would expect that the clay from the walls would be at least as well preserved as that of the floor—there was no raw clay either on or adjacent to the shell footer. These data suggest that the walls were of wood or thatch.

Though intensive excavation at Santa María was restricted to the church interior, we did attempt to discover more about the layout of the mission compound with two transects of posthole tests. If the mission compound had been laid out like the one on St. Catherines Island or like the 1691 plan, we should have intersected a building. In fact, little mission period material was recovered, and what was recovered came from the westernmost postholes. Inspection of the extensive footer trenches for the house subsequently built by the gracious landowners of this property, Gus and Marion Heatwole, revealed no mission period features and few mission period artifacts.

Though our tests were too limited to demonstrate the absence of other buildings, the results are suggestive. The documentary record suggests that the Spanish presence at Santa María was tenuous at best and that there may have been no Spaniards at the site for long periods of time. It may be that a mission compound was never completed at Santa María. Alternatively, we may have misidentified the occupation, and the structure excavated was a *visita*, which might not have had accompanying Spanish structures.

Summary

While all the artifacts from the Harrison Homestead site have been analyzed, it will be years before the site is fully understood. Certainly a better understanding of the site layout will come when other mission excavations are completed so that current hypotheses, such as an ideal layout, can be confirmed or discarded.

At present, it appears that the Amelia Island missions deviated from a theoretical "ideal" on several levels. If our structure functions are correct, there was no quadrangle or triangular plan for the Santa Catalina mission. Building plans also diverged. While the *convento* was within the prescribed Franciscan guidelines of about 14 m × 16 m (Kubler 1948; Saunders 1990:528), the cemetery/church was much smaller than the (possibly erroneous) "average" for *La Florida* or the church on the 1691 plan. This may mean that there was no church over the cemetery, but it is more likely that the small size reflects the dwindling Indian population on Amelia Island in the late seventeenth century. Church size was a reflection of projected burial population in Mexico (Kubler 1948:24, n.); recent archaeological data for *La Florida* seem to indicate that church size did fluctuate to a far greater extent than previously recognized.

The church constructed for the Santa María mission does fall within the predicted range of mission churches in *La Florida*. If other Spanish buildings existed for Santa María, our posthole testing indicates that they were not arranged in a quadrangle plan. On the other hand, because of the ephemeral nature of the Spanish presence at Santa María (Bushnell 1986), it may be that a *convento* and kitchen were never built.

Several mission researchers (McEwan 1991; Marrinan 1990, 1991; Saunders 1990) have become increasingly skeptical of the model of mission layout (Jones and Shapiro 1990) as it is currently used. In general, the model has been imposed on the data, so that, for instance, a structure measuring about 10 m × 20 m is always considered a church, with no independently derived data to support the ascribed function. The model, which should have been considered a testable hypothesis, has become "self-fulfilling" (Marrinan 1990:12). Data from our excavations on Amelia Island, in conjunction with that derived from other, ongoing excavations, might be used to indicate that the social environment was too variable over time and space to support ideal mission layouts in every location (Saunders 1990). In any event, it is a testable hypothesis.

Acknowledgments

This work could never have been started, let alone completed, without the goodwill and patience of George and Dottie Dorion and Gus and

Marion Heatwole, on whose property the remains of the two missions lie. In addition, the Dorions provided substantial funds for several seasons of fieldwork; the Heatwoles also gave money and logistical support. Mission period researchers will always be in debt to these understanding individuals. Financial assistance was also generously provided by the Florida Department of State, Division of Historical Resources. My thanks to all.

Note

1. The Laws of the Indies, codified in 1573, consisted of 148 ordinances governing site selection, town plan, and the political organization of New World towns.

Bibliography

Andrews, Evangeline Walker, and Charles McLean Andrews, eds.
1945 *Jonathan Dickinson's Journal; or, God's Protecting Providence: Being the Narrative of a Journey from Port Royal in Jamaica to Philadelphia, August 23, 1696 to April 1, 1697*. New Haven: Yale University Press.

Arnade, Charles W.
1959 *The Siege of St. Augustine in1702*. Social Sciences Monograph no. 3. Gainesville: University of Florida Press.

Boyd, Mark F.
1948 Enumeration of Florida Spanish Missions in 1675 with Translations of Documents. *Florida Historical Quarterly* 7(2):181–188.

Bullen, Ripley P., and John W. Griffin
1952 An Archaeological Survey of Amelia Island, Florida. *The Florida Anthropologist* 5(3–4):37–64.

Bushnell, Amy T.
1986 *Santa María in the Written Record*. Miscellaneous Project Report Series, no. 21. Gainesville: Department of Anthropology, Florida State Museum.

Geiger, Maynard J., O.F.M.
1940 *Biographical Dictionary of the Franciscans in Spanish Florida and Cuba (1528–1841)*. Franciscan Studies, no. 21. Paterson, N.J.: St. Anthony's Guild Press.

Hann, John H.
1990 Summary Guide to Spanish Florida Missions and *Visitas* with Churches in the Sixteenth and Seventeenth Centuries. *The Americas* 46(4):417–513.

Hann, John H., trans.
1986   General Visitation of the Provinces of Guale and Mocama made by the Capt. Don Juan de Pueyo. Ms. on file, San Luis Archaeological and Historic Site, Tallahassee.

Hardin, Kenneth W.
1986   The Santa María Mission Project. *The Florida Anthropologist* 39(1–2):75–83.

Hemmings, E. Thomas, and Kathleen A. Deagan
1973   *Excavations on Amelia Island in Northeast Florida.* Contributions of the Florida State Museum in Anthropology and History, no. 18. Gainesville.

Jones, B. Calvin, and Gary N. Shapiro
1990   Nine Mission Sites in Apalachee. In *Columbian Consequences.* Vol. 2: *Archaeological and Historical Perspectives on the Spanish Borderlands East*, edited by David Hurst Thomas, 491–509. Washington, D.C.: Smithsonian Institution Press.

Kubler, George
1948   *Mexican Architecture of the Sixteenth Century.* 2 vols. New Haven: Yale University Press.

Larsen, Clark Spencer, and Rebecca Saunders
1987   The Two Santa Catalina Cemeteries. Paper presented at the 44th Annual Meeting of the Southeastern Archaeological Conference, Charleston, South Carolina.

Larson, Lewis H., Jr.
1978   Historic Guale Indians of the Georgia Coast and the Impact of the Spanish Mission Effort. In *Tacachale: Essays on the Indians of Florida and Southeastern Georgia during the Historic Period*, edited by Jerald T. Milanich and Samuel Proctor, 120–140. Ripley P. Bullen Monographs in Anthropology and History, no. 1. Gainesville: University Presses of Florida.

Le Moyne, Jacques
1976   *America.* Edited by Theodore de Bry. In *Discovering the New World*, edited by Michael Alexander, 17–59. New York: Harper and Row.

McEwan, Bonnie G.
1991   San Luis de Talimali: The Archaeology of Spanish-Indian Relations at a Florida Mission. *Historical Archaeology* 25(3):36–60.

Manucy, Albert C.
1962   *The Houses of St. Augustine.* St. Augustine: St. Augustine Historical Society.

1985   The Physical Setting of Sixteenth-Century St. Augustine. *The Florida Anthropologist* 38(1–2):34–53.

Marrinan, Rochelle A.
1990 An Overview of Settlement Plan in the Missions of *La Florida*. Paper presented at the 47th Annual Meeting of the Southeastern Archaeological Conference, Mobile, Alabama.

1991 Archaeological Investigations at Mission Patale, 1984–1991. *The Florida Anthropologist* 44(2–4):228–254.

Milanich, Jerald T., and Rebecca Saunders
1986 *The Spanish Castillo and the Franciscan Doctrina of Santa Catalina, at Santa María, Amelia Island, Florida (8NA41d)*. Miscellaneous Project Report Series, no. 20. Gainesville: Department of Anthropology, Florida State Museum.

Saunders, Rebecca
1987 Investigations of the 1686–1702 Mission/Castillo of Santa María on Amelia Island, Florida. Paper presented at the 1987 Society for Historical Archaeology Conference on Historical and Underwater Archaeology, Savannah, Georgia.

1988 *Excavations at 8NA41: Two Mission Period Sites on Amelia Island, Florida*. Miscellaneous Project Report Series, no. 35. Gainesville: Department of Anthropology, Florida Museum of Natural History.

1990 Ideal and Innovation: Spanish Mission Architecture in the Southeast. In *Columbian Consequences*. Vol. 2: *Archaeological and Historical Perspectives on the Spanish Borderlands East*, edited by David Hurst Thomas, 527–542. Washington, D.C.: Smithsonian Institution Press.

Shapiro, Gary
1987 *Archaeology at San Luis: Broad-Scale Testing, 1984–1985*. Florida Archaeology no. 3. Tallahassee: Florida Bureau of Archaeological Research.

South, Stanley
1983 *Revealing Santa Elena 1982*. Research Manuscript Series, no. 188. Columbia: University of South Carolina, South Carolina Institute of Archaeology and Anthropology.

Thomas, David Hurst
1987 *The Archaeology of Mission Santa Catalina de Guale: 1. Search and Discovery*. Anthropological Papers of the American Museum of Natural History, vol. 63, pt. 2. New York.

1988 Saints and Soldiers at Santa Catalina: Hispanic Designs for Colonial America. In *The Recovery of Meaning: Historical Archaeology in the Eastern United States*, edited by Mark P. Leone and Parker B. Potter, Jr., 73–140. Washington, D.C.: Smithsonian Institution Press.

1990 The Spanish Missions of *La Florida*: An Overview. In *Columbian Consequences*. Vol. 2: *Archaeological and Historical Perspectives on the Spanish*

Borderlands East, edited by David Hurst Thomas, 357–397. Washington, D.C.: Smithsonian Institution Press.

Wenhold, Lucy L., trans.
1936 *A Seventeenth-Century Letter of Gabriel Díaz Vara Calderón, Bishop of Cuba, Describing the Indians and Indian Missions of Florida*. Smithsonian Miscellaneous Collections, vol. 95, no. 16. Washington, D.C.

❂ 3 ❂

The Archaeology of the
Convento de San Francisco

KATHLEEN HOFFMAN

For the past 300 years the Convento de San Francisco has occupied a prominent position along the Matanzas Bay at the northeastern edge of the colonial city of St. Augustine. This friary served as the center of operations for the Franciscan mission effort in *La Florida* during the sixteenth and seventeenth centuries. In this capacity the monastery played a vital role as an intermediary between the outlying missions and the secular town of St. Augustine. As mission headquarters, it also served as a guest house for visiting church officials, and it functioned both as a training center for new friars prior to their departure for their respective mission stations in the provinces of Timucua, Guale, and Apalachee and as a hospice for ill and elderly friars (Matter 1972:11).

Although it was administratively and ecclesiastically linked with the missions, the monastery differed from them in two important ways. First, it was located within the urban, Spanish town of St. Augustine, not in a remote Indian village. Second, the Convento de San Francisco consisted of a community of friars who communicated on a daily basis with the predominantly European population of the Spanish town of St. Augustine, whereas the Franciscans assigned to the missions were isolated not only from fellow missionaries but also from other Spaniards. This chapter is intended to document the spatial organization and material culture of the monastery in order to shed light on its role as a center for religious activity in *La Florida* and as a formal institution organized by the Crown of Spain.

The site (SA-42A) of this Franciscan monastery is located in modern St. Augustine at the corners of St. Francis and Marine streets, property that today houses the Florida Department of Military Affairs Headquarters (fig. 3.1). In 1988 the Florida Museum of Natural History, under the direction of Kathleen Deagan as principal investigator, conducted extensive test excavations in that area of the property known as the quadrangle (Hoffman 1990). These excavations yielded a considerable amount of information regarding the spatial organization of the monastery and provided a glimpse into the material life of the Franciscan friars who lived in *La Florida* during the First Spanish period.

Background

Little is known documentarily about the sixteenth-century monastery except that it was constructed in 1588 (table 3.1), one year after the arrival of the first significant group of Franciscan missionaries. It included a chapel and *convento* of red cedar logs and planks with a thatched roof (Cooper 1962:5; Gannon 1983:37; Eugene Lyon, personal communication 1988). Its location within the colonial city was mandated by the City Planning Ordinances of the Laws of the Indies, and the friars assigned to the new monastery fell under the jurisdiction of New Spain (Crouch, Garr, and Mundigo 1982:114; Geiger 1937:43; Haring 1947:168). No known maps illustrating its configuration exist, but monasteries in other Spanish colonial regions shared a common type of plan that included a courtyard, church, *convento*, and cemetery (Kubler 1948:314–344; Markman 1966:74). Recent investigations at several mission sites in Florida and Georgia have suggested that these mission compounds consisted of three or four rectangular buildings arranged around a quadrangle (Saunders 1990:531), a plan that may have been adhered to during the initial construction of the Franciscan monastery in St. Augustine.

The friary was dedicated to the Immaculate Conception (*La Concepción*) in 1592, and two years later the governor of Spanish Florida, Domingo Martinez de Vendano, died. Following Spanish custom (Koch 1983:221), he was buried in the Franciscan chapel (Geiger 1937:65). Five years later, in 1599, a fire destroyed both the *convento* and the chapel; neither was rebuilt until the very early years of the seventeenth century (table 3.1). The new chapel was apparently constructed by 1603, for at this time the remains of three Franciscan friars, who had been killed in

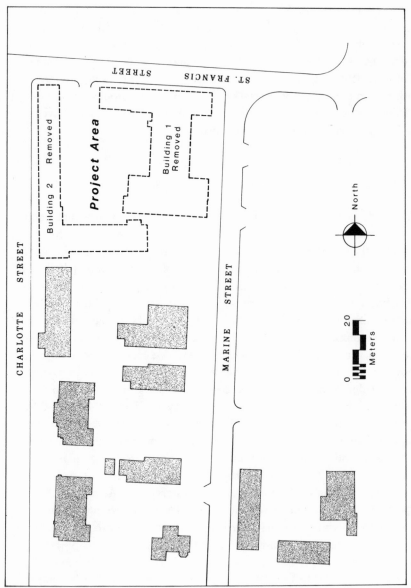

Figure 3.1. Location of project area within the National Guard Headquarters property.

TABLE 3.1. Summary of Known Construction Periods at SA-42A

Pre-1588	Initial construction of nonmasonry church and *convento*
1599-1603	Destroyed by fire and rebuilt
1702	Burned by retreating British troops
Circa 1750	New monastery constructed of coquina

present-day Georgia by the Guale in 1597, were brought to St. Augustine and interred in the friary chapel (Harkins 1990:461, 471). In 1606 the Custody of Santa Elena de la Florida was formed and the mission field was extended west to encompass part of the hinterland. The Convento de San Francisco became the principal convent of this newly formed custody, which included convents in Florida and Cuba (Geiger 1937:227). By 1610 construction of the second monastery had been completed, and two years later Philip III of Spain expanded the administrative duties of the friary when he designated it as a capitular or province house (Geiger 1937:187; Mohr 1929:221). By mid-century, between 35 and 40 missionaries were attached to the monastery (Charles 1928:222; Gannon 1983:57; Thomas 1990:378). The actual number of priests who lived permanently at the friary remains unclear, as does the number of laypersons attached to it. During his 1675 *visita*, Bishop Gabriel Díaz Vara Calderón reported that "three monks, a superior, a preacher, a lay brother, and . . . three curates for the three principal languages of these provinces" resided at the Franciscan convent and administered to the Indians living in St. Augustine (Wenhold 1936:7). The historical record also indicates the presence of an African servant as early as 1589 (Cooper 1962:7), and, given the use of Indian laborers by the Franciscan missionaries (Lyon 1976:118–119; Matter 1973:31), it is possible that Indians also may have been among the residents of *La Concepción*.

In 1702 the church and *convento* were briefly occupied as headquarters for the British army during Colonel Moore's siege of St. Augustine and consequently destroyed by fire during the British retreat from the town, less than two months after their initial attack (table 3.1; Arnade 1959:37, 53–61). An English soldier attached to one of Moore's regiments described the church and *convento* as "large enough to hold 700 to 800 men" (Boniface 1971:78), and several documents mention a library of "Greek and Latin Fathers" as being lost in the fire (Shea 1886:460).

A letter from Governor Antonio de Benavides to the Crown in 1724 noted that the foundations of the burned *convento* measured 56 varas long, 6 varas wide, and 6 varas high (one vara equals approximately 0.84 m; after Manucy 1978:165) and mentioned the existence of a sacristy and a tower, presumably associated with the convent church (Benavides 1724). Although the king of Spain appropriated funds for the construction of a new monastery (the third) in the 1720s, it was not rebuilt until the 1750s (Joyce 1989:74; Mohr 1929:225). From 1702 until that time, the friars lived in wooden huts and used a small coquina structure for their chapel (Gannon 1983:77).

The third friary was constructed of coquina and it is most likely this monastery that appeared on the 1764 Castello map of St. Augustine, the first known depiction of the compound (table 3.1; fig. 3.2). In 1763 the Franciscans vacated the property when Spain ceded *La Florida* to En-

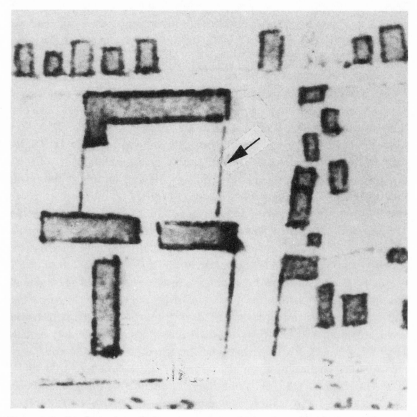

Figure 3.2. Configuration of the monastery as depicted on the 1764 Castello map (arrow indicates monastery compound).

gland under terms of the first Treaty of Paris. During the subsequent British period (1763–1783) the former monastery housed British soldiers and several renovations occurred. In 1766 the commanding officer recommended that the church and *convento* be converted into barracks and construction began in 1767. A two-story building was constructed adjacent to the convent and incorporated the former chapel into its design.

Spain once again gained control of Florida in 1784. During the Second Spanish period (1784–1821) no known construction occurred at the site. Several Franciscan friars briefly reestablished themselves in the monastery from 1786 until 1792. Following this, Spanish soldiers took possession of the property and remained there until Florida became a U.S. territory in 1821 (Mohr 1929:226).

During the first decade of the Territorial period the property was used briefly for a jail. In 1832 it was established as a U.S. military reservation and was occupied as such until 1900, when the U.S. Army abandoned the property. After a temporary occupation by orphans and sisters from the Sisters of St. Joseph convent (Cooper 1962:40), the property was leased to the state of Florida as the state military headquarters. Today the property continues to function as headquarters for the Florida National Guard.

Spatial Organization

Although no complete structures were uncovered during the excavations, sufficient evidence was recovered to determine the construction material and to estimate the dimensions, plans, and orientations of several buildings associated with the sixteenth-, seventeenth-, and eighteenth-century monasteries. Archaeological evidence for these structures and associated activity areas included postmolds, post and trench footings, construction trenches, tabby footings, a crushed coquina walkway, wells, and trash pits. Unfortunately, it was not possible to ascertain the original functions of most of the structures due to the plethora of construction and renovation activities that took place during the nineteenth and twentieth centuries.

SIXTEENTH-CENTURY MONASTERY (CA. 1588)

Associated with the sixteenth-century monastery were a portion of a small wooden post structure (Structure A) and a well construction pit

(Feature 36), both of which were probably constructed shortly after the establishment of the monastery in 1588. As shown in figure 3.2, Structure A consisted of three postmolds, with diameters of 15 cm to 20 cm, spaced 40 cm to 45 cm apart. Their alignment suggests that the building represented by these postmolds was rectangular or square in plan, and the absence of associated daub indicates that it was probably constructed entirely of wood. Both this structure and the well pit, which was approximately 22 m to the northwest, were located in the western half of the quadrangle and appeared to be oriented on a northwest-by-southeast axis. This and the absence of any ca. 1588 features anywhere else on the site suggest that the initial Franciscan occupation was confined to the western half of the property (although this could be a function of sampling bias and postdepositional disturbance).

EARLY SEVENTEENTH-CENTURY MONASTERY (CA. 1600)

In contrast to the brief, early occupation of the ca. 1588 phase, a tremendous amount of activity occurred during the seventeenth century. The amount of construction undoubtedly reflects the growth of mission activity in Florida and the elevation of the monastery to headquarters status. Two discrete occupational phases were identified, dating respectively to ca. 1600 and ca. 1650.

The first phase represents the rebuilding of the monastery following the 1599 fire that destroyed the *convento* and chapel. Evidence for two post-and-trench structures (Structures B and C), two trash pits, and a barrel well was identified (fig. 3.3). Both of the structures and the well were located on the eastern half of the project area, while the trash pits were situated in the far northwestern corner of the site, approximately 23 m from the seventeenth-century buildings. Previous archaeological research in St. Augustine has demonstrated that trash pits are consistently located to the rear of structures, usually at a distance of 7 m to 9 m (Deagan 1983:77). While the great distance between the ca. 1600 trash pits and structures may represent an anomaly, it may also indicate either that a ca. 1600 structure existed on the western half of the property or that the trash pits may in fact be associated with the ca. 1588 occupation, which appeared to be concentrated on the western half of the property. Artifacts recovered from these trash pits were consistent with material found in late sixteenth-century assemblages.

Only a small remnant of Structure B was identified, making it difficult

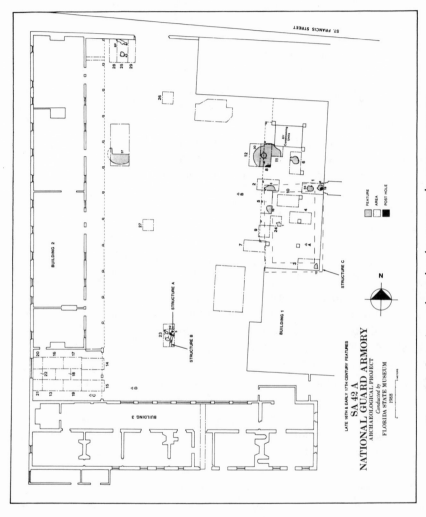

LATE 16TH & EARLY 17TH CENTURY FEATURES

SA 42 A
NATIONAL GUARD ARMORY
ARCHAEOLOGICAL PROJECT
Conducted by
FLORIDA STATE MUSEUM
1988

FEATURE
AREA
POST HOLE

Figure 3.3. Late sixteenth- and early seventeenth-century structures.

to say little more than that it appeared to be a wooden building supported by posts. The posts measured approximately 15 cm in diameter and were set into a narrow trench approximately 12 cm wide (fig. 3.3). This structure was located in the southern end of the quadrangle at a distance of approximately 19 m from the second and larger post structure discussed below.

As seen in figure 3.3, seven postmolds were associated with Structure C, which was located in that area of the quadrangle adjacent to present-day Building 1. These postmolds ranged in diameter from 50 cm to 70 cm, were at least 1 m deep, and were spaced approximately 1 m to 1.5 m apart. They also appeared to be oriented approximately 20° west of north on a northwest-by-southeast axis. The size and depth of these postmolds suggest that they at one time held large posts of 50 cm to 60 cm in diameter and that they supported a substantial amount of weight. Five of these postmolds are in alignment and form a rectangular area that measures approximately 8.3 m by 10 m. The other two postmolds, which were about 3 m to the east and parallel to the rectangular alignment, may have formed the northern boundary of a colonnade that measured about 3 m in width.

Postmolds exhibiting similar dimensions and depths have been reported from several religious sites in Florida and the Caribbean. Thomas noted similar large and deep posts at the seventeenth-century mission of Santa Catalina de Guale on St. Catherines Island in Georgia in association with a structure believed to be the mission chapel (Thomas 1988:94–110; David Hurst Thomas, personal communication 1989). Marrinan also recorded the existence of "post pits" of a similar size and dimension from the Patale mission near Tallahassee and the area believed to be the sixteenth-century church of Puerto Real, a Spanish colonial town located along the north coast of modern Haiti (Marrinan 1982:10–12; Rochelle Marrinan, personal communication 1990). Although the precise function of these "post pits" was not defined, Marrinan postulated that the large pits found at Puerto Real might represent a footing for a colonnade or covered walkway similar to those identified at the fifteenth-century Portuguese town of Qsar es-Seghir off the north coast of Morocco (Marrinan 1982:10–12; Redman 1986).

Although the large postmolds found at the National Guard Headquarters site may simply represent supports for wooden plank walls to a post-and-board structure, which is not inconsistent with the findings of other buildings in St. Augustine or the other known mission sites, their massive size and wide spacing make it more likely that these postmolds may have functioned as footings for a colonnade, as suggested by Marrinan and Redman. Colonnades or arcades, which are defined by Kubler (1948:283) as a row of arches on columns or pillars that support a roof, were common features of sixteenth-century Spanish colonial religious and secular architecture (Baird 1962:23; Manucy 1978:91–92; Markman 1966:74; Newcomb 1973:ix). Ruins of the fifteenth-century Convento de San Francisco at Concepción de la Vega in the Dominican Republic as well as plans of the Convento de San Francisco in Santo Domingo and of several sixteenth-century monasteries in Mexico (specifically those associated with Huejotzingo, Yecapixtla, Tepeyango, Tlaquiltenango, Tezontepec, and Zempoala) all show the existence of arched passageways that often surrounded a square courtyard known as a *claustro*, or cloister (Kubler 1948:314–320; Ortega and Fondeur 1982:131). Similar covered passageways and courtyards were also common features of eighteenth-century Franciscan mission architecture in California (Newcomb 1973:pls. 30–32, 46, 62). There is ample precedent for the existence of *claustros* in the religious architecture of the Franciscans in the Americas, and it is therefore possible that the Franciscan monastery in St. Augustine, which functioned as the headquarters for the entire mission effort in *La Florida*, would have exhibited similar architectural details. Based on this, it is suggested that the postmolds represented by Structure C may have functioned as column supports that formed an arched passageway, approximately 3 m wide, that surrounded a *claustro*.

LATE SEVENTEENTH-CENTURY MONASTERY (CA. 1650)

No complete structures associated with the ca. 1650 building phase were identified, but portions of at least two, and possibly three, distinct post-and-trench structures (Structures D, E, and F), three trash pits, and a possible well construction pit can be associated with the third building phase (fig. 3.4). With the exception of the possible well and one trash pit, all of these features were concentrated in that portion of the quadrangle adjacent to Building 1. As in the previous two phases, all of the structures appeared to be oriented on a northwest-by-southeast axis.

The first structure, Structure E, consisted of a footing trench associated with a wooden-post-and-trench building that was constructed in the approximate location and on top of the earlier ca. 1600 *claustro*. Its east-

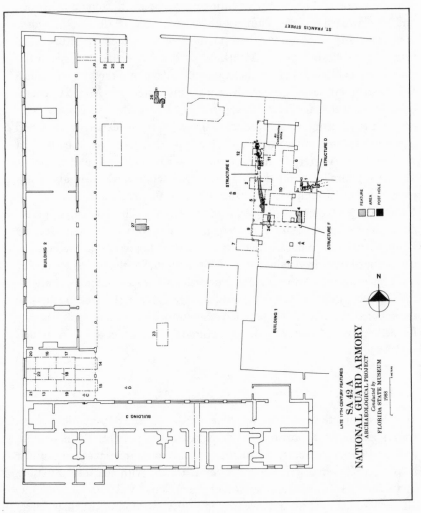

Figure 3.4. Late seventeenth-century structures.

west dimensions are unknown, but it measured at least 9 m along its northwest-southeast axis, which appeared to be oriented approximately 20° west of north. The posts were approximately 15–20 cm in diameter and were spaced approximately 20–30 cm apart. Smaller posts, 3–5 cm in diameter, were found only in the easternmost section of this structure. The trench itself measured 20 cm in width. The absence of daub in or surrounding the trench suggests that the walls consisted of wooden planks.

The second post-and-trench structure, designated Structure F, could conceivably align with the first to form a small 4-m-by-4-m rectangular room attached to the southeastern end of Structure E, but the morphology and depth of this second structure suggest that it instead represents a separate building.

The third building, Structure D, was situated 5 m to the east of Structure E and appeared to be a two-room rectangular building of the common St. Augustine plan described by Manucy (1978:50–53). Because only a portion of this structure was identified, its dimensions remain uncertain, but it measured at least 2.10 m east-west. The presence of two trash pits, 3 m to the northwest of the buildings, indicates a separate activity area used for trash disposal. Because trash pits on Spanish colonial sites are always located outside and to the rear of buildings (Deagan 1985), the proximity (3 m east) of these trash pits to Structure D suggests that either the structure was less than 3 m wide, which seems unlikely, or the remainder of this building extended to the west.

EIGHTEENTH-CENTURY MONASTERY (CA. 1750)

This phase corresponds to the rebuilding of the monastery following Moore's burning of St. Augustine in 1702. Documentary and cartographic evidence indicate that during this time period three rectangular coquina structures were constructed in the approximate locations of existing Buildings 1, 2, and 3 of the National Guard Headquarters (fig. 3.5). The chapel and *convento*, as identified on the key to the Elixio de la Puente map, were arranged around a courtyard with a boxlike chapel forming the eastern border and two buildings, labeled only as the "stone convent of San Francisco," forming the southern and western boundaries of the courtyard (fig. 3.5; Manucy n.d.:17). A fourth rectangular structure, again labeled only as the "stone convent of San Francisco" (Manucy n.d.:17), was approximately 14 m to the southeast of the chapel, a loca-

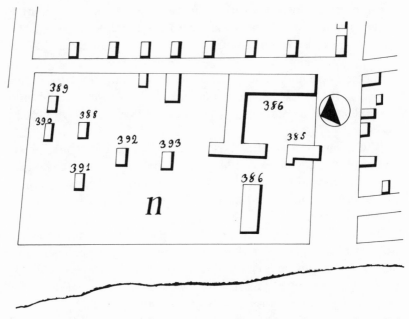

Figure 3.5. Configuration of the monastery as depicted on the 1764 Elixio de la Puente map (arrow indicates monastery compound).

tion that would place it under Marine Street and under a portion of the modern parking lot that fronts the Matanzas River. Burials found to the north of this building during the installation of utilities in 1968 and 1972 (*St. Augustine Record*, 31 January 1968, 24 September 1972) suggest that it was associated with the cemetery, which appears on the historic maps as a walled enclosure, now located underneath Marine Street and the current parking lot situated on the bayfront.

Archaeological excavations confirmed that the central wing of Building 1 was built on top of the tabby footings associated with the ca. 1702–1750 chapel. In addition, the identification of a coquina and limerock column support and an associated trench for a second column suggest that a covered passageway or loggia may have existed along the west elevation of the chapel. This loggia was approximately 90 cm wide and the floor was covered with a crushed coquina surface. The identification of two coquina footings in the southwestern corner of the quadrangle suggests that the eighteenth-century *convento* also lies under extant structures (Buildings 2 and 3).

Material Assemblages

In order to make comparisons between the assemblage from the St. Francis monastery and other sites, the material has been organized by functional categories that follow those developed by South (1977:88–106) and adapted for Spanish colonial sites by Deagan (1983:231–241, 1985:20). Table 3.2 shows the relative frequencies, by major functional groups, of the material associated with the various stages of the Franciscan monastery. It is clear that throughout this occupation ceramic items comprise the major proportion of the assemblage. This is not surprising given the predominance of ceramics on Spanish colonial sites in general (Fairbanks 1972:141–142) and the relatively high frequency of ceramics noted for other sixteenth-, seventeenth-, and eighteenth-century Spanish sites in St. Augustine (Deagan 1983, 1985; King 1984). It is somewhat informative, however, to note the changing frequencies of specific categories of these ceramics through time.

The majority of the European ceramics associated with the establish-

TABLE 3.2. Distribution of Material Associated with the Convento de San Francisco, 1588-1763

Group	Circa 1588		Circa 1600		Circa 1650		Circa 1702	
	#	%	#	%	#	%	#	%
Kitchen								
Majolica	88	12.9	14	10.6	268	13.1	264	12.1
Spanish tableware	5	0.7	1	0.7	10	0.5	13	0.6
Euro-tableware	1	0.2	0	0	20	1.0	60	2.8
Spanish utilitarian	218	32.0	13	9.9	253	12.4	277	12.7
Euro-utilitarian	4	0.6	2	1.5	48	2.4	48	2.2
Aboriginal	366	53.7	101	77.1	1447	70.7	1524	69.7
Subtotal	682	94.0	131	77.4	2046	80.8	2186	73.8
Nonceramic kitchen	15	2.1	6	3.6	107	4.2	289	9.8
Architecture	20	2.8	26	15.4	269	10.6	397	3.4
Arms	1	0.1	0	0	6	0.2	10	0.4
Clothing	5	0.7	3	1.8	87	3.4	44	1.5
Personal	1	0.1	0	0	15	0.6	23	0.8
Activities	1	0.1	0	0	3	0.1	7	0.2
Metal	1	0.1	3	1.8	2	0.1	4	0.1
Total	726	100.0	169	100.0	2535	100.0	2960	100.0

ment of the monastery (ca. 1588) were Spanish in origin, and in fact only five items from the entire ceramic assemblage were non-Spanish. These included one sherd of Guadalajara Polychrome and four unidentifiable coarse earthenware sherds. With the exception of one El Morro sherd and one piece of Redware, all of the utilitarian vessels consisted of fragments of glazed and unglazed olive jars, vessels that functioned as storage containers. Majolica, a tin-enameled ware, was the major tableware used by the Spanish throughout the First Spanish period and was a consistent element of all of the assemblages associated with the Franciscan monastery. During the sixteenth-century occupation, Columbia Plain dominated the majolica group, which accounted for 12 percent of the entire assemblage, but Sevilla Blue on Blue, Yayal Blue on White, Isabela Polychrome, and Santo Domingo Blue on White were also represented. The majority of both the majolica and olive jar fragments were recovered from the ca. 1588 well construction pit found on the western half of the quadrangle. Aboriginal pottery and Spanish utilitarian vessels accounted for 53.7 percent and 31.97 percent, respectively, of the total sixteenth-century ceramic assemblage.

St. Johns pottery, a chalky ware that was manufactured by the Timucuan Indians who resided in and around St. Augustine (Goggin 1952:99–105), represented 72.4 percent of the aboriginal pottery. San Marcos, a coarse, quartz-tempered ware believed to have been made by the Guale Indians of coastal Georgia (Smith 1948:314–316), represented 19.1 percent (table 3.3). Previous research has demonstrated that San Marcos wares supplemented European cooking and storage vessels that were often not available in colonial St. Augustine (Otto and Lewis 1974:102–103), and it has also been suggested that St. Johns pottery served a similar function during the early years of the colony (Herron 1986). Although some of the cooking pots may have been metal (which is poorly represented in the archaeological record due to poor preservation conditions), the frequency of these two types of pottery and the absence of identifiable European cooking wares suggest a reliance on Indian food preparation technology.

Distinctive changes in the ceramic assemblage took place in the early seventeenth century. Although the proportions of most of the categories remained relatively similar, Indian pottery appears to have almost completely replaced Spanish utilitarian wares. The proportion of Spanish utilitarian wares decreased in the assemblage from 32.0 percent to only 9.9 percent, and the proportion of aboriginal wares increased from 53.7

TABLE 3.3. Distribution of Aboriginal Pottery at the Convento de San Francisco, 1588-1763

	Circa 1588		Circa 1600		Circa 1650		Circa 1702	
	#	%	#	%	#	%	#	%
St. Johns	265	72.4	50	49.5	519	35.9	63	4.1
San Marcos	70	19.1	23	22.8	463	32.0	72	4.7
Nonlocal	31	8.5	28	27.7	465	32.1	1389	91.2
Total	366	100.0	101	100.0	1447	100.0	1524	100.0

percent to 77.1 percent (table 3.2). In addition, although St. Johns pottery continued to dominate the Indian pottery assemblage (49.5 percent), the frequency of San Marcos pottery increased (from 19.1 percent to 22.8 percent) and the proportion of unidentified types increased substantially (from 8.5 percent to 27.7 percent).

As in the earlier phase, kitchen items dominated the mid-seventeenth-century assemblage with majolica accounting for 13.1 percent. Spanish utilitarian wares comprised 12.4 percent and other European ceramics comprised less than 5 percent of the total ceramic assemblage. The frequency of Mexico City and Puebla-type majolicas and of non-Spanish tablewares also increased, no doubt related to the shift in responsibility for the Florida *situado* (annual subsidy) from the treasury of Spain to that of Mexico City in 1594 and the emergence of majolica production centers in New Spain during the late sixteenth century (Lister and Lister 1974, 1982; Sluiter 1985:3).

During the ca. 1650 phase Indian pottery comprised 57 percent of the total assemblage and the relative proportions of St. Johns, San Marcos, and nonlocal wares were remarkably similar (table 3.3). The nonlocal wares category, however, contained a greater variety of types than in earlier phases. Although sand-tempered plain and grit-tempered wares continued to be the dominant elements, grog-tempered pottery, red filmed, Lamar-like incised, Ocmulgee Fields, and Altamaha ceramics were also recovered from the late seventeenth-century contexts.

In his analysis of Indian pottery from the Trinity Episcopal site in St. Augustine, Piatek reported a similar increase in the frequency of nonlocal wares during the seventeenth century and suggested a correlation between the presence of nonlocal wares and changes in the tribute system (Piatek 1985:81–89), which was initially introduced by Pedro Menéndez de

Avilés as a source of labor and material commodities (Deagan 1983:293; Lyon 1976:118–119).

The increased frequency of nonlocal wares at the Franciscan monastery during the seventeenth century most likely reflects the increased mission activity that occurred during this period. The early 1600s saw a steady increase in the number of Franciscans stationed in Florida and in the number of *doctrinas* established along the coastal region of Georgia and Florida. By 1632, approximately 40 missions were established and a mission road existed that connected these outlying missions with the Franciscan monastery in St. Augustine (Gannon 1983:49).

Indians from the provinces of Timucua and Guale were brought to St. Augustine throughout the late sixteenth century to provide construction, agricultural, and other services for the Spaniards. This practice of drafting Indian labor continued into the seventeenth century and eventually included Indians from Timucua, Guale, and Apalachee (Bushnell 1981:14–15). The increase in nonlocal Indian pottery may represent earthenware purchased by the Spaniards (Bushnell 1981:11) or a form of tribute collected from the mission Indians, as suggested by Piatek (1985:81–89). However, it may also be indicative of the movement and consolidation of the various Indian groups to the St. Augustine area. The relatively high proportion of nonlocal wares in the late seventeenth-century assemblage suggests that the monastery may have served as a refuge for the various displaced Indian groups.

Only two pieces of colono-ware, an unglazed, hand-built, coarse earthenware pottery made by either African slaves or Indians in imitation of European vessel forms (Ferguson 1978:68), were identified. This type of ware, which can be plain or decorated with a red film, represents a consistent and significant element of the seventeenth-century mission assemblages of San Luis de Talimali in Tallahassee (Vernon 1988:76–82) and of Santa María on Amelia Island (Rebecca Saunders, personal communication 1990). In contrast to the situation at these outlying missions, colono-ware was found in a significantly smaller quantity at the Franciscan mission headquarters site, where only one plain handle and a red filmed plate marley were identified. Other red filmed wares were identified from late seventeenth- and early eighteenth-century contexts, but the sherds were too small to determine whether they exhibited characteristics of European vessels.

The most dramatic shift in ceramic frequencies occurred during the early eighteenth-century occupation. Although the proportion of aboriginal pottery for the whole assemblage was 51.5 percent (lower than that recorded for the earlier phase), a closer analysis of the aboriginal pottery revealed a dramatic increase in the number of nonlocal wares. St. Johns and San Marcos pottery combined accounted for only 4.1 percent of the total aboriginal pottery, whereas 92 percent of the Indian pottery consisted of nonlocal wares. This dramatic increase corresponds to the collapse of the mission system in Florida and may reflect the consolidation of the various Florida Indian groups into St. Augustine following the destruction of the missions in 1702–1704 (Boniface 1971:85; Chatelaine 1941:78).

Other than ceramics, the material assemblage of the various Franciscan occupations was sparse. The Franciscans were a mendicant order and relied on alms and the *situado* for their support (Bushnell 1981:65–66; Gannon 1983:37–38). Therefore it is not surprising that there is little in the material culture to indicate material wealth or surplus. Architectural items, specifically nails and spikes, accounted for 2.8 percent of the ca. 1588 assemblage, 15.4 percent of the ca. 1600 assemblage, 10.6 percent of the ca. 1650 assemblage, and 13.4 percent of the ca. 1702 assemblage. These increased frequencies of architectural items in the later phases most likely reflect the numerous rebuilding episodes following the 1599 fire and the destruction of the monastery by English troops in 1702.

Evidence for non-food-related activities, such as clothing, arms, and personal and ornamental items, was also equally scarce. Throughout the Franciscan occupation, these groups accounted for less than 2 percent of the total assemblages. Several pieces of *bordado* (a metallic thread used to adorn clothing), several straight pins, one aglet (lacing tip), eleven clay pipestems, and a lead fishing weight were identified.

Notably absent from all of the assemblages were explicitly religious items. Although a brass book clasp recovered from a ca. 1650 barrel well could have been part of a religious missal and pieces of *bordado* could have adorned vestments or altar clothes, these items cannot be directly associated with a sacred function. However, the recovery of a brass book clasp from Santa María on Amelia Island, which was similar in size and shape to the one identified at the Convento de San Francisco site, suggests that these book clasps may be standard mission-related items.

This absence of sacred objects is in striking contrast to the assemblage reported from Santa Catalina de Guale, where a number of religious medallions, crucifixes, and other items have been reported (Thomas 1988:99–102). However, almost all of the religious items recovered from

Santa Catalina were associated with the burials. Most likely, the absence of religious paraphernalia at the monastery is related to the fact that the cemetery associated with the monastery was not excavated and to the manner in which this site was abandoned. Unlike the missions, which were forcefully and abruptly abandoned as a result of English raids, the departure of the Franciscans from the monastery in St. Augustine came about because of the transfer of Florida to the British in 1763 (Siebert 1940:148). Because their exodus was planned, the friars had time to pack their possessions and would have taken any sacred paraphernalia and ornaments with them when they departed for Havana.

Summary

Excavations at the Convento de San Francisco have increased our understanding of Franciscan architecture and spatial organization and have provided important information regarding the location of activity areas and how these areas shifted through time. In general, this research showed that the architectural history of this particular site paralleled that which has been previously documented for the St. Augustine colony (see Manucy 1978). The identification of several footing trenches in sixteenth- and seventeenth-century contexts revealed that the earliest monastery buildings were constructed of posts set into shallow trenches, and the absence of any associated daub suggests that these posts supported wooden plank walls. Although no archaeological evidence of roofing material was found, the documentary record suggests that these buildings had thatched roofs that were probably constructed with palmetto fronds (Gannon 1983:44–45). Wood remained the dominant building material until ca. 1702, when the monastery was rebuilt following Moore's raid on St. Augustine. At this time, tabby and coquina replaced wood as a building material, as evidenced by the discovery of tabby footings associated with the ca. 1702 chapel. The locations of structures, when grouped with that of the many wells and trash pits found during the excavation project, have suggested that the initial 1588 occupation may have been concentrated along the western half of the quadrangle but that by ca. 1600 this occupation had expanded to the eastern half of the property. Trash pits and wells were situated to the rear of these early structures, but by the eighteenth century trash disposal within any area of the quadrangle seems to have stopped, as no post-1702 trash pits or wells were identified.

These excavations have also demonstrated dramatic differences between secular, domestic households in St. Augustine, the outlying mission
settlements, and the religious community represented by the monastery.
Most provocative are the relative absence of colono-wares at the monastery and the changing frequencies of various types of nonlocal Indian
pottery in the material assemblage associated with the Convento de San
Francisco. Unlike the situation at the outlying mission sites, where
colono-ware appears to have replaced European tablewares, Spanish tablewares remained a consistent, if small, element of the *convento* assemblages throughout the First Spanish period. Because provisions for the
friars were sent to St. Augustine, where they were stored in the royal
warehouse by the Franciscan custodian (Bushnell 1981:106), the monks
living in St. Augustine, like the townspeople, undoubtedly had greater
access to European supplies than did those in the mission field. Despite
their potential for greater access to provisions, the Franciscans residing at
the monastery increasingly relied on Indian utilitarian wares for storage
and cooking vessels, which suggests a high degree of Franciscan-Indian
interaction. Although the exact nature of this interaction remains unclear,
previous research in St. Augustine has demonstrated a correlation between Indian food preparation technology and the intermarriage of Spanish males with Indian females, a process known as *mestizaje* (Deagan
1973). Marriage was forbidden for members of the Franciscan community, but the presence of Indian utilitarian wares at the Convento de San
Francisco suggests that American Indians, possibly women, played an
important role in food preparation at the monastery.

Not surprisingly, the monastery assemblage also reflects demographic changes in the Indian population of St. Augustine. It is already
known that the decimation of the Timucuans by epidemics and the relocation of the Guale and Mocama to St. Augustine, following the destruction of their missions by the English during the latter half of the
seventeenth century, can be seen archaeologically at domestic sites by the
replacement of St. Johns with San Marcos wares (Deagan 1990:308; King
1984; Piatek 1985). This is reflected also in the material recovered from
the Convento de San Francisco. The movement of several diverse Indian
groups to the St. Augustine area following the collapse of the mission
system in 1704 has previously been documented and can be seen in the
material assemblage of the monastery as a rather startling increase in
the proportion of non-Timucuan and non-Guale pottery associated with
the postmission occupation. This stands in contrast to the assemblages of

domestic nonsecular sites in the town (Deagan 1990:308) and suggests that the Convento de San Francisco continued to be a center of religious activity for the postmission Indian population of St. Augustine. On a more personal level, it may also indicate the church's sense of responsibility for the spiritual and physical welfare of the rapidly declining Indian population.

Acknowledgments

This study was done as part of the St. Augustine project of the Florida Museum of Natural History, with Kathleen Deagan as principal investigator. Funding for this project was provided by the Florida Department of Military Affairs/Florida National Guard under contract 770 and the Florida Museum of Natural History. The assistance and support of the Florida National Guard and the Florida Museum of Natural History is gratefully acknowledged, as is the help and cooperation of the Archaeological Advisory Board, the St. Augustine Historical Society, the Historic St. Augustine Preservation Board, and the St. Augustine Archaeological Society. A special acknowledgment is extended to Kathleen Deagan for her ongoing support and advice throughout this project.

Bibliography

Arnade, Charles W.
1959 *The Siege of St. Augustine in 1702*. Social Sciences Monograph no. 3. Gainesville: University of Florida Press.

Baird, Joseph Armstrong, Jr.
1962 *The Churches of Mexico: 1530–1810*. Berkeley: University of California Press.

Benavides, Antonio de
1724 Letter to the King, 27 October 1724. Archivo General de Indias, Santo Domingo 844, Stetson Collection. P. K. Yonge Library of Florida History, University of Florida, Gainesville.

Boniface, Brian George
1971 A Historical Geography of Spanish Florida, circa 1700. Master's thesis, Department of Geography, University of Georgia, Athens.

Bushnell, Amy
1981   *The King's Coffer: Proprietors of the Spanish Florida Treasury, 1565–1702.* Gainesville: University Presses of Florida.

Charles, Abbott
1928   St. Francis Barracks, St. Augustine: The Franciscans in Florida. *Florida Historical Quarterly* 7:214–233.

Chatelaine, Verne E.
1941   *The Defenses of Spanish Florida, 1565 to 1763.* Carnegie Institute of Washington Publication no. 511. Washington, D.C.

Cooper, Gay
1962   *History of the State Arsenal.* Reprint. Florida Department of Military Affairs Special Archives Publication no. 14. St. Augustine.

Crouch, Dora P., Daniel J. Garr, and Axel I. Mundigo
1982   *Spanish City Planning in North America.* Cambridge: MIT Press.

Deagan, Kathleen
1973   *Mestizaje* in Colonial St. Augustine. *Ethnohistory* 20:55–65.

1983   *Spanish St. Augustine: The Archaeology of a Colonial Creole Community.* New York: Academic Press.

1985   The Archaeology of Sixteenth-Century St. Augustine. *The Florida Anthropologist* 38(1–2):6–33.

1990   Accommodation and Resistance: The Process and Impact of Spanish Colonization in the Southeast. In *Columbian Consequences.* Vol. 2: *Archaeological and Historical Perspectives on the Spanish Borderlands East,* edited by David Hurst Thomas, 297–314. Washington, D.C.: Smithsonian Institution Press.

Fairbanks, Charles H.
1972   The Cultural Significance of Spanish Ceramics. In *Ceramics in America,* edited by I. Quimby, 141–174. Charlottesville: University of Virginia Press.

Ferguson, Leland
1978   Looking for the "Afro-" in Colono-Indian Pottery. *The Conference on Historic Site Archaeology Papers* 1977(12):68–86.

Gannon, Michael V.
1983   *The Cross in the Sand: The Early Catholic Church in Florida, 1513–1870.* Gainesville: University Presses of Florida.

Geiger, Maynard J., O.F.M.
1937   *The Franciscan Conquest of Florida, 1573–1618.* Studies in Hispanic-American History, vol. 1. Washington, D.C.: Catholic University of America.

Goggin, John M.
1952 *Space and Time Perspective in Northern St. Johns Archeology, Florida.* Yale University Publications in Anthropology, no. 47. New Haven.

Haring, Clarence
1947 *The Spanish Empire in America.* New York: Harcourt, Brace and World.

Harkins, Conrad, O.F.M.
1990 On Franciscans, Archaeology, and Old Missions. In *Columbian Consequences.* Vol. 2: *Archaeological and Historical Perspectives on the Spanish Borderlands East,* edited by David Hurst Thomas, 459–474. Washington, D.C.: Smithsonian Institution Press.

Herron, Mary K.
1986 A Formal and Functional Analysis of St. Johns Series Pottery from Two Sites in St. Augustine, Florida. In *Papers in Ceramic Analysis,* edited by Prudence M. Rice, 31–45. Ceramic Notes, no. 3. Gainesville: Florida State Museum.

Hoffman, Kathleen
1990 Archaeological Excavations at the Florida National Guard Headquarters (Site SA-42A) in St. Augustine, Florida. Ms. on file, Department of Anthropology, Florida Museum of Natural History, Gainesville.

Joyce, Edward R.
1989 The St. Francis Barracks: A Contradiction of Terms. *El Escribano* 26:71–90.

King, Julia
1984 Ceramic Variability in Seventeenth-Century St. Augustine. *Historical Archaeology* 18(2):75–82.

Koch, Joan
1983 Mortuary Behavior Patterning and Physical Anthropology in Colonial St. Augustine. In *Spanish St. Augustine: The Archaeology of a Colonial Creole Community,* edited by Kathleen Deagan, 187–227. New York: Academic Press.

Kubler, George
1948 *Mexican Architecture of the Sixteenth Century.* 2 vols. New Haven: Yale University Press.

Lister, Florence C., and Robert H. Lister
1974 Maiolica in Colonial Spanish America. *Historical Archaeology* 8:17–52.

1982 *Sixteenth-Century Maiolica Pottery in the Valley of Mexico.* Anthropological Papers, no. 39. Tucson: University of Arizona.

Lyon, Eugene
1976   *The Enterprise of Florida: Pedro Menéndez de Avilés and the Spanish Conquest of 1565–1568.* Gainesville: University Presses of Florida.

Manucy, Albert
1978   *The Houses of St. Augustine, 1565–1821.* St. Augustine: St. Augustine Historical Society.

Manucy, Albert, trans.
n.d.   Key to the Juan Elixio de la Puente Map of San Augustín de Florida, January 1764. Ms. on file, P. K. Yonge Library of Florida History, University of Florida, Gainesville.

Markman, Sidney David
1966   *Colonial Architecture of Antigua, Guatemala.* Philadelphia: American Philosophical Society.

Marrinan, Rochelle
1982   Test Excavation of Building B (Area 2), Puerto Real, Haiti, Final Report. Ms. on file, Department of Anthropology, Florida State Museum, Gainesville.

Matter, Robert Allen
1972   The Spanish Missions of Florida: The Friars versus the Governors in the "Golden Age," 1606–1670. Ph.D. diss., Department of History, University of Washington, Seattle.

1973   Economic Basis of the Seventeenth-Century Florida Missions. *Florida Historical Quarterly* 50(1):18–38.

Mohr, Charles H.
1929   St. Francis Barracks, St. Augustine: The Franciscans in Florida. *Florida Historical Quarterly* 7(3):214–233.

Newcomb, Rexford
1973   *Franciscan Mission Architecture of California.* New York: Dover.

Ortega, Elpidio, and Carmen Fondeur
1982   *Arqueología Colonial de Santo Domingo.* Fundación Ortega Alvarez, vol. 4. Santo Domingo.

Otto, John Solomon, and Russell Lamar Lewis, Jr.
1974   A Formal and Functional Analysis of San Marcos Pottery from Site SA 16–23, St. Augustine, Florida. *Bureau of Historic Sites and Properties Bulletin* 4:95–117.

Piatek, Bruce J.
1985   Non-Local Aboriginal Ceramics from Early Historic Contexts in St. Augustine. *The Florida Anthropologist* 38(1–2):81–89.

Redman, Charles L.
1986   *Qsar es-Seghir: An Archaeological View of Medieval Life*. New York: Academic Press.

Saunders, Rebecca
1990   Ideal and Innovation: Spanish Mission Architecture in the Southeast. In *Columbian Consequences*. Vol. 2: *Archaeological and Historical Perspectives on the Spanish Borderlands East*, edited by David Hurst Thomas, 527–542. Washington, D.C.: Smithsonian Institution Press.

Shea, John Gilmary
1886   *The Catholic Church in Colonial Days*. New York: John G. Shea.

Siebert, Wilbur H.
1940   The Departure of the Spaniards and Other Groups from East Florida, 1763–1764. *Florida Historical Quarterly* 19(2):145–154.

Sluiter, Engel
1985   *The Florida Situado: Quantifying the First Eighty Years, 1571–1651*. Research Publications of the P. K. Yonge Library of Florida History no. 1. Gainesville: University of Florida.

Smith, Hale G.
1948   Two Historical Archaeological Periods in Florida. *American Antiquity* 13(4):313–319.

South, Stanley
1977   *Method and Theory in Historical Archeology*. New York: Academic Press.

Thomas, David Hurst
1988   Saints and Soldiers at Santa Catalina: Hispanic Designs for Colonial America. In *The Recovery of Meaning: Historical Archaeology in the Eastern United States*, edited by Mark P. Leone and Parker B. Potter, Jr., 73–140. Washington, D.C.: Smithsonian Institution Press.

Thomas, David Hurst, ed.
1990   *Columbian Consequences*. Vol. 2: *Archaeological and Historical Perspectives on the Spanish Borderlands East*. Washington, D.C.: Smithsonian Institution Press.

Vernon, Richard
1988   Seventeenth-Century Apalachee Colono-ware as a Reflection of Demography, Economics, and Acculturation. *Historical Archaeology* 22(1):76–82.

Wenhold, Lucy L., trans.
1936   *A Seventeenth-Century Letter of Gabriel Díaz Vara Calderón, Bishop of Cuba, Describing the Indians and Indian Missions of Florida*. Smithsonian Miscellaneous Collections, vol. 95, no. 16. Washington, D.C.

❂ 4 ❂

St. Augustine and the Mission Frontier

KATHLEEN DEAGAN

The Spanish Franciscan missions of the southeastern United States have long been recognized as the most important Spanish institution for effecting change in seventeenth-century southeastern Indian cultures (Bolton 1917; Fairbanks 1985; Hann 1988; Sturtevant 1962; Thomas 1990a). From a European perspective the missions served not only as a religious agent, bringing conversion, Christianity, and civilization to the southeastern Indians, but also as an efficient and essential mechanism for taming, controlling, and exploiting the vast hinterland holdings of *La Florida* (Bolton 1917; Sturtevant 1962; Thomas 1990a).

In all of these capacities, the Florida mission system was inextricably bound to the colony's capital and only major town, St. Augustine. For more than two centuries, the tiny community of St. Augustine was the ecclesiastical, military, economic, and cultural center for the territorial holdings defined largely by the missions. It was from St. Augustine that friars and their essential supplies were sent to the mission field and, theoretically at least, to St. Augustine that the economic products of the missions accrued.

However, this frontier relationship of the missions to the town, and particularly the ways in which this relationship influenced colonial life in St. Augustine, have been addressed only peripherally in the abundant historical and archaeological literature pertaining to both St. Augustine and to the missions (for the missions, see Thomas 1990b; for St. Augustine, see Deagan 1991). Much of the mission frontier's impact on town life was brought about by the presence of the many Indians who made their way to St. Augustine by virtue of their associations with the missions. These American Indians made direct and indirect choices in their interactions with Spanish colonists which appear to have had subtle but important influences on both the mission frontier and in St. Augustine itself. It is thus relevant to our understanding of the mutuality of Spanish and Indian participation in colonial life in general to consider the nature and effects of the Indians' active participation in both the organization of mission life and the evolution of frontier society in *La Florida*.

Indian Influence in the Missions

It is increasingly evident from mission research under way in both the southeastern and southwestern regions of the United States that the establishment and use of the missions themselves was a process of mutual accommodation between the Indians and the friars (see, for example, Hann 1988; Kessell 1989; Thomas 1990a; Weber 1990). The Florida missions were organized first to bring about conversion and more or less secondarily to support the friars, provide labor and food for the garrison in St. Augustine, and defend the frontier. These ends were to be achieved by a small number of Spaniards working with an Indian population many hundred times larger than their own. Given the enormous discrepancies between the Spanish and Indian population sizes on the mission frontier, it was undoubtedly useful, if not essential, for friars to work through an existing system and take care to avoid serious disruption of traditional lifeways.

The archaeological work reported in this volume and elsewhere (Thomas 1988, 1990a) has documented considerable variation in the flexibility of Franciscan adaptations to diverse Native American political and economic organization. Most of the southeastern people met by the Spanish friars were organized in hierarchical chiefdoms and spent at least part of the year in settled villages (see Milanich 1990; Milanich and Fairbanks 1980; Milanich and Proctor 1978), and the first major missions both conformed to and took advantage of the settlement and social hierarchy of the Indians.

Although the first Franciscan missionaries of *La Florida* were able to adapt the locations and organization of their missions to preexisting

Indian settlement and social patterns, we can also identify many other cases in which American Indian groups made such adaptation impossible and forced the friars to alter their strategies. California, Sonora, and the Texas coast are a few examples of areas in which the Spaniards resorted to *reducción* (congregating) and occasional violence to "convert" the nomadic inhabitants. *Reducción* was also adopted as a strategy by Franciscan missionaries under circumstances of population decline and social upheaval, such as that seen in seventeenth- and eighteenth-century Florida (see Hann 1986, 1989). In still other areas, such groups as the Karankawa, Ais, and Seri in Texas used the mission only when they found it convenient (Corbin, Alex, and Kalina 1980; Gilmore 1989). And in some areas, such as those inhabited by the Georgia Guale (Jones 1978:182–185) and the New Mexico Puebloan peoples (Kessell 1979:84–110), the Indians simply refused to accept the missions and the missionaries were forced to retreat until introduced disease had decimated those groups.

The conformance of the initial Florida missions to preexisting Indian organization of the area was related to the Spaniards' general recognition of the Indian tribes of Florida as legitimate political entities (see Bushnell 1983 for a general discussion of this phenomenon; see Hann 1987 for illuminating specific examples). Caciques were recognized as heads of state and treated accordingly, and it is clear that as late as the late seventeenth century special recognition and privilege were accorded in the mission communities to the chiefs, their families, talented ball game players, and medicine men (Boyd, Smith, and Griffin 1951:34–35; Bushnell 1979, 1983:10; Hann 1988:105–106).

Indian land rights and traditional territorial holdings were also generally acknowledged by the Spaniards (see Hann 1988:138), and only as the formerly occupied areas became depopulated were the lands taken by Spanish entrepreneurs. Hunting lands and gathering areas were carefully guarded and maintained by the Indians of the mission towns, who even extracted promises from the Spaniards to recognize rights to previous hunting and gathering lands after groups relocated (Bushnell 1983:6).

Clearly the caciques of *La Florida* perceived some benefit in allying themselves with the friars. Political and military assistance against other tribes was an important factor in the initial alliances with Spanish interlopers (see, for example, Deagan 1978:105), and these alliances continued to function as a mechanism for the maintenance of chiefly position through much of the colonial period (Hann 1987:13–14).

After missions were established, Indian war councils continued meeting in the traditional manner in the council houses, with Spaniards frequently present (Boyd, Smith, and Griffin 1951:35; Bushnell 1983; Jesús 1633). Raiding over land disputes continued among the Western Timucua and Apalachee into the seventeenth century, and occasionally the Indian fighters would be joined by Spanish soldiers if the offense was made by an "English" Indian or if retaliatory raids on Spanish enemies were required (Bushnell 1983:10).

Mission Impacts on the Frontier Economy

The opportunities to acquire livestock, European technology, and new cultigens were potential—and in many cases abundantly realized—economic benefits to the missions and town alike. The introduction of cattle to the Indians of *La Florida* produced an important change in premission subsistence activities, in that Western Timucuan and Apalachee villages came to own and maintain communal herds of cattle (Bushnell 1978a, 1978b, 1979; Hann 1988:240–241). The cattle were an important resource and could be sold to Havana or to St. Augustine, with the proceeds used for the good of the village or the mission. As skill in handling cattle developed, numbers of Indians left the mission villages to work as hired hands on the Spanish cattle ranches of the interior (Bushnell 1978b; Hann 1988:147), sometimes reducing the available labor pool in the mission towns.

This enthusiastic and successful entry into cattle ranching by Florida Indian frontiersmen assisted by Franciscan friars did not apparently serve to benefit the administrative town of St. Augustine in a demonstrable way. Analysis of faunal assemblages from seventeenth-century St. Augustine households occupied at the peak of mission activity shows no increase (as compared to earlier and later periods)—and in fact shows a slight decrease—in the quantity of beef consumed in the seventeenth century, when the missions and ranches were active (Reitz 1992). Large numbers of cattle, cowhides, and other animal by-products were exported directly to Havana via the Suwannee and St. Marks rivers from the Florida interior during the seventeenth century (Bushnell 1978a, 1978b, 1979; Hann 1988:240–241), and the faunal record of St. Augustine suggests that the garrison families of the town did not find beef more available during the peak of the mission-ranching activity.

This situation underscores a unique aspect of St. Augustine's role as hub of a frontier system, and one that may be related to the fact that the frontier was defined by the missions. Unlike many comparable situations of town-frontier interaction (see, for example, discussions in Lewis 1984:13–17, 297–300), St. Augustine did not appear to accrue the economic benefits—particularly in raw materials—that might be expected by virtue of its administrative and economic centrality. This can be seen not only in the cattle industry bypass of St. Augustine but also in Indian trade, particularly during the seventeenth century. The Apalachee and Western Timucua regions had the largest concentration of mission and ranch activity at that time, and there were several routes to St. Augustine from these areas (Hann 1988:149–151). Indian trade with these areas, however, was often controlled by the friars themselves (Hann 1988:141–142), thereby restricting the St. Augustine entrepreneurs' access to Indian trade goods (particularly deerskins).

Although this proposition is difficult to test archaeologically, it can be documented that ceramic types traditionally associated with the Apalachee and Western Timucua peoples (particularly the Leon-Jefferson Series) are among the Indian wares occurring least frequently in St. Augustine's seventeenth-century households (see summary tables in Deagan 1990:300; King 1984). This may be due in part to the diversion of frontier resources by friars and ranchers on the frontier itself, suggesting that the organization and operation of the mission frontier may have altered or inhibited the expected economic roles and controls of the frontier's capital. It might also be argued that ceramics, being more breakable than other kinds of frontier commodities, were not included as commonly in the overland transport system from the Florida interior. Thus ceramics from this region might be expected to enter the town at a lower rate than ceramics from Guale, from where goods could be shipped by water with less danger of breakage.

Although there is little evidence that the town of St. Augustine benefited materially from the mission-based cattle and trade industries, there is no doubt that at least one frontier resource—labor—was consistently present in the town. The long-term incorporation of a transient labor force from the mission frontier had dramatic impacts not only on fluctuations in St. Augustine's demographic profile over the centuries but also in the material world of its Spanish residents.

This transient labor force (mostly men) came for periods of up to a year as part of the *repartimiento* system organized through the friars and caciques to bring labor and goods to St. Augustine from the frontier.

Workers came as bearers from the interior and stayed as minimally paid (if paid at all) laborers in agricultural fields and on public works. Each *doctrina*, working through the chiefs, was responsible for sending a quota of workers to St. Augustine each year.

This practice may have resulted in alterations in traditional sex roles and division of labor, owing to the absence of a relatively large proportion of adult males each year from the villages (Bushnell 1979:5; Deagan 1985:294). John Hann (1988:142–144) suggests that among the Apalachee the organization of *repartimiento* labor was complicated by increasing numbers of Indian men who chose to leave the villages to become contract labor on Spanish ranches, thereby reducing the traditional labor force in the villages even further.

Pedro Menéndez de Avilés had originally established an obligatory tribute of goods and labor from the Timucua and Guale Indians during the late sixteenth century. This was extended to the Apalachee in 1647, at which time the governor of Florida admitted that all of the other Indians were "nearly used up" (Bushnell 1979:5, 1983:14–15). This *repartimiento* tribute was continued until some unknown date in the early eighteenth century, although the flow of goods seems to have been less significant by the mid-seventeenth century. It was generally paid in the form of corn, animal skins, and labor (Bushnell 1981, 1983; Deagan 1985; Hann 1988:140–146; Lyon 1976:118–119) and resulted in the intermittent presence in St. Augustine of nonlocal Indians and Indian material.

Indian Populations in St. Augustine

The initial settlement of St. Augustine by Pedro Menéndez de Avilés in 1565 was established near the important chiefly town of Seloy (Chaney 1987; Lyon 1976), about one mile north of the present-day Castillo de San Marcos. The first sustained interaction between Spaniards and North American Indians, and probably the earliest attempts at conversion, took place there. The mission of Nombre de Dios was established near this site during the sixteenth century, although the date of its formal beginning is not certain (Gannon 1965:27; Hann 1990:426–427; Seaberg 1991).

Two densely occupied Christian Indian burial areas have been identified and excavated at the site (Goggin 1968:65; Seaberg 1991). The excavations have yielded remains (majolica and beads) that indicate a late sixteenth- and seventeenth-century use of the area.

Conflict with the Timucua of Seloy forced the Spaniards to abandon the first settlement after a year and reestablish their town in its present location (about 3 km to the south). Those Indians who chose to live in proximity of the town remained in small, primarily Christian villages, just outside the walls of St. Augustine. Over the centuries there were always between two and ten of these villages within two miles of the town (see Deagan 1973, 1990:330).

Although the native Saturiwa Timucua population of the St. Augustine region declined steadily after contact, the Indian population of the town did not. This was largely a consequence of mission activities on the frontier. Not only were the temporary *repartimiento* work forces present in the town, but new permanent Indian residents arrived as English encroachment forced the mission frontiers to contract toward St. Augustine (Deagan 1978; Hann 1986, 1987, 1989). Guale mission Indians, for example, were steadily relocated to the St. Augustine area from the 1620s onward (Hann 1987, 1990:501), and a major increase in the Indian population of the town took place after the English invasion of 1704.

These devastating raids led by James Moore brought an end to the Spanish mission system outside of St. Augustine (Arnade 1959; Boyd, Smith, and Griffin 1951; Hann 1987), and refugee Indians from many tribes and areas were relocated to the town. These events—taking place largely on the mission frontier—dramatically affected the population composition of St. Augustine after 1700.

The processes of demographic amplification and diversification in post-1700 St. Augustine can be seen most clearly in the census figures for the refugee mission Indian towns around St. Augustine (see Deagan 1990:301, table 20–2; Hann 1989). In 1689, during the time when the interior Florida missions were still functioning, there were some 100 Timucuas living at Nombre de Dios, with some 125 Guale about eight miles north of St. Augustine at Tolomato. There were 300 more Guale at Santa Cruz de Obadalquini, possibly near St. Augustine at that time, although its locations through various moves during this period are uncertain (Ebelino de Compostela 1689; Hann 1987:6–8, 1990:500–501).

In 1703, just after James Moore's first raid on Florida, there were reported to be eight mission and refugee towns near St. Augustine, including Nombre de Dios at Macaris, Nombre de Dios Chiquito, Timucua, Tama, Jororo, Costa, and Tolomato el Nuevo (Valdés 1729). In 1711 the population was recorded at 401 Indians, and in 1717 the population had risen to more than 950 (Ayala y Escobar 1717). According to

Governor Benavides's account (written ten years later in Mexico), the Indian population around St. Augustine included 1350 Indians (Timucua, Guale, Yamassee, Apalachee, Costas, Macapira, Pojois, Chiluca) living in six villages (Benavides 1738). There were also "about" ten households of Indians living within the city at this date (Benavides 1738).

After this time, however, the Indians in the St. Augustine vicinity began a rapid decline. In 1736 only 466 Indians were counted, and by 1752 there were only 150 adults in five towns (see Deagan 1990:301 for sources). At the time of Spanish departure in 1763, there were just 86 Indians left in St. Augustine.

The consolidation of Native American populations at this predominantly European community greatly increased the natives' susceptibility to European diseases. A series of disease encounters continued to reduce the relocated Indians' numbers, including the smallpox epidemics of 1703 and 1727 (TePaske 1964:67, 112) and the measles epidemic of 1732. During this same period, the seriously weakened demographic circumstances of the Indian populations were exacerbated by repeated raids by English and English-allied Indian enemies (see discussion by Waterbury 1983).

Indian Influence in Spanish St. Augustine

The Indian inhabitants of St. Augustine interacted with the Spanish residents and influenced the life of the Spanish town, particularly through labor arrangements, trade, intermarriage, and concubinage. While the decision to cooperate with the friars and participate in economic activities in the mission community may have primarily benefited the caciques, there was a certain amount of economic opportunity to be had on an individual level in the capital of St. Augustine. This was particularly true for women, who could choose to work in Spanish households, sell pottery or other crafts in the town, or enter into a relationship with a Spanish man.

Spanish-Indian intermarriage began immediately and continued consistently through the two centuries of Spanish occupation (Deagan 1973, 1983). A major material consequence of this interaction—revealed dramatically in the archaeological record—was the incorporation of native pottery into Spanish households as a primary cooking ware.

Various studies (Deagan 1990; King 1981; Piatek 1985) have demonstrated that this phenomenon manifested itself archaeologically in close association with fluctuations in Amerindian populations in St. Augustine. As various Indian peoples declined or increased, Spanish kitchen assemblages adjusted accordingly (Deagan 1990:300–301; Piatek 1985).

The well-documented extent of Indian tradeswomen, cooks, servants, and wives in Spanish St. Augustine—as well as Spanish predisposition to cook in earthenware pots (Fairbanks 1972)—predicts the occurrence of Indian cookware in the town's kitchens and is not remarkable in itself. There are, however, certain particularly notable aspects of the way in which this material evidence of Indian influence is manifested.

THE PHENOMENON OF SAN MARCOS POTTERY

The first of these aspects is the overwhelming dominance (80 percent) of the Indian ceramic ware known as San Marcos in the non-European ceramic assemblage of St. Augustine during the first half of the eighteenth century (Deagan 1990:300, table 20–1). San Marcos ceramics are archaeologically indicated to have been associated with (and presumably produced by) Guale and Yamassee peoples. It is very similar to the Lamar and Irene ceramic traditions of the contact period Georgia and lower South Carolina coasts and bears no resemblance to the St. Johns ceramics produced by the indigenous Timucua peoples of northeast Florida (fig. 4.1; Goggin 1952:58–61; Larson 1978:130; Otto and Lewis 1974; Piatek 1985; Smith 1948; Thomas 1987:61).

When it first appears in St. Augustine's archaeological contexts dating to the late sixteenth century, this ware, which featured stamped, incised, and combinations of stamped and incised designs, is most similar to the ceramic series known as Lamar and Irene and the slightly later but closely related Altamaha ceramics (figs. 4.2 and 4.3; DePratter 1979; Piatek 1985). The "Chicora Ware group" defined at Santa Elena, South Carolina, during this same period (South 1976, 1982:49, 60) also describes this group of ceramics, associated in that area with the Muskhogean-speaking Orista people, who may have formed part of the historic Yamassee. Exchange between St. Augustine and Santa Elena was probably an important source for the early Yamassee-Guale tradition Altamaha–San Marcos wares in Florida.

Through the seventeenth century, details of vessel form and rim treatment of this ceramic ware changed (for example, incising became increasingly rare and was eliminated by the eighteenth century, and circular reed

Figure 4.1. St. Johns ceramics. *Top L-R:* Casuela node handle, FS 26-1-160; plain body sherd, FS 43-1-243. *Bottom L-R:* Check stamped, FS 36-4-394; FS TC.

punctates around the vessel rims were replaced by half-circle or wedge-shaped punctates); however, the basic grit-tempered, paddle-stamped, folded-rim tradition persisted (fig. 4.4). At the same time, this Altamaha–San Marcos ware gradually eclipsed and replaced the indigenous Timucuan St. Johns pottery in St. Augustine (Deagan 1990:300; Piatek 1985).

It is always difficult (and often dangerous) to attempt a correlation between archaeological assemblages and past ethnic groups. In the case of Spanish *La Florida*, however, there is a strong convergence of documentary and archaeological evidence that permits a greater degree of confidence in this exercise than is usually the case. Several seventeenth-century sites are both historically documented to have had Guale mission or town occupation (Jones 1978:fig. 17; Larson 1978) and archaeologically documented to have contained predominantly Irene–Altamaha–San Marcos ceramics during the contact era or later (for summary discussions, see Pearson 1977; Thomas 1987:94–107). These include Santa Catalina de Guale (Jones 1978; Thomas 1987:102–107); the Fort King George site at Darien, Georgia (Kelso 1968:20; Larson 1980; Thomas 1987:98–102); the Southerland Bluff site (possibly the Guale Tolomato mission) and associated sites on Sapelo Island (Larson 1978; Thomas 1987:98–

Figure 4.2. San Marcos line block stamped ceramics. *Top L-R:* FS TC; FS 34-2-903; FS 34-2-105. *Bottom L-R:* RC 4611; FS 34-1-362.

Figure 4.3. San Marcos stamped ceramics. *Top L-R:* Exterior, interior San Marcos cross simple stamped, FS 34-2-94.*Bottom L-R:* San Marcos check stamped, FS 26-1-497.

Figure 4.4. "Altamaha" ceramics. *Top L-R:* Incised/stamped with punctate rim, FS 34-1-312; incised, FS 34-1-176; incised, stamped, FS 34-1-240. *Center L-R:* Incised, FS 26-1-160; incised with punctate rim, FS 34-1-320; incised with punctate rim, FS 34-1-242. *Bottom L-R:* Three punctate rims—FS TC, FS 36-4-214, FS 26-1-71; incised with punctate rim, FS 34-1-320.

102); the Taylor mound on St. Simons Island (Fairbanks 1985:130–131; Wallace 1975:263–264); the Kent mound on St. Simons Island (Cook 1978); the relocated Guale mission of Santa María on Amelia Island (Hemmings and Deagan 1973; Saunders, this volume); and the seventeenth-century mission (populated after ca. 1650 by relocated Guale peoples) at San Juan del Puerto (Hann 1990:436; McMurray 1973).

Altamaha-derived or related San Marcos ceramics dominated the archaeological assemblages of the Spanish households in St. Augustine after the mid-seventeenth century (Deagan 1990:305), replacing the Timucuan St. Johns wares that previously performed the same functions in Spanish kitchens. By the eighteenth century, these wares constituted more than 80 percent of the Indian ceramics in St. Augustine, despite the presence of Timucua, Apalachee, and other Indian groups in the town.

San Marcos ceramics occur in Spanish households at a somewhat higher level than would be predicted by the proportion of Guale people in

St. Augustine's Indian population of the eighteenth century. The Guale and Yamassee, according to the census figures of the same period, comprised only between 30 percent and 60 percent of the Indian population (1711—30 percent, 1717—65 percent, 1726—39 percent, 1737—41 percent; for sources, see Deagan 1990:301, table 20–2). The mean percentage of Guale in the Indian population over this period (calculated to provide comparability to the mean percentage of San Marcos ceramics calculated for this period) is 43.75 percent.

The potential factors leading to this discrepancy have been discussed elsewhere (Deagan 1990:307–308) and strongly suggest that non-Guale native ceramic traditions associated with the missions did not survive the general decimation and decline brought about by relocation in St. Augustine. Guale peoples and ceramics were already well established in St. Augustine and may have dominated and eclipsed other Native American traditions during this period of cultural disruption.

Ethnically, Guale women also dominated the group of Indian women who married Spanish residents of the town, but the proportion of Guale women marrying Spaniards (48 percent) is not significantly different from the proportion of Guale people in the Indian population as a whole during that period (44 percent; see table 4.1). It must be noted that the marriage figures include only those Indian women whose marriages were recorded in the Cathedral Parish Records; many more were undoubtedly recorded in the now-lost Indian *doctrina* records. This in itself was a point of serious contention between Franciscan friars and the town's

TABLE 4.1. Indian-Spanish Marriage Patterns in St. Augustine, 1700-1749

Wife's origin	1700– 1709	1710– 1719	1720– 1729	1730– 1739	1740– 1749	Total
Guale						
"Guale"	1	3	1	1	2	8 30.7
"Tolomato"	1				3	4 14.8
"San Juan"			1			1 3.7
(Subtotal)	(2)	(3)	(2)	(1)	(5)	(13) 48.1
"Apalachee"	2	1		4	1	8 30.7
Mocamo ("Palica")					3	3 11.5
"Timucua"			2			2 7.7
Total	4 15.4	4 15.4	4 15.4	5 19.2	9 34.6	26

Source: St. Augustine Parish Register, Book of Marriages (1700-1750) and Pardos (1735-1750), St. Augustine Historical Society.

Figure 4.5. Miscellaneous nonlocal incised wares. *Top L-R:* Bold incised, FS 34-1-344; unidentified gritty incised, FS 34-1-394; Lamar-like Bold Incised, FS 36-4-88. *Bottom L-R:* Ocmulgee Fields Incised, FS 35-2-23; FS 35-2-23; Aucilla-like Incised, FS 36-4-92.

secular clergy, since the former insisted that Indian marriages fell under their domain and not that of the St. Augustine Parish priests, despite the continued inclusion of Indians in the town's records (TePaske 1964:175–177).

Additional excavation of the refugee mission villages of the same time period will be essential to test the possibility that Spanish preference for Guale women as marriage partners influenced the dominance of San Marcos ceramics in the households of St. Augustine. If this was in fact the case, St. Augustine's eighteenth-century Indian communities should not contain predominantly Guale-origin San Marcos and Altamaha but rather a mix of wares known to be associated with the various tribal groups (fig. 4.5; for example, the Leon-Jefferson wares associated with the Apalachee or St. Johns wares associated with the Timucua).

The limited amount of preliminary work done to date does not support the hypothesis that the dominance of San Marcos ceramics was a town-specific pattern. Although none of the eighteenth-century refugee Indian sites has been systematically and extensively excavated, the results of a series of test projects suggest that Guale material traditions dominated the material world of these eighteenth-century Indian settlements as well as that of the Spanish town. These test projects have been carried out in areas thought to have been associated with a variety of eighteenth-century Indian settlements, including portions of the Fountain of Youth Park site occupied by the town of Nombre de Dios (Chaney 1986, 1987; Luccketti n.d.; Merritt 1977, 1983; Seaberg 1991); North St. Augustine, in the vicinity of the 1764 Castello map location of Macaris (Chatelaine 1941; Smith and Bond 1981); the La Leche Shrine, part of the Nombre de Dios mission in the eighteenth century (Chaney 1988; Luccketti n.d.); and the Abbott tract, where Costa and other Indian settlements are shown on an anonymous 1765 map (Chaney 1986; Luccketti n.d.; St. Augustine Historical Society Map no. 133). Although only limited excavation has been done, all of the tests so far indicate that Guale ceramics consistently outnumber all other kinds of native pottery in these outlying Indian settlements.

COLONO-WARES IN ST. AUGUSTINE HOUSEHOLDS

A second arresting feature of native ceramic influence in both the Spanish and Indian sites of St. Augustine is the fact that the great majority of aboriginal pottery is unmodified from its traditional forms; for the overwhelming majority of ceramics, neither shape nor decoration show European influence. This stands in contrast to the frontier missions, where directed change by friars and sometimes associated settlers often led to the production of European-inspired colono-ware (see McMurray 1973:77–79; Rebecca Saunders, personal communication 1991; Symes and Stephens 1965:7; Vernon 1988; Vernon and Cordell, this volume). This phenomenon of directing native potters to produce European forms is not restricted to the Florida missions and has been documented in the missions of the western and southwestern borderlands, where it is known as "Mission wares" (Hoover and Costello 1985:30–32; Snow 1984).

However, traditional Amerindian forms persisted in a largely unaltered state through the entire colonial period in St. Augustine. Even after the relocation to St. Augustine of mission groups known to have made colono-wares, such wares are rare in the archaeological record of the eighteenth-century town. Colono-wares seem instead to have been a mission-related phenomenon.

Either there was no serious directed effort on the part of the Spaniards in St. Augustine to influence change in favor of Spanish tastes, or there was native resistance to and disinterest in this aspect of European influence. It is also likely that Indian cooks did not perceive a need to alter their vessels in favor of less familiar Spanish forms, particularly when European tablewares were already available in the town.

It is nevertheless worthy of note that this native southeastern pottery, made by people in daily contact with Europeans, persisted unmodified for nearly 200 years of Spanish-Indian interaction. Despite the disruption to mission Indian society from disease, directed change, relocation, and consolidation, at least some systems for the transmission of crafts and symbolic information persisted unaltered through generations. This in itself implies a remarkable cultural resiliency, at least on the part of the Guale. The implications of this for the complex interactions among the various relocated Indian groups, the resident Indian groups, and the European and African residents of St. Augustine are less clear and await archaeological study.

Summary

There is no doubt that the town of St. Augustine—administrative, political, military, and religious center for the mission-defined frontier of *La Florida*—was closely tied to the missions throughout its 200-year Spanish occupation. There is also little doubt that the missions themselves evolved as a process of mutual accommodation between Spanish and Indian systems and that actions by the Indian peoples on the mission frontier directly and indirectly influenced life in the Spanish town center.

The economic benefits expected of an agricultural and trading frontier—cattle trade and Indian trade—do not appear to have been enjoyed extensively by the Spanish residents of St. Augustine. Spanish (sometimes including friars) and Indian cattle owners tended to bypass St. Augustine in the sale of their goods, and friars appear to have diverted much of the frontier Indian trade from the town to the missions.

There was a pronounced influence, however, in St. Augustine's demographic patterns and fluctuations, caused by the movements of mission groups in and out of the town during the late sixteenth and seventeenth centuries. This is reflected clearly in the marriage patterns and material assemblages of the Spanish households.

The demographic impact of the missions became even more pronounced after 1700, when the majority of surviving mission towns were relocated to the immediate vicinity of St. Augustine. The presence and consolidation of multiple tribal groups as well as European and African peoples in eighteenth-century St. Augustine pose a number of potentially fruitful anthropological questions related to multiethnic exchange, migration, competition, and survival. It will require the combined efforts of archaeology and history in the refugee communities of eighteenth-century St. Augustine—outside the town walls—to realize this potential.

Acknowledgments

This paper has been substantially revised following a detailed and extremely insightful review and comment by Dr. John Hann. I would also like to thank Dr. Jane Landers and Dr. Bonnie McEwan for their helpful suggestions, although I assume responsibility for any remaining errors of fact or interpretation.

Bibliography

Arnade, Charles
1959 *The Siege of St. Augustine in 1702.* Social Sciences Monograph no. 3. Gainesville: University of Florida Press.

Ayala y Escobar, Juan de
1717 Letter to the King, St. Augustine, 18 April 1717. Archivo General de Indias, Santo Domingo 843, Stetson Collection. P. K. Yonge Library of Florida History, University of Florida, Gainesville.

Benavides, Antonio de
1738 Letter to the King, 24 April 1738. Archivo General de Indias, Santo Domingo 865, Stetson Collection. P. K. Yonge Library of Florida History, University of Florida, Gainesville.

Bolton, Herbert E.
1917 The Mission as a Frontier Institution in the Spanish-American Colonies. *American Historical Review* 23:42–61.

Boyd, Mark F., Hale G. Smith, and John W. Griffin
1951 *Here They Once Stood: The Tragic End of the Apalachee Missions.* Gainesville: University of Florida Press.

Bushnell, Amy
1978a The Menéndez Marquéz Cattle Barony at La Chua and the Determinants of Economic Expansion in Seventeenth-Century *La Florida. Florida Historical Quarterly* 56(4):407–431.

1978b "That Demonic Game": The Campaign to Stop Indian *Pelota* Playing in Spanish Florida, 1675–1684. *The Americas* 35:1–19.

1979 Patricio de Hinachuba: Defender of the Word of God, the Crown of the King and the Little Children of Ivitachuco. *American Indian Culture and Research Journal* 3(July):1–21.

1981 *The King's Coffer: Proprietors of the Spanish Florida Treasury, 1565–1702.* Gainesville: University Presses of Florida.

1983 Cross, Pole and Banner: The Balance of Power in the Provinces of Seventeenth-Century Florida. Paper presented at the annual meeting of the Southern Historical Association, Columbia, South Carolina.

Chaney, Edward
1986 Survey and Evaluation of Archaeological Resources in the Abbott Tract and North City, St. Augustine. Ms. on file, Department of Anthropology, Florida State Museum, Gainesville.

1987 Report on the 1985 Excavations at the Fountain of Youth Park (8-SJ-31), St. Augustine, Florida. Ms. on file, Department of Anthropology, Florida State Museum, Gainesville.

1988 Preliminary Report of Test Excavations at the Nombre de Dios Mission Site, St. Augustine. Ms. on file, Department of Anthropology, Florida Museum of Natural History, Gainesville.

Chatelaine, Verne E.
1941 *The Defenses of Spanish Florida, 1565 to 1763.* Carnegie Institute of Washington Publication no. 511. Washington, D.C.

Cook, Fred
1978 *The Kent Mound: A Study of the Irene Phase on the Lower Georgia Coast.* Master's thesis, Department of Anthropology, Florida State University, Tallahassee.

Corbin, James E., Thomas Alex, and Arlan Kalina
1980 *Mission Dolores de los Ais.* Papers in Anthropology, no. 2. Nacogdoches, Tex: Stephen F. Austin State University.

Deagan, Kathleen A.
1973 *Mestizaje* in Colonial St. Augustine. *Ethnohistory* 20:55–65.

1978 Cultures in Transition: Fusion and Assimilation among the Eastern Timucua. In *Tacachale: Essays on the Indians of Florida and Southeastern Georgia during the Historic Period,* edited by Jerald T. Milanich and Samuel Proctor, 89–119. Ripley P. Bullen Monographs in Anthropology and History, no. 1. Gainesville: University Presses of Florida.

1983 *Spanish St. Augustine: The Archaeology of a Colonial Creole Community.* New York: Academic Press.

1985   Spanish-Indian Interaction in Sixteenth-Century Florida and the Carib-
        bean. In *Cultures in Contact,* edited by W. Fitzhugh, 281–318. Washing-
        ton, D.C.: Smithsonian Institution Press, Anthropological Society of
        Washington.

1990   Accommodation and Resistance: The Process and Impact of Spanish Col-
        onization in the Southeast. In *Columbian Consequences.* Vol. 2: *Archae-
        ological and Historical Perspectives on the Spanish Borderlands East,*
        edited by David Hurst Thomas, 297–314. Washington, D.C.: Smithso-
        nian Institution Press.

Deagan, Kathleen, ed.
1991   *America's Ancient City: A Sourcebook on First Spanish Period St. Au-
        gustine.* New York: Garland Press.

DePratter, Chester
1979   Ceramics. In *The Anthropology of St. Catherines Island: 2. The Refuge-
        Deptford Mortuary Complex,* edited by David Hurst Thomas and Clark
        Spencer Larsen, 109–132. Anthropological Papers of the American Mu-
        seum of Natural History, vol. 56, pt. 1. New York.

Ebelino de Compostela, Diego
1689   Letter to the King, Havana, 28 September 1689. Archivo General de
        Indias, Santo Domingo 151, Stetson Collection. P. K. Yonge Library of
        Florida History, University of Florida, Gainesville.

Fairbanks, Charles H.
1972   The Cultural Significance of Spanish Ceramics. In *Ceramics in America,*
        edited by I. Quimby, 141–174. Charlottesville: University of Virginia
        Press.

1985   From Exploration to Settlement: Spanish Strategies for Colonization. In
        Alabama and the Borderlands: From Prehistory to Statehood, edited by
        R. Reid Badger and Lawrence A. Clayton, 128–139. Tuscaloosa: Univer-
        sity of Alabama Press.

Gannon, Michael V.
1965   *The Cross in the Sand: The Early Catholic Church in Florida, 1513–
        1870.* Gainesville: University of Florida Press.

Gilmore, Kathleen
1989   The Indians of Mission Rosario: From the Books and from the Ground. In
        Columbian Consequences. Vol. 1: *Archaeological and Historical Perspec-
        tives on the Spanish Borderlands West,* edited by David Hurst Thomas,
        231–244. Washington, D.C.: Smithsonian Institution Press.

Goggin, John M.
1952   *Space and Time Perspective in Northern St. Johns Archeology, Florida.*
        Yale University Publications in Anthropology, no. 47. New Haven.

1968 *Spanish Majolica in the New World.* Yale University Publications in Anthropology, no. 72. New Haven.

Hann, John H.

1986 Demographic Patterns and Changes in Mid-Seventeenth-Century Timucua and Apalachee. *Florida Historical Quarterly* 64(4):371–392.

1987 Twilight of the Mocama and Guale Aborigines as Portrayed in the 1695 Spanish Visitation. *Florida Historical Quarterly* 66(1):1–24.

1988 *Apalachee: The Land between the Rivers.* Ripley P. Bullen Monographs in Anthropology and History, no. 7. Gainesville: University of Florida Press.

1989 St. Augustine's Fallout from the Yamassee War. *Florida Historical Quarterly* 68(2):180–200.

1990 Summary Guide to Spanish Florida Missions and *Visitas* with Churches in the Sixteenth and Seventeenth Centuries. *The Americas* 46(4):417–513.

Hemmings, E. Thomas, and Kathleen A. Deagan

1973 *Excavations on Amelia Island in Northeast Florida.* Contributions of the Florida State Museum in Anthropology and History, no. 18. Gainesville.

Hoover, Robert L., and Julia G. Costello, eds.

1985 *Excavations at Mission San Antonio, 1976–1978.* Monograph no. 26. Los Angeles: Institute of Archaeology, University of California.

Jesús, Francisco Alonso de

1633 Relación de Fray Francisco Alonso de Jesús, Custodio de la Florida, 25 June 1633. Archivo General de Indias, Seville, leg. 302, Stetson Collection. P. K. Yonge Library of Florida History, University of Florida, Gainesville.

Jones, Grant D.

1978 The Ethnohistory of the Guale Coast through 1684. In *The Anthropology of St. Catherines Island: 1. Natural and Cultural History,* edited by David H. Thomas, Grant D. Jones, Roger S. Durham, and Clark S. Larsen, 178–210. Anthropological Papers of the American Museum of Natural History, vol. 55, pt. 2. New York.

Kelso, William

1968 *Excavations at the Fort King George Historical Site.* Georgia Historical Commission Archaeological Series, no. 1. Atlanta.

Kessell, John L.

1979 *Kiva, Cross, and Crown.* Washington, D.C.: National Park Service, U.S. Department of Interior.

1989 Spaniards and Pueblos: From Crusading Intolerance to Pragmatic Accommodation. In *Columbian Consequences.* Vol. 1: *Archaeological and His-*

torical Perspectives on the Spanish Borderlands West, edited by David Hurst Thomas, 127–138. Washington, D.C.: Smithsonian Institution Press.

King, Julia

1981   An Archaeological Investigation of Seventeenth-Century St. Augustine, Florida. Master's thesis, Department of Anthropology, Florida State University, Tallahassee.

1984   Ceramic Variability in Seventeenth-Century St. Augustine, Florida. *Historical Archaeology* 18(2):75–82.

Larson, Lewis H., Jr.

1978   Historic Guale Indians of the Georgia Coast and the Impact of the Spanish Mission Effort. In *Tacachale: Essays on the Indians of Florida and Southeastern Georgia during the Historic Period,* edited by Jerald T. Milanich and Samuel Proctor, 120–140. Ripley P. Bullen Monographs in Anthropology and History, no. 1. Gainesville: University Presses of Florida.

1980   The Spanish on Sapelo. In *Sapelo Papers: Researches in the History and Prehistory of Sapelo Island,* edited by D. P. Juengst, 35–45. West Georgia College Studies in the Social Sciences, no. 19. Carrollton.

Lewis, Kenneth E., Jr.

1984   *The American Frontier.* New York: Academic Press.

Luccketti, Nicholas

n.d.   Preliminary Report on the Sub-Surface Survey of North St. Augustine and the Fountain of Youth Park. Ms. on file, Department of Anthropology, Florida Museum of Natural History, Gainesville.

Lyon, Eugene

1976   *The Enterprise of Florida: Pedro Menéndez de Avilés and the Spanish Conquest of 1565–1568.* Gainesville: University Presses of Florida.

McMurray, Judith Angley

1973   The Definition of the Ceramic Complex at San Juan del Puerto. Master's thesis, Department of Anthropology, University of Florida, Gainesville.

Merritt, James D.

1977   Excavation of a Coastal Eastern Timucuan Village in Northeast Florida. Master's thesis, Department of Anthropology, Florida State University, Tallahassee.

1983   Beyond the Town Walls: The Indian Element in Colonial St. Augustine. In *Spanish St. Augustine: The Archaeology of a Colonial Creole Community,* edited by Kathleen Deagan, 125–150. New York: Academic Press.

Milanich, Jerald T.

1990   The European Entrada into *La Florida*: An Overview. In *Columbian Con-*

sequences. Vol. 2: *Archaeological and Historical Perspectives on the Spanish Borderlands East*, edited by David Hurst Thomas, 3–29. Washington, D.C.: Smithsonian Institution Press.

Milanich, Jerald T., and Charles H. Fairbanks
1980   *Florida Archaeology*. New York: Academic Press.

Milanich, Jerald T., and Samuel Proctor, eds.
1978   *Tacachale: Essays on the Indians of Florida and Southeastern Georgia during the Historic Period*. Ripley P. Bullen Monographs in Anthropology and History, no. 1. Gainesville: University Presses of Florida.

Otto, John S., and Russell L. Lewis, Jr.
1974   A Formal and Functional Analysis of San Marcos Pottery from Site SA-16-23, St. Augustine, Florida. *Bureau of Historic Sites and Properties Bulletin* 4:95–117.

Pearson, Charles
1977   Evidence of Early Spanish Contact on the Georgia Coast. *Historical Archaeology* 11:74–83.

Piatek, Bruce J.
1985   Non-Local Aboriginal Ceramics from Early Historic Contexts in St. Augustine. *The Florida Anthropologist* 38(1–2):81–89.

Reitz, Elizabeth
1992   Vertebrate Fauna from Seventeenth-Century St. Augustine. *Southeastern Archaeology* 11(2):79–94.

Seaberg, Lillian
1991   Report on the Indian Site at the "Fountain of Youth." In *America's Ancient City: A Sourcebook on First Spanish Period St. Augustine*, edited by Kathleen Deagan. New York: Garland Press. Reprint. Ms. on file, Department of Anthropology, Florida Museum of Natural History, Gainesville, 1951.

Smith, Hale G.
1948   Two Historical Archaeological Periods in Florida. *American Antiquity* 13(4):313–319.

Smith, Jimmy, and Stanley Bond
1981   Phase III Archaeological Survey of St. Augustine, Florida. Ms. on file, Historic St. Augustine Preservation Board, St. Augustine, Florida.

Snow, David H.
1984   Spanish-American Pottery Manufacture in New Mexico: A Critical Review. *Ethnohistory* 31(2):93–113.

South, Stanley
1976   *An Archaeological Survey of Southeastern Coastal North Carolina*. Insti-

tute of Archaeology and Anthropology Notebook no. 8. Columbia: University of South Carolina.

1982 *Exploring Santa Elena 1981.* Institute of Archaeology and Anthropology Research Manuscript Series, no. 184. Columbia: University of South Carolina.

Sturtevant, William C.
1962 Spanish-Indian Relations in Southeastern North America. *Ethnohistory* 9(1):41.

Symes, M. I., and M. E. Stephens
1965 A 272: The Fox Pond Site. *The Florida Anthropologist* 18(2):65–76.

TePaske, John Jay
1964 *The Governorship of Spanish Florida, 1700–1763.* Durham: Duke University Press.

Thomas, David Hurst
1987 *The Archaeology of Mission Santa Catalina de Guale: 1. Search and Discovery.* Anthropological Papers of the American Museum of Natural History, vol. 63, pt. 2. New York.

1988 Saints and Soldiers at Santa Catalina: Hispanic Designs for Colonial America. In *The Recovery of Meaning: Historical Archaeology in the Eastern United States*, edited by Mark P. Leone and Parker B. Potter, Jr., 73–140. Washington, D.C.: Smithsonian Institution Press.

1990a The Spanish Missions of *La Florida*: An Overview. In *Columbian Consequences.* Vol. 2: *Archaeological and Historical Perspectives on the Spanish Borderlands East*, edited by David Hurst Thomas, 357–397. Washington, D.C.: Smithsonian Institution Press.

Thomas, David Hurst, ed.
1990b *Columbian Consequences.* Vol. 2: *Archaeological and Historical Perspectives on the Spanish Borderlands East.* Washington, D.C.: Smithsonian Institution Press.

Valdés, Bishop Gerónimo
1729 Letter to the King, 14 January 1729. Archivo General de Indias, Santo Domingo 865, Stetson Collection. P. K. Yonge Library of Florida History, University of Florida, Gainesville.

Vernon, Richard
1988 Seventeenth-Century Apalachee Colono-ware as a Reflection of Demography, Economics, and Acculturation. *Historical Archaeology* 22(1):76–82.

Wallace, Ronald
1975 An Archaeological, Ethnohistoric, and Biochemical Investigation of the

Guale Aborigines of the Georgia Coastal Strand. Ph.D. diss., University of Florida, Gainesville.

Waterbury, Jean P.
1983   The Castillo Years, 1668–1763. In *The Oldest City, St. Augustine: Saga of Survival*, edited by J. P. Waterbury, 57–89. St. Augustine Historical Society, St. Augustine.

Weber, David
1990   Blood of Martyrs, Blood of Indians: Toward a More Balanced View of Spanish Missions in Seventeenth-Century North America. In *Columbian Consequences*. Vol. 2: *Archaeological and Historical Perspectives on the Spanish Borderlands East*, edited by David Hurst Thomas, 429–448. Washington, D.C.: Smithsonian Institution Press.

❂ 5 ❂

The Mayaca and Jororo and Missions to Them

JOHN H. HANN

The people of south-central Florida living along the upper St. Johns River and the Oklawaha and throughout the lake districts north and south of Orlando are among the least known of the state's aboriginal tribes archaeologically and historically. Some of that region's tribes probably disappeared without even their names having been recorded. But obscurity persists even for the groups whose names appear most often in the historical record. Blurred perception characterizes knowledge of the Mayaca in particular, leaving in doubt the linguistic identity of the people with whom the name Mayaca was associated in different eras and to some degree the location of the village bearing that name. The people alluded to as Mayaca from the 1560s into the early seventeenth century have often been considered to have been Freshwater Timucua despite evidence linking the Mayaca with the Ais. Even people who concede that the issue is in doubt treat the Mayaca as though they were Freshwater Timucua (Deagan 1978:110). For the late seventeenth century and early eighteenth century, the Mayaca are recognized as speakers of a language distinct from Timucua known as Mayaca, which they shared with the Jororo and which was probably akin to Ais (Ayala y Escobar 1717; Dickinson 1981:60; Milanich 1978:60). Erroneous identifications of the names of other distinct villages as variants of Mayaca have added to the confusion over the Mayaca's identity, and the presence of Yamassee at the late seventeenth-century Mayaca mission has compounded the confusion.

The purpose of this chapter is to assemble and analyze what is known about the Mayaca and Jororo to try to dispel some of the mist in which their history has been shrouded and to clear up some of the misidentifications and establish whether the Mayaca of the sixteenth and early seventeenth centuries were one with those who bore that name later. The close association of the Mayaca's name with the Freshwater Timucua in accounts from the 1560s to the early seventeenth century requires that attention be given to the Freshwater Timucua as well. Evidence of links between the Surruque and the Mayaca also makes passing mention of them necessary.

Historical Archaeological Background

Beginning in the 1560s the name Mayaca was applied to a particular chief, the village he headed, two temporally distinct missions at the same site, a province, a culture, and a language. The name survives today in Port Mayaca, eastern terminus for the Lake Okeechobee Waterway. The name Myakka, given today to a river, lake, two settlements, and a state park in western south-central Florida, may be a variant of Mayaca. The name Jororo, also spelled Hororo, first appeared only in the late seventeenth century. The name Jororo was applied to a particular village and the people who inhabited it and to at least several neighboring villages, which, in Spanish eyes, constituted the province of Jororo. But those Jororo settlements were also linked with Mayaca in what Spaniards designated as the province of Mayaca and Jororo.

Eugene Lyon has provided the clearest definition to date of the boundaries of the Mayaca culture (fig. 5.1): "I feel that a line drawn south of Lake George eastward to the seacoast and one from the Orlando metropolitan area to the Cape would probably define the northern and southern boundaries of the Mayaca culture" (Lyon 1983:168–169, n. 15). Lyon based his "outline of the lands under direct or indirect control of Chief Mayaca" on two Spanish rutters (*derroteros*). One is from 1566, the era in which the name Mayaca first appeared. The other is the Mexía *derrotero* of 1605.

The 1566 guide was composed for Gonzalo de Gayón when Pedro Menéndez de Avilés sent the pilot Gayón south "from St. Augustine to seek Mayaca from the seacoast" to ransom some Frenchmen who were reported to be with Chief Mayaca and in his territory. Gayón "stated that

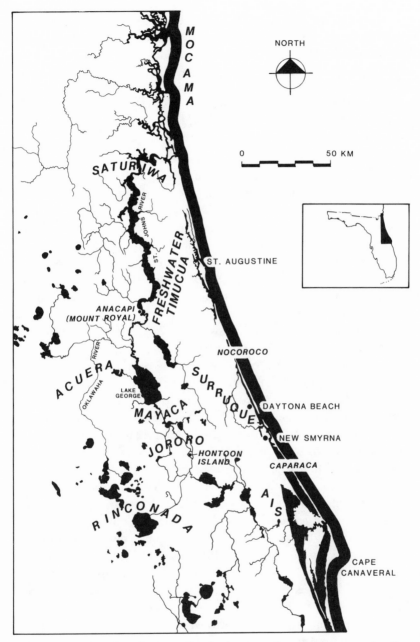

Figure 5.1. Map of northeastern Florida showing tribes and places mentioned.

the villages near the coast owed allegiance to Mayaca" (Lyon 1983:169, n. 15; Provanza 1566:60–61). Spaniards then considered Mayaca a village of some importance. Alvaro de Mexía identified what may be those coastal villages. He recorded that "midway on the trail [from Nocoroco to Caparaca] a small sweet-water river enters, which descends from the hinterland and there are many clusters of villages [*rancherías*] by the mouth of said river to which one may go from the Mayaca village located on the San Mateo River [the St. Johns] in one day" (Griffin and Smith 1949:340–343; Mexía 1605a). Irving Rouse (1951:270, n. 16) placed the location of those villages as "probably Turnbull's Bay and Creek."

References in the two *derroteros* along with data from explorations of the St. Johns River by Menéndez de Avilés and by Frenchmen under the jurisdiction of René de Laudonnière converge to indicate a location for Mayaca just south of Lake George where the river begins to narrow. Mexía's Nocoroco is in today's Tomoka State Park and his Caparaca at New Smyrna (fig. 5.1; Griffin and Smith 1949:340–343; Rouse 1951:270). Laudonnière's account reveals that the French expedition that pushed farthest upriver reached the lake but did not cross it. Menéndez, sailing 50 leagues upriver and advancing 2 leagues farther than the French had gone, went to a point where the river began to narrow in a land under the jurisdiction of a chief Mocoya or Macoya, alluded to as "very powerful throughout this region." Barrientos spelled it Mocoya and Solís de Merás as Macoya (Barrientos 1965:117–118; Bennett 1975:114–115; Solís de Merás 1923:204–205). Menéndez himself gave the name as Mayacuya (Hann 1991:302). All three obviously were speaking of Mayaca. When the original mission at Mayaca was last mentioned in 1655, it was 36 leagues from St. Augustine, a figure compatible with Menéndez's 50-league sail up the river and identical with that given for the late seventeenth-century Mayaca mission. Manuel Serrano y Sanz (1912:133), in his version of the 1655 mission list drawn from Juan Díez de la Calle (1659), presented the name as "San Salvador de Macaya," approximating the variants of the 1560s such as Macoya. However, the name is written as "Sn Salbador de Mayaca" in a manuscript version of the list that belonged to Díez de la Calle, which is held by Madrid's Biblioteca Nacional. (Mary L. Mitchell graciously provided a photographic copy of the manuscript to this writer.) Charles Hudson and Jerald Milanich noted a dense distribution of sites south of Lake George, observing that it was most likely the territory of Mayaca and other south Florida native groups (Milanich and Hudson 1993:204). To date no site has been registered in Florida's Master Site File as the location of the 1560s village or the two missions bearing the names San Salvador de Macaya and San Salvador de Mayaca.

The name Mayaca as such does not appear in French sources from the 1560s, but those sources' Mayarqua and Mathiaqua (or Mathiaca) have been construed as variants of the Spaniards' Mayaca (Lussagnet 1958:115, 131, 136, 262; Milanich 1978:68, 212). Neither Mayarqua nor Mathiaqua corresponds to the Spaniards' Mayaca. The Le Moyne map (Lorant 1946:34–35) depicts Mathiaca and Mayarqua as distinct sites, both downriver from Lake George. Lussagnet (1958:136, n. 4) also noted that Mayarqua was distinct from Mathiaca. Laudonnière's description of Mathiaqua as 30 leagues north of Lake George seems to rule it out definitively (Bennett 1975:114–115). Although Mayarqua's given distance of 80 leagues from Fort Caroline seems compatible with its being the Spaniards' Mayaca, the distance is obviously an exaggeration, as Lussagnet (1958:115, n. 2) has observed. Mayarqua is clearly north of Ouae Outina's village, as the French stopped there in going from Fort Caroline to Outina's place. Mayarqua seems to have been visited by the French prior to the trip that took them to Lake George, that is, during the expedition that Laudonnière dispatched to send prisoners back to the Freshwater Timucua Chief Outina. If the French Mayarqua were the Spaniards' Mayaca south of Lake George, that would eliminate the need for the subsequent voyage on which the French discovered the lake (Bennett 1975:90–91, 114–115). Additionally, the Le Moyne map places Mayarqua well downriver from the lake, farther down indeed than Mathiaca.

If any of the villages named by the French are variants of Mayaca, Mayrra seems the most likely candidate, although no one seems to have suggested such an identification. Le Moyne depicts Mayrra as farther upriver than either Mayarqua or Mathiaca. But his placement of Mayrra still downriver from the lake, if it is reliable, would also rule it out. Nevertheless, Laudonnière's references to Mayrra suggest that it could be Mayaca. Mayrra was three long days' journey upriver from the village of Molona, which was subject to Chief Outina. Mayrra's chief was described as "rich in gold and silver" (Lussagnet 1958:100). That description is applicable to Mayaca, as will be seen below from Fontaneda's remark about Mayaca.

More difficult to resolve than uncertainties about Mayaca's general location are the uncertainties relating to its inhabitants' linguistic affiliation in the sixteenth and early seventeenth centuries. Kathleen Deagan (1978:110) remarked that "it is not clear whether Mayaca was considered part of the Agua Dulce province by the Spanish." But after that prefatory caution she added, "Since they shared material culture and, possibly, linguistic elements with the Agua Dulce, however, they will be considered part of the Agua Dulce here." In the light of the evidence from the 1560s and above all that from the early seventeenth century, which provides most of our knowledge about the Freshwater missions, her position is not unreasonable.

Both in the 1560s and in the early seventeenth century the evidence for Mayaca's linguistic affiliation is equivocal. For the 1560s it is scant and largely circumstantial. Macoya was an ally of the Saltwater Timucua chieftain Saturiwa and an enemy of the Freshwater chieftain Aotina. That enmity suggests that they were not part of the Agua Dulce as Deagan suggested they might be. It led Mayaca to join with Potano and Saturiwa to make war on the Freshwater paramount Aotina in the summer of 1567 in retaliation for Aotina's alliance with the Spaniards (Lyon 1983:198). Twenty leagues upriver from Macoya's village was definitely Ais territory. Menéndez's guide and interpreter for his trip upriver had once been a slave of the above-mentioned Ais chief and knew Macoya. That suggests friendly relations between Macoya and the Ais (Barrientos 1965:117–118; Solís de Merás 1923:205–207). Remarks by Fontaneda suggest linguistic and political ties between the Mayaca and the Ais. Speaking of another Spaniard who had been a captive among the Indians like him, Fontaneda remarked, "He understands well the language of the Ais and the language of other places mentioned which are spoken as far as Mayaca and Mayajuaca, places toward the north" (Fontaneda 1944:18). His remark indicates that in moving northward beyond Mayaca one crossed a linguistic frontier. Lussagnet (1958:115, n. 3) also interpreted Fontaneda's remarks as meaning that Mayaca and Mayaguaca marked "the northern limit of the dialects Ais, Guacata and Jeaga," although she described all three as "related to Timucua." Fontaneda also noted that Mayaguaca and Mayaca were among the chieftains with whom the cacique of Ais divided the gold and silver from shipwrecks along the southeast coast. Such a distribution suggests a political tie.

The somewhat fuller evidence from the early seventeenth century is more equivocal, with some Spaniards seemingly viewing Mayaca as part of the province of Rio Dulce. Before considering that evidence, it is advisable to look briefly at the upriver villages mentioned. For the 1560s

French and Spanish sources identify Mathiaca, Mayaguaca, Mayarca, Outina or Aotina, Coya, Edelano, Patica, Chilile, Calanay or Calabay, Enaguape or Encacque, Molona, Mayrra, and Mayaca or Macoya or Mayacuya as villages located on or close to the river. Outina's Olata Ouae Outina was head chief for most of those upriver villages with the exception of Mayaca. Laudonnière mentions others as vassals of Outina but does not indicate where they were located. In a 1602 inquiry Spaniards with long service in Florida identified Tocoy, San Julian, Antonico, Calabay, Nyaautina, Filache, and Mayaca as villages along upper portions of the river in which Christianization had begun. Other early seventeenth-century sources mention Equale, Anacabile (also spelled Anacabili), and Enacape (usually spelled Anacape later) similarly. Enacape and Anacabile may be one and the same (Montes 1602; Oré 1936:126; Valdés 1602). In 1602 Antonico was the head chief for the Rio Dulce rather than Nyaautina, who seems to represent Aotina or Outina of the 1560s.

During the 1602 inquiry, when witnesses mentioned Mayaca they always did so in conjunction with their mention of the Freshwater missions and *visitas*. But some witnesses omitted mention of Mayaca or mentioned Mayaca separately in ways that could be interpreted as meaning that it was not part of Rio Dulce Province. For example, the first witness mentioned a number of Rio Dulce villages without mentioning Mayaca. But in a separate context in which the witness spoke of principal chiefs from the region whom he had seen visit St. Augustine, he mentioned the chief of Antonico as head chief for Rio Dulce Province and then remarked separately, "Similarly I have seen the cacique of Mayaca and some of his vassal Indians come to this presidio daily from their land as friends." On the other hand, several witnesses seemed to include Mayaca as part of Rio Dulce, as did the fourth witness. He remarked that "in the Rio Dulce and San Sebastian, where Gaspar, Antonyco, and Mayaca are chiefs . . . there is a number of Christian Indians." However, in using the term Rio Dulce, he and the others may have been thinking of those riverine settlements only in geographical terms rather than intending to make a statement about their sharing a common tribal affiliation. And the fourth witness's mention of Mayaca's chief in conjunction with Chief Gaspar and Chief Antonico, head of the Freshwater Province, raises the possibility that Mayaca also was a head chief in a distinct polity (Valdés 1602). The 8 leagues that separated Mayaca from villages clearly identified as part of the Freshwater Province might be interpreted as a buffer zone indicating that Mayaca was part of a separate entity (Montes 1602).

Fray Francisco Pareja (1602) indicated clearly that such was the case, noting that there were six or more villages with Christians in the land of the Agua Dulce that lacked a friar and "other Indians whom they call of Mayaca" similarly without a friar.

A 1605 service record for a soldier-interpreter killed by the Surruque in 1597 while he was on his way to Ais links Mayaca's cacique more definitely with both the Surruque and the Ais. Mayaca's cacique in 1597 was a father-in-law of the cacique of Ais. The Surruque killed the soldier-interpreter because he had made war earlier on the cacique of Mayaca, killing or imprisoning many of Mayaca's people (Méndez de Canzo 1602; John Worth, personal communication 15 July 1991). The Indians then reportedly quartered and roasted the interpreter's body, presenting each quarter to their chief, after which they ate him (Junco 1605).

Sources from the late seventeenth century and early eighteenth century clearly indicate that the Mayaca were more closely related to the Ais and other south Florida peoples than to the Timucua. There is little reason to believe that the name Mayaca was applied then to a different people than it had been in the earlier periods. The Mayaca of the late mission period along with the Jororo spoke a language distinct from Timucua. In a 1717 census of the mission villages in the vicinity of St. Augustine, the Jororo, who had been neighbors of the Mayaca in the 1690s and had been spoken of then as belonging to the province of Mayaca and Jororo, were described as Mayaca-speakers (Ayala y Escobar 1717). In mentioning the killing of a friar working among the Jororo in 1696, Jonathan Dickinson (1981:60) described the friar as having been "murdered by some of the Cape Indians." In authorizing departure from Spain of a 1695 mission band destined for Florida, the Crown specified that they were to work exclusively among the Calusa and the Ais. Upon their arrival, those not sent to Calusa were assigned to the missions of Mayaca and Jororo (Hann 1991:119, 125, 130, 135–136, 140). This suggests that Mayaca and Jororo were considered to be missions among the Ais (fig. 5.1).

If that is the case, as it seems to be, the Mayaca and the Ais in general on the Timucua's southern borders are analogous to the Mocama and possibly other Timucua on Guale's southern border. The Mocama's ceramics are of the San Marcos type that characterizes the Guale, but the Mocama spoke Timucua rather than the Guale's Ibaja language. The Mocama example shows that ceramics are not always a reliable indicator of linguistic boundaries. Therefore, in the face of other evidence linking the Mayaca to the Ais, the Mayaca's sharing of the Timucua's St. Johns ceramic tradition need not be interpreted as meaning that the Mayaca were Timucua.

After Menéndez de Avilés's time no contact appears to have been made with the Mayaca until the beginning of mission work among them and the Freshwater Timucua of the St. Johns valley in the 1580s or early 1590s. A friar or friars worked intermittently in Mayaca sometime before 1597, baptizing the chief and an undetermined number of his people (Méndez de Canzo 1602; Valdés 1602). Of that effort Fray Blas de Montes (1602) wrote: "To the south of this city at the edge of a freshwater river at a distance of twenty-four leagues there are seven villages of Christians whose names are Tocoy, San Julian, Filache, Antonico, Equale, Anacabile, and Mayaca, and they would have something like two hundred Christian Indians. And in the last village, as it is eight leagues away from the nearest of the six, there would be more than 100 yet to be baptized." Governor Gonzalo Méndez de Canzo revealed a reason for the relative lack of progress at Mayaca down to 1602, noting that since his arrival in 1597 no friar had gone to Mayaca. He attributed the friars' neglect to their "lack of enthusiasm [*tibieza*]" toward both the people and the land "as being cursed [*mal dicta*] and swampy and [having] other problems" (Méndez de Canzo 1602). A similar distaste of friars of a later era for working with the Jororo and other Indians from south Florida suggests that one of the "other problems" was that the Mayaca were seasonally nomadic fisher-hunter-gatherers rather than agriculturalists (Hann 1991:110, 111, 115, 377). In view of the earlier Spanish conflict with Chief Mayaca and Mayaca's ties with the Ais and Surruque, simple prudence may have deterred the friars from going to Mayaca after 1597. Soon after his arrival in 1597 Governor Méndez de Canzo had sent Juan Ramírez de Contreras, the above-mentioned soldier-interpreter, to visit the Ais chief. In retaliation for the Surruque's killing of Contreras, the governor sent soldiers who killed up to 80 of the Surruque and brought 55 women and children to St. Augustine as captives (Alas 1599; Geiger 1937:137–139; Rouse 1951:53). Surruque's proximity to Mayaca and ties to it make the friars' reluctance to venture there understandable, especially in the wake of the killing of five friars in Guale in 1597.

Nothing more is known about relations between Mayaca and the Surruque. No mention of Mayaca appears in the documentation of the intensive contact between the Surruque and the governor in the first years of the seventeenth century following the above-mentioned incidents. At the start of the seventeenth century the Surruque were allied to the Ais and enemies of the Timucua of Nocoroco, as the Mayaca had been of Chief Outina a generation or so earlier (Mexía 1605b). The Surruque at Turtle Mound appear to have been the coastal equivalent of the Mayaca in the sense of being border chieftains with the obligations typical of the leader of a march territory.

Whether the natives of the upper St. Johns River were horticulturists or simply fisher-hunter-gatherers is another matter for which the evidence is seemingly contradictory, at least temporally. In separate contexts Governor Méndez de Canzo characterized Freshwater Timucua in general and the Mayaca as nonagriculturalists. Noting that in 1602 no religious lived at Tocoy, Antonico, or Mayaca, he remarked that "it is a wretched [*miserable*] people who sustain themselves with nothing but fish." In a similar vein he observed later that the natives "of the Freshwater district, Tocoy, Antonico, and Mayaca, never paid tribute, as they are people who live solely from fish and roots from the swamps and woods" (Méndez de Canzo 1602). For Tocoy and Antonico at least, either the governor was exaggerating or native life-styles had changed drastically since the 1560s. The latter could well be the case. The 1602 figure of only about 200 Christians among the Freshwater Timucua and Mayaca combined and the small number of villages mentioned as compared to the 1560s suggest a drastic decline in population had occurred, which may have disrupted established cultural patterns.

Both French and Spanish sources from the 1560s indicate that maize was grown in Freshwater Timucua villages, and French sources record the planting of maize as far upriver as Outina. But horticulture was conceivably not a major source of their food supply. The foodstuffs Outina and his people furnished to the French when the French were short of food indicates a considerable reliance on gathering. On one occasion Outina sent 12 or 15 baskets of acorns and 2 of pinocqs. Laudonnière described pinocqs as "little green fruit growing in the grass of the river and about the size of cherries" (Bennett 1975:125; Lussagnet 1958:145). Publishers of Laudonnière's accounts have identified pinocqs variously as "water chinquapens, more technically named *Nelumbo lutea*," (Bennett 1975:-224, n. 94) and *Apios tuberosa* (Lussagnet 1958:145, n. 2). Laudonnière's description seems to rule out *Apios*, which is harvested for its potatolike tuber. Pinocqs are probably the *pinoco* of later Spanish sources (see Florencia 1695; Hann 1986:201). In 1695 inhabitants of Salamototo complained that ranchers were preventing them from harvesting *pinoco* along the river. The growing of maize at Aotina is attested to dramatically in its chief's request to Menéndez de Avilés that he pray for rain to save his parched maize fields as he had successfully done earlier for the cacique of Guale (Barrientos 1965:115–116). But Spanish sources from the 1560s make no mention of maize upriver beyond Aotina. In threatening retaliation if he were not well received as he proceeded upriver from Aotina, Menéndez spoke only of burning down the villages and destroying canoes and fish weirs.

For the Freshwater Timucua, archaeology provides little data to resolve this issue. In their excavations at Nocoroco on the coast John W. Griffin and Hale Smith found no positive evidence for agriculture at the site. But they concluded that "while archaeological exploration gave direct evidence only of hunting, fishing, and shellfish gathering, it is to be assumed from the relatively small amount of evidence of these pursuits in relation to the total midden bulk that agriculture and root and seed gathering were also practiced" (Griffin and Smith 1949:345, 359).

Hontoon Island excavations provide data for the Mayaca-speaking region south of Lake George. Although cultivated species were found in historic-era contexts, Lee A. Newsom (1987:47, 77) concluded that "the inhabitants remained primarily non-horticultural, pursuing a hunting-gathering-fishing economy." She even suggested that maize and the larger pepos found there may have been introduced by native intruders from the north during the latter half of the seventeenth century. Worthy of note is her remark that the territory just south of Lake George is "bisected by Larson's (1980:213) inferred southern limit for agriculture." When Yamassee moved into the region in the late 1670s they also pursued the nomadic life of fisher-hunter-gatherers for much of the year (Bushnell 1990:481–482).

Missions to the Mayaca and Jororo

Little is known about the establishment of the first mission at Mayaca. In 1602 Mayaca was not among the places where friars had erected a church, although its chief had been converted by that time (Valdés 1602). In 1597 Mayaca's chief was among the native leaders who came to St. Augustine to render obedience to newly arrived Governor Méndez de Canzo. Soldiers in 1602 placed him among those who frequented the city but did not specify the times of those visits. There is no mention of him after that date. In 1606 Mayaca's chief did not appear on the roll of chiefs whom Bishop Juan de las Cabezas de Altamirano confirmed. In 1614 Oré went only 20 leagues upriver to San Antonio Anacape (rendered as Enacape by Oré) mission on his visitation, where he met a friar who came from Avino (San Luis de Acuera). The first phase of the mission at Mayaca was mentioned for the first and last time on the 1655 mission list, where it appears as San Salbador de Mayaca, located 36 leagues from St. Augustine (Diez de la Calle 1659). Neither Mayaca nor San Antonio Anacape appears on either of the mission lists from 1675.

But both Anacape and Mayaca reappear on a listing of the missions drawn up in December 1680 by the newly installed governor, Juan Marques Cabrera. He described both as "new conversions," seemingly indicating that most or all of the missions' earlier populations had disappeared since 1655. Marques Cabrera placed both missions under his heading "Provinces of Timuqua" (Marques Cabrera 1680).

The circumstances of the reemergence of missions at Anacape and Mayaca are ill defined. Both sites are first mentioned anew in passing in the latter half of 1679 by Governor Pablo de Hita Salazar and Fray Jacinto de Barreda. The inhabitants of both sites were identified as Yamassee who had left their homeland to escape attacks by Westo. The governor spoke of heathen Yamassee at Anacape having asked for a friar. After looking into the matter, Fray Barreda informed the governor that the Yamassee at Anacape showed no interest in becoming Christians, but he said that he had instructed Fray Bartolomé de Quiñones, who was stationed in Mayaca, to exhort and prepare the Yamassee at Anacape to become Christians. Barreda promised to send a second friar to Mayaca soon so that he might work with the people at Anacape "disposing their spirits" until divine providence should move them to desire to become Christians (Hann 1990:88–89; Hita Salazar 1680; Solana 1679).

The promise was fulfilled by October 1680. Fray Juan Miguel de Villareal testified on 12 April 1682 that he had been stationed at Anacape for about a year and a half. He identified his mission's population as consisting of "four grown men [hombres hechos]—two Caciques, one without vassals, the other with them—one blind Christian male—four little boys [mocitos] up to three years old more or less—two young Christian males [chiquillos]—and one young Christian female [chiquilla], all of about four years of age more or less—and two heathen nursing infants—three women, with another two very old ones" (Villareal 1682). In several weeks of archaeological exploration at the believed site of Anacape (Mount Royal) in the vicinity of Palatka, B. Calvin Jones found much Spanish material scattered over 40 acres, which he believes belongs exclusively to the early 1600s Spanish presence. He has not sufficiently studied the native ceramics he found to venture an assessment of their cultural affiliation (Goggin 1952:25, n. 11; Hann 1990:23–24, 90; B. Calvin Jones, personal communication 1988, 1991).

The testimony given by Fray Villareal was part of an investigation into the advisability of continuing the two missions after Fray Quiñones abandoned his post at Mayaca sometime in 1681. Remarks by one of Mayaca's chiefs indicated that Quiñones had been absent a number of times since the mission was revived. The last of his departures precipitated the above-mentioned investigation. He made that departure more dramatic and definitive when he took the mission's two bells and the church ornaments and vestments with him on leaving, telling the chief that the governor had ordered the closing of the mission, something the governor had not done.

The inadequacy of the friar's diet and the strains imposed by the hunter-gatherer subsistence strategy of Mayaca's inhabitants seem to have been the reasons for Quiñones's abandonment of his post. He had become ill from attempting to follow the Yamassee in their wanderings through the woods in search of greens and starchy roots and from being forced to share the natives' diet on many occasions because of inadequate supplies from St. Augustine.

In his sworn statement for the inquiry, Quiñones gave Mayaca's population as "twenty-eight grown men—twenty-one women—eight young *doctrina* girls [*chiquillas*]—ten young *doctrina* boys [*pequatas*]—twelve [other children] between nursing infants and children up to the age of three" (Quiñones 1682).

The royal officials noted that five unruly (*lebentes*) male Indians had left Mayaca, that up to nine of the same sort had departed from Anacape during the preceding year or earlier, and that they, as royal officials, had done what was possible to assist the chiefs in this matter. The officials confirmed that those who remained ordinarily lived in the woods, as they were not in the habit of farming or having the form of a village, and that the roots that they gathered in the fields were their principal sustenance (Menéndes Marques and Rocha n.d.).

Mayaca's chiefs, Francisco and Matheo, protested to the governor that the king had given the bells and other church furnishings to that village and to no other one at the time the mission was revived. They asked that if Quiñones did not wish to continue to work among them, they be given another friar who would stay in order "to teach both those vassals of the said chiefs who were Christians and those who were heathens and the rest who were being attached to them" and that the church furnishings that Quiñones had removed to Salamototo be returned to Mayaca. They argued that in view of Mayaca's population of 28 men, not to mention its women and children, it merited a friar, pointing out that the population could have been much larger if Quiñones had not objected to the heathens living with the Christians. One of Mayaca's chiefs insisted that, inasmuch as both heathens and Christians were his vassals, the heathens could not be dismissed out of hand but rather they should be accepted as such so that they might become Christians with continued exposure to the teaching of the law of God (Leturiondo 1682).

In response to those petitions, the governor characterized Quiñones's actions as inopportune, for the natives were left without any spiritual recourse and were liable to disperse to the woods on a more or less permanent basis. Consequently he asked the Franciscan provincial to provide a remedy (Marques Cabrera 1682). There is no information about what immediate steps, if any, were taken to remedy the situation.

In June 1681, Anacape's friar Villareal, while remaining at his post, had questioned Anacape's viability, with its present population of only 5 working men and total population of no more than 30 people. To remedy this he asked the governor for permission to bring in some Yamassee who were then living at the places of Santa María and San Pedro and, in particular, 8 people identified by name. They included 5 who had left Anacape to go to Santa María and San Pedro: Pacuqui, a man; Micayoga, a man; Hulatapale, a woman; Nuscha, a boy; and Tasigaia (meaning warrior), a man. Two others were living among the Chachises (probably Salchiches, as suggested by a penciled note in the Connor transcript), next to San Phelipe in the province of Guale. They were a woman named Quiypa and a boy named Saquila. Villareal argued that if he, the chief, and a soldier were allowed to bring them back, the governor's support of this move would influence many others to follow them and he would have an adequate number of people with whom to work. He suggested that, even if those individuals did not presently wish to become Christians, they would in time because "they are like the monkeys in that they do what they see others doing" (Villareal 1681).

In reply the governor commended his zeal but remarked that it would be counterproductive to try to force those heathen Indians to return to

Anacape and that God's grace would be more likely to move their hearts at Santa Cathalina, which was where they wanted to be. He noted as well that they were needed in Santa Cathalina because of its exposed frontier position. The governor suggested that he await God's bringing about an increase in Anacape's population by inspiring people from the Rinconada (for meanings of *rinconada* see Hann 1991:6–7), who belonged to caciques who had just come to St. Augustine to visit him, to move to that mission (Marques Cabrera 1681).

Mayaca next appeared in the records only in 1689. It then contained 30 families, or 150 individuals (Ebelino de Compostela 1689). But like many other missions during this period when many friars were being shifted to Cuba, Mayaca appears to have been without a friar much of the time during the first several years after 1689. At the end of August 1690 Florida's governor spoke of Fray Salvador Bueno as having been at Mayaca three or four months earlier, implying that Mayaca had lacked a friar since then (Quiroga y Losada 1690). Before April 1692, however, persistent orders from the Crown to send friars to work among the Ais and Calusa of south Florida moved Franciscan authorities to return a friar to Mayaca and establish the first two Jororo missions, Concepción de Atoyquime and San Joseph de Jororo. As of April 1692, 108 people had been baptized at San Salvador de Mayaca, 30 of them adults. Only 4 of the 108 were natives of Mayaca. The remaining 104 were natives of villages named Malao, Afafa, and Hipaha. Our knowledge of the earlier presence of Yamassee in the area and the name Hipaha's resemblance to de Soto's Yupaha suggest that some, if not all, of the 104 were Yamassee. At Jororo, Fray Francisco Camacho had baptized 53 children by April 1692. At Anacape, 18 adults and 25 children had been baptized by then and up to 10 more people were under instruction (Barreda 1692). By 1693 more than 400 people had been Christianized in the four missions of Anacape, Mayaca, Jororo, and Atoyquime. The friars then were hopeful of winning many more in territories surrounding those existing missions. They described that land and its surrounding territory as having "the form of a triangle terminating on the Cape of Canaveral on the southeast side. And on that of the east running along the coast of Florida to the north, and along that of the south in the Keys of the Bahama Channel and along that of the southwest and west to the Mexican Gulf, in the inner parts and edges of which that covered more than three hundred leagues there is an abundance of nations, some idolaters, other heathens [*gentiles*] with the provinces being differentiated in accord with the languages" (Carmenatri and Provincial Chapter 1693; Menéndez Marques and Florencia 1697). By 1696 a third Jororo mission existed at Atissimi or Jizime and a people known as Aypaja or Piaja had begun to be converted.

To some degree creation of these new missions of Mayaca and Jororo can be attributed to Governor Hita Salazar's interest in promoting missions among the previously neglected natives of south Florida. He informed the Crown early in 1680 that he had promised himself that the friars would move forward with the conversion of south Florida's natives and that his fondest desire was to see missions established from Ais to Calusa as a legacy of his administration. His alerting of the Crown to this unmet need led the Crown to press for a mission to the Calusa as early as 1681 and later to insist on expansion of the missions to the Ais in terms that suggest that the Mayaca-Jororo missions of the 1690s were a beginning of those missions to the Ais (Hann 1991:27, 28–29, 51, 119, 125, 130).

In 1693, after informing the Crown of the progress of the new missions, the friars asked for financial support for expeditions to establish contact with new peoples beyond the reach of the existing missions and for the purchase of iron tools with which to convert the region's largely fisher-hunter-gatherer peoples into sedentary agriculturalists. The friars' remarks at that time that these people "on the whole do not work at plantings" but "are able to sustain themselves solely with the abundance of fish that they catch and some wild fruits" suggest that some of those people engaged in agriculture to a minimal degree (Carmenatri and Provincial Chapter 1693).

Although data are available for the distances between the five Mayaca-Jororo missions of the 1690s, they do not permit an exact location of the Jororo missions. In 1697 Mayaca was still 16 leagues from Anacape on or near the first-phase mission of 1655. San Joseph de Jororo was 16 leagues from Mayaca and 9 from Atissimi. Atoyquime in its turn was 9 leagues from Atissimi (Menéndez Marques and Florencia 1697). Jororo Province was largely swamp (or subject to flooding—*añegadiza*) with places full of brambles and an abundance of lakes, some of which were large (Torres y Ayala 1697).

Mayaca served as headquarters for the province. By 1696 it had a resident deputy-governor and his soldier assistants. His appointment may have been recent for Governor Laureano de Torres y Ayala, who arrived in Florida only in 1693, spoke of having placed the deputy-governor in the province (Torres y Ayala 1697).

The friars' 1693 hopes for an abundance of converts and ongoing success were dashed in 1696 and 1697. The troubles began at Atoyquime in late October 1696, when natives there killed their friar, Luis Sánchez, apparently because of his having disciplined some errant natives. Dickinson's differing account appears to be a garbled version of the events. Dickinson observed that "the Caseekey of this town they gained on to embrace the Roman faith, but all his people were much incensed against the friars, and therefore would have their caseekey renounce his faith and put the friars to death; but he would assent to neither; therefore they killed him and one friar" (Dickinson 1981:60). The murdered native leader was cacique of Aypaja rather than chief of Atoyquime, and he was killed because of his opposition to the killing of the friar. Two Guale boys who assisted the friar at Mass were also killed. Initially the other villages remained calm and permitted the two other friars in Jororo Province to withdraw safely to Mayaca. On reaching Mayaca, Fray Salvador Bueno, the friar at San Joseph de Jororo, informed the lieutenant about "how the people of the said place had come to his convent weeping and saying that the people of the said place of Atoquime [*sic*] had killed the priest, Fray Luis Sánchez, and that they had seen the habit reduced to shreds and bloodied" (Torres y Ayala 1697).

On learning of the event at Atoyquime, the governor dispatched 6 and then an additional 11 soldiers to restore calm, secure the church furnishings, seek to capture the assailants, and learn what motivated the killing of the friar. Despite the governor's instructions to the soldiers to treat the peaceful Indians amicably and to make no demands on them for food during their stay, the trouble spread not long after the arrival of the second group of soldiers, when the soldiers set out to capture those responsible for the friar's death. When the lieutenant and the first soldiers visited the remaining Jororo villages, they had received a friendly reception and many of the natives of some villages offered to assist the Spaniards in their search for the inhabitants of Atoyquime, who were reported to have fled toward the coast to a village named Yuamajiro (rendered also as Guamajiro). That goodwill had been feigned, however, and the soldiers' two Jororo guides led them astray "onto swampy and gravelly trails [*caminos variales y cascales*] that were so difficult that they were able to advance only at the cost of much labor and delay" (Torres y Ayala 1697). At a point where the trail branched, the Spaniards sent the Jororo scouts with a Guale Indian to try to capture an Indian from Yuamajiro who might serve better as a guide. Their guides then abandoned them in an area full of brambles, swamps, and ponds, as did the porters who carried the provisions. When the soldiers returned to Jororo three days after having left it, they found the village deserted, the church desecrated, and a soldier dead whom they had left behind to recuperate from a punctured foot. The Jororo had also killed two Guale who served the mission as sacristans. Although Atissimi's people were not involved in the violence, they also took to the woods at this juncture, probably fearful of retaliation by the Spaniards. When the soldiers withdrew to Mayaca with the church furnishings they had salvaged, they found that Mayaca's people had fled as well without taking anything from church or convent or doing any harm. Convinced that under the circumstances any further attempt then to apprehend the assailants or to bring back those who had fled would be futile, the soldiers returned to St. Augustine with the church furnishings, attributing their failure to the harshness of the trails, the Indians' residence on islands and very large lakes that made canoes a necessity, and "that they would always be bound to be detected beforehand."

Before the governor had completed his inquiry in January 1697, Mayaca's people had returned to their village. St. Augustine's leaders in assembly decided that in view of difficulties posed by the winter rains and the lack of provisions no further expedition should be mounted at that time. They advised the governor to strive to attract the Indians back to their villages with kindness and to seek to capture the Indian captain of Atoyquime, who was the principal instigator of the trouble, and his closest followers. To that end the governor issued a general pardon to all the Indians of the Mayaca-Jororo Province who had fled except those directly involved in the killings and promised 25 pesos for the capture and delivery of Atoyquime's captain. The governor gave responsibility for implementation of this policy to his lieutenant at Mayaca (Torres y Ayala 1697).

Except in the matter of apprehending those responsible for the killings, the governor's policy was largely successful in the short term. In response to a Crown request for information on the matter, the governor reported in September 1699 that friars were working in Anacape and Mayaca, whose people he characterized as "never having rebelled." He placed Aypaja's people in the same category, reporting that they had been resettled at Anacape at their own request. Two groups of Jororo had also returned, asking to be resettled in two areas, one called Las Cofas, where about 100 were established, and the other, the woods of Afafa, with about 60 people. The 10 or so from Atoyquime involved in the murders had retreated "to a very unknown region," and the rest of the 30 or so people from that village had scattered into different areas. The governor suspected that some of the returnees may have been people from Atoyquime who were not party to the murders. "Out of all this province of San Salvador de Mayaca," he concluded, "only those of the village of Atisme remain to be resettled." He also characterized them as having simply withdrawn to the woods rather than revolting. His agents who were in contact with them were hopeful of resettling them. The four existing settlements were each two days' journey from one another. At that moment the friars from Anacape and Mayaca were visiting Las Cofas and Afafa, but the governor had made provisions for two friars to live in the new Jororo settlements (Torres y Ayala 1699).

On 1 January 1701 trouble flared again at Mayaca as its 21 to 23 inhabitants fled to the woods anew along with others of the Malao nation (possibly the Malica of Laudonnière's time, according to Swanton 1922:326) who also had been living there. An Indian named Martinillo, whom Governor Torres y Ayala had imprisoned for a time in St. Augustine's castillo, precipitated the flight with a false report that Spaniards were coming to kill Mayaca's inhabitants. To bring back the fugitives and to attempt anew to capture the natives responsible for the killings in Jororo Province in 1696–1697, Governor Zúñiga ordered Joachín de Florencia to lead a mixed force of 20 soldiers, 11 Guale, and 60 Apalachee and Chacato into the Mayaca region. In that search, if possible, Florencia was to reconnoiter the portion of south-central Florida referred to as the Rinconada all the way to the Lake of Maymi and the borders of the land of Carlos. If at all possible the force was to avoid hostilities and was not to initiate them under any circumstances. And even if hostilities proved unavoidable, the men were to exercise moderation in the hope that during the breaks in the action the natives might have a change of heart (Zúñiga y Zerda 1701a, 1701b, 1701f). The Apalachee and Chacato warriors apparently did not materialize. The force that accompanied Florencia to Mayaca consisted of 26 soldiers and 30 Indians from Timucua and Guale. The expedition penetrated that territory as deeply as it was able to without finding the fugitive Mayaca, "because," as the governor phrased it, "of the roughness [*agrio*] of the land of swampy woods [*montes atascaderos*] and very tangled reed-mace swamps [*espadañales mui embarazosos*] in which they ordinarily lived." He reported that the Indians of the place of Jororo remained quiet, as did those of San Antonio and Las Cofas as well as some other chiefs from that region who had come recently to render obedience to the king at Florencia's suggestion. Florencia's force succeeded in capturing three heathen natives said to be involved in the earlier killings at Atoyquime (rendered here as Atoycuime) and Jororo. Governor Zúñiga reported regretfully that in disobedience to his orders some of the Timucua on the expedition, without Florencia's consent, killed some unreduced heathen natives of that region whom they encountered by chance wandering through the woods. Speaking of this incident, the governor lamented what he termed "the native's destructive passion for killing each other for no other reason than to lessen each other's numbers." The incident prompted him to issue a general ban on the taking of scalps or dancing with them (Zúñiga y Zerda 1701b, 1701c, 1701d, 1701e, 1701f).

After Florencia's arrival back in St. Augustine, the governor reported confidently that the fugitives from Mayaca would soon return because of the friendly overtures to them that Florencia had made through the medium of the other Spanish-allied settlements in the region. His prediction proved correct. On 15 November 1701 he reported that most of the fugitives had returned and that the chiefs had promised that they would secure the return of those who were still absent (Zúñiga y Zerda 1701c, 1701f).

After the questioning of the three natives accused of involvement in the earlier killings in Jororo Province, Governor Zúñiga officially closed the case on the basis of the inquiry's findings. The detainees indicated that a number of the others who had been involved in the killings had died already. The first of the detainees to be questioned died of natural causes only three days after making his statement, receiving baptism at his own request before his death. The second of the detainees, named Sique, was condemned to six years of exile from Florida, to be served either in Havana or in Caracas. The governor absolved and freed the third detainee, named Yvo, for lack of proof of the charges against him. Yvo maintained that his only involvement was to dig the pits for the burial of those killed and that he had done that under duress as a subject (Zúñiga y Zerda 1701c, 1701f).

During this period a number of Spanish ranches continued to exist in this southern region. The ranch of Alonso de Esquivel was described as being "in the environs [contornos] of the province of Mayaca." It was Esquivel who advised the governor of the return of the Mayaca fugitives to their village (Zúñiga y Zerda 1701f).

In September 1704, the governor spoke of the "provinces of the

south—Rinconada, Jororo, Mayaca, Tisimea, Tocuime, and other populations" as enjoying peace. However, he expressed fear of their being attacked by Indians allied to the English and informed the Crown that he
could do nothing to prevent such attack (Zúñiga y Zerda 1704). Four years
later the succeeding governor reported that such attacks had begun to
affect parts of Mayaca and Jororo and that among the Jororo and Mayaca
who had sought refuge near St. Augustine 28 women had been captured
while out in the countryside in search of roots for sustenance. Four of them
escaped to bring word of the incident (Córcoles y Martínez 1708).

Mayaca, Jororo, and other Indians from south Florida continued to
live near St. Augustine intermittently in some number over the next several decades. In 1717 a village bearing the name San Joseph de Jororo
housed 33 people who spoke the Mayaca language. Their chief, don Juan
Romo, and 4 leading men were Christians. Only 2 of the 11 identified as
warriors were Christian and only 3 out of 13 women. Out of 4 children
only 1 had been baptized (Hann 1989:185). Between 1718 and 1723, 4
children and 26 adults were baptized in the Jororo village (Benavides
1723). A 1726 census of the Indian villages near St. Augustine did not
mention the Jororo. But in a description of those villages and their inhabitants written in 1728, a friar reported that the Jororo had been living in a
village 9 leagues south of St. Augustine united with Pojoy and Amacapira
until an epidemic struck in 1727. Most of the villagers died in the epidemic. The few survivors then returned to their former homelands (Bullones 1728). A few Jororo reappeared in the early 1730s. Initially they
lived in a camp described as "a rifle-shot's distance" from a village of
other south Floridians, inhabited by Pojoy, Alafaya, and Amacapira. But
at the insistence of a new governor, who assumed office in 1734, the
Jororo were united with Casapullo in the mission of Puríssima Concepción de Casapullos, from which they soon fled southward again (Montiano 1738). That is the last mention of the Jororo.

There is little mention of the Mayaca per se during these first decades
of the eighteenth century. In 1735 Franciscans prematurely reported the
complete annihilation of the Mayaca (Deagan 1978:111). A Jesuit expedition to the Miami area in 1743 reported that remnants of the Maymi,
Santaluzo, and Mayaca numbering about 100 were living together about
four days' journey to the north (Alaña and Monaco 1743).

The Piaja or Aypaja of the Jororo territory and other Indians from
that region also migrated to the vicinity of St. Augustine during this
period. In 1726, 38 heathens of the Piaja nation from the Rinconada of

Carlos were living in a village near St. Augustine (Benavides 1726). They are not mentioned thereafter. Twenty-four Amacapiras, 18 of whom were recently converted Christians, were living with Chiluca (Mocama) at San Buenaventura in 1726 (Benavides 1726). When last mentioned in the early 1730s, they were living with Alafaya and Pojoy.

The most durable of the south Florida natives who migrated to the vicinity of St. Augustine were people whom Spaniards called Costas, who have been identified variously as Ais, Keys Indians, and Alafaya (Hann 1989:198). The Costa first appeared on a 1723 list as the "village of the Costa nation Guasacara," in which 15 children and 39 adults had been baptized since 1718 (Benavides 1723). In 1726 the Costa village of San Antonio held 88 people, only 38 of whom were Christians. An imbalance of 55 men to 13 women suggests that many of the women had been lost to slave raiders, probably while out on a foray looking for the roots that were a staple of their diet (Benavides 1726). By 1728 the gender imbalance had been rectified somewhat by the disappearance of many of the men, as there were then 20 men, 18 women, and about 14 children (Bullones 1728). By 1734 the Costa village had only 10 men above the age of fourteen (Swanton 1922:105). Their village was last mentioned in 1738 and 1739. By 1738 it had only 19 people, the majority having died at the hands of their enemies (Montiano 1738). Nine heathen Costa were still living in one of St. Augustine's two native settlements in 1759 (Ruís 1759).

The friars had a low opinion of the Costa and all the other immigrant groups from south Florida because of their adherence to their own no-madic ways and religious beliefs. Of the Jororo, Amacapira, and Pojoy, Fray Bullones remarked: "They were all idolaters and heathens except two or three. . . . They maintained themselves with their Minister, although with great difficulty, because neither did they have a secure territory, nor did they sow, nor did they work. And they wander about all year, women as well as men, searching for the marine life with which they sustain themselves, killing alligators and other unclean animals, which is delectable sustenance to them." He characterized the Costa as "vile by nature" and useless, noting that when they felt like it they left their camp to go off to eat palm fruit and alligators (Bullones 1728).

Summary

There are solid indications that the Mayaca of the sixteenth and early seventeenth centuries, like those who bore the name later, were not Freshwater Timucua but people related to or identical with the Mayaca-speaking Jororo and probably related to the Ais and other peoples of south-central Florida. The village and mission of Mayaca was on the upper St. Johns River a little south of Lake George and distinct from the French sources' Mathiaca and Mayarqua. The Mayaca and Jororo were mainly, if not exclusively, fisher-hunter-gatherers rather than horticulturists. The revolt of 1696–1697 began in Jororo's Atoyquime and did not involve the inhabitants of the Mayaca mission except for their temporary flight from their village. St. Johns–type ceramics seem to be the Mayaca and Jororo's only significant link with the Freshwater Timucua, which is probably no more than a parallel to the Mocama's ceramic ties with the Guale. Early eighteenth-century raids into south-central Florida by Indians allied with the English drove many of that region's peoples to seek refuge near St. Augustine, where most perished in epidemics and in warfare. The Mayaca appear to have made their last stand on Lake Okeechobee, which bears the name Lake Mayaca on maps from the 1820s (Buchon 1825; Carey 1822; Finley 1827).

Bibliography

Alaña, Joseph Xavier, and Joseph María Monaco
1743   Report that Fathers Joseph María Monaco and Joseph Xavier Alaña of the Company of Jesus Present to the Most Excellent Señor Don Juan Francisco Güemes de Horcasitas . . . about the State in which They have Found the Indians of Southern Florida and its Keys, Along with what they Considered Necessary for its Permanent Reduction, Havana, 1743. Archivo General de Indias, Santo Domingo 860, Stetson Collection. P. K. Yonge Library of Florida History, University of Florida, Gainesville. Translated by John H. Hann. In *Where the River Found the Bay: Historical Study of the Granada Site, Miami, Florida.* Vol. 2: *Archaeology and History of the Granada Site*, by Arva Moore Parks, 56–65. Tallahassee: Florida Division of Archives, History, and Records Management, 1985.

Alas, Alonso de Las
1599   Letter to the King, St. Augustine, 20 March 1599. Archivo General de Indias, Santo Domingo 229, reel 3, Jeannette Thurber Connor Collection. P. K. Yonge Library of Florida History, University of Florida, Gainesville.

Ayala y Escobar, Juan de
1717   Letter to the King, St. Augustine, 18 April 1717. Archivo General de Indias, Santo Domingo 843, Stetson Collection. P. K. Yonge Library of Florida History, University of Florida, Gainesville.

Barreda, Jazintho de
1692 Petition to Diego de Quiroga y Losada, St. Augustine, 16 April 1692.
      Archivo General de Indias, Santo Domingo 228, doc. no. 42, vol. 4, John
      Tate Lanning Collection. Thomas Jefferson Library, University of Mis-
      souri at St. Louis.

Barrientos, Bartolomé
1965 Pedro Menéndez de Avilés, Founder of Florida. Translated by Anthony
      Kerrigan. Gainesville: University of Florida Press.

Benavides, Antonio de
1723 Letter to the King, St. Augustine, 8 March 1723. Archivo General de
      Indias, Santo Domingo 865, Stetson Collection. P. K. Yonge Library of
      Florida History, University of Florida, Gainesville.

1726 Record of his visitation of the native settlements, 1 December 1726. Ar-
      chivo General de Indias, Santo Domingo 866. [Microfilm copy furnished
      by Victoria Stapells-Johnson.]

Bennett, Charles E., trans.
1975 Three Voyages, René Laudonnière. Gainesville: University Presses of Flor-
      ida.

Buchon, Jean Alexandre C.
1825 Map. Tallahassee: Florida State Library.

Bullones, Joseph de
1728 Letter to the King, St. Augustine, 5 October 1728. Archivo General de
      Indias, Santo Domingo 865, Stetson Collection. P. K. Yonge Library of
      Florida History, University of Florida, Gainesville.

Bushnell, Amy Turner
1990 The Sacramental Imperative: Catholic Ritual and Indian Sedentism in the
      Provinces of Florida. In Columbian Consequences. Vol. 2: Archaeological
      and Historical Perspectives on the Spanish Borderlands East, edited by
      David Hurst Thomas, 475–496. Washington, D.C.: Smithsonian Institu-
      tion Press.

Carey, Henry Charles
1822 Map. Tallahassee: Florida State Library.

Carmenatri, Juan de, and Provincial Chapter
1693 Letter to the King, St. Augustine, 5 December 1693. Archivo General de
      Indias, Santo Domingo 235. [Microfilm copy furnished by Victoria
      Stapells-Johnson.]

Córcoles y Martínez, Francisco de
1708 Letter to the King, St. Augustine, 14 January 1708. In Here They Once
      Stood: The Tragic End of the Apalachee Missions, by Mark F. Boyd, Hale

G. Smith, and John W. Griffin, 90–91. Gainesville: University of Florida Press, 1951.

Deagan, Kathleen A.
1978 Cultures in Transition: Fusion and Assimilation among the Eastern Timucua. In *Tacachale: Essays on the Indians of Florida and Southeastern Georgia during the Historic Period*, edited by Jerald T. Milanich and Samuel Proctor, 89–119. Ripley P. Bullen Monographs in Anthropology and History, no. 1. Gainesville: University Presses of Florida.

Dickinson, Jonathan
1981 *Jonathan Dickinson's Journal; or, God's Protecting Providence: Being the Narrative of a Journey from Port Royal in Jamaica to Philadelphia, August 23, 1696 to April 1, 1697.* Edited by Evangeline Walker Andrews and Charles McLean Andrews. Stuart: Florida Classics Library.

Díez de la Calle, Juan
1659 *Noticias Sacras i Reales Delos dos Ymperios Delas Indias Occidentales Dela Nveva España.* 2 vols. [Mary Mitchell found that Díez de la Calle was official mayor of the Secretaria de la Nueva España and that the 1655 mission list was composed to assist the work of the *cronista* mayor.]

Ebelino de Compostela, Diego
1689 Letter to the King, Havana, 28 September 1689. Archivo General de Indias, Santo Domingo 151, Stetson Collection. P. K. Yonge Library of Florida History, University of Florida, Gainesville.

Finley, Anthony
1827 Map. Tallahassee: Florida State Library.

Florencia, Joachín de
1695 Visitation of Timucua. Archivo General de Indias, Escribanía de Cámara, leg. 157A, cuaderno I, folios 89–109. Translated by John H. Hann. In *Visitations and Revolts in Florida, 1656–1695.* Florida Archaeology no. 7. Tallahassee: Florida Bureau of Archaeological Research. Forthcoming.

Fontaneda, D⁰ d'Escalante
1944 *Memoir of D⁰ d'Escalante Fontaneda Respecting Florida.* Rev. ed. Translated by Buckingham Smith, Miami.

Geiger, Maynard J., O.F.M.
1937 *The Franciscan Conquest of Florida, 1573–1618.* Studies in Hispanic-American History, vol. 1. Washington, D.C.: Catholic University of America.

Goggin, John M.
1952 *Space and Time Perspective in Northern St. Johns Archeology, Florida.* Yale University Publications in Anthropology, no. 47. New Haven.

Griffin, John W., and Hale G. Smith
1949 Nocoroco, a Timucua Village of 1605. *Florida Historical Quarterly* 27(4):340–361.

Hann, John H., ed. and trans.
1991 *Missions to the Calusa.* Ripley P. Bullen Series. Gainesville: University of Florida Press.

1989 St. Augustine's Fallout from the Yamasee War. *Florida Historical Quarterly* 68(2):180–200.

1990 *Summary Guide to Spanish Florida Missions and Visitas with Churches in the Sixteenth and Seventeenth Centuries.* Washington, D.C.: Academy of American Franciscan History.

Hann, John H., ed. and trans.
1991 *Missions to the Calusa.* Ripley P. Bullen Series. Gainesville: University Press of Florida.

Hita Salazar, Pablo de
1680 Letter to the King, St. Augustine, 1680. Archivo General de Indias, Santo Domingo 226, reel 3, Jeannette Thurber Connor Collection. P. K. Yonge Library of Florida History, University of Florida, Gainesville.

Junco, María de
1605 Letter accompanying service record of Juan Ramírez de Contreras, St. Augustine, mid-October 1605. Archivo General de Indias, Santo Domingo 24. [Document furnished by John E. Worth.]

Larson, Lewis H.
1980 *Aboriginal Subsistence Technology on the Southeastern Coastal Plain during the Late Prehistoric Period.* Ripley P. Bullen Monographs in Anthropology and History, no. 2. Gainesville: University Presses of Florida.

Leturiondo, Domingo de
1682 Petition, 7 [March?] 1682, in Juan Marques Cabrera 1682, q.v.

Lorant, Stefan, ed.
1946 *The New World: The First Pictures of America.* New York: Duell, Sloan, and Pearce.

Lussagnet, Suzanne
1958 *Les Français en Amérique pendant la Deuxième Moitié du XVIe Siècle: Les Français en Floride.* Paris: Presses Universitaire de France.

Lyon, Eugene
1983 *The Enterprise of Florida: Pedro Menéndez de Avilés and the Spanish Conquest of 1565–1568.* Gainesville: University Presses of Florida.

Marques Cabrera, Juan
1680 Report on the religious existing in the missions of Florida and on the

villages in which there are *doctrinas*, St. Augustine, 6 December 1680. Archivo General de Indias, Santo Domingo 226, reel 4, Woodbury Lowery Collection. Strozier Library, Florida State University, Tallahassee.

1681 Letter to Juan Miguel Villareal, St. Augustine, 22 June 1681. Archivo General de Indias, Santo Domingo 226, reel 3, Jeannette Thurber Connor Collection. P. K. Yonge Library of Florida History, University of Florida, Gainesville.

1682 Letter to the King, St. Augustine, 7 October 1682. Archivo General de Indias, Santo Domingo 226, reel 3, Jeannette Thurber Connor Collection. P. K. Yonge Library of Florida History, University of Florida, Gainesville.

Méndez de Canzo, Gonzalo
1602 Letter to the King, St. Augustine, 22 September 1602. Archivo General de Indias, Santo Domingo 224, reel 2, Jeannette Thurber Connor Collection. P. K. Yonge Library of Florida History, University of Florida, Gainesville.

Menéndes Marques, Antonio, and Francisco de la Rocha
n.d. In Juan Marques Cabrera 1682, q.v.

Menéndez Marques, Thomás, and Joachín de Florencia
1697 Letter to the King, St. Augustine, 20 April 1697. Archivo General de Indias, Santo Domingo 230, reel 4, Jeannette Thurber Connor Collection. P. K. Yonge Library of Florida History, University of Florida, Gainesville.

Mexía, Alvaro de
1605a Beneficial and useful *derrotero* and true in everything of the rivers, channels, lagoons, woods, settlements, landing places, shoals [and] hamlets which extend from the city of St. Augustine to the bar of Ais. Archivo General de Indias, Patronato 19, reel 1, Jeannette Thurber Connor Collection. P. K. Yonge Library of Florida History, University of Florida, Gainesville.

1605b Letter to Pedro de Ibarra, Urubia, 15 June 1605. Archivo General de Indias, Patronato 19, reel 1, Jeannette Thurber Connor Collection. P. K. Yonge Library of Florida History, University of Florida, Gainesville.

Milanich, Jerald T.
1978 The Western Timucua: Patterns of Acculturation and Change. In *Tacachale: Essays on the Indians of Florida and Southeastern Georgia during the Historic Period*, edited by Jerald T. Milanich and Samuel Proctor, 59–88. Ripley P. Bullen Monographs in Anthropology and History, no. 1. Gainesville: University Presses of Florida.

Milanich, Jerald T., and Charles Hudson
1993 *Hernando de Soto and the Indians of Florida*. Gainesville: University Press of Florida.

Montes, Blas de
1602   Letter to the King, St. Augustine, 16 September 1602. Archivo General de Indias, Santo Domingo 232, reel 2, Woodbury Lowery Collection. Strozier Library, Florida State University, Tallahassee.

Montiano, Manuel
1738   Letter to the King, St. Augustine, 4 June 1738. Archivo General de Indias, Santo Domingo 865, Stetson Collection. P. K. Yonge Library of Florida History, University of Florida, Gainesville.

Newsom, Lee A.
1987   Analysis of Botanical Remains from Hontoon Island (8-VO-202), Florida: 1980–1985 Excavations. *The Florida Anthropologist* 40(1):47–84.

Oré, Luís Gerónimo de
1936   *The Martyrs of Florida (1513–1616).* Translated and edited by Maynard J. Geiger. Franciscan Studies, no. 18. New York: Joseph F. Wagner.

Pareja, Francisco
1602   Letter to the King, St. Augustine, 14 September 1602. Archivo General de Indias, Santo Domingo 235, Stetson Collection. P. K. Yonge Library of Florida History, University of Florida, Gainesville.

Provanza hecha a pedimiento de Gonzalo de Gayón
1566   Archivo General de Indias, Santo Domingo 11, Stetson Collection. P. K. Yonge Library of Florida History, University of Florida, Gainesville.

Quiñones, Bartolomé de
1682   Sworn Statement, 11 March 1682, in Juan Marques Cabrera 1682, q.v.

Quiroga y Losada, Diego de
1690   Letter to the King, St. Augustine, 31 August 1690. Archivo General de Indias, Santo Domingo 228, doc. no. 42, vol. 4, John Tate Lanning Collection. Thomas Jefferson Library, University of Missouri at St. Louis.

Rouse, Irving
1951   *A Survey of Indian River Archeology, Florida.* Yale University Publications in Anthropology, no. 44. New Haven.

Ruís, Alonso
1759   Census of the Indian village of Nra. Señora de la Leche of the jurisdiction of this Presidio of St. Augustine of Florida for this year of seventeen hundred and fifty-nine, made by me Fray Alonso Ruís of the order of our seraphic father St. Francis, *doctrinero* of the said village, on the fourth of February of the year mentioned. Archivo General de Indias, Santo Domingo 2604. [Photocopy furnished by Jane Landers.]

Serrano y Sanz, Manuel
1912   *Documentos Históricos de la Florida y la Luisiana, Siglos XVI al XVIII.* Madrid: Librería General de Victoriano Suárez.

Solana, Alonso
1679   Certification, St. Augustine, 31 October 1679. Archivo General de Indias, Santo Domingo 226, reel 3, Jeannette Thurber Connor Collection. P. K. Yonge Library of Florida History, University of Florida, Gainesville.

Solís de Merás, Gonzalo
1923   *Pedro Menéndez de Avilés, Adelantado, Governor and Captain-General of Florida, Memorial.* Translated by Jeannette Thurber Connor. Deland: Florida State Historical Society.

Swanton, John R.
1922   *Early History of the Creek Indians and Their Neighbors.* Bureau of American Ethnology Bulletin no. 73. Washington, D.C.: Government Printing Office.

Torres y Ayala, Laureano de
1697   Letter to the King, St. Augustine, 3 February 1697. Archivo General de Indias, Santo Domingo 228, reel 3, Jeannette Thurber Connor Collection. P. K. Yonge Library of Florida History, University of Florida, Gainesville.

1699   Letter to the King, St. Augustine, 16 September 1699. Archivo General de Indias, Santo Domingo 228, reel 3, Jeannette Thurber Connor Collection. P. K. Yonge Library of Florida History, University of Florida, Gainesville.

Valdés, Fernando de
1602   The Valdés Inquiry, St. Augustine, 1602. Archivo General de Indias, Santo Domingo 2533. [Microfilm copy furnished by Eugene Lyon.]

Villareal, Juan Miguel
1681   Letter to Juan Marques Cabrera, San Antonio, 21 June 1681, in Juan Marques Cabrera 1682, q.v.

1682   Sworn Statement, 12 April 1682, in Juan Marques Cabrera 1682, q.v.

Zúñiga y Zerda, Joseph de
1701a   Order to Joachín de Florencia, Florida, 20 January 1701. Archivo General de Indias, Santo Domingo 840, reel 5, Jeannette Thurber Connor Collection. P. K. Yonge Library of Florida History, University of Florida, Gainesville.

1701b   Letter to the King, St. Augustine, 10 March 1701. Archivo General de Indias, Santo Domingo 840, reel 5, Jeannette Thurber Connor Collection. P. K. Yonge Library of Florida History, University of Florida, Gainesville.

1701c   Letter to the King, St. Augustine, 11 March 1701. Archivo General de Indias, Santo Domingo 840, reel 5, Jeannette Thurber Connor Collection. P. K. Yonge Library of Florida History, University of Florida, Gainesville.

1701d   Order, St. Augustine, 14 March 1701. In *Here They Once Stood: The Tragic End of the Apalachee Missions,* by Mark F. Boyd, Hale G. Smith, and John W. Griffin, 35–36. Gainesville: University of Florida Press, 1951.

1701e Letter to the King, St. Augustine, 3 October 1701. Archivo General de Indias, Santo Domingo 840, reel 5, Jeannette Thurber Connor Collection. P. K. Yonge Library of Florida History, University of Florida, Gainesville.

1701f Letter to the King, St. Augustine, 15 November 1701. Archivo General de Indias, Santo Domingo 840, reel 5, Jeannette Thurber Connor Collection. P. K. Yonge Library of Florida History, University of Florida, Gainesville.

1704 Letter to the King, St. Augustine, 15 September 1704. In *Here They Once Stood: The Tragic End of the Apalachee Missions*, by Mark F. Boyd, Hale G. Smith, and John W. Griffin, 68–69. Gainesville: University of Florida Press, 1951.

❂ 6 ❂

Mission Santa Fé de Toloca

KENNETH W. JOHNSON

Santa Fé de Toloca was one of the earliest and long-lived seventeenth-century Spanish missions in northern Florida. The mission was destroyed by raids from the Carolinas in 1702, and the location was soon lost. This chapter summarizes the historical background of Mission Santa Fé de Toloca, describes archaeological investigations at the site, and correlates the Santa Fé site (8AL190) with the mission of Santa Fé.

Historical Background

Santa Fé operated simultaneously with several other mission stations in northern Florida, including San Francisco de Potano and San Martín de Timuqua (Geiger 1940:126; Hann 1990). Santa Fé de Toloca (or Teleco or Toloco or Señor Santo Tómas de Santa Fé; Boyd 1939:261) was established between 1606 and 1616. The first recorded reference was in 1616, when the mission was visited by Father Luís Gerónimo de Oré (Geiger 1940:123). Santa Fé's founder was probably Father Martín Prieto, who also established the nearby San Francisco mission. Like other early missions, Santa Fé was almost certainly established near an existing Indian village.

Bubonic plague may have struck the native people at Santa Fé in 1613–1617 (Dobyns 1983:278). Major epidemics of yellow fever and smallpox struck Florida in 1649 and 1653, respectively (Dobyns 1983:279–280), and presumably included Santa Fé. In 1655 the mission was still in operation, as its name appears on the visitation list that year

(Geiger 1940:126). In 1656 the Western Timucuans, including the residents at Santa Fé, rebelled against Spanish authority in what may have been a native revitalization movement. Spanish military forces from St. Augustine put down the rebellion, burned several villages, and hanged several chiefs, including the chief at Santa Fé. In 1659 a measles epidemic swept through Florida (Dobyns 1983:280), probably including Santa Fé.

Other historically documented events may have occurred at another, later site of Santa Fé. The Santa Fé site (8AL190) was occupied during the first half of the seventeenth century, but there is no archaeological evidence that it was occupied after this time. It was probably abandoned as a result of the rebellion of 1656 or the epidemic of 1649, 1653, or 1659. The mission complex must then have been rebuilt at a different location that has not been identified. Later events in the documentary record, such as the arrival of other ethnic groups to repopulate the mission village, Bishop Calderón's visit in 1675, epidemics in 1675 (Dobyns 1983:281) and 1686 (Dobyns 1983:282), and the 1702 attack and destruction of Santa Fé, evidently took place at this later Santa Fé site. The attack, led by Colonel James Moore, came from the British colony of Carolina. The British led a large force of their Indian allies. The village and the church were burned, but the attack was repulsed from the *convento*.

The attack was described in a letter from the governor of Florida to the king of Spain. This description of the later Santa Fé gives us insights into what the earlier Santa Fé may have been like: "They entered in the dawn watch and burned and devastated the village of Santa Fé, one of the principal towns of the Province of Timuqua, Saturday, the 20th of May of this year 1702, making an attack on the convent with many firearms and arrows and burning the church, although not the images which with some risk were saved. Finally, the fight having lasted for more than three hours, our force repulsed them, after the hasty strengthening of an indefensible stockade which served as a fence to the gate of the convent. The enemy retired with some injury, and . . . our side had some killed and wounded" (Zúñiga in Boyd, Smith, and Griffin 1951:37).

Archaeological Results

Dating

The Santa Fé site (8AL190) dates from approximately 1610 to 1650, based on documentary evidence (Geiger 1940:123; Wenhold 1936:8)

TABLE 6.1. Aboriginal Ceramics from Santa Fé, Controlled Surface Collection

Type	Count	Percentage
Linear marked (brushed, wiped, or simple stamped)	14	13.7
Cord marked or fabric impressed	2	1.9
Check stamped	2	1.9
Incised (mostly single line)	7	6.8
Roughened	1	0.9
Curvilinear complicated stamped	4	3.9
Rectilinear complicated stamped	8	7.8
Complicated stamped	6	5.8
Leon Check Stamped	1	0.9
St. Johns (plain and check stamped)	25	24.5
Simple stamped?	1	0.9
Cross simple stamped?	2	1.9
Stamped	1	0.9
Miller Plain ring base sherd	1	1.9
Miller Plain European vessel form (1 beaker, 1 bowl?)	1	1.9
Jefferson rims (folded; folded and notched or with nodes folded and pinched)	11	10.7
Other rims (1 flattened, 3 rounded, 2 notched but not folded, 7 others [especially outward flair])	13	12.7
Punctated and incised	1	0.9
Total decorated[a]	102	100.0

a. Summary of decorated versus plain: 102 total decorated (52.0%); 94 total plain (47.9%); 196 total classified (100.0%).

and majolica production dates. The aboriginal ceramic inventory includes mostly plain sherds and small amounts of Indian Pond complex pottery but no cob-marked Alachua tradition ceramics (table 6.1). The Indian Pond complex was associated with the Utina Indian group (Johnson 1991; Johnson and Nelson 1990). The introduced Leon-Jefferson pottery series is present, but it does not dominate the assemblage. The low number of Leon-Jefferson sherds and the types of majolica recovered (table 6.2) indicate that 8AL190 is the earlier Santa Fé, not the Santa Fé destroyed in 1702.

Previous Research

In addition to the Santa Fé site, at least 57 archaeological sites of all time periods are known in the Robinson Sinks area of northwestern Alachua County, a dozen of which have Spanish mission period compo-

TABLE 6.2. European Tablewares from the Santa Fé Site, Controlled Surface Collections and Excavations, 1988 Field Season

Type	Date	Count
Mexico City White	1550–1650+?	33
San Luis Blue on White	1550–1650+?	10
Puebla Polychrome	1650?–1725	3
Panama Plain	1575?–1624+?	3
Blue on White Faience	1500–18th c.	1
Unidentified majolica		11
Total		61

nents (Johnson 1991). The first recorded archaeological investigations in the Robinson Sinks vicinity were by the Simpson family of High Springs (Simpson n.d.). John Goggin's research in this locality apparently began when J. C. Simpson showed him several sites. Goggin's students at the University of Florida recorded numerous sites in the vicinity in the 1950s, including 8AL190. They characterized it only as a "sherd area" and did not recognize it as the location of a Spanish mission. The interpretation changed after investigations began in 1986 (Johnson 1991).

METHODS OF INVESTIGATION

Research methods used at the Santa Fé site include the following, listed in the approximate sequence in which they were undertaken:

1. General surface collections
2. Shovel tests
3. 1-m-by-1-m test pits (nine units excavated)
4. Metal detector survey
5. Soil cores
6. Soil resistivity survey
7. 2-m-by-2-m test pits (nine units excavated)
8. Controlled surface collections
9. Remote sensing
10. Auger testing and posthole testing (periphery of the site)
11. Mechanical stripping of the plow zone (in a small portion of the cemetery)

The site was initially thought to be a seventeenth-century farmstead or hamlet. Low numbers of artifacts and poor surface visibility obscured the nature and size of the site. Interpretation of the site changed during the metal detector survey. The survey located and recovered dozens of wrought iron nails and spikes and showed that a large structure and thus a prominent site were present (Leader and Nelson 1989). Later, plowing, controlled surface collecting, and other investigations revealed the size and internal arrangement of the site.

Clear acetate overlays were produced for each class of artifacts from the controlled surface collecting and metal detector survey, including aboriginal ceramics, Spanish ceramics, fired clay fragments, and each nail type (Types 1 through 10; South, Skowronek, and Johnson 1988). Soil cores, a soil resistivity survey, and remote sensing images were used in selecting test pit locations. Test pits produced structural evidence such as postholes, pinpointing the location of the probable church and of residential structures. Electronic multispectral remote sensing images of the Santa Fé site were produced by David Wagner, Stennis Space Center, Mississippi. The images also show the location of the old Spanish road, possible boundaries of the cemetery, and several unexplained shaded areas within the site.

These various lines of evidence are drawn together in the following sections. They describe the locations of structures, the cemetery area, and residential areas; define the community pattern; and produce estimates of the number of residences and residents.

STRUCTURES AND BURIALS

Structure 1. The locations of several structures and burials were identified (figs. 6.1 and 6.2). Structure 1 was located through soil coring, three 2-m-by-2-m test pits, the metal detector survey (fig. 6.3), and controlled surface collections (fig. 6.4). Findings at Structure 1 included at least one large post, a small remnant of intact floor or post support pad, a thin stratum of red-stained soil at the base of the plow zone, and the plow-zone distribution of nails, spikes, and fired clay fragments.

Just below the plow zone was a thin layer of soil that was stained red by leaching from the clay fragments. The cores producing this soil formed a rectangle approximately 8 m by 16 m, oriented generally northwest-southeast (fig. 6.2). The rectangle of red soil, in combination with the floor remnant, nails, and large post, suggested the location of a building,

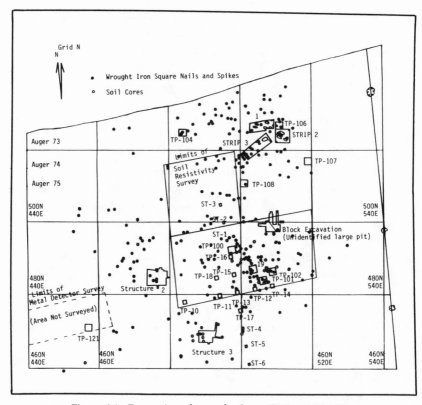

Figure 6.1. Excavation plan at the Santa Fé site (8AL190).

Structure 1 (fig. 6.5). It is possible to make two different interpretations of the size and precise orientation of the structure based on the red soil and post, but they differ only slightly (fig. 6.5).

The remnant of floor or support pad was hard-packed clayey sand rather than pure clay. This section of floor or support pad is found immediately below the base of the plow zone and adjacent to a large postmold. The postmold contained a large chunk of charcoal that has been identified as pine (Donna Ruhl, personal communication June 1990). The postmold was 45 cm in diameter and extended to 85 cm below the surface, apparently representing a major support post. The location of the post in relation to the areal extent of red-stained soil suggests that this may have been the southern corner of the structure. The size of the postmold suggests a large building (e.g., a church or other large building) rather than a small structure.

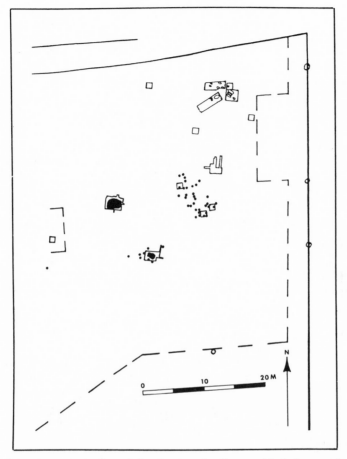

Figure 6.2. Locations of clay floors, red soil cores (*black dots*), and excavations at the Santa Fé site.

Time permitted the excavation of only three 2-m-by-2-m test pits (TP-100, -101, and -102) within Structure 1. The soil was screened through 1/4-inch mesh. The low number of artifacts per volume of soil in Test Pit 100 (table 6.3) is typical.

There is evidence for two episodes of Spanish occupation. Below the level of the top floor in Test Pit 102, there was a second stratum also containing Spanish artifacts. These artifacts extended across the entire 2-m-by-2-m test pit at 27 cm to 37 cm below surface (table 6.4). This may have been a floor that predated the compact clayey sand floor, suggesting

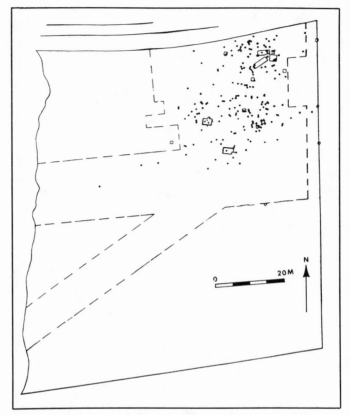

Figure 6.3. Wrought iron square nails and spikes (*black dots*), limits of metal detector survey (*dashed black line*), and excavations at the Santa Fé site.

rebuilding or refurbishing. Both episodes must have occurred in the first half of the seventeenth century.

The structure does not appear to have had wattle-and-daub walls. Fired clay fragments are present but only in small amounts, suggesting that clay was used for something other than walls. Cliff Nelson (personal communication 1990) suggests that the fragments may represent chinking or clay plaster rather than true daub. This suggestion is based on the thin cross sections, intact surfaces, low number of specimens across the site, and scarcity of wattle impressions or fiber inclusions. These fragments are different from the true daub found at Structure 6 (see below).

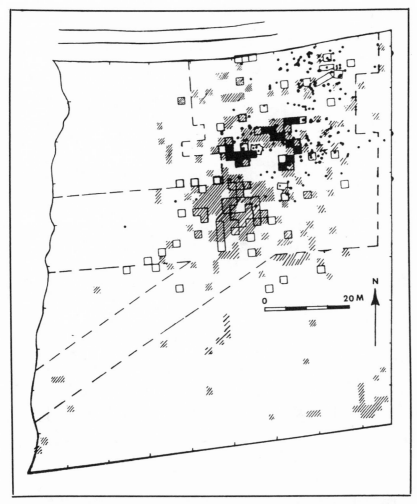

Figure 6.4. All maps combined. Surface locations of fired clay fragments (*solid black shading*), Spanish artifacts (*open boxes*), aboriginal sherds (*diagonal shading*), and subsurface locations of wrought iron square nails and spikes (*black dots*). Also shown are the limits of metal detector survey (*dashed black line*) and excavations. Controlled surface collection units are 3.5 m in width. Chert flakes are excluded. Santa Fé site (8AL190).

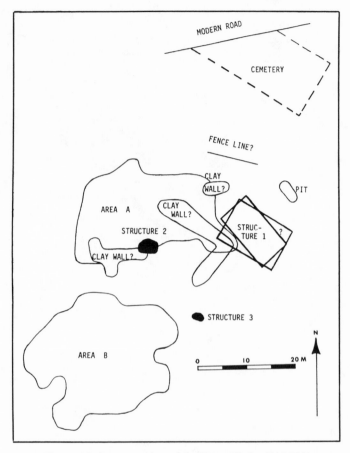

Figure 6.5. Interpretation of the Santa Fé site (8AL190).

Some of the clay at Structure 1 may represent support pads for posts. A possible function of the clay pads may have been to discourage termites. Termite damage can occur within weeks in northern Florida. Rotting also might account for the apparent rebuilding.

Structure 1 may represent either the church or the *convento* (Spanish priest's house). It was originally identified as a church for the following reasons. First, the structure is the focal point of the site; it sits on precisely the highest point of the hill, even higher by a few centimeters than the cemetery at Structure 4. Second, the structure and overall layout of the site complex correspond with the general layout of other known mission complexes in Florida and Georgia (Jones and Shapiro 1990; Saunders

TABLE 6.3. Results from Test Pit 100

Depth below surface	Count	Description
0–10 cm	22	Fired clay fragments (23.2 g)
	50	Fragments of clay and sand mix construction material (100.7 g)
	4	Fragments of clay and sand mix, possible plaster (11.4 g)
	8	Chert flakes
	18	Grog-tempered sherds, too small to classify
	1	Gastrolith rock
	2	Leon-Jefferson folded and notched rim sherds
	1	Green-glazed olive jar sherd (burned?)
	1	Majolica sherd (included in table 6.2)
10–20 cm	20+	Fragments of fired clay (36.1 g)
	17	Chert flakes
	13	Grog-tempered sherds, too small to classify
	1	Grog-tempered plain sherd
	1	Leon-Jefferson folded and notched rim sherd
	1	Green-glazed olive jar sherd
20–26 cm	20	Fired clay fragments (24.6 g)
	20+	Possible fired clay fragments (37.6 g)
	7	Charcoal flakes
	10	Chert flakes
	10	Grog-tempered sherds, too small to classify
	1	Grog-tempered rim sherd with node
	1	Green-glazed olive jar sherd
26–32 cm	50+	Fired clay fragments (158.4 g)
	100+	Fragments of clay and sand mix, some burned (177.9 g)
	2	Triangular-shaped fragments of clay and sand mix
	41	Charcoal flakes
	5	Fragments of near ceramic (clay?)
	6	Chert flakes
	8	Grog-tempered sherds, too small to classify
32–38 cm	50+	Fired clay fragments
	20+	Charcoal and charred wood fragments
	5	Chert flakes
	1	Gastrolith rock
	2	Grog-tempered sherds, too small to classify
	1	Sand-tempered sherd, too small to classify
38–42 cm	9	Fired clay fragments (10.9 g)
	3	Chert flakes

TABLE 6.4. Layer of Artifacts Indicating Lower Level of Occupation, Test Pit 102, Zone 2, Level 1

Description	Depth below surface
Wrought iron square-headed nail	28 cm
Unidentified metal fragment	27 cm
Green-glazed olive jar sherd	33 cm
Unidentified metal fragment	31 cm
Green-glazed olive jar sherd	N/A
Majolica, too small to identify	27.5 cm
Wrought iron square-headed nail, 8.0 cm	N/A
Green-glazed (both sides) olive jar sherd	37 cm
Marine shell (fossilized?)	37 cm
1 grog-tempered sherd, 1 fired clay fragment, and 1 concreted mass	34–37 cm
1 fragment fired clay or chinking with fiber impressions	39 cm
Additional map specimens in TP-102 found at a deeper level:	
Wrought iron square nail, 4.6 cm long	46 cm
Nail fragment	49 cm

1990). Third, artifact distributions indicate a residential area (Residential Area A) nearby, which is a likely candidate for the location of the *convento*. Fourth, Structure 1 was identified as the church because the cemetery (see Structure 4 below) was found in association with it.

However, Structure 1 seems too small to be the church, assuming that its dimensions (approximately 8 m × 16 m) were correctly identified. Recent excavations at nearby Mission San Martín (which may have been built by the same missionary) have shown that the church was much larger than originally thought (Rebecca Saunders, personal communication July 1991; Weisman 1988).

The proportions (twice as long as wide) but not the size of Structure 1 match Mission Santa Catalina de Guale on Amelia Island (13.5 m × 26 m; Saunders 1990:530–531) and Santa Catalina de Guale on St. Catherines Island (11 m × 20 m; Thomas 1987). It is also smaller than many structures in Apalachee Province that have been identified as churches (Boyd, Smith, and Griffin 1951:107–136; Jones and Shapiro 1990). Two Spanish-style structures were found at Baptizing Spring in Utina Province (Loucks 1979 and this volume), but the functions were not positively identified. Saunders suggests that the larger one, 8 m × 10 m, was a three-walled chapel (Saunders 1990:535). The existence of both a chapel and a church at a single site was the normal pattern at mission compounds in Mexico and possibly also in Florida (Saunders 1990:527). Perhaps Structure 1 at Santa Fé was a chapel.

Structure 4 and Burials. The burial area or cemetery was identified on the basis of one burial that was excavated and 18 burial pit outlines that were mapped but not excavated (fig. 6.6). Structure 4 is identified from the large number of spikes and nails in the cemetery area (figs. 6.1, 6.3, and 6.4) and one or two possible large posts (see below). As at Santa Catalina, San Martín, San Luis, and elsewhere, it is possible that the

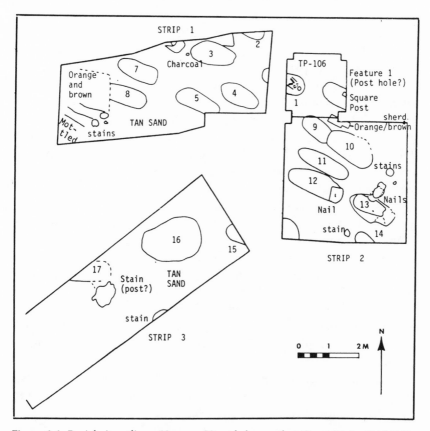

Figure 6.6. Burial pit outlines, 40 cm to 50 cm below surface, Santa Fé site (8AL190). All burial pits are mottled tan and brown sand with small orange clay inclusions; all pit outlines are very faint.

Santa Fé cemetery was actually located within the church, with burials interred beneath the floor of the building. Other possibilities are that Structure 4 was an open pavilion over the cemetery or other structure(s) within or adjacent to the cemetery.

The Santa Fé cemetery/Structure 4 contains a surprisingly large number of spikes and nails, which were mapped and recovered during the metal detector survey. A single test pit, Test Pit 106, was first excavated within this nail cluster in an attempt to locate and identify structures, but burial pits were encountered instead (fig. 6.6). Only one burial, Burial 1, was exposed. The top of the skull was encountered at 80 cm below the surface. Examined in situ by Dr. William Maples, Florida Museum of Natural History, the individual was a female, 17 to 25 years old, and most likely 20 years plus or minus 2 years. The incisors were shovel shaped, with some double shoveling, indicating Native American ancestry. Her hands were folded across her chest in Christian burial fashion. No artifacts accompanied the individual.

Feature 1, within the same test pit, was the same size, shape, and orientation as Burial 1 but may have been a large post. When excavated, no burial was present. The upper levels contained a small square charred post (fig. 6.6), and the deeper levels tapered to a point, unlike a flat-bottomed burial pit. It is unclear whether this was an interior post or outside wall post for Structure 4, because it is not known whether any additional burials are present farther to the northeast.

Subsequent to exposure of Burial 1, the question remained whether this was a cemetery or an isolated burial. Therefore the plow zone was removed from three small areas in order to determine whether additional burials were present and, if so, to determine their extent. Approximately 58 square meters were mechanically stripped using a jeep with a blade attachment. The stripped areas were then shovel skimmed and troweled to 30 cm or 40 cm below surface, and the pit stains were outlined and mapped in plan view. The pit outlines were difficult to see in the leached, sandy soils. Several instances of charcoal and/or nails within the burial pit outlines may be the remains of posts or wooden headstone markers.

A total of 18 burial pits were mapped in the 58 square meters. Other than Burial 1, no other skeletons were exposed. The burials were aligned generally northwest to southeast, matching the alignment of Structure 1. From Burial 1 we assume that all of the heads are to the southeast. A large rounded feature, Feature 2, was encountered beyond which there were no more burials. The feature was not excavated, but it may be a large postmold marking the southwestern boundary of the cemetery, a church wall post, or open-air pavilion. Feature 2 is 10 m southwest of Feature 1, perhaps indicating the width of Structure 4. The length of Structure 4 (assuming all the burials were within the structure) was not fully determined but is at least 11 m.

Using South's typology for wrought iron square nails and spikes (South, Skowronek, and Johnson 1988:33–47), medium-sized Type 6 nails were the most common type at both Structures 1 and 4 (Leader and Nelson 1989). Like Structure 1, Structure 4 contained some large Type 10 spikes. In contrast to Structure 1, Structure 4 contained no fired clay, suggesting it was a different kind of construction from Structure 1.

After archaeological field investigations began, remote sensing investigations were conducted over the site, and images were produced by David Wagner from the National Aeronautics and Space Administration's National Technology Laboratory Space Remote Sensing Center in Stennis, Mississippi, using a Daedalus 1260 multispectral scanner on board low-flying aircraft. The cemetery, first located archaeologically, could then be recognized on the remote sensing images (thermal infrared). The cemetery's location can also be seen on the archaeologically produced controlled surface collection maps. There is a sparse but distinct ring of surface artifacts marking the apparent boundaries of the cemetery and possible church. This technique may also be useful for finding cemeteries (or structures) at other sites with good surface visibility.

By using these methods it is possible to measure the area of the burials and estimate how many burials may be present. The controlled surface collections and the remote sensing results produce two different but overlapping estimations of burial area boundaries and thus lead to two somewhat different estimates of the number of burials potentially present. Based on the arrangement and spacing of the 18 known burial pits, and the reconstructed boundaries and size of the cemetery according to controlled surface collections, the projected burial area has a capacity to hold at least 180 burials. By using the remote sensing estimation of burial area boundaries, it is estimated that up to 320 burials may be present.

Recent computer enhancement of photographs by Cliff Nelson indicates that there may be additional burials not visible to the naked eye and not recognized during the field investigations. These burial pits may lie at 90° angles to the previously recognized burials. Two different burial areas may thus be present. If so, then there are even more burials than predicted and they may represent different time periods. Thus the two methods of determining burial area boundaries—remote sensing and controlled surface collecting—may both be correct but may be identifying different episodes.

The data from the metal detector survey also appear to indicate the location of a fence in an otherwise "empty area" between Structures 1 and 4. Evidence for a wall or fence is a long row of nails. The row of nails appears to be too long to be associated with a structure and is in an area generally devoid of other artifacts. The orientation of the line of nails matches the alignment of the burials and Structure 1 but is midway between them. One of the artifacts recovered along this line is a small wrought iron latch, perhaps indicating the location of a gate where a pathway led from Structure 1 to Structure 4.

Residential Structures. Structures 2 and 3 appear to be habitation structures within the residential portion of the site. These residential areas are identified by the distribution of aboriginal sherds, chert flakes, and other residential-type debris.

Structure 2 (fig. 6.7) may have been the *convento* or another residential structure. It had a partially intact red clay floor and may have been surrounded by a courtyard with clay walls (figs. 6.4 and 6.5). This house is part of Residential Area A, which is closer to Structure 1 than is Residential Area B (see below).

Structure 2 is approximately 4 m by 5 m in size and is situated 16 m to 20 m west of Structure 1, depending on how the size and orientation of Structure 1 are interpreted. Structure 2 is much smaller than Structure 1. The plow zone was stripped off by shovel to reveal the remaining portions of the floor and the features that penetrate it. The edges of the clay floor have been destroyed by plowing, and the exact orientation of the structure is unclear.

Numerous small features penetrated the clay floor. Some were excavated, including small posts or smudge pits, in addition to a clay-lined hearth. The hearth contained at least two layers of clay, representing reuse or rebuilding. The dense, black, formless mass of charcoal fill indicates a low-oxygen, low-temperature, slow-burning fire, thus presumably a large smudge fire rather than a true hearth. This "hearth" is on the south side of the structure, not in the center. The metal detector survey indicated very few nails at this structure. The scarcity of nails, the presence of the

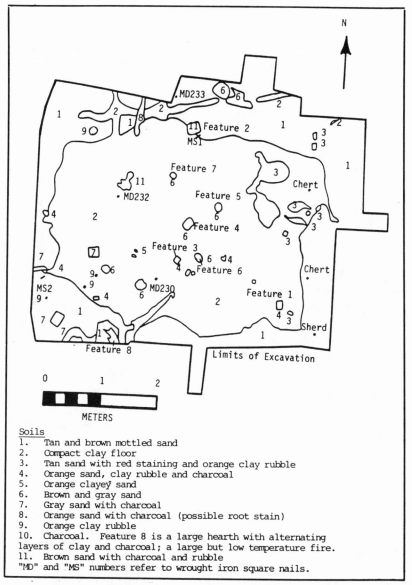

Soils
1. Tan and brown mottled sand
2. Compact clay floor
3. Tan sand with red staining and orange clay rubble
4. Orange sand, clay rubble and charcoal
5. Orange clayey sand
6. Brown and gray sand
7. Gray sand with charcoal
8. Orange sand with charcoal (possible root stain)
9. Orange clay rubble
10. Charcoal. Feature 8 is a large hearth with alternating layers of clay and charcoal; a large but low temperature fire.
11. Brown sand with charcoal and rubble
"MD" and "MS" numbers refer to wrought iron square nails.

Figure 6.7. Compact red clay floor and associated features, Structure 2, plan view at base of plow zone. Santa Fé site (8AL190).

hard clay floor, and the structure size indicate a different architectural style from that of Structure 1.

Structure 3, slightly southeast of Structure 2 (figs. 6.2 and 6.5), is not as well defined. It consists of an area of puddled clay, ashes, and charcoal, approximately 1.7 m × 2.5 m in size. This oval shape is aligned northwest-southeast like the cemetery and the church. Three to four small square features (possible square posts) frame the edges of the clay, but they were not excavated. Majolica and olive jar sherds were found in the plow zone at distances of 1 m to 4 m east and northeast of the clay. This "puddle" of clay is not fire-hardened despite the abundant mixture of charcoal and ashes. It is not clear whether this large ashy clay feature represents a portion of a floor, an activity area, or simply debris such as from cleaning out a fireplace.

Structure 3 may be a special structure of some kind, such as a gate house, as suggested by its location on the remote sensing images. These images show a large teardrop-shaped pattern encompassing much of the Santa Fé mission complex. This teardrop shape encloses all of Structure 1 and parts of the cemetery and residential area. The teardrop tapers to a point at Structure 3, where the teardrop narrows and merges into an old road also visible on the images. This road was a part of a major north-south trail, the Santa Fé trail (Johnson 1991). It is visible on the aerial remote sensing images but not on the ground or on the earliest aerial photographs taken in 1937. The teardrop shape is interpreted here as a fork in the road that encircled the mission complex. Structure 3 is situated within this fork and is thus interpreted as a special-use structure.

DISCUSSION

The sizes, location, and arrangement of the known structures can be compared with the controlled surface collection maps and other data in order to estimate how many other structures may have existed at the site. Based on artifact distributions, there may be two separate residential areas at the site, designated Residential Areas A and B (fig. 6.5). The two are distinguished because they contained different kinds of artifacts and are separated spatially.

Controlled surface collection maps show linear concentrations of fired clay fragments that appear to represent the locations of former clay walls. The distribution may indicate a wall around a courtyard or small plaza with the center of the area being essentially devoid of artifacts. This possible courtyard separates two parts of the site, Areas A and B.

Residential Area A contained Spanish and Indian ceramics, nails, and heavy concentrations of fired clay fragments, including Structure 2 with its red clay floor. Residential Area B, in contrast, contained the highest concentrations of Indian ceramics anywhere on the site and also had some Spanish ceramics but contained few nails or fired clay fragments. The structures in Area A must have been architecturally different from those in Area B, as shown by the different amounts of nails and fired clay.

Area A is roughly rectangular, approximately 20 m × 40 m in size, situated immediately adjacent to Structure 1. Structure 2 lies within and along the south-central perimeter of this area. This area is surrounded (at least in part) by what seem to be clay walls, indicated by surface distributions of small fired clay fragments. The distributions are linear, but the pattern is not the result of modern plowing. The bands of fired clay fragments are 15 m to 22 m long and 3 m to 5 m wide. One band has the same orientation as Structure 1 and the burials. Another band intersects it at right angles, immediately adjacent to Structure 1. If these linear bands of fired clay had been the result of modern plowing, then plowing in one direction would have obliterated the patterns in the other directions.

Residential Area B is approximately 45 m × 45 m or larger in size, based on surface distributions of artifacts and depending on how boundaries are drawn. The boundaries used here were drawn by excluding all collection units that contained no artifacts or only one artifact per grid unit and by drawing a line around collection units containing two or more artifacts each on the surface. Collection units were 3 m × 3.5 m in size, between rows of planted pine seedlings.

Area A is west of Structure 1 and north of Area B. Structure 1 and Area A are separated from Area B by an area of 10 m to 20 m in diameter that contains practically no artifacts. This open area may be a courtyard or small plaza. The distribution of fired clay fragments shown on the map may thus indicate the locations of clay walls around the courtyard.

The courtyard and its clay walls may have surrounded the *convento*, not the church. If the later Santa Fé was built on the same plan as the earlier Santa Fé, then this arrangement would help explain the events of the 1702 attack in which the church was destroyed but the attack was successfully repulsed from the *convento*.

Area A, including Structure 2, may be the Spanish priest's residential and activity area, and Area B may be the Indian residential area. An alternative hypothesis is that Area B represents the *cocina* (kitchen).

From the concentrations of sherds and fired clay fragments, it is estimated that Area A contained from 3 to 6 structures, assuming that Structure 2 is typical. Area B is estimated to have contained from 5 to 15 houses, depending on how the boundaries of Area B are drawn. The heaviest concentration of sherds, in the center of Area A, may represent something more than an ordinary house. If there were 4 people per household, then there may have been 20 to 60 people living in Area B, assuming that all the houses were contemporaneous.

ADDITIONAL SITE AREAS

An area immediately east of the religious complex, called the East of Shealy area, contains a sparse scatter of seventeenth-century artifacts on the surface. The nature of this occupation and whether it was another residential area are unclear. Investigations were limited to general surface collecting. Artifact densities indicated the apparent locations of two structures, Structures 5 and 6. Both contain true daub, which is not found elsewhere on the Santa Fé site. True daub refers to thick fragments of fired clay with wattle impressions and abundant fiber inclusions.

Structure 5. Structure 5 is located approximately 70 m to 80 m southeast of and downslope from Structure 1. It consists of a rectangular or oval-shaped area marked by a surface distribution of slightly dark stained soil and fragments of charcoal and true daub. Artifact density is higher than elsewhere in the East of Shealy area, but it is only moderate (table 6.5), roughly comparable to Residential Areas A and B.

The surface limits of the stained soil, daub, charcoal, and artifacts within the plowed field indicate that the structure was approximately 28 m east-west (or east-northeast by west-southwest) and 16 m north-south, which is larger than Structure 1. The structure is aligned slightly west of north, similar to the alignment of Structure 1 and the burial pit outlines.

A large feature is found at each end of Structure 5. Each is approximately 4 m in diameter and is visible on the surface as black-stained soil and numerous small fragments of charcoal but no daub. Both are interpreted as hearths or fireplaces. Another feature is a 5-m-diameter surface concentration of burned bone, sherds, small chert flakes, charcoal, darkened soil, and fired clay fragments but not much other building rubble. Found just outside or at the northwest corner of the structure, it is the

TABLE 6.5. Artifacts from Structure 5 and Immediate Vicinity, General Surface Collection

Description	Count
Majolica, 1 burned and 1 too small to identify	2
Olive jar sherds, including 1 neck	3
Leon-Jefferson Curvilinear Complicated Stamped, grog-tempered	3
Ceramic handle, Miller Plain	1
Grog-tempered Plain	1
Grog-tempered sherds, too small to classify	3
Chert flakes	11
Fragment of clay chinking	1
Burned bone fragment	1

only feature that was observed to contain food remains (i.e., burned bone fragments), sherds, and chert flakes. This may be a food preparation area, which suggests that Structure 5 may have been a residential structure such as a dormitory for neophytes or children or barracks for soldiers.

The flat exterior surface of more than one daub fragment from Structure 5 is coated with a white substance that may be lime whitewashing. Such whitewashing and true daub were not found elsewhere at the site, suggesting that Structure 5 received special attention.

Structure 6. Structure 6 is located 5 m south of Structure 5 and consists of an area approximately 20 m to 22 m in diameter, visible only as a surface scatter of daub in the plowed field. Sherds, lithics, and charcoal fragments are scarce at Structure 6, indicating a different function from that of Structure 5.

The Josh Site (8AL188B)

The Josh site was classified as a separate site but may be part of Mission Santa Fé de Toloca, as it is separated only by a modern road. The time period is uncertain but the site has yielded at least one Fort Walton sherd (collected by John Goggin's students), which may indicate a Spanish mission period occupation. No ground surface was visible for collecting. Three 1-m-by-1-m test pits were excavated, and the number of sherds recovered (135) indicates a habitation area. Most sherds are sand-tempered plain (15), grog-tempered plain (9), or too small to classify

(105). The presence of grog tempering suggests that a Spanish period component is present.

Other sites also in the vicinity, such as the Goodwin (8AL453) and Carlisle sites (8AL2599), appear to be associated with the Santa Fé de Toloca mission, based on artifact assemblages. Some are situated within 0.5 km, that is, within the sound of the bell that would have called the workers to daily vespers. Other slightly more distant sites appear to be outlying satellite settlements and farmsteads but are components of the larger Santa Fé cluster. Many are distributed in a linear pattern, as though dispersed along roads. The Palmore site (8AL189) is another large nearby site. Palmore may have been the existing Indian village near which the mission of Santa Fé was originally founded, and it may have also been the village of Cholupaha, which was captured by Hernando de Soto's army 70 years before the founding of Santa Fé de Toloca (Johnson 1991).

Summary

The correlation of site 8AL190 with the mission of Santa Fé de Toloca has been supported by several lines of evidence. The distribution of seventeenth-century sites in northern Florida and the geographic position of 8AL190 relative to other known mission sites are consistent with this identification. Also, the 1778 Purcell-Stewart map of northern Florida (Boyd 1939) indicates "Santa Fé old fields" in this vicinity.

Archaeological investigations have also supported this interpretation. Features from the site verify the presence of an early seventeenth-century Spanish mission, including a cemetery with Christian-tradition aboriginal burials and several Hispanic-style structures. Interestingly, Indian Pond complex pottery was recovered from the excavations, but no Alachua tradition cob-marked ceramics were found. Modern scholars have assumed that Santa Fé was a Potano mission based on its location on the south bank of the Santa Fé River as shown on a 1680 map and the assumption that the river was probably the boundary between the Potano and the Utina. However, the presence of Indian Pond complex pottery suggests that Santa Fé may have been a Utina mission.

Now that the location of Mission Santa Fé de Toloca has been identified, additional research at the site and adjacent areas is needed to understand better the nature of the mission community and the cultural affiliation of its native population.

Acknowledgments

Initial testing at the Santa Fé site (8AL190) was funded by the Florida Division of Recreation and Parks under a grant to the Florida Museum of Natural History, University of Florida, to locate the sites of Indian villages contacted by Hernando de Soto and the sites of seventeenth-century Spanish missions. A full field season of investigations at this site was funded by a grant from SantaFe HealthCare, Inc. The Division of Sponsored Research and the Center for Early Contact Studies at the University of Florida provided additional support. All work was conducted by the author under the supervision of Jerald T. Milanich, curator, Florida Museum of Natural History, University of Florida, Gainesville. Artifact analysis was completed by B. C. Nelson and the author.

Bibliography

Boyd, Mark F.
1939 Mission Sites in Florida. *Florida Historical Quarterly* 17:254–280.

Boyd, Mark F., Hale G. Smith, and John W. Griffin
1951 *Here They Once Stood: The Tragic End of the Apalachee Missions.* Gainesville: University of Florida Press.

Dobyns, Henry F.
1983 *Their Number Became Thinned: Native American Population Dynamics in Eastern North America.* Knoxville: University of Tennessee Press.

Geiger, Maynard J., O.F.M.
1940 *Biographical Dictionary of the Franciscans in Spanish Florida and Cuba (1528–1841).* Franciscan Studies, no. 21. Paterson, N.J.: St. Anthony's Guild Press.

Hann, John H.
1990 Summary Guide to Spanish Florida Missions and *Visitas* with Churches in the Sixteenth and Seventeenth Centuries. *The Americas* 46(4):417–513.

Johnson, Kenneth W.
1991 The Utina and the Potano Peoples of Northern Florida: Changing Settlement Systems in the Spanish Colonial Period. Ph.D. diss., Department of Anthropology, University of Florida, Gainesville.

Johnson, Kenneth W., and Bruce C. Nelson
1990 The Utina: Seriations and Chronology. *The Florida Anthropologist* 43(1):48–62.

Jones, B. Calvin, and Gary N. Shapiro
1990 Nine Mission Sites in Apalachee. In *Columbian Consequences*. Vol. 2: *Archaeological and Historical Perspectives on the Spanish Borderlands East*, edited by David Hurst Thomas, 491–509. Washington, D.C.: Smithsonian Institution Press.

Leader, Jonathan, and Bruce C. Nelson
1989 Technometric and Functional Analysis of Metal Artifacts from the Seventeenth-Century Santa Fé de Toloca Mission, Florida. Paper presented at the 1989 Annual Meeting of the Florida Anthropological Society, Jacksonville, Florida.

Loucks, Lana Jill
1979 Political and Economic Interactions between Spaniards and Indians: Archeological and Ethnohistorical Perspectives of the Mission System in Florida. Ph.D. diss., University of Florida. Ann Arbor: University Microfilms.

Saunders, Rebecca
1990 Ideal and Innovation: Spanish Mission Architecture in the Southeast. In *Columbian Consequences*. Vol. 2: *Archaeological and Historical Perspectives on the Spanish Borderlands East*, edited by David Hurst Thomas, 527–542. Washington, D.C.: Smithsonian Institution Press.

Simpson, J. Clarence
n.d. Unpublished notebook on file, Department of Anthropology, Florida Museum of Natural History, Gainesville. Circa 1920–1940.

South, Stanley, Russell K. Skowronek, and Richard E. Johnson
1988 *Spanish Artifacts from Santa Elena*. Anthropological Studies, no. 7. Columbia: Occasional Papers of the South Carolina Institute of Archaeology and Anthropology, University of South Carolina.

Thomas, David Hurst
1987 *The Archaeology of Mission Santa Catalina de Guale: 1. Search and Discovery*. Anthropological Papers of the American Museum of Natural History, vol. 63, pt. 2. New York.

Weisman, Brent
1988 *1988 Excavations at Fig Springs (8CO1), Season 2, July–December 1988*. Florida Archaeological Reports, no. 4. Tallahassee: Florida Bureau of Archaeological Research.

Wenhold, Lucy L., trans.
1936 *A Seventeenth-Century Letter of Gabriel Díaz Vara Calderón, Bishop of Cuba, Describing the Indians and Indian Missions of Florida*. Smithsonian Miscellaneous Collections, vol. 95, no. 16. Washington, D.C.

☀ 7 ☀

Archaeology of Fig Springs Mission, Ichetucknee Springs State Park

BRENT R. WEISMAN

Fig Springs (8CO1) is a seventeenth-century Spanish mission site in Ichetucknee Springs State Park (fig. 7.1) on a small tributary of the Ichetucknee River approximately one mile south of the headspring. The site contains an underwater component, probably a refuse deposit, discovered in 1949 by John Goggin (fig. 7.2; Goggin 1949) and, on the upland adjacent to the springs, an extensive associated terrestrial component that first came to light in limited test excavations and survey conducted by the Florida Museum of Natural History (FMNH) in 1986 (Johnson 1987, 1990). Here are found the well-preserved remains of a seventeenth-century Spanish mission, including areas of the site interpreted as a mission church, *convento*, cemetery, plaza, and mission village.

In 1988–1989 the Florida Bureau of Archaeological Research (FBAR), under contract with the Florida Department of Natural Resources, Division of Recreation and Parks (DNR), undertook archaeological investigations at Fig Springs with the purposes of defining the site plan and excavating the presumed church and *convento* as well as aboriginal structures in the mission village. The archaeology of these structures was to be used as the basis for their architectural reconstruction, which was to occur in conjunction with the construction of an interpretive center in the park showcasing the major themes of local natural and

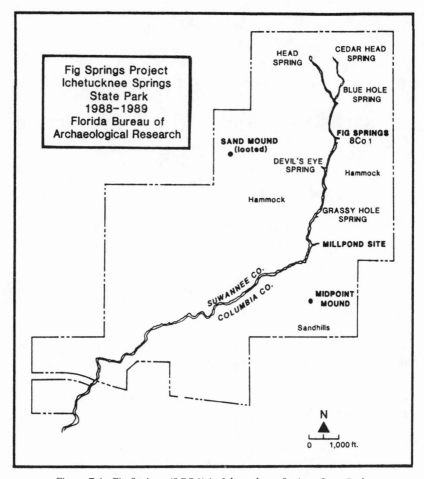

Figure 7.1. Fig Springs (8CO1) in Ichetucknee Springs State Park.

cultural history. Unfortunately, plans for the public interpretation of the Fig Springs mission and Fig Springs archaeology have since been scuttled by DNR, at least on the scale as was originally proposed. This in no way diminishes the significance of the site and its potential to contribute to our understanding of the Spanish mission period in Florida.

The 1988–1989 archaeological investigations at the Fig Springs mission produced a rich yield of new information about architecture, site plan, and material culture of a seventeenth-century interior Florida mission. Overall interpretation of the site was enhanced by an archaeological

Figure 7.2. A Goggin student using glass-bottom bucket to search for artifacts, Fig Springs, early 1950s.

approach that combined detailed architectural excavations and the simultaneous investigation of functionally distinct areas of the mission community. Four new points of information about mission archaeology of the Florida interior are of particular interest and will be briefly summarized here.

First, stratigraphic excavations of a structure interpreted as a chapel-like church have revealed a construction sequence that involved a great deal of planning and site preparation. After the building site had been selected, construction began by first removing the topsoil and humus from within the building area. A layer of clean sand then was placed where the humus had been, and was graded to have a slight fall from east to west. Roof support posts, vertical board walls, and a pine sill plate or "grade beam" were placed on or in this fill. A prepared clay floor covered the sand fill in the north and west areas of the building. Finally, after the building had burned and been abandoned, a mantle of orange and yellow sand, virtually free of artifacts, was placed to cover the building ruins.

Second, zooarchaeological and archaeobotanical analysis of remains collected from trash-filled pits and cooking hearths associated with a mission period aboriginal structure indicates that the residents of this building shared a continuity with the basic prehistoric aboriginal subsistence pattern of north Florida, with a dietary emphasis on both wild plant and animal foods. In the study of 1165.95 g of faunal material from aboriginal features, it was found that wild terrestrial animals accounted for 90.42 percent of the estimated proportional biomass contributing to the diet, with deer alone comprising 77.99 percent of the biomass (Newsom and Quitmyer 1992). Eleven plant species were identified in the botanical analysis, including three definite Old World domesticates (watermelon, peach, wheat); two domesticates of New World origin (bean, maize); four wild fruits (persimmon, maypop, cabbage palm, saw palmetto); and two wild nuts (hickory, acorn) (Newsom and Quitmyer 1992).

A third point of interest is that while the pattern of artifact distribution shows that certain types of artifacts are not evenly distributed across the site (86.6 percent of all projectile points obtained were found in the aboriginal structure and 78.9 percent of all straight pins came from the church; see table 7.1), it is difficult to define presumed Spanish and Indian site areas of the mission period component on the basis of artifact counts and percentages. This perhaps suggests that mission society at Fig Springs was an open community, where the boundaries between priest and Indian were not rigidly maintained through material means.

A fourth notable point is that roughened, cob-marked, and punctated pottery surface treatments, present in the prehistoric pottery tradition in the Fig Springs area (the Suwannee Valley Series), appear as surface treatments on about 1.8 percent of the grog-tempered Jefferson Series ceramics, the aboriginal pottery of the seventeenth-century mission period at Fig Springs. This suggests that while there was without question a major ceramic transformation subsequent to the founding of the missions, there is some demonstrated continuity between the prehistoric inhabitants of Fig Springs and the Indians of the mission period.

The 1988 Auger Survey

The first objectives of the FBAR project at Fig Springs were to define the area of the presumed mission site and, if possible, to determine the architectural arrangement of the site. This delineation was to include the specific locations of mission and aboriginal structures and an evaluation of the potential of the archaeological remains to yield specific information about construction techniques and building appearance.

The initial phase of investigation consisted of a power auger survey and topographical mapping of a 30-acre area adjacent to the springs thought to contain the mission site (including the one-acre area tested in 1986 by FMNH). Beginning in February 1988, ten weeks of survey work were conducted, in which 1341 auger tests were drilled at 10-m intervals across the site and 5000 topographical readings were taken over the same area (Weisman 1988a). With the assistance of the Florida Bureau of Survey and Mapping (DNR), a horizontal grid was established prior to the archaeological survey, with grid points marked with iron rebar and/or concrete monuments, and vertical benchmarks were set and marked in elevations of meters above mean sea level (mmsl).

A total of 724 of the 1341 auger holes (54 percent) contained artifacts. Of these, 324 contained only lithic flakes or tools, while the remaining 400 (55.3 percent) variably contained aboriginal pottery, Spanish materials, lithics, and faunal remains. The densities of artifacts and the presence/absence distributions of artifacts such as Spanish majolica and wrought nails in these 400 tests were used to derive a preliminary interpretation of the Fig Springs site plan. Of particular importance for the subsequent seasons of excavation was the contour map of aboriginal pottery density produced at the end of the auger season. By contouring the weights of aboriginal pottery obtained in the auger holes at 10-g intervals, as had been done early in the San Luis project (Shapiro 1987a), the locations and alignments of the major activity areas of the 20-acre site began to take shape (see fig. 7.4).

Cultural Identity of the Mission Indians

In addition to providing the archaeological evidence necessary to support an architectural reconstruction of the mission buildings, there was some concern with determining the cultural or tribal identity (or identities) of the Indians who inhabited the Fig Springs mission. It had become customary among archaeologists (Deagan 1972; Johnson and Nelson 1990; Loucks 1979; Milanich 1978), following Swanton (1946:201), to refer to the north Florida mission Indians as the Utina, a term that appears in the names of several towns encountered by Hernando de Soto in 1539 after leaving Potano, an aboriginal center presumed to have been in the general vicinity of present-day Gainesville.

Unfortunately, use of this term has led to the conflation of the north Florida mission Indians with the peoples encountered by de Soto and with the Outina (Utina) Indians of the central St. Johns River area (Gatschet 1877:627) who figure so famously in the French narratives of the 1560s (Lorant 1946). While there may have been some interaction and a degree of cultural relationship between the sixteenth-century Outina of the St. Johns, the residents of the Utina-named towns of the de Soto chronicles, and the north Florida mission Indians of the seventeenth century, it seemed unwise to carry forward the name Utina in referring to this latter group, particularly in that extensive documentary research conducted by Amy Bushnell (1988) and John Hann (Bullones 1728; Jesús 1630; López 1602; Machado 1597; San Antonio 1657) in the early stages of the Fig Springs project indicated that the Spanish did not use the term Utina as a name of a mission province nor did they write of any tribal, ethnic, or linguistic group of that name.

Instead, the colonial Spanish documents consistently refer to the land or province of Timucua (Oré 1936), the principal town of which in 1597 was reported in a location 50 leagues inland from the San Pedro mission on Cumberland Island. This location fits well with the Fig Springs vicinity, using a measurement of 2.6 miles to the league (John Hann, personal communication 10 August 1988). In 1597 Timucua consisted of five major towns with an estimated total population of 1500 persons (López 1602). References throughout the seventeenth century persist in referring to Timucua Province, which grew to encompass the territory between the St. Johns River west to the Aucilla River (Geiger 1940:127–131). Thus, in terms of historical accuracy the term Timucua is preferred over Utina to refer to the protohistoric and historic period aboriginal peoples of the area described.

This terminology decision does little to resolve the question of the cultural identity of the Indians making and using the "bull's-eye" complicated stamped pottery (Jefferson Series) that seems to dominate ceramic assemblages in Timucua in the mid-seventeenth century. In archaeological terms, this stamping appears abruptly and does not appear to derive from the pottery of the prehistoric Timucua in the Fig Springs area, which consists primarily of varieties of the type Fig Springs Roughened, Prairie Cord Marked, Alachua Cob Marked, varieties of Lochloosa Punctated, and other Alachua tradition-related types.

The problem really is one of finding evidence to support either a model of rapid population replacement in Timucua in the early to mid-1600s or the idea that the native population quickly adopted an entirely new pottery tradition, one with ultimate origins to the west in Apalachee or in the Georgia Lamar area. There is no conclusive evidence either way at the present time. Indeed, there are indications in the documents and from archaeological results that both population replacement and cultural continuity were simultaneous processes shaping the cultural landscape of Spanish Florida. Recent research in the Spanish archives of Seville by John Worth will go far in bringing clarity to this situation.

The Historical Identity of the Fig Springs Mission

There also was the related concern regarding the historical identity of the Fig Springs mission, particularly because the site (as known from Goggin's collections) had been named in the literature as the mission Santa Catalina de Afuerica (or Ahoica; Deagan 1972, 1987:11; Johnson 1987; Milanich 1978), a mission known from the documents to have been in existence in the general vicinity of Fig Springs between about 1675 and 1685. Goggin's majolica seriations, however, which have held up as being generally accurate, suggested a pre-1650 date for the mission (Goggin 1968:74), a dating that is generally accepted for the site (Deagan 1987:5). Either the Ahoica mission existed much earlier than the known dates, which increasingly seemed more improbable as more documentary research was done, or Fig Springs was not Santa Catalina. On this latter premise, the mission San Martín de Timucua (also referred to as San Martín de Ayaocuto; see Hann 1990), founded in 1608 by Fray Martín Prieto in the main village of Timucua (Oré 1936) at a distance later recorded in 1655 to be 34 leagues (88.4 miles) from St. Augustine (Geiger 1940:126), compares well to the Fig Springs site, located some 82 air miles from St. Augustine. San Martín evidently was destroyed in the 1656 Timucua rebellion and largely abandoned then or shortly thereafter; it fails to appear by that name on subsequent mission lists.

The 1988–1989 Excavations

Based on the positive results of the auger survey, two seasons of archaeological excavations were funded by DNR in areas interpreted as the central mission complex and mission village. Fieldwork consisted of a five-month season of 2-m-by-2-m test excavations (fig. 7.3; Weisman 1988b) in a sampling of site areas, followed by a ten-month season of major block excavations expanded from the tested areas (fig. 7.4). Results

Figure 7.3. Season 2 excavation of the sill plate and door threshold, east end of church. Note pedestaled artifacts and vertical wall boards perpendicular to north and south ends of sill plate. At upper left is a clay support pad, a portion of which was uncovered in 1986. View is to the north.

and conclusions of excavations in the site areas shown in figure 7.4 are summarized below.

THE CHURCH

Beneath a 10–15 cm layer of humus and below a second 10–15 cm layer of what appears to have been an intentionally placed sand cap or mantle are the ruins of what was most likely a chapel-like mission church, indicated by areas of prepared clay floor, charred hewn support posts, charred vertical wall boards, and a hewn sill plate or "grade beam" with an associated door threshold of wood (fig. 7.5; see also fig. 7.3) at the eastern end of the structure. Major roof support posts, each about 10 cm square, seem to have rested on clay pads, several of which show impressed or burnt areas where the posts actually sat. The roof appears to have covered an area measuring about 10.5 m north-south and 8 m east-west. Elevation of the clay floor rises in steps from west to east, with an overall rise of some 20 cm relative to the mission period ground surface outside the building.

Wattle-and-daub construction was not used, although clay chinking was squeezed between the vertical wall boards at the east end of the structure. The building probably was open on three sides, with the back (east) wall at the sill plate closed by a board wall. Excavations to depths of over 1 m below the ground surface through several areas of the floor indicate that the original humus had been stripped from the building site and a 20-cm layer of clean sand fill brought in and graded out to serve as a subfloor. The sand floor of an interior room was almost completely free of artifacts, suggesting the presence of a raised floor or platform of wood. The raised floor seems to have been open on the west side, facing the clay floor, as there is no evidence of plank walls in this area. The wood architecture, consisting of vertical board walls, hewn pine posts, threshold, and pine sill plate, is generally similar to the architecture of the excavated "church" at the Pine Tuft (8JE2) or Aspalaga mission in Apalachee (Morrell and Jones 1970).

Artifacts were not abundant but include majolica and olive jar— together combining for the highest percentage (18.8) of Spanish versus aboriginal pottery present in any of the excavation areas—aboriginal pottery sherds along wall lines, an iron sewing needle, and iron and brass straight pins (table 7.1), all of which were found in fill around burnt posts. Charred peach pits and burnt mud dauber nests were also found.

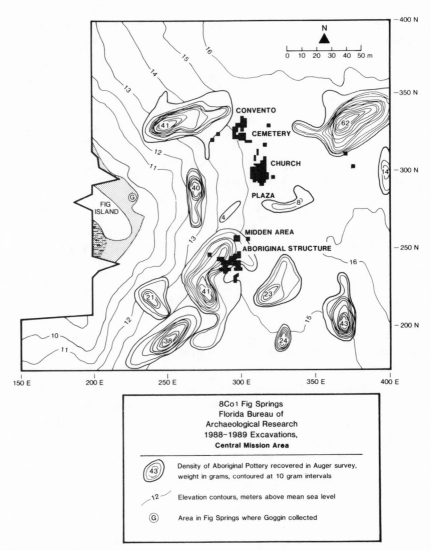

Figure 7.4. Plan view of excavations in the central mission area. Excavated areas are indicated in black.

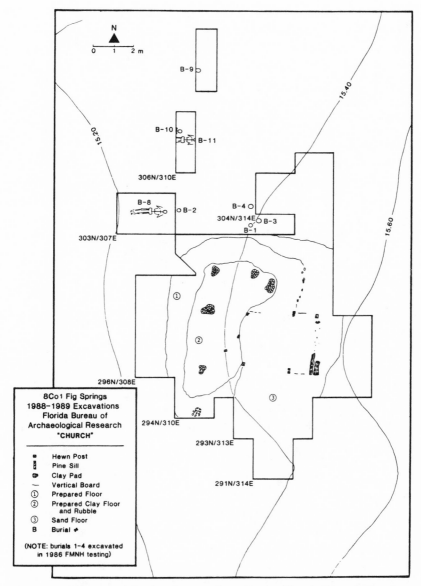

Figure 7.5. Plan view of the church excavations. Contour lines indicate surface elevations.

TABLE 7.1. Frequency of Major Artifact Types Found in Excavation Areas

Artifact	Count	% of Total Found in Excavation Area						Total
		Ch[a]	Co[b]	Cem[c]	A.S.[d]	A.M.[e]	So. End[f]	
Nails and spikes (intact)	112	33.3	38.4	6.3	17.8	4.5	0.0	100.0
Nails and spikes (fragment)	163	37.4	30.7	2.5	28.2	1.2	0.0	100.0
Glass (fragment)	61	27.9	24.6	0.0	47.5	0.0	0.0	100.0
Aboriginal pottery	4421	7.8	6.3	1.3	70.3	8.3	6.0	100.0
Majolica	57	45.6	17.5	1.8	29.8	5.3	0.0	100.0
Olive jar	157	34.4	10.8	0.0	48.4	6.4	0.0	100.0
Glass beads	164	1.2	2.4	1.2	90.9	4.3	0.0	100.0
Straight pins	19	78.9	15.8	0.0	5.3	0.0	0.0	100.0
Lead shot	12	8.3	0.0	8.3	75.0	8.3	0.0	100.0
Shell artifacts (inc. shell bead)	12	8.3	0.0	0.0	83.3	8.3	0.0	99.9
Projectile points	225	2.7	2.7	0.4	86.6	4.9	2.7	100.0

a. Ch = church.
b. Co = *convento*.
c. Cem = cemetery.
d. A.S. = aboriginal structure.
e. A.M. = aboriginal midden.
f. So. End = south end of village excavation.

THE CEMETERY

Burials are found along the north wall of the church and cover an estimated area about 30 m north-south by 10 m east-west. There is evidence of at least seven orderly rows of burials with an eighth intrusive row on the western side. Results of excavations in the central area of the cemetery in 1990 and 1991 by the Florida Museum of Natural History (see Hoshower and Milanich, this volume) suggest that less formal burial practices may have prevailed here and that at least some of the burials in the central area may intrude on a poorly preserved clay-floored structure, possibly a larger (and later) church than the structure we excavated.

Heads are to the east, facing west, with the burials aligned with the presumed east-west axis of the church. Burial pits are easily seen as areas of mottled sand and clay fill in a matrix of tan sand subsoil. Six burials were partly or completely cleaned in the FBAR excavations, all of which were supine and with hands typically folded over the chest. Burials were encountered from 48 centimeters below surface (cmbs) to 88 cmbs. None of these burials (including four burials partially exposed in the same area in 1986) was interred beneath the floor of a structure as is the case in other Florida missions (Jones and Shapiro 1987), because excavation profiles show them to be intrusive through humus deposits, unlike the cultural deposits noted in the building areas. All burials were backfilled in place after mapping and photography. Only one burial (no. 8) was cleaned in its entirety so as to allow an age and sex determination. This was a female, estimated to be between 35 and 45 years of age at the time of death (see Weisman 1992, appendix B).

A single blue glass seed bead was found in water-screening soil from the neck region of one burial; otherwise, grave goods, personal possessions, or evidence of clothing such as shroud pins was not found in direct association with the interments.

The *Convento*

The presumed *convento* is west of the cemetery and northwest of the church and is roughly defined by alignments and/or clusters of wrought nails and spikes found in association with majolica, olive jar, and aboriginal sherds; glass vial fragments (see fig. 7.6b); an iron trunk lock (fig. 7.6a); several straight pins; and several glass beads. Tentative identification of this area as the remains of the mission *convento* is made based on its placement in the site plan—that is, so as not to obstruct the view of the church from the plaza and aboriginal village—and the lack here of the special construction sequence described previously for the presumed mission church.

A single charred hewn post was found, the top of which was almost 40 cm below the tops of posts in the church, suggesting that the *convento* was built at an elevation lower than the church, a relationship not immediately apparent when looking at the present topography. The *convento* post, which is rectangular, not square, is oriented with its long axis east-west, thus suggesting that this structure was not aligned exactly with the church or with the burials identified in the FBAR project. A total of 38.4 percent of the intact nails and spikes recovered in the entire excavation came from the *convento* area, the largest percentage of any single excavation area (see table 7.1). Six of eight "L-head" type flooring nails (South, Skowronek, and Johnson 1988) were found here. Evidence of other architectural features was elusive, and it does not appear as if the building had vertical wall board construction and a prepared clay floor as did the church. Evidence for wattle-and-daub architecture is lacking.

The stratigraphy in this area of the site is disturbed and difficult to

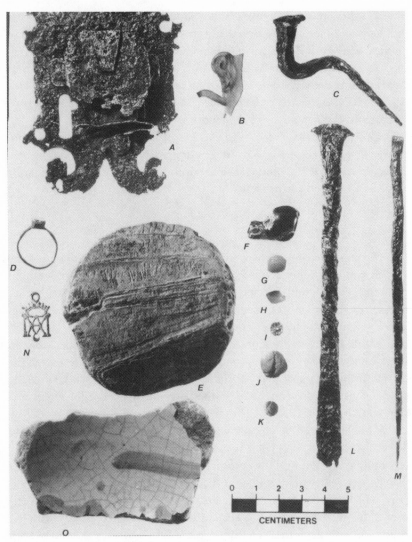

Figure 7.6. Selected artifacts from the Fig Springs excavations: (A) iron trunk lock (*convento*); (B) ornamental glass handle (*convento*); (C) bent nail associated with burnt post in church; (D) brass finger ring (aboriginal midden); (E) shell disk (aboriginal midden); (F) five-layered heat-altered chevron bead (probable village area); (G–H) Ichtucknee Blue glass beads; (I) gilded fluted bead; (J–K) clay balls; (L) iron chisel/knife, Feature 16 (trash-filled pit, aboriginal structure); (M) iron "awl," Feature 16; (N) "Ave Maria" gold *venera* medallion or pendant (aboriginal structure); (O) Fig Springs Polychrome majolica sherd (aboriginal structure).

interpret, due in part to soil mixing from tree falls and active erosion that is removing the western edge of the cultural deposit (see the downhill "creep" of pottery from the *convento* area in fig. 7.4). The main concentration of *convento* artifacts was found in an area of about 7 m east-west by 10 m north-south and came from a 10-cm-to-20-cm-thick occupation stratum consisting of tan, brown, and orange mottled sand with red clay inclusions, 20 cm to 30 cm below the present ground surface.

PLAZA

The plaza is an area of low artifact density separating the church--*convento*-cemetery complex from the mission village (see fig. 7.4). Strata in this area consist of a loose dry sand underlain by a sticky gray to tan clay, which is a natural deposit very close to the surface along the edge of the terrace above the springs (defined by the 15-m contour line).

ABORIGINAL STRUCTURE

The aboriginal structure is a rectangular 9-m-by-13-m structure (fig.7.7) south of the plaza and at the north end of the mission village (fig. 7.8). It is notable both for the quantity of artifacts recovered and the number of cultural features, many of which were filled with food refuse and discarded artifacts.

Seven types of features were identified (fig. 7.9). Cob-filled pits (total of 19) are bell-shaped and are thought to have been smudge pits located along the inside wall of the structure. Wood-filled pits (total of 24), also bell-shaped (fig. 7.10), contain dense layers of charcoal in the pit bottom and are associated with the cob pits.

Postholes or charred post features (total of 18) are found along the presumed wall line of the structure and at several places in the interior. Charred posts appear to be round, not hewn as in the church. Major wall posts typically are 1.7 m apart (the same distance from the clay support pads in the church to the edge of the floor). The remains of smaller interior posts and the restricted placement of the smudge pits suggest that benches lined the inner wall of the building, as has been suggested at other historic period aboriginal sites (Milanich 1972; Shapiro 1987b).

Just outside the north and presumed west walls of the structure were found seven linear to oval-shaped trash-filled pits (Features 7, 16, 31, 32,

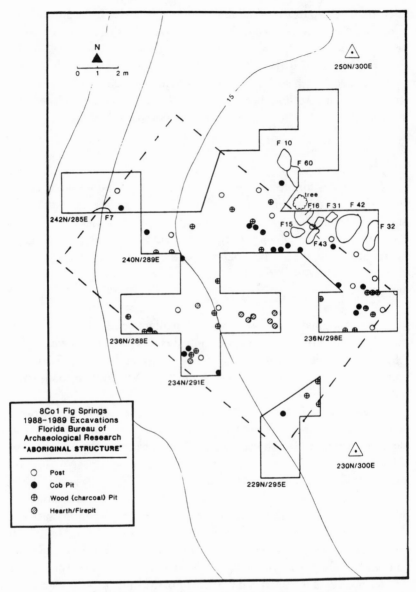

Figure 7.7. Plan view of excavations in aboriginal structure.

Figure 7.8. East end of the excavated aboriginal structure, view to the southeast. The cooking/roasting pits (Features 10, 60) are in left foreground. Pedestal in center is charred wall post.

34, 42, 43; see fig. 7.7). These pits were particularly rich sources of artifacts, including about 70 percent of the glass beads recovered in the entire excavation and other Spanish-derived items such as an iron chisel/knife and iron awl (see fig. 7.6l–m) that may have been cached. An iron hoe, similar to one found previously in the springs (Deagan 1972), came from a shallow pit feature (Feature 31). Hickory nut shells and an acorn hull have been identified in botanical analysis of trash-filled pit soil, as well as peach pit fragments and, of most interest, a single grain of wheat. Faunal remains from trash-filled pits include deer (minimum number of individuals present, or MNI, totaled 3); pig (1 MNI); turkey (1 MNI); sunfishes (6 MNI); catfish (3 MNI); gar (1 MNI); bass (1 MNI); turtle (1 MNI); and gopher tortoise (1 MNI) (Newsom and Quitmyer 1992).

On the outside of the building beyond the north wall are two 60-cm-deep oval pits (Features 10 and 60, fig. 7.7) interpreted as cooking or

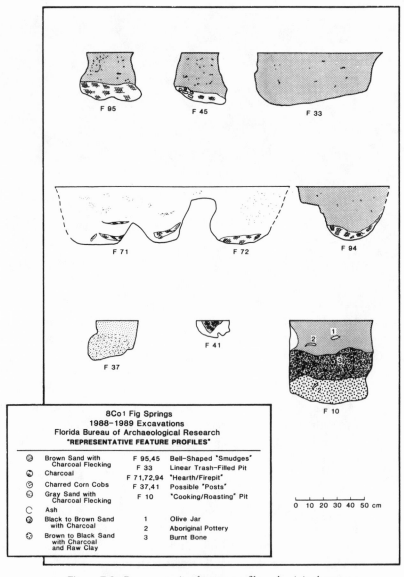

Figure 7.9. Representative feature profiles, aboriginal structure.

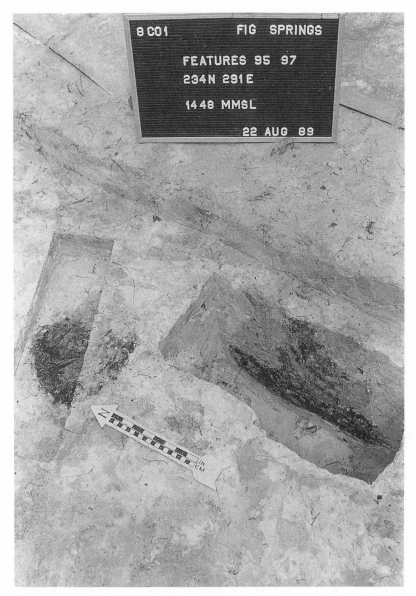

Figure 7.10. Profile of bell-shaped wood-filled "smudge pit," aboriginal structure.

roasting pits (these are seen in the left foreground of fig. 7.8). Fill consisted of layers of midden soil mixed with charcoal and lenses of ash. Most of the artifacts found in Feature 10 fill, including olive jar sherds found in the single greatest density on the site, were burnt. Botanical remains from Feature 10 consist of hickory nut and acorn fragments, maize cob and cupule fragments, saw palmetto seeds, maypop, sandspur, a possible hazel nut, possible domestic bean, and four watermelon seeds. Faunal remains include specimens of deer (1 MNI); opossum (1 MNI); gray fox (1 MNI); skunk (1 MNI); and gopher tortoise, mud turtle, and bowfin, each represented by 1 MNI.

Inside the structure, in what is interpreted as a large, open central room (around which the benches were placed), were found five 50-cm-deep basin-shaped hearths or fire pits with layers of ash and charcoal but few if any artifacts and no faunal remains.

The most curious feature associated with the aboriginal structure is a dog burial located just inside the north wall of the structure (fig. 7.11).

Figure 7.11. The dog burial exposed in the burial pit, north wall of aboriginal structure. Circular charcoal area in right center is a wall post. North of the dog burial is the quadrant excavation of trash-filled pit Feature 16 (in progress).

The flexed articulated skeleton, about the same size as an adult German shepherd, was found in the bottom of a pit evidently dug solely for the purpose of interring the animal. No artifacts were found with the skeleton, and the pit fill contained few artifacts, suggesting that burial occurred relatively early in the occupation of the structure. An undisturbed mission period cultural stratum covered the top of the pit intrusion, making it certain that the burial dates to the seventeenth century.

Spanish-derived artifacts found in the occupation stratum of the structure include sherds of Fig Springs Polychrome majolica (see fig. 7.6o) and a cast gold religious medallion (fig. 7.6n) with the interlocked letters M and A topped by a crown, thought to symbolize an early seventeenth-century Virgin Mary cult.

MIDDEN AREA

Associated with all known structures at Fig Springs but most strongly evident around the aboriginal structure are deposits of sheet midden, containing numerous Spanish and aboriginal artifacts and occasional faunal remains. The midden between the north side of the aboriginal structure and the south boundary of the plaza contains a notable density of artifacts, which are found in a cultural deposit 30–40 cm thick beneath modern humus. It appears that the midden in this area accumulated in natural low spots and around trees. Artifacts found in the midden north of the aboriginal structure include a brass finger ring with its stone setting still in place (see fig. 7.6d) and a shell disk (fig. 7.6e).

SOUTH END VILLAGE EXCAVATIONS

During the auger survey an area was identified in the southern portion of the mission village, some 200 m south of the excavated mission period aboriginal structure, that contained no complicated stamped pottery and no Spanish artifacts. Aboriginal pottery belonged exclusively to the Suwannee Valley Series. This area was interpreted as pure premission component. Archaeological testing here in 1989 and again by John Worth in 1990 (Worth 1991) was instrumental in developing the concept of the Suwannee Valley ceramic series and the Suwannee Valley culture, which, on the basis of a series of radiocarbon dates obtained by FBAR (Weisman 1992) and Worth (Worth 1991), was the indigenous Woodland-like cul-

ture in existence in post–Weeden Island times from about the tenth century A.D. through the sixteenth century.

Revised Aboriginal Pottery Typology

Early in the 1989 season a revised typology of Fig Springs aboriginal
pottery was adopted, in large part because existing typologies of mission
period ceramics developed from work at San Luis, Baptizing Spring, and
elsewhere in Timucua and Potano were not yielding the kinds of specific
information about culture and chronology that were hoped for. The
premise of the Fig Springs typology is that pottery temper is a good
chronological indicator, at least in Timucua, and the typology is based on
the archaeological observation that mission period pottery at Fig Springs
is almost exclusively grog-tempered, while early mission and premission
pottery is sand-tempered. Use of the typology is leading to understand-
ings of the cultural dynamics of the mission period, particularly in dem-
onstrating some degree of continuity between the premission and mission
period aboriginal Timucua population.

Five pottery series, based on temper, are used to classify the Fig
Springs collections. First is the Jefferson Series, with a grog-tempered
paste, containing varieties of bull's-eye and other complicated stamped
motifs (fig. 7.12e), check stamping (fig. 7.12d), punctated, cob-marked,
incised, and roughened surface treatments. The type Jefferson Plain accounts for almost 49 percent (by count) of the entire Fig Springs pottery
assemblage. The Suwannee Valley Series, sand-tempered wares, contains
varieties of the type Fig Springs Roughened (fig. 7.12b–c) and types of the
Alachua tradition. This is the pottery of the premission Timucua.

The third series is the shell-tempered Goggin pottery, which is present
only in mission contexts and contains plain (fig. 7.12a), incised, and cord-
marked types. The fourth series is Lamar, on a grit paste, and has plain,
complicated stamped, incised, and check-stamped types. Context appears
to be mission period although some late premission dating (late sixteenth
century?) is indicated. The fifth is the familiar St. Johns Series, which
comprises a minor (generally less than 2 percent in the different site areas)
but consistent part of the premission and mission period assemblages. A
total of 10 sherds of Fort Walton Incised was found in the aboriginal
structure.

Figure 7.12. Selected aboriginal pottery from Fig Springs: (A) Goggin Plain with notched appliqué strip; (B) Fig Springs Roughened variety Ichetucknee; (C) Fig Springs Roughened variety Santa Fé; (D) Jefferson Check Stamped variety Fort White; (E) Jefferson Complicated Stamped variety Early.

Comparison to Other Sites

The similarity between the wooden architecture of the Fig Springs and Aspalaga (Pine Tuft) "churches" has been pointed out, with the exception that the Fig Springs building is smaller and evidence for a compound wall is lacking. In terms of general similarities in site plan, the best comparison is with Baptizing Spring (8SU65). This perhaps is not too surprising given that both sites are interior Timucua missions dating to approximately the same time. Aboriginal structures C and D at Baptizing Spring contained cob-filled, wood-filled, trash-filled, and hearth features (Loucks 1979:141 and this volume) similar to those excavated in the aboriginal structure at Fig Springs. Curiously, the singular finds of religious medallions at both sites also came from an aboriginal structure.

As regards the interest among archaeologists in comparing the relative percentages of Spanish versus aboriginal pottery present in different site areas, the Fig Springs excavations add to a growing body of comparative data. In the Fig Springs church and *convento* areas, Spanish pottery (majolica and olive jar combined) accounts for an average of 13 percent of the total pottery assemblage, while this percentage is 1.5 percent for aboriginal areas. At Baptizing Spring, Spanish pottery accounts for 11.4 percent of the assemblage in the two presumed Spanish structures excavated and 2.9 percent in the village area. During preliminary test excavations at San Luis, Spanish pottery accounted for 8.3 percent of the total pottery from the church-*convento* areas and 2.1 percent from the suspected Apalachee village (Shapiro 1987a:111). It is also interesting to note that the percentages of majolica alone present in the Fig Springs church (6.1 percent) and *convento* (3.3 percent) relative to aboriginal pottery generally fall within the range of majolica percentages reported for sixteenth-century Spanish households in St. Augustine (Deagan 1985:28).

Much remains to be worked out at Fig Springs concerning the chronology of occupation, changes through time in site plan, and the relationship of this site to nearby sites such as Mill Pond (8CO43), where testing in 1989 (Weisman 1992) and 1990 (Worth 1991) has yielded Spanish artifacts, burnt patches of possible clay floor, and a pottery sequence showing the replacement of Suwannee pottery by ceramics of the Jefferson Series.

Bibliography

Bullones, Joseph de
1728   Letter to the King, St. Augustine, 5 October 1728. Archivo General de
       Indias, Santo Domingo 865, Stetson Collection. P. K. Yonge Library of
       Florida History, University of Florida, Gainesville. Translated by John H.
       Hann. In *Missions to the Calusa*, edited and translated by John H. Hann,
       371–380. Gainesville: University of Florida Press, 1991.

Bushnell, Amy
1988   Translation of Three Documents from the Edict on Afuyca, 22 March
       1685. Archivo General de Indias, Santo Domingo 838. Ms. on file, Flor-
       ida Bureau of Archaeological Research, Tallahassee.

Deagan, Kathleen A.
1972   Fig Springs: The Mid-Seventeenth Century in North-Central Florida. *His-
       torical Archaeology* 6:23–46.

1985   The Archaeology of Sixteenth-Century St. Augustine. *The Florida Anthro-
       pologist* 38(1–2):6–33.

1987   *Artifacts of the Spanish Colonies of Florida and the Caribbean, 1500–
       1800*. Vol. 1: *Ceramics, Glassware, and Beads*. Washington, D.C.:
       Smithsonian Institution Press.

Gatschet, Albert S.
1877   The Timucua Language. *Proceedings of the American Philosophical Soci-
       ety* 17:490–504.

Geiger, Maynard J., O.F.M.
1940   *Biographical Dictionary of the Franciscans in Spanish Florida and Cuba
       (1528–1841)*. Franciscan Studies, no. 21. Paterson, N.J.: St. Anthony's
       Guild Press.

Goggin, John M.
1949   Field Book for Florida, 1949. Box 9, Goggin Collection. P. K. Yonge
       Library of Florida History, University of Florida, Gainesville.

1968   *Spanish Majolica in the New World*. Yale University Publications in An-
       thropology, no. 72. New Haven.

Hann, John H.
1990   Summary Guide to Spanish Florida Missions and *Visitas* with Churches in
       the Sixteenth and Seventeenth Centuries. *The Americas* 46(4):417–513.

Jesús, Francisco Alonso de
1630   Petition, 1630. Archivo General de Indias, Santo Domingo 235, microfilm

28K, reel 36, Stetson Collection. P. K. Yonge Library of Florida History, University of Florida, Gainesville. Translated by John H. Hann. Ms. on file, Florida Bureau of Archaeological Research, Tallahassee.

Johnson, Kenneth W.

1987 *The Search for Aquacaleyquen and Cali: Archaeological Survey of Portions of Alachua, Bradford, Citrus, Clay, Columbia, Marion, Sumter, and Union Counties, Florida.* Miscellaneous Project Report Series, no. 33. Gainesville: Department of Anthropology, Florida State Museum.

1990 The Discovery of a Seventeenth-Century Spanish Mission in Ichetucknee State Park, 1986. *Florida Journal of Anthropology* 15:39–46.

Johnson, Kenneth W., and Bruce C. Nelson

1990 The Utina: Seriations and Chronology. *The Florida Anthropologist* 43(1):48–62.

Jones, B. Calvin, and Gary Shapiro

1987 Nine Mission Sites in Apalachee. Paper presented at the 1987 Society for Historical Archaeology Conference on Historical and Underwater Archaeology, Savannah, Georgia.

López, Baltazar

1602 Letter to Blas de Montes, St. Augustine, 15 September 1602. Archivo General de Indias, Santo Domingo 235, reel 2, Woodbury Lowery Collection. Strozier Library, Florida State University, Tallahassee. Translated by John H. Hann. Ms. on file, Florida Bureau of Archaeological Research, Tallahassee.

Lorant, Stefan, ed.

1946 *The New World: The First Pictures of America.* New York: Duell, Sloan, and Pearce.

Loucks, Lana Jill

1979 Political and Economic Interactions between Spaniards and Indians: Archeological and Ethnohistorical Perspectives of the Mission System in Florida. Ph.D. diss., University of Florida. Ann Arbor: University Microfilms.

Machado, Francisco

1597 [Testimony by; June–July 1597.] Account of the clothing, flour, iron tools, and other things that have been given to the Indians. Archivo General de Indias, Santo Domingo 231, Woodbury Lowery Collection. Strozier Library, Florida State University, Tallahassee. Translated by John H. Hann. Ms. on file, Florida Bureau of Archaeological Research, Tallahassee.

Milanich, Jerald T.

1972 Excavations at the Richardson Site, Alachua County, Florida: An Early

Seventeenth-Century Potano Indian Village (with Notes on Potano Culture Change). *Bureau of Historic Sites and Properties Bulletin* 2:35–61.

1978 The Western Timucua: Patterns of Acculturation and Change. In *Tacachale: Essays on the Indians of Florida and Southeastern Georgia during the Historic Period*, edited by Jerald T. Milanich and Samuel Proctor, 59–88. Ripley P. Bullen Monographs in Anthropology and History, no. 1. Gainesville: University Presses of Florida.

Morrell, L. Ross, and B. Calvin Jones
1970 San Juan de Aspalaga: A Preliminary Architectural Study. *Bureau of Historic Sites and Properties Bulletin* 1:25–43.

Newsom, Lee, and Irvy R. Quitmyer
1992 Appendix E: Archaeobotanical and Faunal Remains. In *Excavations on the Franciscan Frontier: Archaeology at the Fig Springs Mission*, by Brent R. Weisman, 206–233. Gainesville: University Press of Florida.

Oré, Luís Gerónimo de
1936 *The Martyrs of Florida (1513–1616)*. Translated and edited by Maynard J. Geiger. Franciscan Studies, no. 18. New York: Joseph F. Wagner.

San Antonio, Francisco de, and Provincial Chapter
1657 Letter to the King, St. Augustine, 10 September 1657. Archivo General de Indias, Santo Domingo 235, reel 3, Woodbury Lowery Collection. Strozier Library, Florida State University, Tallahassee. Translated by John H. Hann. Ms. on file, Florida Bureau of Archaeological Research, Tallahassee.

Shapiro, Gary
1987a *Archaeology at San Luis: Broad-Scale Testing, 1984–1985*. Florida Archaeology no. 3. Tallahassee: Florida Bureau of Archaeological Research.

1987b Inside the Apalachee Council House at San Luis. Paper presented at the 44th Annual Meeting of the Southeastern Archaeological Conference, Charleston, South Carolina.

South, Stanley, Russell K. Skowronek, and Richard E. Johnson
1988 *Spanish Artifacts from Santa Elena*. Anthropological Studies, no. 7. Columbia: Occasional Papers of the South Carolina Institute of Archaeology and Anthropology, University of South Carolina.

Swanton, John R.
1946 *The Indians of the Southeastern United States*. Bureau of American Ethnology Bulletin no. 137. Washington, D.C.: Smithsonian Institution.

Weisman, Brent R.
1988a *Archaeological Investigations at the Fig Springs Mission (8CO1)*. Florida

Archaeological Reports, no. 11. Tallahassee: Florida Bureau of Archaeological Research.

1988b *1988 Excavations at Fig Springs (8CO1), Season 2, July–December 1988.* Florida Archaeological Reports, no. 4. Tallahassee: Florida Bureau of Archaeological Research.

1992 *Excavations on the Franciscan Frontier: Archaeology at the Fig Springs Mission.* Gainesville: University Press of Florida.

Worth, John E.
1991 Prehistory in the Timucua Mission Province: Archaeological Investigations at Ichetucknee Springs State Park, 1990. Draft report in the possession of John Worth.

❂ 8 ❂

Spanish-Indian Interaction
on the Florida Missions:
The Archaeology of
Baptizing Spring

L. JILL LOUCKS

Interest in the Spanish mission system of Florida has existed since the Spaniards first established the missions in the late 1500s. Naturalists, geographers, and historians have expressed curiosity over the ruins, the "old fields," and the documents for the past 200 years or more. Archaeological interest can be traced to the 1940s, when Dr. Hale G. Smith carried out the first research-oriented excavation of a Spanish mission in the former province of Apalachee (Smith 1948, 1951b). Since that time, archaeological investigation has waxed and waned according to funding and the pressures of other responsibilities. During the late 1960s and early 1970s, it appeared that archaeological work at the Florida missions was under way on a full scale at last when the state of Florida, through the Division of Archives, History, and Records Management, began to test and excavate a number of mission sites in northern and northwestern Florida (B. C. Jones 1970a, 1970b, 1971, 1972, 1973; Morrell and Jones 1970). Unfortunately, even the state is subject to funding problems. A final and comprehensive report is still forthcoming. Archaeologists had not been idle in eastern Florida during this period, and several mission and mission period sites have been investigated since the late 1940s (Benton 1976; Deagan 1978; Goggin 1953, 1968, 1970; Griffin 1960; W. M. Jones 1967; McMurray 1973; Seaberg 1951). A few mission sites were also studied in north-central Florida (Deagan 1972; Milanich 1972, 1978; Seaberg 1955; Symes and Stephens 1965).

As archaeology became more anthropological and scientific, mission period archaeology began to take a similar turn in Florida as archaeologists began to discuss acculturation processes and change in native Floridian subsistence and social patterns. The thesis summarized herein is the result of cumulative changes in emphasis in archaeological and anthropological theory to date. The author has had the benefit of time and these changes and past research in mission archaeology upon which to build. In the vein of current anthropological theory (and attempting to live up to its expectations), it was felt that even though acculturation had been approached in mission period archaeology, the final product lacked the holistic metal for which anthropologists claim they are searching. Indians and Spaniards who lived and worked at the missions were still ephemeral; changes in material culture could be diagnosed, but the meaning of these changes, their magnitude, and their impact remained veiled.

Economic anthropology is concerned not only with material objects and tangible (i.e., quantifiable) outcomes but also with the social significance of human interactions. Because the material objects are present in archaeological sites, it is only a step further to investigate the interactions and actions that might have produced and distributed them. If one is to investigate acculturation, then the interactions and intangible significance of production, distribution, and consumption of physical objects cannot be overlooked.

The basic goal of the archaeological research at the Baptizing Spring site (8SU65) in Suwannee County, Florida, was to give substance to some of the questions concerning acculturation processes that had been broached by past researchers. From the point of view of the author, this substance was to be behavioral (personal) as well as material. Artifacts, the hard and preserved remains of past cultures, had intangible meaning to those who once used or owned them. One has only to look at one's own possessions to be able to see what would be assumed from their physical characteristics versus what would not be learned about their emotional or symbolic meaning.

The objectives of this project were twofold: to build a model of Spanish-Indian interactions using historical data and to test certain hypotheses relating to these interactions using archaeological information.

The analysis of historical data, which was largely carried out prior to field research, was undertaken from an anthropologic-economic point of view. The outcome suggested that the so-called golden age of the Florida missions was a significant misrepresentation of the facts, a conclusion that is not unique to this author (Spellman 1965). It was shown that, very probably, Indian values and demands were little affected by Spanish goals of directed change. Many Indians did become "good" converts, but the primary motivation for adapting to Spanish behavioral expectations appears to have been economic and political, not to mention survival. When goods stopped moving in *both* directions and "exchange" became decidedly one-way, the native Floridians rebelled not only against the Spaniards but also against their own leaders, or caciques (Loucks 1979).

Spaniards and Indians assumed two primary sets of roles: missionary-convert and patron-client. However, one cannot separate these behavioral roles, for missionaries were patrons, providing goods and services, and favored clients were probably good converts. Economic, political, and religious benefits seem to have been awarded in conjunction (Loucks 1979).

Baptizing Spring

The Baptizing Spring site (fig. 8.1) was tentatively identified as the Utina mission of San Agustín de Urica.[1] This mission was occupied at least as late as 1655 (Geiger 1940:125–126) and probably was abandoned as a result of the Timucuan uprising in 1656; it is not mentioned after that date. Although the date of its founding is unknown, Spanish ceramics recovered from the site suggest that the period of greatest activity was early in the seventeenth century, probably around the early to mid-1620s. A religious medallion that probably postdates 1640 was recovered from one of the two aboriginal structures excavated, indicating that the village was still occupied around this time.

Although Spanish friars, especially Father Baltasar López from the mission on Cumberland Island, Georgia, made visitations to the interior as early as the late 1500s (Geiger 1940), it is not known whether these forays greatly affected Indian culture change or whether Spanish artifacts were introduced in large numbers. One can assume that the establishment of the interior missions in 1606–1610 (Geiger 1937) had much greater impact on Indians living in the north-central and northern parts of Florida.

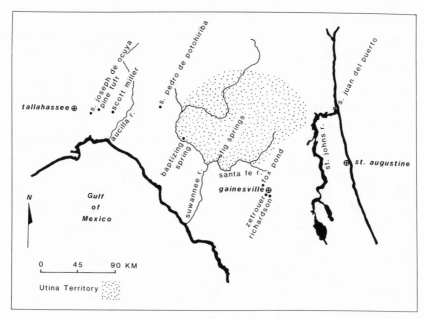

Figure 8.1. Location of sites discussed.

The tentative identification of the Baptizing Spring site as San Agustín de Urica suggests that the village was indeed a mission rather than a *visita*. There is virtually no accepted way of distinguishing the two types of settlements archaeologically; the historical documents have been relied upon to provide that information through the provision of names. Comparison of the material assemblage of Baptizing Spring with that of the Potano (north-central Florida) village Richardson site, which has been tentatively identified as the *visita* of Apalo (Milanich 1972),[2] indicates that the former claims a greater number and variety of Spanish artifacts than does the latter (tables 8.1, 8.2). The Potano mission site Fox Pond, however, has a greater variety of Spanish artifacts than does Baptizing Spring. For these reasons the site under investigation has been designated a mission, a village with a resident priest, rather than a *visita*, although the Baptizing Spring mission appears to have been relatively poor in material wealth.

The main mission village of Baptizing Spring, which included Indian and Spanish structural remains and covered approximately 2.83 ha, was small and assumed to be less well-off economically than the more impor-

TABLE 8.1. Classified Majolica Types for Nine Florida Mission or *Visita* Sites

Type	E. Timucua	Potano		Utina		Apalachee		
	San Juan del Puerto	Fox Pond[a]	Richardson[a]	Fig Springs	Baptizing Spring	Scott Miller[a]	Pine Tuft[a]	San Joseph de Ocuya[a]
Columbia Plain	1	6	5	58	23			
Green-Glazed Columbia Plain					1			
La Vega B/W[b]	4							
Isabela Polychrome	1		1	3				
Santo Domingo B/W	1	7		12	49			
Ichtucknee B/B	1	1	12	43	7			
Ichtucknee B/W	7	22		43	145			
Fig Springs Polychrome	18	54		66	3			
San Luis B/W	13	40			4	21	7	1
Tallahassee B/W		3		17		9	9	19
Mt. Royal Polychrome	3	1				1		1
Aucilla Polychrome	13					10		11
San Luis Polychrome	19					55	57	7
Abo Polychrome	4					42	7	2
Puaray Polychrome		1						
Puebla Polychrome	12	3				54	401	27
Castillo Polychrome	7							
San Agustin B/W	12							
Aranama Polychrome	1							
Total	117	138	18	242	232	192	481	68

Note: Types represented reflect periods of occupation. Majolica types are listed from earliest to latest.

a. Supplemented counts with data from Goggin (1968) added to data from later excavations or listed only in Goggin.

b. Blue on White majolica is abbreviated B/W; Blue on Blue is abbreviated B/B.

TABLE 8.2. Nonceramic Spanish Artifacts Compared between Spanish Mission Period Sites in Florida

Description	Baptizing Spring	Fig Springs	San Juan del Puerto	Richardson	Fox Pond	Scott Miller	San Joseph de Ocuya
Containers							
Goblet			x				
Medicine vial		x					
Hardware							
Nails, spikes	x	x	x	x	x	x	x
Hinges						x	
Locks, bolts						x	
Keys			x				
Clothing							
Buttons			x				
Buckles			x		x		
Thimble		x					
Ornaments							
Glass bead	x	x	x	x	x	x	x
Copper bead	x						
Lead bead			x				
Copper rectangles	x		x				
Religious medal	x		x				
Crucifix/corpus		x	x			x	
Brass finger ring			x				
Rosary			x				
Metal scraps							
Brass			x				x

Copper	x						
Whelk shell	x	x					
Pendant and dipper				x			
Tools and weapons							
Knives	x						
Ramrod tip					x		
Pistol/musket parts		x	x			x	
Gunflints							
Native	x					x	x
European			x				
Musket ball, shot	x	x	x		x	x	
Lance head						x	
Sword/dagger					x	x	
Chisel					x	x	
Anvil						x	
Spur rowel						x	
Hoes			x			x	
Axe						x	
Miscellaneous							
Coins			x				
Coin weight			x				
Tobacco pipes			x				
Book clasp			x				
Olive jar/majolica		x	x				
Gaming disks							x
Bone counters?	x						
Gaming pieces							

TABLE 8.3. Cultures Represented by Identifiable Aboriginal Ceramics at Eight Florida Mission Period Sites (%)

Site	St. Johns	Weeden Island	Alachua	San Marcos	"Creek"	Leon-Jefferson	Fort Walton	Total %
E. Timucua								
San Juan del Puerto	5.24	0.06	5.48	86.86		2.37		100.01
Potano								
Richardson	14.02	0.11	85.16			0.72		100.01
Fox Pond	27.03	2.82	25.70			44.44		99.99
Zetrouer	8.46		22.08	68.86		0.73		100.13
Utina								
Fig Springs	24.59		5.96	1.32	10.43	57.04	0.66	100.00
Baptizing Spring	6.44	1.32	2.45		6.86	82.93		100.00
Apalachee								
Scott Miller			0.14			99.86		100.00
San Joseph de Ocuya		0.31			0.93	95.04	3.72	100.00

tant missions in Apalachee, Potano, and near St. Augustine. It was, however, in an area that seemed to have experienced greater tribal mixing.
Whereas the west Florida, east Florida, and central north Florida mission
villages appear to contain fairly homogeneous aboriginal ceramic complexes, the Utina assemblages reveal a high degree of variety even though
certain ceramic types predominate (table 8.3).

The Baptizing Spring site is situated in an area proximal to riverine,
floodplain, hardwood hammock, and pine–turkey oak habitats. Soil fertility in the area, however, is low to moderate without modern alteration,
but the clay substrate in the vicinity of the village could have enhanced
natural fertility and made sedentism based on horticulture more practica-
ble. Intensive agricultural pursuits and high productivity, however, were
probably beyond the capacities of the soil. Perhaps for this reason, precontact human activity in this region was minimal. Although our knowledge of precontact settlement in this area is practically nil, present data
suggest that large-scale villages and ceremonial centers were not established here. Outside the immediate area of Baptizing Spring the only other
evidence of prehistoric activity suggests impermanent settlements of small
groups of hunters and gatherers (Loucks 1978). There is as yet no indication that prehistoric population density was ever very great in southwestern Suwannee County.

Acculturation and Economics at Baptizing Spring

The hypotheses that were to be tested were aimed at discovering whether
native political and economic roles and values were maintained during
the mission period. The site was approached with the idea that settlement
patterning would reflect retention of prehistoric/protohistoric location
(as identified through ethnohistoric and prehistoric archaeological data)
of important residences and buildings on rises near a central plaza. If
these elite households/structures could be identified, then it was anticipated that the associated material culture would also exhibit differentia-
tion on the basis of status. If aboriginal reckoning of high status was
maintained and if the precontact elite maintained their positions by virtue
of Spanish reinforcement, then it was hypothesized that prestige and
nonlocal goods of both Indian and European origins would be nonrandomly distributed within the village in association with high-status dwellings. It was also anticipated that Spaniards living at missions would have

enjoyed more of the material wealth of both Spanish and aboriginal realms than the Indians would have.

Four probable aboriginal living areas were encountered during the one-and-a-half seasons of work at Baptizing Spring (fig. 8.2), but only two of these—Structures C and D—were extensively excavated. The remains of two wattle-and-daub Spanish buildings, possible church (Structure B) and convent (Structure A), were also excavated.[3] The small amount of site coverage precludes definite conclusions regarding village settlement pattern. The larger of the two Spanish structures, the possible church, was situated in the highest portion of the core village and might have bordered a central plaza. The other Spanish building was behind (to the north of) this structure at the base of the rise. The latter also appears to have been located at the northern boundary of the main village. The two extensively investigated aboriginal structures were approximately the same distance from the "church" although Structure D was located nearer the spring. If the four probable Indian structures are considered, it appears that they were arranged around the central plaza, 20–25 m apart, in a linear fashion. The relationships between these structures, however, are subject to sampling bias and cannot be accepted with any degree of certainty. There is too much of the village left to be excavated before actual community arrangement can be determined.

Information recovered from Baptizing Spring indicates that the Spaniards affected little change in the material culture of the native inhabitants. If anything, priests were required to adapt to the new environment to a greater extent than the Indians were. The Spanish element appears to have enjoyed certain restricted access to European, nonlocal, and locally manufactured goods. Table 8.4 compares European-derived artifacts found in the two Spanish structural areas and the rest of the village. It is notable that Spaniards had greater access to hardware and European ceramics. This becomes more significant if the relative size of Spanish and Indian populations is considered. Table 8.5 compares aggregated aboriginal ceramic types between Spanish and Indian contexts. Presumed and known nonlocal ceramic groups include Ocmulgee Fields Incised (2.23 percent in the Spanish area versus 0.14 percent in the village), St. Johns types (15.99 percent Spanish, 2.99 percent aboriginal), Chattahoochee Brushed (0.97 percent Spanish, 0.55 percent aboriginal), and "Georgia-like complicated stamped" types (3.06 percent Spanish, 1.20 percent aboriginal). The possible nonlocal "Alachua types," which were better represented in the village, will be discussed below. Of the presumed lo-

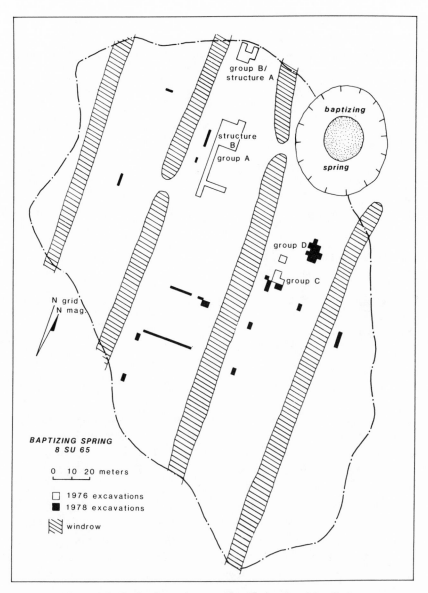

Figure 8.2. Predominant features identified at Baptizing Spring.

TABLE 8.4. European Artifacts from Baptizing Spring:
Spanish versus Indian Contexts

Description	Spanish		Indian	
	Count	% of total	Count	% of total
Copper rectangles	0	0.00	4	2.96
Copper bead	0	0.00	1	0.74
Sheet copper	1	0.31	0	0.00
Religious medal	0	0.00	1	0.74
Glass bead	1	0.31	1	0.74
Cf. knife blade (iron)	1	0.31	2	1.48
Wrought nails/spikes	21	6.42	2	1.48
Lead shot/musket ball	2	0.61	2	1.48
Olive jar/storage jar	89	27.22	99	73.33
Honeyware	3	0.92	0	0.00
Santo Domingo Blue on White	39	11.93	10	7.41
Ichtucknee Blue on Blue	6	1.83	1	0.74
Ichtucknee Blue on White	141	43.12	4	2.96
Columbia Plain	21	6.42	2	1.48
Fig Springs Polychrome	0	0.00	3	2.22
San Luis Blue on White	1	0.31	3	2.22
Green-Glazed Columbia Plain	1	0.31	0	0.00
Total	327	100.00	135	100.00

cally manufactured ceramics, "scraped" types were higher in frequency in the village (6.76 percent versus 2.23 percent in the Spanish area) and Jefferson Complicated Stamped Type B (Smith 1951a) was slightly greater in the village area (9.62 percent versus 7.23 percent). Notably, two variants of a unique, nested-cross design complicated stamped type—"loop" and "solid" cross—were better represented in the Spanish area (5.84 percent and 5.98 percent, respectively) than in the aboriginal village (2.76 percent and 2.67 percent, respectively). These variants of complicated stamped motifs are not known to have prehistoric precedents and it is possible that the use of a cross element for decorating ceramics was instigated by the priests.

Although Indians may have manufactured the "cross-motif" complicated stamped ceramics largely for the Spaniards, it is evident that they were not restricted to Spanish proveniences. A better indication of special manufacture and restricted consumption is the ceramic vessels manufactured by Indians in European forms. Forms represented included small,

TABLE 8.5. Aggregated Aboriginal Ceramics from Baptizing Spring: Spanish versus Indian Contexts

Description	Spanish[a]	Indian[a]
Ocmulgee Fields Incised	16 (2.23)	3 (0.14)
Alachua types	4 (0.56)	78 (3.59)
St. Johns types	115 (15.99)	65 (2.99)
Chattahoochee Brushed	7 (0.97)	12 (0.55)
Scraped	16 (2.23)	147 (6.76)
Georgia-like complicated stamped	22 (3.06)	26 (1.20)
Loop-Cross complicated stamped	42 (5.84)	60 (2.76)
Solid-Cross complicated stamped	43 (5.98)	58 (2.67)
Jefferson Complicated Stamped		
Type A	4 (0.56)	6 (0.28)
Type B	52 (7.23)	209 (9.62)
Type C	3 (0.42)	1 (0.05)
Type D	1 (0.14)	3 (0.14)
Total identifiable decorated ceramics[b]	719	2173

a. Percentages in parentheses reflect proportion of total identifiable decorated ceramics.

b. Total includes additional ceramics other than those listed in this table (see Loucks 1979, table 9).

footed bowls (resembling Oriental handleless cups); plates; and handled bowls or pitchers. Most of these were thin-walled, fine-textured, and well-smoothed. No ceramics of this ware were found in the village and sherds from these vessels were primarily restricted to the smaller Spanish structure, where they comprised at least three, possibly four, of the small, footed bowls, at least one plate, and a small bowl with a pinched spout. Coarser Jefferson ware European forms were also present, including a small handle and several sherds from a flat-bottomed, flared-footed vessel. The latter were recovered from Structure D and, although it could not be reconstructed, the vessel appears to have been copied from a recovered, (partial) Santo Domingo Blue on White majolica jar. A portion of a Jefferson ware plate was also recovered from Structure A, the convent. One footring sherd similar to those found in the convent was recovered from Structure C, the other aboriginal structure. The final European vessel form identified was part of a Columbia Plain–like bowl base found in the convent. It was neither Jefferson ware nor the finer, thinner ware type.

In addition to the apparent differential access to ceramic goods, food also seems to have been nonrandomly distributed between Spaniards and

Indians. The overall subsistence pattern at Baptizing Spring does not seem to be significantly different from known prehistoric patterns in Florida. Certain Indian households consumed introduced domesticates such as pig, cow, and peaches, and these domesticates are also represented in the Spanish sectors. They do not, however, appear to have been important in either area. It is cautioned that the organic sample was small and that any conclusions must be treated with deliberation. The major difference between Spanish and Indian food consumption was the lower variety of animal species utilized by Spaniards (primarily gopher tortoise and deer; table 8.6) and the apparent monopolization of the meatier portions of deer by the priests. In Structures C and D only one-third of the identifiable deer elements derived from the hindquarters, versus roughly 90 percent in the Spanish sector. The variety of elements present in the aboriginal area was much greater: scapular fragments, manus and pes elements, forelimb elements, dentaries, teeth, and vertebrae. The less complete inventory of elements in the Spanish sector suggests that butchering was carried out elsewhere and that priests received the meatier (hind limb) portions almost to the exclusion of other portions. Disparities in the sections of deer represented not only in Spanish versus Indian areas but also in Structure C versus Structure D suggest that products of the hunt were being distributed according to a specified pattern.

On a material level, therefore, the Spaniards were consumers and "produced" little by way of providing a means of acquiring and/or distributing externally derived wealth and goods. More goods flowed to the priest from the Indians than vice versa, and the nonlocal goods that Indians did receive were primarily of a religious (i.e., Christian-reinforcing) and ornamental (copper bangles and copper and glass beads) nature (table 8.4). European ceramics that Indians may have used as vessels or perhaps collected as sherds were largely utilitarian olive jar or storage jar.

Among the Indians, status positions seem to have been maintained and validated through acquisition of Spanish goods and nonlocal aboriginal goods (tables 8.7, 8.8). It is possible that some of these goods (i.e., Alachua tradition ceramics associated with the Potano area), if indeed they were nonlocal, were not always channeled through the priests. Presumed nonlocal aboriginal ceramics—olive jar, majolica, St. Johns types, Georgia-like complicated stamped types (CSGA)—were significantly nonrandomly distributed between the two aboriginal structures (table 8.8). Majolica, St. Johns types, and CSGA were more abundant in Struc-

TABLE 8.6. Faunal Species and Classes Represented in Spanish and Indian Contexts at Baptizing Spring: MNI, (% MNI), Number of Fragments

Classification	Spanish Area		Indian Area	
	MNI (%)	# of fragments	MNI (%)	# of fragments
Bos taurus (cow)	1 (7.69)	2	1 (2.86)	2
Sus scrofa (pig)	1 (7.69)	1	2 (5.71)	92+ [a]
Odocoileus virginianus (deer)	4 (30.77)	29+	12 (34.29)	72
Procyon lotor (raccoon)			1 (2.86)	1
Sciurus sp. (squirrel)			1 (2.86)	1
Sigmodon hispidus (cotton rat)			1 (2.86)	1
Artiodactyl (deer or pig?)				26
Unidentified mammal		13+		120
Gopherus polyphemus (gopher tortoise)	6 (46.15)	109+	8 (22.86)	127
Chrysemys sp. (pond turtle) C. cf. *scripta* ($n = 1$)			3 (8.57)	5
Terrapene carolina (box turtle)			2 (5.71)	2
Unidentified turtle		23+		65
Alligator mississipiensis (alligator)			2 (5.71)	5
Colubridae (racer)	1 (7.69)	1		
Passerine (song bird)			1 (2.86)	1
Mugil sp. (mullet)			1 (2.86)	1
Unidentified bony fish				8
Total identifiable MNI	13		35	
% mammal	46.15		54.54	
% reptile	53.85		38.66	
% bird			2.22	
% fish			4.55	
% domestic	15.38		8.57	
% wild	84.62		91.43	

a. This total reflects part of a pig carcass (ribs, scapula, vertebral column found in one aboriginal structure, Structure D).

ture D. Alachua types were also significantly more common in Structure D. The former three groups seem to be Spanish "markers" when Spanish and aboriginal contexts are compared; the latter Alachua group—plus the "scraped" group—is definitely an Indian "marker."

In addition to differences in ceramic assemblages, the two aboriginal structures varied according to the variety and types of other introduced

TABLE 8.7. Aggregated Ceramic Groups Compared between the Two Aboriginal Structures (C and D) at Baptizing Spring: Adjusted Frequencies[a]

OLIVEJAR										
C:	16	14	4	4	4	3	3	3	0	0
D:	5	0	0	0	0	0	0	0	0	0
MAJOLICA										
C:	1	0	0	0	0	0	0	0	0	0
D:	7	3	2	2	2	2	0	0	0	0
STJOHNS										
C:	9	3	1	1	0	0	0	0	0	0
D:	12	10	9	7	5	5	3	2	0	0
LOOPCRS (nested "loop" or open cross complicated stamped)										
C:	9	6	6	4	4	4	3	1	0	0
D:	5	3	2	2	2	0	0	0	0	0
SOLIDCRS (nested cross complicated stamped with solid central element)										
C:	10	4	3	1	1	0	0	0	0	0
D:	10	3	2	2	2	0	0	0	0	0
ALACHUA										
C:	4	1	1	1	0	0	0	0	0	0
D:	21	21	16	14	14	10	9	9	2	0
CSGA (Georgia-like complicated stamped types)										
C:	3	1	1	1	0	0	0	0	0	0
D:	7	5	5	2	2	2	2	2	0	0
OTHERGA (Ocmulgee Fields Incised and Chattahoochee Brushed)										
C:	1	1	0	0	0	0	0	0	0	0
D:	9	3	2	0	0	0	0	0	0	0
CSTYPB (Jefferson Complicated Stamped Type B)										
C:	21	18	13	10	7	7	6	3	1	0
D:	21	19	19	17	16	14	14	10	10	7
SCRAPED										
C:	34	24	3	3	3	1	1	0	0	0
D:	33	33	22	21	10	10	9	9	7	0

a. To standardize ceramic frequencies, raw counts were divided by the excavated area within the structural areas (Structure C = 68 square meters; Structure D = 58 square meters) then multiplied by 10.0 to produce whole numbers.

artifacts, some of which are classified as prestige items. Significance of these differences must be inferred, however, since their numbers were small. Structure D yielded remains of floral and faunal domesticates such as peach hulls and pig remains, Spanish-origin prestige items such as a glass bead and three copper rectangles, and possible aboriginal prestige items such as whelk shell and shark tooth ornaments. This structure also yielded two possible iron knife blades, a lead shot, and an aboriginally

TABLE 8.8. F Values of One-way Analysis of Variance between Structures C and D by Ceramic Type/Group (with 1 and 18 Degrees of Freedom)

Ceramic type/group	Structure C			Structure D			
	Mean	SD	Sum	Mean	SD	Sum	Fa
OLIVEJAR	5.10	5.45	51	0.50	1.58	5	6.58
MAJOLICA	0.10	0.32	1	1.80	2.15	18	6.12
STJOHNS	1.40	2.84	14	5.30	4.16	53	5.99
LOOPCRS	3.70	2.87	37	1.40	1.71	14	4.74
SOLIDCRS	1.90	3.18	19	1.90	3.07	19	0
ALACHUA	0.70	1.25	7	11.60	7.07	116	24.30
CSGA	0.60	0.97	6	2.70	2.26	27	7.28
OTHERGA	0.20	0.42	2	1.40	2.88	14	1.71
CSTYPB	7.28	7.11	86	14.70	4.57	147	6.79
SCRAPED	6.90	11.95	69	15.40	11.27	154	2.68

a. At $p = .05$, $F_{1,18} = 4.41$.
  At $p = .01$, $F_{1,18} = 8.28$.
  At $p = .001$, $F_{1,18} = 15.38$.

manufactured gunflint. The fact that aboriginal and European prestige items clustered suggests that certain rights to these goods were controlled and that these rights were upheld by both Spaniards and Indians.

There is no evidence at Baptizing Spring that Spanish-introduced agricultural tools or domesticates produced significant impacts on subsistence activities. Archaeological data from other mission sites imply that this was not true in all areas, but access to tools and retention of yields have not been examined. It is known that at missions in Apalachee and eastern Florida iron tools were present in Spanish areas of sites (table 8.2). This does not mean, however, that they were plentiful (or numerically adequate) or widely distributed among Indians. Historical documents indicate that immense quantities of iron were forged to produce tools for Indian consumption. Where these tools actually ended up is unknown; they do not appear to have remained in archaeological contexts at the missions.

The abundance and variety of lithic tools at Baptizing Spring suggest that European subsistence tools and weapons did not replace aboriginal counterparts (table 8.9). Even though an aboriginally manufactured gunflint and lead shot were recovered, the tool and weapon assemblage was predominantly aboriginal. The occurrence of a lead musket ball that was undistorted and the gunflint implies that some Indians had access to,

TABLE 8.9. Summary of Worked and Utilized Lithic Artifacts from Spanish and Indian Contexts at Baptizing Spring (% of Class)

Description	Spanish area	Indian area
Small projectile points	5 (8.62)	142 (30.87)
Medium-large projectile points	17 (29.31)	77 (16.74)
Drills	0	20 (4.35)
Awls	0	5 (1.09)
Gravers	1 (1.72)	3 (0.65)
Scrapers	12 (20.69)	80 (17.39)
Knives	5 (8.62)	36 (7.83)
Knife/scraper	0	3 (0.65)
Spokeshaves	1 (1.72)	0
Spokeshave/scraper	0	6 (1.30)
Graver/scraper	0	2 (0.43)
Heavy chopper/scraper	0	1 (0.22)
Adze	1 (1.72)	5 (1.09)
Chopper/hammer–pecking stone	6 (10.34)	8 (1.74)
Gunflint	0	1 (0.22)
Square biface; gunflint blank?	0	6 (1.30)
Unidentifiable biface	7 (12.07)	39 (8.48)
Unidentifiable uniface	1 (1.72)	15 (3.26)
Unidentifiable worked fragment	2 (3.45)	11 (2.39)
Total worked	58 (99.97)	460 (99.80)
Scrapers	90 (68.70)	671 (66.37)
Knives	4 (3.05)	93 (9.20)
Gravers	13 (9.92)	61 (6.03)
Spokeshaves	11 (8.40)	125 (12.36)
Perforators	0	4 (0.39)
Scraper/spokeshave	9 (6.87)	15 (1.48)
Scraper/graver	1 (0.76)	9 (0.89)
Scraper/knife	0	12 (1.19)
Graver/knife	0	5 (0.49)
Spokeshave/graver	0	2 (0.20)
Perforator/scraper	0	1 (0.10)
Spokeshave/knife	0	1 (0.10)
Spokeshave/graver/knife	0	3 (0.30)
Battered cf. pecking stone	1 (0.76)	7 (0.69)
Utilized core	0	2 (0.20)[a]
Total utilized	131 (99.99)	1011 (99.99)[b]

a. One of these core tools is a palm-sized, prism-shaped gouging tool made from silicified coral.

b. This total includes only chert and silicified coral tools. A quartzite grinding stone was recovered from the village (Structure C).

perhaps ownership of, European weapons. Again, the lack of extensive excavation over the entire village precludes conclusive statements regarding access to and distribution of European tools and/or weapons. However, the possibility that restricted access was a factor cannot be dismissed.

Summary

The unfortunate concentration of previous research on Spanish occupational areas, or on village areas whose affiliation could not be determined, has failed to provide data that could be used to examine the interactions between Spaniards and Indians at the Florida missions. At Baptizing Spring it may be tentatively concluded that the items Indians received from Spaniards were primarily prestige goods. These goods, although they had little impact on actual lifeways, were socially important in that they served to reinforce traditional native roles and politico-economic position within village society. It is not the goods themselves that are significant but the right to acquire and own these items that is important. Spanish recognition and validation of Indian roles within the new colonial system would have created strong ties between high-status Indians and Spaniards. These symbolic goods would have been important as long as effective economic control over Indians, and the force to back up this control, was maintained.

Analysis of historical documents suggests that control was largely a matter of power rather than authority during the mission period and, as noted by Emerson (in Hall 1972:205), power resides in the control of valued items. The postulated close relationship between Spaniards and high-status Indians, and their mutual interest in maintaining power, would have set them apart from the rest of the Indian community.[4] Caciques may have become, in the view of the community, more a part of the Spanish organization than they remained part of the Indian social system. In effect, high-status Indians and subordinate Indians were no longer part of the same "moral community" (Salisbury 1976:42). The former position of the cacique, which was based on authority, was later substantiated by Spanish power, and therefore the chiefly authority was destroyed.

As the Spanish/high-status-Indian ability to wield power through the control of valued items and provision of necessities waned—owing largely to cutbacks in supplies from Spain and New Spain—their ability to control the large proportion of the native population also deteriorated. The British, however, could and did offer material benefits, and it is probable that the distribution of these goods was less restrictive. The ungovernable Indian migration and emigration, which occurred throughout the mission period and accelerated during the latter half of the period (Pearson 1968:246, 256–258, 259), testify to the existence of a moribund colonial system long before the advent of external destructive forces in the form of Yamassee and Carolinian raiders.

Editor's Note

This paper was written by L. Jill Loucks in 1983 prior to her untimely death. Although a significant number of mission studies have been undertaken in the intervening years, Jill's thoughtful work at Baptizing Spring continues to make an important contribution to mission research.

Acknowledgments

This article is adapted from the concluding chapter in Loucks (1979). Research at the Baptizing Spring site was funded by the National Endowment for the Humanities (Dr. Charles H. Fairbanks, principal investigator).

Notes (prepared by Jerald T. Milanich and Bonnie G. McEwan)

1. Based on documentary evidence, John Worth (1992:59) suggests that Baptizing Spring is the mission of San Juan de Guacara, which, after the Timucuan rebellion of 1656, was moved to near Charles Spring on the Suwannee River. If true, the site dates to the period ca. 1610–1656. Mission San Agustín de Urica is most likely in southern Hamilton County east of the confluence of the Suwannee and Alapaha rivers (Worth 1992:fig. 2, 70–71).

2. Apalo has since been identified as a mission. See Hann 1990.

3. Structures A, B, and C were excavated in the summer of 1976 by a University of Florida archaeological field school under the direction of Jerald T. Milanich. Nineteen students participated in the two-week project, which was funded by the Wentworth Foundation, whose president, William Goza, also participated in the excavations. Field school students included Joan Ling and Arlene Fradkin, the graduate assistants, and Ann Cordell, Thomas DesJean, Robert

Johnson, Jeffrey Mitchem, and Arthur Rountree. The site was originally discovered by DesJean and Rountree. Ling, aided by other students, prepared a detailed site report on the 1976 excavations, which, along with field notes and collections, were provided to Jill prior to her 1978 excavations.

In 1979 Milanich submitted two radiocarbon samples to the University of Miami Radiocarbon Dating Laboratory for analysis. The first, a charred square-cut pine wall post from Structure B, the possible church, yielded an uncorrected date of 510 ± 70 years: A.D. 1440 (UM-1786). The second, charred wood from a small pit in aboriginal Structure C, was dated at 250 ± 75: A.D. 1700 (UM-1787). Applying the University of Washington Quaternary Isotope Lab radiocarbon calibration program 1987 (Stuiver and Becker 1986) produces ranges of, in the first instance, A.D. 1329–1440 (at one sigma), with the most likely being 1418, and in the second, A.D. 1523–1955 (one sigma), with the most likely being 1650. Averaging the two (at one sigma) yields ranges of A.D. 1437–1519 (80 percent area under the probability distribution) and A.D. 1595–1621 (20 percent area under the probability distribution). These data sets support the contention that the site dates from the first half of the seventeenth century. All collections from the site, including a large sample of charred maize cobs from Structure C, are available for study at the Florida Museum of Natural History.

4. Documentary evidence suggests that this may not have been true. For example, in a letter written by the friars of Apalachee, they remark that "[the natives] discuss their problems with one another. And on such occasions, the cacique and the one who is not are all Indians. And as such, they are easily swayed to come to an agreement on an opinion" (Hann 1993).

Bibliography

Benton, Dale
1976   An Auger Survey of the North St. Augustine Area. Ms. on file, Historic St. Augustine Preservation Board, St. Augustine, Florida.

Deagan, Kathleen A.
1972   Fig Springs: The Mid-Seventeenth Century in North-Central Florida. *Historical Archaeology* 6:23–46.

1978   Cultures in Transition: Fusion and Assimilation among the Eastern Timucua. In *Tacachale: Essays on the Indians of Florida and Southeastern Georgia during the Historic Period*, edited by Jerald T. Milanich and Samuel Proctor, 89–119. Ripley P. Bullen Monographs in Anthropology and History, no. 1. Gainesville: University Presses of Florida.

Geiger, Maynard J., O.F.M.
1937   *The Franciscan Conquest of Florida, 1573–1618*. Studies in Hispanic-American History, vol. 1. Washington, D.C.: Catholic University of America.

1940 *Biographical Dictionary of the Franciscans in Spanish Florida and Cuba (1528–1841)*. Franciscan Studies, no. 21. Paterson, N.J.: St. Anthony's Guild Press.

Goggin, John M.
1953 An Introductory Outline of Timucua Archaeology. *Southeastern Archaeological Conference Newsletter* 3(3):4–17.

1968 *Spanish Majolica in the New World*. Yale University Publications in Anthropology, no. 72. New Haven.

1970 *The Spanish Olive Jar: An Introductory Study*. Yale University Publications in Anthropology, no. 62. New Haven.

Griffin, John W.
1960 A Report on Test Excavations at San Juan del Puerto. *Papers of the Jacksonville Historical Society* 4:63.

Hall, R. H.
1972 *Organizations: Structure and Process*. Englewood Cliffs, N.J.: Prentice-Hall.

Hann, John H.
1990 *Summary Guide to Spanish Florida Missions and Visitas with Churches in the Sixteenth and Seventeenth Centuries*. Washington, D.C.: Academy of American Franciscan History.

1993 *Visitations and Revolts in Florida, 1656–1695*. Florida Archaeology no. 7. Tallahassee: Florida Bureau of Archaeological Research.

Jones, B. Calvin
1970a Missions Reveal State's Spanish-Indian Heritage. *Archives and History News* 1(2):1, 3.

1970b Seventeenth-Century Spanish Mission Cemetery Is Discovered near Tallahassee. *Archives and History News* 1(4):1–2.

1971 State Archeologists Unearth Spanish Mission Ruins. *Archives and History News* 2(4):2.

1972 Spanish Mission Sites Located and Test Excavated. *Archives and History News* 3(6):1–2.

1973 A Semi-Subterranean Structure at Mission San Joseph de Ocuya, Jefferson County, Florida. *Bureau of Historic Sites and Properties Bulletin* 3:1–50.

Jones, William M.
1967 A Report on the Site of San Juan del Puerto, a Spanish Mission Site, Fort George Island, Duval County, Florida. Ms. on file, Department of Anthropology Archeological Laboratory, University of Florida, Gainesville.

Loucks, Lana Jill

1978 Suwannee County Survey Report, Fall 1977: An Account of Sites Located on Property Owned by Owen-Illinois, Inc. Ms. on file, Department of Anthropology, University of Florida, Gainesville.

1979 Political and Economic Interactions between Spaniards and Indians: Archeological and Ethnohistorical Perspectives of the Mission System in Florida. Ph.D. diss., University of Florida. Ann Arbor: University Microfilms.

McMurray, Judith Angley

1973 The Definition of the Ceramic Complex at San Juan del Puerto. Master's thesis, University of Florida, Gainesville.

Milanich, Jerald T.

1972 Excavations at the Richardson Site, Alachua County, Florida: An Early Seventeenth-Century Potano Indian Village (with Notes on Potano Culture Change). *Bureau of Historic Sites and Properties Bulletin* 2:35–61.

1978 The Western Timucua: Patterns of Acculturation and Change. In *Tacachale: Essays on the Indians of Florida and Southeastern Georgia during the Historic Period*, edited by Jerald T. Milanich and Samuel Proctor, 59–88. Ripley P. Bullen Monographs in Anthropology and History, no. 1. Gainesville: University Presses of Florida.

Morrell, L. Ross, and B. Calvin Jones

1970 San Juan de Aspalaga (a Preliminary Architectural Study). *Bureau of Historic Sites and Properties Bulletin* 1:23–43.

Pearson, Fred L.

1968 Spanish-Indian Relations in Florida: A Study of Two *Visitas*, 1657–1678. Ph.D. diss., University of Alabama. Ann Arbor: University Microfilms.

Salisbury, R. F.

1976 Transactions or Transactors? An Economic Anthropologist's View. In *Transactions and Meaning*, edited by B. Kapferer, 41–59. Philadelphia: Institute for the Study of Human Tissues.

Seaberg, Lillian M.

1951 Report on the Indian Site at the "Fountain of Youth," St. Augustine. Ms. on file, Department of Anthropology Archeology Laboratory, University of Florida, Gainesville.

1955 The Zetrouer Site: Indian and Spanish in Central Florida. Master's thesis, University of Florida, Gainesville.

Smith, Hale G.

1948 Two Historical Archaeological Periods in Florida. *American Antiquity* 13(4):313–319.

1951a Leon-Jefferson Ceramic Types. In *Here They Once Stood: The Tragic End of the Apalachee Missions*, by Mark F. Boyd, Hale G. Smith, and John W. Griffin, 163–174. Gainesville: University of Florida Press.

1951b A Spanish Mission Site in Jefferson County, Florida. In *Here They Once Stood: The Tragic End of the Apalachee Missions*, by Mark F. Boyd, Hale G. Smith, and John W. Griffin, 107–136. Gainesville: University of Florida Press.

Spellman, Charles W.
1965 The Golden Age of the Florida Missions, 1632–1674. *Catholic Historical Review* 51:354–372.

Stuiver, Minze, and Bernd Becker
1986 High-Precision Decadal Calibration of the Radiocarbon Time Scale, A.D. 1950–2500 B.C. *Radiocarbon* 28(2B):863–910.

Symes, M. I., and M. E. Stephens
1965 A 272: The Fox Pond Site. *The Florida Anthropologist* 18(2):65–76.

Worth, John E.
1992 The Timucuan Missions of Spanish Florida and the Rebellion of 1656. Ph.D. diss., University of Florida.

❂ 9 ❂

Excavations in the Fig Springs Mission Burial Area

LISA M. HOSHOWER
JERALD T. MILANICH

The seventeenth-century Fig Springs mission site is believed to be the mission of San Martín de Timucua. The mission complex was originally located and tested by Kenneth Johnson in 1986 (Johnson 1987, 1990). Earlier, archaeologists had recovered and studied mission period Spanish and aboriginal artifacts from a spring adjacent to the mission complex (Deagan 1972; Goggin 1953). Following Johnson's initial work, Brent Weisman conducted systematic testing of the site and excavated mission structures and portions of the aboriginal village (Weisman 1988a, 1988b, 1989, and this volume). The tests by Johnson and Weisman pinpointed the location of the burial area, thought to be a cemetery or *campo santo*, making it possible for the 1990 fieldwork to focus on that feature of the site (fig. 9.1).

The 1990 excavations in the burial area were a six-week pilot project to (1) determine the feasibility of on-site osteological analysis (with re-burial of human remains following immediately) and (2) gather bio-anthropological data on the mission population, the northern Utina Indians, a Timucuan-speaking people reported in seventeenth-century documents to have suffered from epidemic diseases (for information on the northern Utina, see Johnson 1991:72–108; see Milner 1980, on epidemics in the Southeast; and see Newman 1976).[1] Hoshower served as bioanthropologist for the project and provided the data for this report. Milanich was project director and archaeologist.

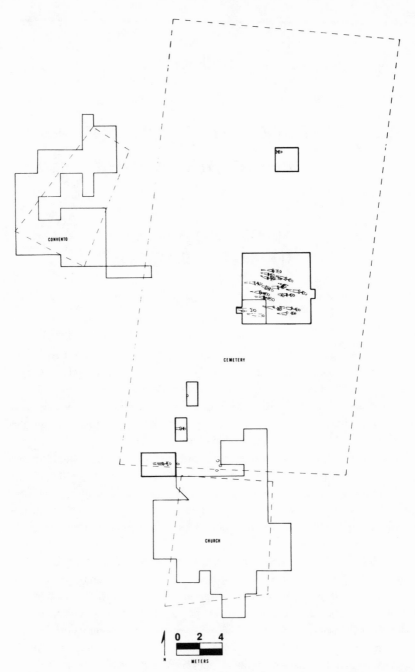

CONVENTO

CEMETERY

CHURCH

0   2   4
METERS
N

Figure 9.1. Architectural features at the Fig Springs site. The locations of the church
and *convento* indicated by dashes are based on Weisman's previous excavations
(1988a, 1988b, 1989), the outlines of which are shown. Similarly, the reconstructed

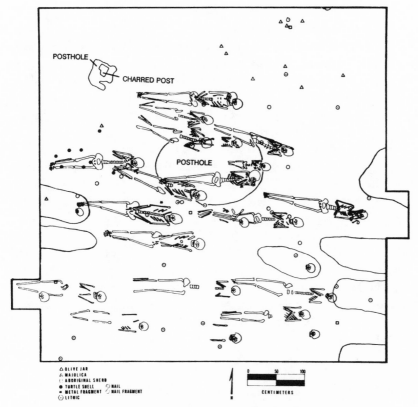

Figure 9.2. 1990 excavations with interments and artifacts.

As it turned out, the archaeology of the burial area was more complex than anticipated and a third goal emerged: to interpret architectural features—nails and spikes, a post, and a possible clay floor—present in what was thought to be a cemetery (see fig. 9.2). Adding to the complexity of the archaeological situation was a high density of interments, including intrusive burials and multiple burials. In the excavated portion of the burial area, the interments and archaeological remains more closely resembled the subfloor interments reported for the church of Mission Santa Catalina de Guale on the Georgia coast (Larsen 1990; Thomas

---

extent of the cemetery (also shown by dashes) is based on data recovered by Weisman's tests and augering. The 6-m² unit in the cemetery (north of the church) was excavated in 1990 and encompasses one of Weisman's tests (in the southwest corner).

1987) than they did the cemetery burials of Mission Santa Catalina on Amelia Island, Florida (Saunders 1988).

The clay floor(s) as well as most of the artifacts recovered were on the seventeenth-century ground surface 10–15 cm below the present surface. Because of the overlapping nature of graves, it was almost impossible to recognize individual burial pits at the level of the floor or even just below it. At times, individual graves could only be distinguished when the remains of the person interred in the grave were being cleared. At this elevation, roughly 1.5 m below the floor, the darker, mottled fill of individual grave pits (at times with clay in the fill) could be distinguished from the sand matrix.

Two hypotheses emerged to explain the clay floor: it was the floor of a large structure; or the clay was from several small (in horizontal extent) floors, perhaps floors of small chapels or other structures erected in a cemetery (such structures might have been for family or other kin groups interred below the building floors). In the short time in the field neither hypothesis was negated. However, the presence of a single small post (charred) and a possible large posthole (see fig. 9.2), as well as many nail and nail fragments, supported the contention that some type of structure(s) was present.

Fig Springs Demographic Profile

During the six weeks of fieldwork, a total of 23 skeletons were excavated from four contiguous 3-m-by-3-m excavation units (see fig. 9.3; the entire 36 m^2 was not excavated; the extent of the burial area, based on Weisman's tests and shown in figure 9.1, and the density of interments encountered in 1990 suggest there could be as many as 900 individuals in the burial area). While overall preservation at the burial area was good, the majority of the pubic symphyseal faces were subject to taphonomic forces that precluded complete and intact retrieval from the soil matrix. Determination of adult age was therefore based on the auricular surface of the ilium (Lovejoy et al. 1985) and dental wear (Miles 1962, 1963, 1978). Immature individuals were aged through patterns of dental development, diaphyseal length of long bones (Ubelaker 1978), and epiphyseal closure of the long bones (Bass 1987). Determination of sex was based on general robusticity, sexual dimorphism (Bass 1987; Krogman and Iscan 1986), and pelvic morphology (Phenice 1969).

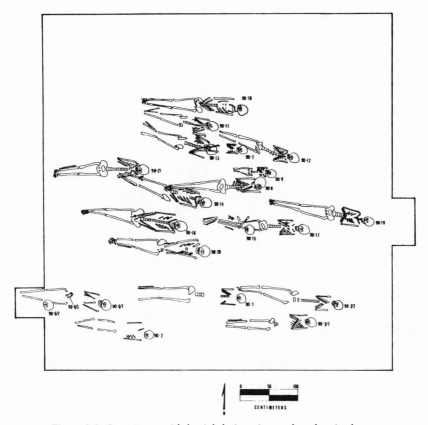

Figure 9.3. Interments with burial designations referred to in the text.

Common to all biological anthropological analyses of skeletal populations is the basic and necessary assumption that the skeletal collection is
a mortality sample of the living population from which it came (Cook
1981). A representative demographic profile is essential for the interpretation of the impact of social, environmental, and biological consequences
on archaeological populations. It has been demonstrated that inclusions
of individuals in the cemetery implies inclusion of those individuals in the
corporate group (Binford 1971; Charles and Buikstra 1983; O'Shea
1981, 1984). Analysis of the Fig Springs population was conducted
within these parameters. Tables 9.1–9.3 provide demographic summa-
tions for the 23 individuals and tables 9.4–9.6 provide summaries of
pathology data; figure 9.4 shows adult stature.

It is necessary that one proceed with extreme caution when attempt-

TABLE 9.1. Sex Ratio

Sex	Number	% of total
Female	5	22
Male	9	39
Subadult	5	22
Adult	4	17
Total	23	100

ing to generalize about a population from a small and spatially localized sample. Preliminary data suggest, however, that peak mortality for both genders fell between 25 and 30 years of age (see tables 9.2 and 9.3). The biological data indicate that males were more affected by systemic and specific diseases than were females. This gender-biased distribution suggests that the Spanish mission system impacted more heavily on the adult male cohort. As the incidence and distribution of enamel hypoplasias show that both female and male preadults were equally subjected to the adverse effects of the mission environment, an explanation must be sought for the observed dichotomy in adult disease involvement. It may be suggested that this pattern is a correlate of the *repartimiento*, the native labor force organized by the Spanish and composed of the male members of the mission population.

Several rather consistent trends have been noted in temporally and

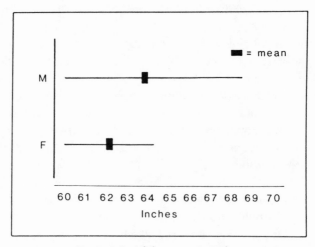

Figure 9.4. Adult stature in inches.

TABLE 9.2. Estimated Biological Age at Death Based on Dental Wear Patterns

Age	Number
Infant	1
2.5–3.0 yrs	1
4.0–5.0 yrs	1
4.5–5.5 yrs	1
13–15 yrs	1
20–25 yrs	2
25–30 yrs	8
30–35 yrs	4
35–40 yrs	2
40–45 yrs	0
45+ yrs	1
Mature adult	1
Total	23

spatially distinct archaeological populations. Most common is the under-enumeration of infants and individuals over 50 years of age. Typically the underrepresentation of infants and young children has been attributed to rapid disintegration of incompletely calcified bones by taphonomic forces (Gordon and Buikstra 1981). Older adults are particularly vulnerable to bone loss with advancing age (osteoporosis), suggesting that these fragile remains may be increasingly susceptible to disintegration after burial (Walker, Johnson, and Lambert 1988). Although such taphonomic forces may explain the underenumeration of infants, young children, and older adults in the Fig Springs collection, future research will focus on the synergistic relationships that exist among social, cultural, environmental, behavioral, nutritional, systemic, and pathogenic stressors.

TABLE 9.3. Combined Adult Sex and Age Data

Age	Female	Male	?
20–25 yrs	1	1	0
25–30 yrs	3	3	2
30–35 yrs	0	3	1
35–40 yrs	0	2	0
45+ yrs	1	0	1
Total	5	9	4

Method of Interment

The mortuary program at Fig Springs is similar to those followed at other archaeologically documented burial areas in *La Florida* (e.g., Jones and Shapiro 1990; Larsen 1990; Saunders 1988; Thomas 1987, 1990). At Fig Springs individuals were interred fully articulated (extended), supine, and in an east-west direction, with heads placed east. All burials were aligned parallel to the long axis of the nearby presumed church. The hands of some of the deceased were clasped beneath the mandible (chin). For others the arms were folded across the chest or crossed on the abdomen. There is no physical evidence for the presence of coffins or burial shrouds.

Five of the 23 individuals are represented by incomplete and disarticulated remains. These individuals may represent initial interments that were subsequently disturbed by later burials. Crowded cemetery conditions lend credence to this conclusion. Burial 90-1 included an articulated male, 25–30 years of age, with numerous cranial fragments representing one infant and one adult scattered across the top of the grave. Burial 90-6, an articulated 25-to-30-year-old individual, also included cranial fragments of two additional adults in the pit fill. Burial 90-15, whose disarticulated remains included cranial fragments, left femur and os coxae, and numerous rib fragments, was found scattered directly across the articulated remains of Burial 90-17.

Within the excavated portion of the burial area there exists no discernible pattern of age or sex distribution. In addition, lack of burial furniture precludes any distinction of social status. Only three burials were loosely associated with grave goods. Burial 90-17, a 45+-year-old female, had a chert knife (?) point resting directly upon her right scapula. Analysis of the surrounding osteological tissue failed to reveal any trauma to the area. Nineteen small blue glass beads were found near the feet of Burial 90-18. It is unclear whether these beads were remnants of an anklet or adornment on foot garb. Under the feet of Burial 90-21, a male 30–35 years of age, a wrought iron Spanish nail was discovered, and numerous fragments of turtle carapace were found scattered across the surface of the grave pit fill. In addition, numerous Spanish nails and nail fragments, as well as a few aboriginal Leon-Jefferson potsherds and Spanish olive jar and majolica sherds, were recovered both from the old ground surface and in burial pit fill (fig. 9.2). No pattern of artifact distribution was discerned.

Depth of interment, measured at the top of each cranium, varies between 13 cm and 63 cm below ground surface. The wide range of depths, coupled with clear evidence of intrusive burial episodes, strongly indicates that the burial area was in use for at least several years. At present it is impossible to provide a more concise temporal evaluation. A single radiocarbon date was obtained from a square-cut charred post in a shallow posthole (fig. 9.2). That date is 450 ± 50 B.P.: A.D. 1500 radiocarbon years (C_{13} adjusted age; Beta-41052). This yields a calibrated date (at two sigmas) of A.D. 1334–1337, 1410–1520, or 1600–1616 (based on Stuiver and Reimer 1986; the calibration curve offers three possibilities for 450 B.P.). When these data are considered, there is a 95 percent chance the true calibrated date is between A.D. 1334–1616 with the most likely date being A.D. 1437.

The 1990 excavations revealed two patterns (fig. 9.3). In the southern portion of the excavation unit are the remains of nine individuals. Burial 90-2 is a single interment episode with a clearly defined burial pit. Burials 90-1 and 90-6 are also individual interments and each was within a distinct burial pit. Included in the pit fill of both individuals, however, were the remains of two additional disarticulated individuals, indicating Burials 90-1 and 90-6 were intrusive interments. Burial 90-3 is a multiple burial, also with a clear burial pit outline. (Multiple burials are defined here as the interment of two or more individuals.) Individuals 1 and 2, of Burial 90-3, were interred at virtually the same depth and north-south axis, with approximately 5 cm separating the humeri. Given the obviously fleshed condition of the remains at burial, it is logical to assume that a single burial episode had occurred. The unexcavated burial immediately south of Burial 90-3, Individual 2, is likely part of the same burial episode. The individual skeletons in this southern portion of the excavation unit are less well preserved than their more northerly counterparts (fig. 9.3). This suggests that the southern individuals were interred in different circumstances from those of the interments of the more northerly individuals.

The second mortuary pattern, present in the center of the excavation unit, is not as readily defined. Within this area are 14 burials, some of which were intrusive, indicating repeated use of this portion of the cemetery. One of two distinct burial pit outlines was located directly at excavation grid point 319N319E. Excavation was initiated at this point, with the area of excavation expanded as the presence of additional elements was discerned.

Reconstruction of the sequence of burial events within this area focused on body position, missing skeletal elements (due to intrusion of later interments), and depth-below-surface of interments. The following scenario is suggested (see fig. 9.3):

1. Burials 90-10, 90-11, 90-13, 90-14, 90-18, and 90-20 appear to be oriented along the same north-south axis, suggesting some burials were made in ordered rows. Five of the six burials are osteologically complete and the depths of the six crania range between 39 cm and 59 cm below ground surface. The even spacing of the six interments further suggests either a single interment episode for the six or that some type of grave marker was in use.

2. Burial 90-21 was interred after the burial of the six individuals described above. Burial 90-14 is missing all the bones of both feet. Several scattered metatarsals and tarsals were discovered in the pit fill for Individual 90-21, suggesting the foot bones of Burial 90-14 were disturbed during the burial of 90-21.

3. Burial 90-12, a 21-to-25-year-old female, Burial 90-7, a 2.5-to-3.0-year-old child, and Burial 90-9, a 4-to-5-year-old child, seem to represent a multiple burial. Both juvenile crania are buried at a depth of 33 cm below ground surface, with the adult cranium at 43 cm below ground surface. Burial 90-7 was placed in direct contact with the adult female, Burial 90-12.

4. When compared to the multiple burial described above, Burial 90-8, a 30-to-35-year-old male, appears to represent a distinct yet temporally and spatially contemporaneous interment episode. While a distinct and separate pit outline was observed, this individual's cranium rests 34 cm below ground surface and is in direct contact with the left radius of Individual 90-9. The left humerus of 90-9 was completely missing, and the left ulna was discovered resting beside the cranium of 90-8.

5. Because all the foot bones are missing from Burials 90-7 and 90-12, it is likely they were interred before Burials 90-11 and 90-13, respectively.

6. Burials 90-15, 90-17, and 90-19 appear not to be directly associated with any of the above episodes. Burial 90-17, missing all the foot bones, was probably an earlier interment disturbed by the burial of Individual 90-15.

The only other contemporary Spanish mission cemetery for which there is published bioanthropological and archaeological data is the site of Santa Catalina de Guale on the Georgia coast (Larsen 1990). Excavation of 431 individuals from a 20-m-by-11-m portion of the church revealed the following traits: (1) a high degree of disturbance as a result of intrusive burial episodes and extensive use; (2) a majority of interments of single individuals; (3) no clear patterns of distribution by age or sex; and (4) an artifact-rich inventory (Larsen 1990; Thomas 1987; nearly all the Santa Catalina artifacts were either beads interred with individuals or artifacts from the end of the church where the altar may have stood). The results of the Fig Springs excavations are somewhat similar, but, as indicated above, the majority of the excavated Fig Springs interments (61 percent) are multiple burials, and the artifact inventory, especially objects accompanying individuals, is small. The interment of multiple individuals in a single grave, relatively common at Fig Springs, may be a way to save labor (Milner 1980) and could reflect fatal disease epidemics that necessitated such a practice.

Osteological Pathologies

Degree of skeletal representation is a key variable in the analysis of pathology in archaeological samples. The various stages of skeletal completeness for the 23 individuals are as follows: 8 individuals complete; 5 individuals represented by disarticulated fragments only; 4 individuals virtually complete, missing feet only; 1 individual virtually complete, missing hands and feet; and 5 individuals missing various combinations of hands, feet, ribs, and/or vertebrae.

This analysis of pathologies must therefore be tempered by the variation in numbers of observable osteological elements. Unfortunately, given the fragmented and incomplete nature of several remains, there is an uncontrollable bias built into this analysis. The inherent nature of the bias predisposes toward a conservative profile, as it is a virtual certainty that additional pathologies would be revealed by total skeletal representation. Evaluation of the Fig Springs pathologies was conducted within these parameters (see table 9.4).

Seven individuals displayed no signs of pathology. Four of these individuals—Burial 90-1/2, an infant; Burial 90-1/3, an individual 13–15 years of age; Burial 90-6/2, a 25-to-30-year-old; and Burial 90-6/3, an

TABLE 9.4. Bone Pathology Data Summary

MNI	23
# observable for pathologies	23
# with no pathologies	7 (30%)
Periosteal lesions	12 (52%)
Porotic hyperostosis	7 (30%)
Periosteal reaction, porotic hyperostosis, enamel hypoplasias	12 (52%)
Trauma	3 (13%)
Osteoarthritis	6 (26%)

adult—are represented by cranial fragments only. Three burials— 90-3/1, a 25-to-30-year-old male; 90-6/1, a 25-to-30-year-old; and 90-15, a 4.5-to-5.5-year-old child—are virtually complete.

Five individuals—Burial 90-1, a 25-to-30-year-old male; Burial 90-2, aged 30–35; Burial 90-12, a 21-to-25-year-old female; Burial 90-17, 45+-year-old female; and Burial 90-7, a 2.5-to-3.0-year-old child—were affected by periosteal reactions of the lower limb elements. All skeletons were virtually complete.

Burial 90-2 also displayed a compression fracture of the third and fourth cervical vertebrae. Unfortunately, the seven cervical vertebrae were the only preserved spinal elements. Burial 90-3/2, a 25-to-30-year-old female with a virtually complete skeletal inventory, showed some slight lipping on the olecranon of the left ulna.

In 10 individuals various combinations of pathologies were present. Individual 90-8 (skeleton complete), a 30-to-35-year-old male, displayed a fractured and completely remodeled left fourth metacarpal; slight lipping of all articular surfaces; Schmorl's nodes on the first, second, and third lumbar vertebrae; and platycynemia. In addition, there were bone spicules on the posterior portions of the tibular medial malleoli.

Individual 90-9, 4–5 years old (missing the foot bones), displayed symmetrically active and remodeled cribra orbitalia, active pinpoint porotic hyperostosis on the left and right parietals and at nasion, and slight eburnation on the auricular surface of the left ilium. In addition, the right superior articular facet of the first cervical vertebra was flattened, with a small amount of lipping on the posterior rim and a small, slightly porous depressed area that articulated with a raised porous portion of the right occipital condyle.

Individual 90-10, a 25-to-30-year-old female (skeleton complete), was affected by a slight amount of osteoarthritis on the articular joints of the elbow, patellae, tali, and calcanei. Degenerative changes were also present on the vertebral bodies. There was a slightly remodeled periosteal reactive area along the entire posterior shaft of the right fibula, a button osteoma on the distal posterior shaft of the right tibia, and active porotic hyperostosis on the occipital protuberance.

Burial 90-11, a 20-to-25-year-old male (skeleton complete), showed evidence of several forms of cranial pathology. Healed and active porotic hyperostosis was observed on the frontal and left parietal bones. A remodeled depression fracture was evident near the glabella. The right ulna displayed a small healed periosteal reactive area.

Individual 90-13, a 25-to-30-year-old female (skeleton complete), displayed active pinpoint porotic hyperostosis on the frontal and occipital bones. Six small button osteomas, three on each parietal bone, were present. The vertebral column showed a significant amount of osteophytosis, especially pronounced in the cervical region. In addition, there were Schmorl's nodes on the inferior body of the fifth and the superior body of the sixth cervical vertebra. Both vertebral bodies were collapsed, with pronounced osteophyte development.

Individual 90-14, a 35-to-40-year-old male (skeleton virtually complete), showed active symmetrical pinpoint porotic hyperostosis of the parietal bones. There were active periosteal areas along the medial shaft of the left tibia and medial distal shaft of the right humerus.

Burial 90-18, a 20-to-25-year-old male (skeleton complete), displayed active pinpoint porotic hyperostosis on the frontal bone. A slight amount of arthritic degeneration was observed along the superior and inferior aspects of the vertebral bodies, elbow joints, and femoral epicondyles. A slight amount of active periostitis was present along the diaphyses of both fibulae and the left ulna and right tibia. The right humerus displayed evidence of osteomyelitis, with a small remodeled cloaca surrounded by an area of remodeled periosteal activity on the anterior aspect of the proximal diaphysis.

Individual 90-19, a 25-to-30-year-old male (missing only the thoracic vertebrae), showed slight arthritic degeneration on the superior and inferior bodies of the cervical and lumbar vertebrae, the lateral articular surfaces of the clavicles, and the proximal articular facets of the metatarsals. A slight amount of periosteal reaction was observed on the right femur and fibula. Although lacking any indication of infection or remodeling, the hand phalanges appeared expanded.

Burial 90-20, a 35-to-40-year-old male (skeleton complete), displayed slight active periosteal reactions on the right fibula and tibia. Porotic hyperostosis was evident on the occipital bone.

Individual 90-21, a 30-to-35-year-old male (missing foot phalanges only), showed a slight amount of arthritic degeneration on all articular long bone surfaces and vertebral bodies, with pronounced osteophyte activity on the superior border of the fifth lumbar vertebra, which was collapsed along with the superior body of the first sacral vertebra. In addition, the fourth and fifth cervical vertebrae were fused at the right pedicles. There was a small amount of active periostitis on the humeri and the left third and fourth metatarsals. The bones of the arms appeared asymmetrical. The left humerus, ulna, and radius showed no signs of infection or remodeling. The diaphyses were, however, noticeably expanded in comparison to their right counterparts. In addition, the left ulna and radius had sharp interosseous crests. The left femur was heavily remodeled, with lateral torsion of the proximal shaft. These two processes appeared to be the result of remodeling associated with a greenstick fracture during the growth stage. Both tibiae shafts were expanded, the right more so than the left, yet they did not display any macroscopic evidence of pathology.

Seven of the 23 individuals (30 percent) analyzed exhibited no evidence of pathology. Twelve (52 percent) individuals were affected with periosteal inflammation. The major areas were along the lateral shafts of the tibiae and the medial shafts of the fibulae; expression was slight. All age segments of the sample were affected, and males (30 percent) were more than twice as likely to be affected than were females (13 percent). This pattern of involvement is unlike that reported by Powell (1988, 1990) in a diagnosis of endemic treponematosis among the Irene Mound (coastal Georgia) skeletal collection. In the Irene population the major focus of periosteal inflammation was localized along the anterior crests of the tibiae. Additional indicators of treponematosis in the Irene Mound population included more extensive pathological involvement (of the tibiae) approaching the classic deformity known as "sabre shins," remodeling indicative of extensive healing and quiescence of the disease prior to death, and gummatous ulcers known as "caries sicca" (Powell 1990:28–29). This etiology is completely lacking in the Fig Springs population.

Three trauma-related skeletal lesions were observed: a compression fracture of the third and fourth cervical vertebrae (of a 25-to-30-year-old adult of unknown sex), a fractured fourth metacarpal (a 35-to-40-year-old male), and a depression fracture at glabella (a 25-to-30-year-old male). Osteoarthritis affected 26 percent of the population, with males twice as likely as females to exhibit the condition. Porotic hyperostosis was present in 7 individuals (30 percent of the population), with males twice as likely as females to exhibit the disease.

Dental Pathologies

No teeth were recovered for three individuals, and another was represented by only a healthy upper-right second permanent molar. Of the other individuals, only two—Burial 90-7, a 2.5-to-3.0-year-old child, and Burial 90-1, a 25-to-30-year-old male—displayed a total lack of dental pathology (table 9.5).

Nineteen individuals (83 percent) with virtually intact dental arcades were scored for occlusal wear—enamel enfacets, dentin cupping, secondary dentin exposure, pulp cavity exposure, and coalescing cusps. These remains all displayed rates of attrition that are relatively severe and are likely attributable both to diet and to food preparation techniques.

The reconstruction of a representative demographic profile in archaeological populations is dependent on accurate age estimation at the individual level. It is essential that the remains be evaluated by as many independent indicators of age and sex as possible. At the Fig Springs site the dental remains are both better preserved and more abundant than postcranial skeletal elements typically used by biological anthropologists for aging. One of the authors (Hoshower) has chosen to develop age stages from seriation of occlusal wear patterns for the Fig Springs Native

TABLE 9.5. Dental Pathology Data

MNI	23
# observable for pathologies	19
# with no pathologies	2 (10.5%)
Enamel hypoplasias	15 (78.9%)
Incidence of caries	4.2%
Incidental rate of abscesses	1.8%
Calculus	7 (36.8%)
Periodontal disease	0
Dental crowding	6 (31.6%)

American remains based on the method developed by Miles (1962, 1963, 1978). Not only does the Miles method allow for the establishment of a population-specific age profile, but numerous researchers have also demonstrated it to be a reliable indicator of age at death (e.g., Kieser, Preston, and Evans 1983; Lovejoy 1985; Nowell 1978; Smith 1984; Walker, Dean, and Shapiro 1991; Wolpoff 1979). Of special importance for the Fig Springs population is the fact that Russell and co-workers have shown that modifications to the Miles system are both highly accurate and reliable for the Spanish period Guale, a collection from the Georgia coast contemporary with the Fig Springs population (Russell, Choi, and Larsen 1990).

It should be noted that this seriation was developed on the remains excavated in the 1991 field season at Fig Springs, the results of which were then applied to the dental charts of the 1990-excavated population (reported here), which had been scored using Brothwell (1963, 1967) as a reference. As a result, all but two individuals 20–25 years of age were reclassified. This procedure permitted a population-specific demographic profile to be developed for the Fig Springs interments.

Fifteen (88 percent) of the 17 observable individuals show evidence for enamel hypoplasias. Enamel hypoplasias are transverse linear depressions that form in the enamel during dental development as a response to a variety of systemic stressors, including nutrition, infectious disease, localized trauma, or metabolic systemic stress. Because the growth of dental tissue is cumulative and once formed remains unaltered, these disrupted growth patterns may be used to estimate an individual's developmental age at time of defect formation (Rose, Condon, and Goodman 1985).

A population subset of eight individuals was drawn from the "best-teeth" analysis for enamel hypoplasias (Goodman et al. 1984). In the Fig Springs population the most hypoplasias occurred between the ages of 2.0 to 5.0 years, which is consistent with the hypothesis that enamel hypoplasias are indicators of systemic or nutritional stress associated with weaning (Rose, Condon, and Goodman 1985).

Preliminary analysis of the 1991 data indicates a similar age of occurrence. In both the 1990 and 1991 samples, all individuals lacking enamel hypoplasias were also void of bone pathologies. Data from the 1991 analysis appear to indicate that at Fig Springs the incidence rate of enamel hypoplasias increased through time. It may be suggested that a dynamic relationship exists between hypoplastic formation, weaning, nutritional stress, and epidemic-induced stress. Investigators of archaeological populations repeatedly remark on the commonality of high morbidity at approximately age 2, a critical period in postnatal human life, especially the period following weaning from mother's milk (Wood 1983). In an epidemic, such as measles, no active immunity exists. Passive immunity is acquired by those individuals who survive the disease. Mothers who have survived a measles outbreak will confer passive immunity on their children transplacentally during the last month of pregnancy. The measles antibody has a half-life of 21 days. The amount of antibody present in an infant is dependent on the amount conferred at birth. During stress episodes amino acids typically earmarked for skeletal growth will be mobilized in the fight to adapt to the stress (Acheson 1960). Nutritional deficiencies develop as these nutrients, vital to skeletal growth, are redirected for survival. An increase in the frequency of hypoplastic banding of the enamel may be correlate of such a dynamic relationship among weaning, nutritional deficiency, and epidemic episodes.

Occlusal surface caries were present in 16 of 381 observable teeth, an incidence rate of 4.2 percent. No interproximal caries were observed. Pronounced calculus was present on 7 of the 19 (36.8 percent) observable individuals.

Dental caries is a disease process characterized by the focal demineralization of dental hard tissues by organic acids produced by the bacterial fermentation of dietary carbohydrates, especially sugars (Larsen 1987:375). Maize is an example of a highly cariogenic food, known to promote tooth decay, because it contains a relatively large amount of the simple sugar sucrose, which acts as a pathway for oral bacteria, such as lactobacilli or streptococci (Keyes 1968). The bacteria produce an acid that destroys the enamel and eventually the underlying dentine. Thus dental caries is a pathological process that affects either the occlusal or interproximal tooth surfaces or, after destruction of the enamel or recession of the gingiva, the tooth root.

There is general agreement that prevalence of dental caries increases as populations shift to agricultural subsistence patterns (Cohen and Armelagos 1984; Larsen 1987; Powell 1985). Hutchinson (1991:125) reports that Larsen and co-workers found that populations from the Georgia coast known to have had maize-dependent diets displayed carious lesions rates in excess of 7 percent. He also reports a carious lesion rate of 6.1

percent in the Tatham Mound skeletal series, a Timucuan population from west-central Florida thought not to be heavily dependent on maize (Hutchinson 1991).

The combined data for the 1990 and 1991 Fig Springs samples indicate a rate of carious lesions (1489 teeth examined; 72 caries for a 4.7 percent rate of incidence) that is lower than both the St. Catherines and Tatham Mound data. However, this relatively low prevalence of caries is not consistent with the generally accepted characterization of the northern Utina peoples as maize agriculturists. Factors beside or in addition to agriculture may be causal in the prevalence of caries in these three southeastern U.S. populations.

Although the difference is not significant, the fact that an appreciatively higher portion of the males (55 percent versus 20 percent of females) displayed carious lesions is a reversal of the generally held pattern of relatively greater occurrence of dental caries in females (see review in Larsen 1987). Various explanations have been generated for this pattern: greater ingestion of plant carbohydrates by females; earlier age of tooth eruption in females; and physiological stresses associated with pregnancy. It will be interesting to see whether this pattern of a sexually dimorphic rate of occurrence in dental caries continues with increased sampling.

Five individuals (22 percent) showed evidence for dental crowding. Although dental crowding may be an indication of nutritional or chronic, severe stress in archaeological populations (Goodman et al. 1984), genetic, environmental, or even evolutionary factors may be more common causes. Future research at Fig Springs will help clarify this issue.

Summary

Excavations in the burial area associated with the Fig Spring mission complex have produced evidence of architectural features thought to be associated with a structure or structures. As is evident from figure 9.1, the projected size of the burial area (approximately 20 m by 37 m, based on data from Johnson's and Weisman's tests) makes it unlikely that all the burials were within a single structure.

However, the projected 20-m width of the burial area is well within the range of the St. Catherines Island and Amelia Island churches, which did contain burials. Perhaps a portion of the burial area was within a church (or churches) and the remainder was a cemetery immediately adjacent. Another possibility is that the clay floors are from small structures erected in a cemetery and serving individual families or other kin groups.

Excavations did not reveal any evidence for preferential burial treatment. Nor did there appear to be any relationship between age of death and/or sex and disease expression (table 9.6). Initial skeletal analysis indicates the Fig Springs population will display symptoms of cumulative episodes of systemic stress. Disease may have been chronic, with health generally compromised and punctuated by episodic stress. It is entirely possible, therefore, that any of the epidemics described by the Franciscan priests could have had a profound and detrimental effect on the Fig Springs population. At Fig Springs, evidence for death by epidemic may be inferred from (1) multiple burials and (2) lack of severe pathological expressions (death from an epidemic would not permit sufficient time for osseous tissue remodeling). Continued excavation of the Fig Springs burial area will expand the bioanthropological data base and help clarify these issues.

Finally, we learned that on-site analysis of the burial population, followed by immediately reburial, was only partially successful, because it did not allow sufficient comparative analysis. It is recommended that future research at this and other sites where reburial is called for allow sufficient opportunity not only for analysis of individuals but for comparative studies of the entire sample as well.

Postscript

In 1991 additional, more extensive excavations were carried out in the Fig Springs burial area. Rebecca Saunders served as field archaeologist and Hoshower again provided the bioanthropological analysis.

It was determined that the burial area was much smaller than the 20-m-by-37-m area projected based on earlier testing. More important, it was found that the burials had been placed through the floor(s) of a structure measuring approximately 15 m by 25 m, most likely the mission church of San Martín. No separate cemetery was present. The church, which was rebuilt or refloored at least once, originally had a dirt floor that was later replaced with a clay floor. It is now estimated that 400–500 interments were made through the floors of the church. The location of this

TABLE 9.6. Skeletal Pathology

Burial	Age[a]	Sex	Skeletal representation	Pathology observed
90-1/1	25–30	M	Virtually complete	Periosteal reactive area on lower limbs
90-1/2	Infant	?	Cranial fragments	None
90-1/3	13–15	?	Cranial fragments	None
90-2	30–35	?	Virtually complete	Compression fracture C3-4; periosteal reactive area on lower limbs
90-3/1	25–30	M	Virtually complete	None
90-3/2	25–30	F	Virtually complete	Slight osteoarthritis (elbow)
90-4			Not excavated	
90-5			Not excavated	
90-6/1	25–30	?	Virtually complete	None
90-6/2	25–30	?	Cranial frags. and teeth	None
90-6/3	Adult	?	Cranial fragments	None
90-7	2.5–3.5	?	Virtually complete	Periosteal reactive area on lower limbs
90-8	30–35	M	Complete	Schmorl's nodes L1, 2, 3; fractured MC; slight osteoarthritis; retroverted tibiae
90-9	4–5	?	Missing feet	Active and healed cribra and porotic hyperostosis; lipping C1 and occipital condyle; eburnation
90-10	25–30	F	Complete	Slight osteoarthritis at joints; healed periosteal areas; active porotic hyperostosis; button osteoma on tibia
90-11	30–35	M	Complete	Healed porotic hyperostosis; periostitis; depression fracture glabella
90-12	21–25	F	Virtually complete	Periosteal reactive area on lower limbs
90-13	25–30	F	Complete	Active porotic hyperostosis; 3 button osteomas on parietals, osteoarthritis; collapsed C5-6; osteophytosis
90-14	35–40	M	Complete	Active porotic hyperostosis; periosteal reactive areas
90-15	4.5–5.5	?	Virtually complete	None
90-16			Not excavated	
90-17	45+	F	Virtually complete	Periosteal reactive areas on lower limbs

TABLE 9.6. *(Continued)*

Burial	Age[a]	Sex	Skeletal representation	Pathology observed
90-18	20–25	M	Complete	Active periosteal areas and porotic hyperostosis, slight osteoarthritis on vertebrae and joints
90-19	25–30	M	Missing thoracic	Slight osteoarthritis on vertebrae and vertebrae joints; periosteal area on femur; expanded hand phalange shafts
90-20	35–40	M	Complete	Active porotic hyperostosis and periosteal areas
90-21	30–35	M	Missing foot phalanges	Slight osteoarthritis on joints and vertebrae; L5 and S1 collapsed; osteophyte activity; C4-5 fused; greenstick fracture on femur

a. Age is given in years.

church is approximately the central one-third of the burial area labeled in figure 9.1 as "cemetery"; the church extends slightly west of the dotted line in that figure that delineates the west edge of the "cemetery" into the "*convento*." We believe that the "*convento*" represents architectural features and debris from the western end of the church (the long axis of which is oriented approximately east-west).

Presence of a second burial area was verified in 1991. That burial area is found around the structure labeled "church" in figure 9.1 and excavated by Weisman. It encompasses the three burials just north of that structure (see fig. 9.1; two of the burials were only partially cleared in the testing project and are shown as such in the figure). We believe that this relatively small "church" was an early church at the mission and that interments were made around it, at least on the north, east, and south sides. On the north and east sides the burials abutted the wall of the structure.

The two-floored church with subfloor burials whose presence was verified in 1991 is to the north of the early, small church and was probably later in time. The 1991 excavations demonstrated that the burials around the early church do not extend north to the two-floored church with its subfloor burials.

Additional excavations are planned for the site to gather more information on the presumed later church and to gather a larger skeletal sample from both burial areas.

Acknowledgments

We are grateful to the Florida Department of Natural Resources, Division of Recreation and Parks, for their support of this project. Azell G. Nail, Craig N. Parenteau, Paul E. Perras, and Lanette H. Radel are due special thanks. James J. Miller (Florida Division of Historical Resources) and Joe A. Quetone (Florida Governor's Council on Indian Affairs) also facilitated our work. Credit is also due our field crew, especially Megan Donnelly, who assisted in the bioanthropological analysis. Jane E. Buikstra and George J. Armelagos offered advice and were kind enough to critique an earlier version of this paper, as did three anonymous reviewers.

Note

1. The data that form the basis for most of this analysis were gathered in 1990; however, additional data from the 1991 field season were also incorporated to a limited degree. Rebecca Saunders served as field archaeologist during the 1991 investigations.

Bibliography

Acheson, R. M.
1960   Effects of Nutrition and Disease on Human Growth. In *Human Growth*, edited by James M. Tanner, 73–92. New York: Pergamon Press.

Bass, William
1987   *Human Osteology: A Laboratory and Field Manual.* 3d ed. Special Publication no. 2. Columbia: Missouri Archaeological Society.

Binford, Lewis R.
1971   Mortuary Practices: Their Study and Their Potential. In *Approaches to the Social Dimensions of Mortuary Practices*, edited by James A. Brown, 6–29. Society for American Archaeology Memoir no. 25.

Brothwell, Don R.
1967   *Digging Up Bones.* 2d ed. London: British Museum of Natural History.

Brothwell, Don R., ed.
1963   *Dental Anthropology.* New York: Pergamon Press.

Charles, D. K., and Jane E. Buikstra
1983   Archaic Mortuary Sites in the Central Mississippi Drainage: Distribution, Structure, and Behavioral Implications. In *Archaic Hunters and Gatherers in the American Midwest*, edited by James L. Phillips and James A. Brown, 117–145. New York: Academic Press.

Cohen, Mark, and George Armelagos
1984   Paleopathology at the Origins of Agriculture: Editors' Summation. In *Paleopathology at the Origins of Agriculture*, edited by Mark Cohen and George Armelagos, 585–601. New York: Academic Press.

Cook, Della C.
1981   Mortality, Age-Structure and Status in the Interpretation of Stress Indicators in Prehistoric Skeletons: A Dental Example from the Lower Illinois Valley. In *The Archaeology of Death*, edited by R. Chapman, I. Kinnes, and K. Randsborg, 133–144. Cambridge: Cambridge University Press.

Deagan, Kathleen A.
1972   Fig Springs: The Mid-Seventeenth Century in North-Central Florida. *Historical Archaeology* 6:23–46.

Goggin, John M.
1953   An Introductory Outline of Timucua Archaeology. *Southeastern Archaeological Conference Newsletter* 3(3):4–17.

Goodman, Alan, D. Martin, George Armelagos, and G. Clark
1984   Indications of Stress from Bone and Teeth. In *Paleopathology at the Origins of Agriculture*, edited by Mark Nathan Cohen and George J. Armelagos, 13–49. New York: Academic Press.

Gordon, Claire C., and Jane E. Buikstra
1981   Soil pH, Bone Preservation, and Sampling Bias at Mortuary Sites. *American Antiquity* 46(3):566–571.

Hutchinson, Dale L.
1991   Postcontact Native American Health and Adaptation: Assessing the Impact of Introduced Diseases in Sixteenth-Century Gulf Coast Florida. Ph.D. diss., Department of Anthropology, University of Illinois, Urbana.

Johnson, Kenneth W.
1987   *The Search for Aquacaleyquen and Cali: Archaeological Survey of Portions of Alachua, Bradford, Citrus, Clay, Columbia, Marion, Sumter, and Union Counties, Florida.* Miscellaneous Project Report Series, no. 33. Gainesville: Department of Anthropology, Florida State Museum.

1990   The Discovery of a Seventeenth-Century Spanish Mission in Ichetucknee State Park, 1986. *Florida Journal of Anthropology* 15:39–46.

1991   The Utina and the Potano People of Northern Florida: Changing Settlement Systems in the Spanish Colonial Period. Ph.D. diss., Department of Anthropology, University of Florida, Gainesville.

Jones, B. Calvin, and Gary N. Shapiro
1990   Nine Mission Sites in Apalachee. In *Columbian Consequences*. Vol. 2: *Archaeological and Historical Perspectives on the Spanish Borderlands East*, edited by David Hurst Thomas, 491–509. Washington, D.C.: Smithsonian Institution Press.

Keyes, P.
1968   Research in Dental Caries. *Journal of American Dental Association* 76:1357–1370.

Kieser, J. A., C. B. Preston, and W. G. Evans
1983   Skeletal Age at Death: An Evaluation of the Miles Method of Ageing. *Journal of Archaeological Science* 10(1):9–12.

Krogman, W. M., and M. Y. Iscan
1986   *The Human Skeleton in Forensic Medicine*. 2d ed. Springfield, Ill.: Charles C. Thomas.

Larsen, Clark Spencer
1987   Bioarchaeological Interpretations of Subsistence Economy and Behavior from Human Skeletal Remains. In *Advances in Archaeological Method and Theory*, vol. 10, edited by Michael Schiffer, 339–445. San Diego: Academic Press.

1990   Biological Interpretation and the Context for Contact. In *The Archaeology of Mission Santa Catalina de Guale: 2. Biological Interpretation of a Population in Transition*, edited by Clark Spencer Larsen, 11–25. Anthropological Papers of the American Museum of Natural History, no. 68. New York.

Lovejoy, C. Owen
1985   Dental Wear in the Libben Population: Its Functional Pattern and Role in the Determination of Adult Skeletal Age at Death. *American Journal of Physical Anthropology* 68:1–14.

Lovejoy, C. Owen, R. Meindl, T. Pryzbeck, and R. Mensforth
1985   Chronological Metamorphosis of the Auricular Surface of the Ilium: A New Method for the Determination of Adult Skeletal Age at Death. *American Journal of Physical Anthropology* 68:15–28.

Miles, A. E. W.
1962   Assessment of Ages of a Population of Anglo-Saxons from Their Dentitions. *Proceedings of the Royal Society of Medicine* 55:881–886.

1963   The Dentition in the Assessment of Individual Age in Skeletal Material. In

Dental Anthropology, edited by Don R. Brothwell, 191–209. New York: Pergamon Press.

1978 Teeth as an Indicator of Age in Man. In *Development, Function, and Evolution of Teeth*, edited by Percy M. Butler and Kenneth A. Joysey, 455–464. New York: Academic Press.

Milner, George
1980 Epidemic Disease in the Post-Contact Southeast: A Reappraisal. *Midcontinental Journal of Archaeology* 5:39–56.

Newman, M. T.
1976 Aboriginal New World Epidemiology and Medical Care and the Impact of Old World Disease Imports. *American Journal of Physical Anthropology* 45:667–672.

Nowell, G. W.
1978 An Evaluation of the Miles Method of Aging Using the Tepe Hissar Dental Sample. *American Journal of Physical Anthropology* 49:271–276.

O'Shea, John M.
1981 Social Configuration and the Archaeological Study of Mortuary Practices: A Case Study. In *The Archaeology of Death*, edited by R. Chapman, I. Kinnes, and K. Randsborg, 133–144. Cambridge: Cambridge University Press.

1984 *Mortuary Variability: An Archaeological Investigation*. New York: Academic Press.

Phenice, Terrell W.
1969 A Newly Developed Visual Method of Sexing the Os Pubis. *American Journal of Physical Anthropology* 30:297–301.

Powell, Mary Lucas
1985 The Analysis of Dental Wear and Caries for Dietary Reconstruction. In *The Analysis of Prehistoric Diets*, edited by R. I. Gilbert and J. H. Mielke, 307–338. New York: Academic Press.

1988 *Status and Health in Prehistory: A Case Study of the Moundville Chiefdom*. New York: Academic Press.

1990 On the Eve of the Conquest: Life and Death at Irene Mound, Georgia. In *The Archaeology of Mission Santa Catalina de Guale: 2. Biocultural Interpretations of a Population in Transition*, edited by Clark Spencer Larsen, 26–35. Anthropological Papers of the American Museum of Natural History, no. 68. New York.

Rose, Jerome, K. Condon, and Alan Goodman
1985 Diet and Dentition: Developmental Disturbances. In *The Analysis of Prehistoric Diets*, edited by R. I. Gilbert and J. H. Mielke, 281–305. New York: Academic Press.

Russell, Katherine F., Inui Choi, and Clark Spencer Larsen
1990   The Paleodemography of Santa Catalina de Guale. In *The Archaeology of Mission Santa Catalina de Guale: 2. Biocultural Interpretations of a Population in Transition*, edited by Clark Spencer Larsen, 36–49. Anthropological Papers of the American Museum of Natural History, no. 68. New York.

Saunders, Rebecca
1988   *Excavations at 8NA41: Two Mission Period Sites on Amelia Island, Florida*. Miscellaneous Project Report Series, no. 35. Gainesville: Department of Anthropology, Florida Museum of Natural History.

Smith, B. H.
1984   Patterns of Molar Wear in Hunter-Gatherers and Agriculturists. *American Journal of Physical Anthropology* 63:39–56.

Stuiver, Minze, and Paula J. Reimer
1986   A Computer Program for Radiocarbon Age Calibration. *Radiocarbon* 28(2B):1022–1030.

Thomas, David Hurst
1987   *The Archaeology of Mission Santa Catalina de Guale: 1. Search and Discovery*. Anthropological Papers of the American Museum of Natural History, vol. 63, pt. 2. New York.

1990   The Spanish Missions of *La Florida*: An Overview. In *Columbian Consequences*. Vol. 2: *Archaeological and Historical Perspectives on the Spanish Borderlands East*, edited by David Hurst Thomas, 357–397. Washington, D.C.: Smithsonian Institution Press.

Ubelaker, Douglas
1978   *Human Skeletal Remains, Excavation, Analysis, and Interpretation*. Chicago: Aldine.

Walker, P., J. Johnson, and P. Lambert
1988   Age and Sex Biases in the Preservation of Human Skeletal Remains. *American Journal of Physical Anthropology* 76(2):182–187.

Walker, P. L., G. Dean, and P. Shapiro
1991   Estimating Age from Tooth Wear in Archaeological Populations. In *Advances in Dental Anthropology*, edited by Marc A. Kelley and Clark Spencer Larsen, 169–178. New York: Wiley-Liss.

Weisman, Brent R.
1988a   Archaeological Investigations at the Fig Springs (8CO1) Mission, Season 1, January–July 1988. Ms. on file, Florida Bureau of Archaeological Research, Tallahassee.

1988b   *1988 Excavations at Fig Springs (8C01), Season 2, July–December 1988*.

Florida Archaeological Reports, no. 4. Tallahassee: Florida Bureau of Archaeological Research.

1989   Excavation Summary, 1989 Season, Fig Springs Mission Church, Fig Springs Site (8CO1), Ichetucknee Springs State Park. Ms. on file, Florida Bureau of Archaeological Research, Tallahassee.

Wolpoff, M. H.
1979   The Krapina Dental Remains. *American Journal of Physical Anthropology* 50:67–114.

Wood, C.
1983   Early Childhood: The Critical Stage in Human Interactions with Disease and Culture. *Proceedings of the Royal Society of Medicine* 17:79–85.

☼ 10 ☼

Archaeological Investigations
at Mission Patale, 1984–1992

ROCHELLE A. MARRINAN

This paper has two goals. First, it presents information resulting from nine field sessions at the Apalachee mission site of San Pedro y San Pablo de Patale (fig. 10.1). Initial excavation of the site was conducted by B. Calvin Jones during the summer of 1971. In 1984 a long-term project for research and education was begun by the Department of Anthropology, Florida State University. The first years included broad-scale testing, remote sensing, areal site survey, and excavation projects designed to answer questions generated by a consortium of mission period researchers in the Tallahassee area. Later years have seen specific attention paid to the religious complex. While a series of annual papers has been presented (Bryne 1985; Bryne and Marrinan 1984; Marrinan 1984, 1985a, 1985b, 1985c, 1986a, 1986b, 1986c, 1987, 1988, 1990, 1991a, 1991b; Marrinan and Bryne 1987; Marrinan and Rust 1992; Marrinan, Alldredge, and Stanton 1992; Shapiro and Marrinan 1986), this paper represents the most comprehensive discussion of current site data and information from allied projects.

The second goal is equally important and has been prompted by my experiences at the Patale mission and the work of colleagues in other Florida missions. Archaeological data relevant to mission structures and settlement layout have been used to develop a predictive "mission model" best stated by Jones and Shapiro (1990). A systematic study of these data reveals that they are highly variable for Florida-area missions compared

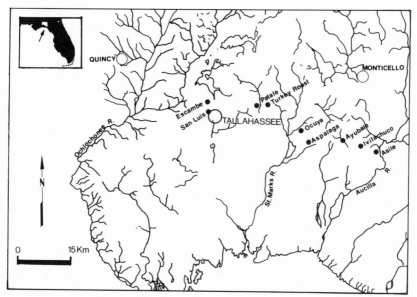

Figure 10.1. The location of the mission of San Pedro y San Pablo de Patale and the Turkey Roost sites in relation to other mission sites in Leon and Jefferson counties.

with the regularity of Franciscan mission plans in Arizona, New Mexico, New Spain, California, and Texas. By contrast, these Florida mission data seem aberrant. A comparison of the Florida data and data from comparable mission systems elsewhere will be presented.

The involvement of the Department of Anthropology of Florida State University in research at Mission San Pedro y San Pablo de Patale began with a telephone call from prospective owners. Dr. Frank and Eveline Bilek purchased the property from the Dickinson family in the fall of 1983. The Dickinsons had owned the property since the early 1970s, and it was their residential construction that gave B. Calvin Jones of the Bureau of Archaeological Research, Division of Archives, History, and Records Management, the opportunity to confirm the presence of a mission site. Jones was able to make preliminary excavations as the Dickinsons converted the site from pasture to residence and lawn.

Patale was the site of at least one mission. After the congregation left this hilltop location, other Spanish residential or agricultural activity may have occurred on the site. Patale is often mentioned as the ranch of Marcos Delgado, but we do not know whether this indicates a residential use or that Delgado simply ran his cattle on the *chicasa* (old fields, abandoned place) of Patale (Jones, Hann, and Scarry 1991:16–17). After the fall of the mission chain in the early 1700s, the area was abandoned. To date, there has been little evidence of Creek or Seminole use of the site. During antebellum times the area was in crop agriculture. Up until about 1960 the site was a tung orchard (for the production of tung oil). At present most of the site is in pasture with occasional crop production. Agricultural use of this land has caused significant feature loss.

The site is located on a ridge at about 70-m elevation. The substrate is red clay, but there is considerable sandy loam that remains on top of the ridge. In addition to agricultural activities, another source of site disturbance is the presence of centuries of pocket gopher (*Geomys pinetis*) burrows. These rodents have honeycombed the site with their burrows and caused the displacement of cultural materials and the destruction or severe alteration of many features.

In 1971 Jones identified a complex of three structures (fig. 10.2): mission church with subfloor burials, *convento*, and *cocina* (kitchen/storage structure). These findings and interpretations have been recently reported (Jones, Hann, and Scarry 1991). Between 1968 and 1984 Jones also conducted preliminary excavations at a number of other mission sites in Apalachee Province and in neighboring Timucua Province. These data have been reported in several brief publications (Jones 1970a, 1970b, 1971b, 1972, 1973; Morrell and Jones 1970) and a recent paper (Jones and Shapiro 1990) in which these data are synthesized. Jones's data have been used to generate a predictive model for Florida Franciscan mission sites.

Research Orientation

In late 1983, when the opportunity to work at Patale came, a review of the literature revealed several internal patterns: (1) the earliest anthropologically trained archaeologists working in Florida missions had specifically addressed the topic of acculturation and viewed their work in missions as important for this reason; (2) the majority of work in mission sites had focused on the sacred complex of structures, primarily the church—indeed, finding fully extended supine burials was a certain way to discriminate between native styles of interment and one that embraced the Catholic norm; (3) only a few of the potentially numerous mission

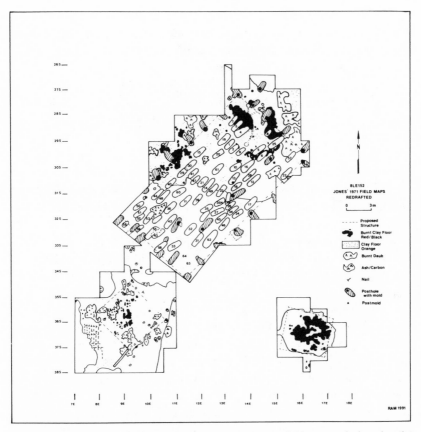

Figure 10.2. A redraft (Marrinan) of Jones's (1971a) field map of the church/ *convento/cocina* area of the Patale mission.

locations had been identified; and (4) little was known about the native residential areas of mission settlements.

At the outset it was not clear that the Patale project would be as long-term a project as it has been. The research orientation for the first year (1984) was modest. Identification of and preliminary excavation in the native settlement were specific goals. Such an approach was intended to add to information gained by Jones's 1971 work in the central area/religious complex and provide a broader view of mission life. Broad-scale subsurface testing would be the initial tool used to evaluate the distribution of materials across the site. Concentrations of burned clay (daub) would be used to indicate previous locations of residential areas. Because the church, *convento*, and *cocina* were located in the front yard of the Bilek residence, the project would not involve those areas after preliminary data gathering had been completed.

In the native settlement, information that would assist in interpreting cultural change would be sought. It would be possible to assess the quantity of introduced material, the relative quantity of ceramic copywares, the pattern of the settlement around the mission structures, the form of the residences, and patterns of material possessions that might indicate status differences.

Since 1984, annual excavation goals have been motivated by different conditions. The work during several sessions has been directed by findings from previous years (1985, 1986, 1990, 1991, 1992) or requested by the Bileks to clear areas that they wished to use (1987, 1988, 1989). Findings from each of these sessions will be summarized below.

A number of questions have guided the research strategy through the years.

1. *What was the nature of the Patale settlement?* This question includes determination of the chronological affiliation of the site. It also involves examining whether this mission site represents a new location or an extant settlement in which a mission was established. If it is determined to be a new location, what is the arrangement of the various elements (sacred structures, support structures, native village, etc.) relative to each other? If an extant village became a mission site, have mission structures been incorporated or are these elements adjacent to the village?

2. *What are the limits of the mission/village?* Identifying the limits and nature of the cultural deposit at the site will help to determine whether the village is tightly nucleated or dispersed. Using a broad-scale approach, is it possible to determine whether there are outlying elements (e.g., farmsteads) that are affiliated with the mission?

3. *Can historically known dependencies or other locations of the Patale congregation be identified?* From the history of this congregation available to date, there are two reported *visitas*: Ajamano and Talpahique (Jones, Hann, and Scarry 1991:14). Documentary research has indicated that the position of the Patale mission was not constant. One site, the Turkey Roost site (8LE157), has been proposed by Jones (Jones and Shapiro 1990:499) as another location of the Patale congregation. Can this site be verified as related to Patale? Can the *visitas* be located?

4. *Is there adherence to a recognizable Franciscan plan?* In other

areas, Franciscan missions with regularized plans were established within the time frame of the Florida missions. Does Patale reflect a basic Franciscan plan, or is there some arrangement of structures that indicates a modification or accommodation that is unique to Florida?

Testing, Survey, and Remote Sensing

Work began at Patale just as the state of Florida purchased the site of Mission San Luis de Talimali and was designing its research strategy. A group of collaborators, composed of the late Gary Shapiro (who headed the San Luis effort until 1988), John Scarry, Richard Vernon, John Hann, Stephen Bryne, Charles Poe, B. Calvin Jones, and, later, Bonnie McEwan, formed to discuss research goals and strategies. This consortium of scholars has provided local critical appraisal of research strategy and methodology for mission and temporally related projects. Given the similarities and differences expected in the two sites, many of the same research questions and field approaches were adopted.

SURFACE COLLECTION

In 1984 the Bilek and some of the adjacent Dickinson properties were gridded and a controlled surface collection based on 20-m squares was made. Low temperatures in December 1983 inhibited growth of new pasture grass to the north, south, and west, but some areas, particularly on the east side of the house, could not be collected given the thickness of pasture grass. Figure 10.3 shows the results of the surface collection. It is clear that the occurrence of European-derived majolicas and olive jar is near the known church, *convento*, and *cocina* area. The occurrence of aboriginal ceramics indicates a large but concentrated residential area.

BROAD-SCALE TESTING

A broad-scale subsurface testing program was initiated in 1984 and continues to the present. The subsurface testing program used manual posthole diggers (an average 18 cm in diameter). All test fill was screened through 1/4-inch screen. Positive tests were assigned field catalog numbers and segregated by grid coordinates. Data for each test were collected on individual forms and the soil profile recorded before the test was backfilled. Distribution frequency maps were generated to indicate areas

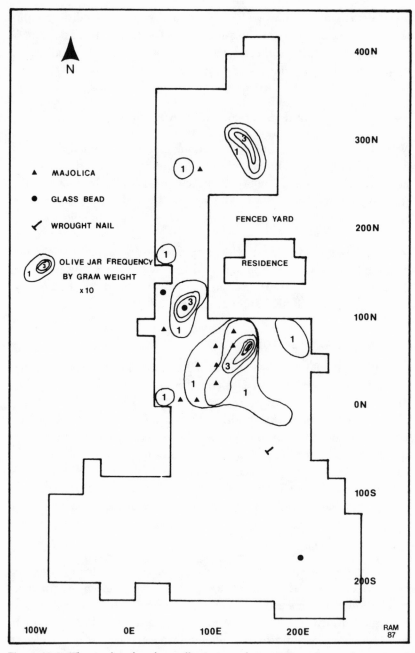

Figure 10.3. The results of surface collections made in 1984 on the north, west, and south unsodded areas of the Patale mission site.

likely to contain remains that could provide data appropriate to research questions.

To date, over 3500 tests representing an area of approximately 350,000 m² (35 ha) have been made at 10-m intervals across the Patale site and adjacent properties. Within this area, the habitation area (represented by the occurrence of aboriginal or European-introduced ceramics) comprises about 220,000 m² (22 ha) or 63 percent of the area tested. Figure 10.4 illustrates the area tested to date and the tests positive for period ceramics (there is also a small early twentieth-century occupation that is not included among the data presented here). Of the 3569 tests that have been conducted, 485 (13.58 percent) were positive for ceramics of the period.

Areas of high burned clay (daub) concentration were initially thought to be indicators of residential activity: floors or wall fall accumulations. These areas received first attention for remote sensing preparatory to excavation. In retrospect, burned clay (daub) seems to be of dubious quality for determination of residential space at Patale. First, it is important to define what is meant by daub. Donna Ruhl (1987) has shown that materials used in the construction of wattle-and-daub walls contain discernible quantities of vegetal inclusions. When hardened by fire, these remnants have the appearance of fiber-tempered clay. The color ranges from blackened to deep reds and red oranges. At Patale some of the daub recovered in the posthole tests is truly resultant of wall construction, but it is apparent that daublike material can be created by naturally occurring fires and burning tree-root systems.

As a consequence of these findings, definition of residential areas has depended on the occurrence of pottery, both aboriginal and European-derived. From the subsurface survey results, it is clear that the primary residential area has been well defined to the south and east (fig. 10.4). Definition is less clear for the north and west, where testing continues with each field session. It is also clear that minor pottery scatters do occur away from the main concentration. These may indicate earlier sites or contemporaneous habitations, or some other interpretation may be appropriate.

AREAL SURVEY

Early in the discussions among San Luis and Patale researchers, survey of a region around a known mission site was proposed. Such a study

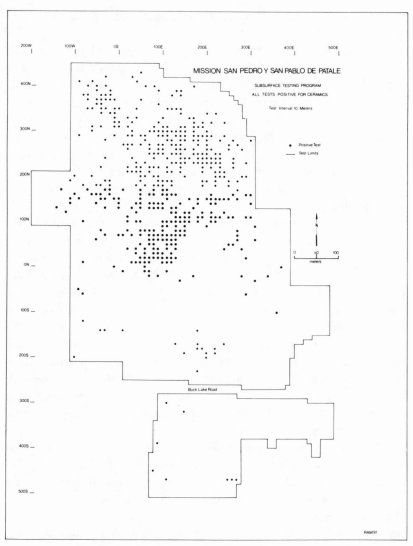

Figure 10.4. The distribution of subsurface tests positive for ceramics at the Patale mission site. These findings represent all field seasons from 1984 to 1992.

would allow identification of other mission sites, mission dependencies, and possible nonmission residential occupations. The Patale mission, in a rural setting, was chosen for this study. The library research, fieldwork, and laboratory analysis for the Apalachee-Mission Archaeological Survey were conducted in 1985 with Survey and Planning Grant funds from the

Department of State matched by monies from the Bilek Fund for Archaeology.

The survey considered all Florida Master Site File entries that reported period aboriginal ceramics or European materials in Leon County. Collections from these sites (curated by the Department of State and by Florida State University) were examined and the sites were relocated and visited when possible. Jones and Shapiro (1984) produced a list of site locations near Patale not then recorded on the Master Site File. The project began with a population of 69 reported and unreported sites in the Tallahassee area plus other locations thought likely to be sites. Bryne used students from the Florida State University Archaeological Field School on a rotating basis during the spring and a small paid crew during the summer months.

The Apalachee-Mission Survey final report (Marrinan and Bryne 1986) summarizes information for 118 sites in the Patale survey area. Of these, 67 were new sites. Bryne tested 21 of these sites using screened shovel tests on 30-m grid intervals. The sites exhibited a high percentage of multicomponent use (46 percent; Marrinan and Bryne 1986:17). Perhaps the most alarming statistic was the condition of sites. In the study population only 13.5 percent were considered in stable condition (mostly residential situations that were stable in 1986). An alarming 80 percent of the sites were rated threatened, damaged, or damaged/destroyed (Marrinan and Bryne 1986:18). Since 1986 several of the sites placed in the stable category have been sold for large subdivision developments. (Site-specific information can be found in Marrinan and Bryne 1986, settlement analysis in Bryne 1986.)

Testing at the Turkey Roost Site

The Turkey Roost Site (also called Patale II) was visited in 1985 as part of the Apalachee-Mission Archaeological Survey. Because the site was planted in row crops, no testing was undertaken at that time. During three weeks of testing in 1986 and 1987, a total of 122,500 m^2 (12.25 ha) were tested at 10-m intervals. Overall, this area seems to represent a small part of a large site. One transect, a quarter mile in length, revealed a spread of cultural debris a considerable distance away from the area of Jones's 1969 excavations. Figure 10.5 illustrates the findings from the area tested and indicates that the site is not well defined on any side.

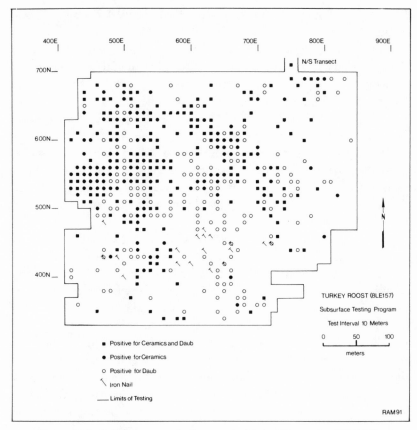

Figure 10.5. Subsurface test findings at the Turkey Roost site (8LE157).

REMOTE SENSING

Several kinds of remote sensing have been applied to the Patale site. First, aerial photographs were consulted to determine whether features of the mission were apparent on the surface. These were uninformative.

As a result of the subsurface testing program, a number of areas were selected for soil resistivity survey (Resistivity Areas 1 through 5). While more than 16,000 m² were surveyed and mapped, the technique failed to be a diagnostic tool at this site. In retrospect, the problem seems to be the extent of agricultural damage to the upper 50 cm of the site.

A magnetic survey (using a White 9100 metal detector) was performed in an attempt to delimit concentrations of iron (Brewer 1984).

This technique did not identify any concentrations that could be positively related to the mission era. One late twentieth-century steel-reinforced cement drainage pipe was identified, however.

The Excavation Program

Excavation projects undertaken to date have primarily been located in one of three general areas of the site: the South Excavation Area, the Northeast Yard Excavation Area, and the Church Excavation Area. Excavation units were 2-m squares (a site standard). Metrical levels (10 cm) were used. Figure 10.6 presents a composite of excavation areas.

The South Excavation Area

The South Excavation Area (includes Resistivity Areas 4 and 5) is located in fields outside the fenced residence yard. Two areas in which resistivity values were highly variable were exposed. Area 4 excavations revealed a clay deposit stratigraphically higher than usual based on the subsurface test profiles. While it now seems that this clay deposit is natural, at the time questions about the archaeological signature of a decomposed, but not burned, wattle-and-daub structure were posed. No evidence of structural features was exposed, however.

Area 5 was the most productive of structural evidence. The first postmolds were exposed in this area. Post pits were not evident for most of these molds, suggesting an advanced state of feature loss. An often extreme (50–70 cm) plow-disturbed depth was also revealed. Excavations were conducted there from 1984 to 1986, in 1989, and again in 1992. Four structural entities were identified (fig. 10.7).

Given data from previous years (Marrinan 1991a:235–237), Structure 1 was thought to be a roughly oval or circular domestic structure 10 m in diameter. That interpretation now seems incorrect in light of data from continued excavation in this area in 1992. Feature 203, at the approximate center of the structure(s), is a large sloping post pit (shallow northeast sloping to a deep southwest end) with postmold in the southwest end. Native American and European-derived ceramics were recovered from the Structure 1 area and Feature 203 (Gray, Kelly, and McEvoy 1992). The fact that none of the 70 postmolds exposed in this area is

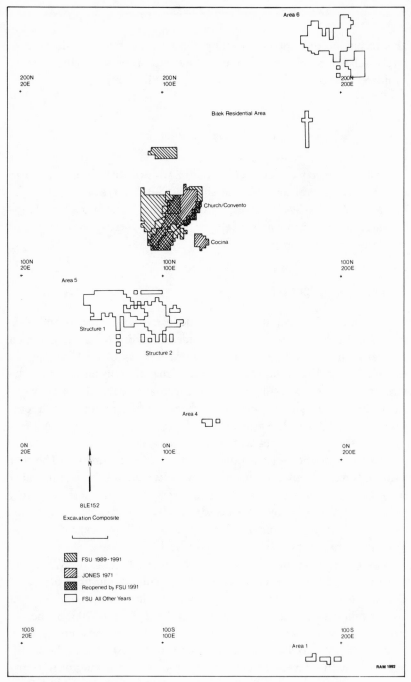

Figure 10.6. An excavation composite for the Patale mission site indicating all areas that have been open to excavation.

Figure 10.7. Excavation findings in the South Excavation Area (Area 5) at the Patale mission site.

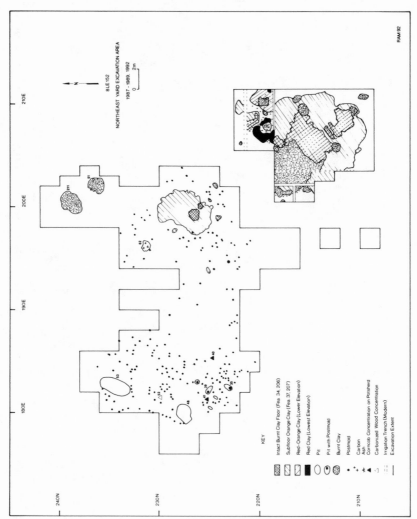

Figure 10.8. Excavation findings in the Northeast Yard Excavation Area (Area 6) at the Patale mission site.

intrusive further complicates the interpretation. However, this finding may argue for a single structure.

The superimposed remains of three structures were exposed to the east of Structure 1. Structure 2 was identified in 1986 and has been interpreted as an Apalachee council house. It lies 16 m to the southeast of Structure 1 and has a diameter of 12 m (Keel 1989). A palisade line intrudes on this council house and is in turn intruded upon by a series of large, historic post pits. The palisade line has been followed 35 m to date and seems to turn toward the north. The large, historic post pits indicate a long structure (about 21.5 m by 6.5 m have been exposed) with a northeast to southwest orientation.

The Northeast Yard

In 1987 excavation was begun in the northeast quadrant of the residence yard at the Bileks' request. This area would receive our attention until 1989 and produce a large number of postmolds, none of which has been related successfully to discrete structures (fig. 10.8). Because of the area's location northeast of the church area, it has been proposed that this quadrant might contain remains of the mission era council house, but to date such an interpretation is not firm.

In 1992 excavation was resumed in this area. Initially, a group of excavation units was opened directly east of the Bilek residence (170N to 190N on the 180E line). This area produced no clearly cultural features.

Farther to the northeast, excavation units were placed outside the residence fence where recent plowing for a firebreak had exposed burned clay. This area has revealed a surprising degree of preservation. Figure 10.8 has been updated to illustrate Feature 206/207, an area of intense burned clay and daub rubble (Feature 207) over a still-intact burned clay floor (Feature 206). A large quantity of olive jar (over 4 kg), unglazed earthenware (over 700 g), and majolica (31 g) has been recovered (Harris and Sweiderk 1992). A single fragment of blue-on-white porcelain was also recovered there. The floor area is, at best estimate, about 6.5 m by 5 m. However, a yellow clay subfloor deposit extends the area's dimensions to 11 m by 9 m. This floor differs from other structural features at Patale in that its orientation is northwest to southeast. Feature 34/27, another area of intact burned clay floor with subfloor yellow-orange clay deposit, seems to be related.

To the north, Feature 51 (first noted in 1988) was completed in 1992.

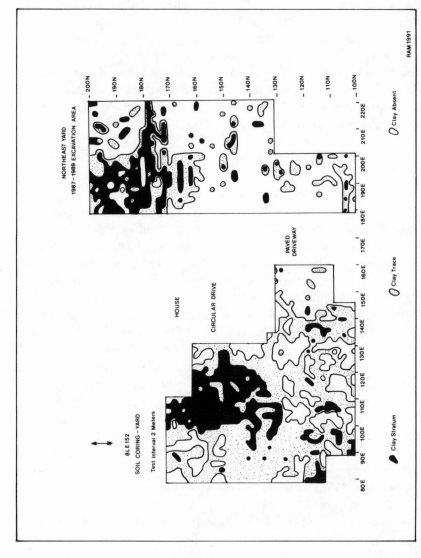

Figure 10.9. Subsurface coring in the vicinity of the church.

First thought to be another area of burned clay floor, it was found to be a large and deep pit filled with disturbed soil and clay with an upper deposit of burned clay. It was about 1.5 m in diameter and reached a depth of 1.6 m. There was no discernible postmold. Feature 211 may be a related or comparable feature.

THE CHURCH AREA

In 1989 a small, L-shaped area was opened on the northeast end of the church (identified by Jones in 1971) at the request of B. Calvin Jones, who was finalizing the architectural data for the publication of the Patale report (Jones, Hann, and Scarry 1991). He wanted information on the closure of the northeast end of the church. One of the outcomes of this project was the exposure of many types of postmolds, post pits, and features. Some of them seemed to be related to the church structure, but others were not as easily interpreted. In addition, cross-sectioning of two of the largest post pits and postmolds suggested that the structure had been rebuilt after a fire. It seemed that the same plan had been followed, but the posts had been pulled up in their pits about 1 m. Historic post pits previously excavated (in the South Excavation Area) had clearly been single-event features. These findings, and a growing concern for data that produced some coherent settlement plan, provided the impetus for continuing to examine the original church/*convento*/*cocina* complex.

Because the data for the church seemed to be the most secure, the area on the northwest side of the church was opened in 1990. Another motivation for opening this area resulted from Hann's and Marrinan's visits to a number of southwestern Franciscan mission ruins and active reservation churches during the summer of 1989. The disparity between the Florida data and the southwestern data prompted new questions about our research strategies and interpretations.

In 1990 and 1991, auger testing at 2-m intervals was conducted prior to excavation to determine the distribution of clay beneath the present surface of the residence yard in the vicinity of the church/*convento*/*cocina* complex (fig. 10.9). Figure 10.10, which details the 1990 excavation findings, illustrates evidence of a continuation of the north wall line to the west (Feature 113 and features to the southwest). There is also the suggestion of structural debris on the north side of the church Jones identified in 1971.

In 1991 the northwest church area was reopened along with the

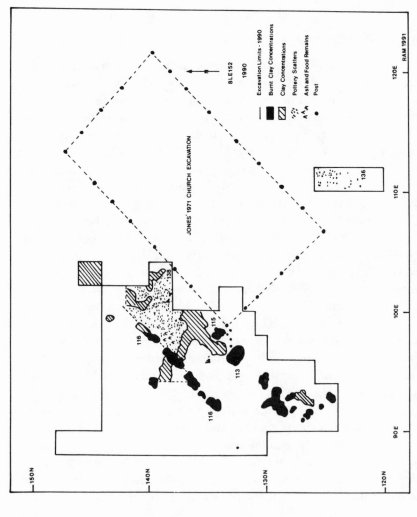

Figure 10.10. An excavation composite of 1990 excavation findings at the Patale mission site.

majority of Jones's 1971 western church excavation area and *convento* area (fig. 10.5). The *convento* area identified by Jones in 1971 was definitely relocated from the field map drafts. Figure 10.11 shows the results. If we are correct about the position of Jones's church wall post placements, the *convento* area seems to be connected to the church and considerably lengthens this structure. In addition, there is another line of post pits and postmolds that represent some other rebuilding or alteration of this structure.

Architectural Summary

THE PREMISSION EVIDENCE

Interpretation of structural function is hampered by the lack of a comparative sample of architectural data from Apalachee Province. A recent paper by Scarry and McEwan (1991) on domestic architecture relied heavily on Velda site (8LE44) and Martin site (8LE853b) data for appropriate comparisons. In general, most architectural data from Apalachee are from structures that were not completely exposed (e.g., Bear Grass—8LE473 [Tesar 1980:777–779]; Apalachee Hill—8LE148 [Bierce-Gedris 1981:184–230]). The most complete structural data are from the Velda site (Scarry 1984b), the Martin site (Scarry and McEwan 1991), and the Spanish Hoe site (8LE667; Bryne 1989).

At Patale there are two structures that seem to be related to events at the site prior to the mission settlement (fig. 10.7). Patale's Structure 2 is called a council house. This interpretation has been made because of the structure's similarities to the council house at San Luis. The structure has double rows of posts (inner tightly placed row and outer wider-spaced row). In form it is one-third the size of the mission-era council house at San Luis (Shapiro and McEwan 1992). Burials were not encountered beneath the floor of this structure or at the mission-era council house of San Luis (McEwan 1990). One other Apalachee council house has been identified by Jones (1990:83–86) at the Borrow Pit site (8LE170). This structure was approximately 11 m (35 ft) in diameter with eight deep interments beneath the floor.

Several questions are appropriate here. First, are any of these structures council houses? The most conclusive data come from San Luis (Shapiro and McEwan 1992). The Patale and Borrow Pit council houses

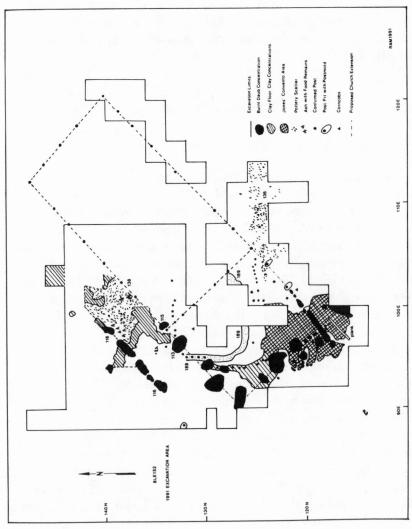

Figure 10.11. An excavation composite of 1991 excavation findings at the Patale mission site.

are roughly the same size and have the same configuration. The Patale council house (Structure 2) varies significantly from Structure 1 at Patale in the clarity of its archaeological footprint. If Jones's structure is a council house, is burial beneath a council house floor a late prehistoric custom? Some scholars maintain that mound burial ceases in late prehistoric times and cite the absence in the chronicles of early explorers of any mention of mound-building activities (see Shapiro 1987:4–5). Does the council house area acquire functions previously filled by mounds? On the other hand, is Jones's structure domestic in function and are the individuals excavated at Borrow Pit members of a family group?

A second premission construction is a palisade that clearly overlies the council house structure and is in turn overlain by a series of large post pits from the mission or postmission period. This palisade features small postmolds with rounded bases that have been spaced about 40 cm to 50 cm apart. At the present time, our best evidence indicates a curving to the north. We have currently identified 35 m of palisade line.

Structure 1 and the council house (Structure 2) can no longer be proposed as chronological correlates. It may be significant to note that the palisade line has not been identified within the Structure 1 area. Nor have we excavated far enough to the north or west of Structure 1 to encounter the palisade again. One conclusion that may be drawn is that the soil-disturbing activities of Structure 1 have obliterated evidence of the palisade. Such a conclusion would imply that Structure 1 is later than the palisade and possibly related to the historic structure with the large post pits (only partially exposed). Another conclusion is that the palisade extended no further.

The council house and superimposed palisade line suggest that following the occupational episode in which the council house was built, the site was abandoned. Either sufficient time had passed that the location of the council house was forgotten or previous council house locations did not carry importance beyond a specific occupation. Evidence suggests that a new, enclosed settlement was built to the north of the palisade.

In summary, at least two occupational events occurred on the Patale site prior to the founding of a mission settlement. Ceramics recovered from the area suggest a late Mississippian period (Fort Walton) affiliation. The earlier episode is represented by the council house and the later episode by the palisade line that may have formed a village perimeter.

Evidence from the Mission Period

Jones's excavation in 1971 revealed the presence of three structures—church, *convento*, and *cocina*—and suggested the possibility of others (Jones, Hann, and Scarry 1991:25–57).

The Patale Church and Convento. Given the findings of subfloor burials in other mission settings, notably on St. Catherines Island, Georgia (Larsen 1990:19), and Amelia Island, Florida (Saunders 1988), the church at Patale seems to be the most secure structural identification. As defined by Jones, it was 26 m in length by 10.5 m in width and oriented northeast by southwest on its long axis (fig. 10.2). He suggests the presence of a door along the northwest wall and another possible door socket on the northeast end wall. Jones believes that the altar was located on the northeast end of the church. He has identified a drainage feature, lying in the nave near the northeast end, that he associates with a baptismal font. Jones's excavation also exposed structural evidence closely adjacent to the southwest end wall of the church. There he found evidence of several postmolds and a clay floor and interpreted this area as the *convento*. It lies approximately 5 m distant.

At this juncture I would like to address orientation of the religious features of the Patale church. Unlike Jones, I must argue for the altar placement on the southwest end of the church. There are several reasons. First, the burials identified by Jones in 1971 are interred in a supine position with the head of the grave to the northeast. Thus, the congregation faces southwest. Only one individual is buried in the opposite manner (Burial 43). The hypothesis that this individual was a priest or religious functionary does not seem to be supported by the osteological analysis. The individual has been identified as a subadult of undetermined sex (Storey and Widmer 1991:191).

Second, greater incidence of subadult burials near the altar is a feature noted by Larsen and Saunders (1987:6) on Amelia Island. At Patale, children are more numerous at the southwestern end of the nave (Jones, Storey, and Widmer 1991:fig. 60).

A third reason for suggesting a southwest altar placement is the presence of the "baptismal font" feature in the northeast nave area (Jones, Hann, and Scarry 1991:fig. 19A). The usual placement of baptismal fonts in sixteenth- and seventeenth-century mission churches elsewhere is near the door opposite the altar (e.g., the Franciscan missions of New Mexico, specifically Abó [Delong and Schofield n.d.], Gran Quivira

[Carroll, Fuller, and Schofield n.d.], and Quarai [National Park Service n.d.]). Jones has identified a possible door socket from the area.

Figure 10.11 updates Jones's map and shows several important differences. First, evidence of large postmolds continues to the southwest along the line that Jones identified in 1971. This proposed extension indicates that the "*convento*" area may be a part of the church, specifically, I would argue, the sanctuary area of the structure (in which the altar is placed). This extension would increase the length of the structure to as much as 35 m or 36 m. Jones identified clay floor on the northeast end of the church and there is clay floor on the southwest end (Jones's former "*convento*" area). I suggest that postmission agricultural activities have removed a large part of the church floor on an east-west line. This may be related to access roads within the tung grove during the 1940s and 1950s or earlier. In addition, the clay floor clearly continues past the post perimeter of Jones's north wall (fig. 10.2). The situation on the south side is less certain.

If Jones's *convento* area is a part of the church, specifically the sanctuary of the church, the dimensions of the church fall between a four-to-one (4:1) ratio that Kubler (1948:242–247) reports for Franciscan churches in New Spain and a three-to-one (3:1) ratio seen in many New Mexico churches (Kubler 1972). We might expect to identify additional burials beneath the sanctuary floor, but to date none has been identified. It is possible that no burials within the sanctuary area proper were made since these would lie beneath the altar (which may have been a permanent fixture).

Feature 116. This 10-m-long deposit of rubble (burned daub and occasional wrought nails) paralleled the north wall line of the church at a distance of about 4 m (figs. 10.10 and 10.11). In 1990, when this feature was first exposed, we projected the same relationship to the south wall (to see whether Jones's 1971 church lay within some larger, symmetrical structure) and opened three contiguous units designed to cross such a feature. An identical line of rubble near the south wall was not identified in 1990, or in 1991 when the area was enlarged. What we did find was a concentration of pottery (see discussion of ceramics from Feature 136). Limited investigation of Feature 116 in 1991 has suggested that the feature may represent a wall line but that the wall does not have large post pits (by comparison with the size of post pits and postmolds on the church itself). What Feature 116 may represent is a garden wall or screen type of construction that lacks large or deep posts.

Between this feature and the north church wall line we have exposed pottery concentrations that appear to be partitioned by linear clay deposits (e.g., Feature 138). These clay deposits have not yet been investigated for the possibility of being wall remnants. Several areas of ashy deposits have been encountered within which most of the preserved vertebrate fauna has been recovered at Patale. It is also clear (fig. 10.11) that there are other post pits and postmolds inside the church area. Just what these represent is not known at present. Jones's map does not offer comparable features.

Feature 189. This feature may represent some sort of premission structure. At present, it is comprised of a north-south line of postmolds on its west side. A contiguous soil stain lacking discernible postmolds continues to the south and east. On the north side, we have identified an east-west line of postmolds. In 1990 postmolds were identified beneath and adjacent to Feature 113, a large daub-filled post pit immediately adjacent to Jones's excavation limits. Jones's backfill was removed in 1991 and more postmolds were identified in this line. It is not clear at what level these postmolds originated, but if they relate to the west-side posts, they may have been intersected by Jones's excavation in 1971. Time did not permit locating the eastern side of this proposed structure during the 1991 session, but we can say that it is oriented east-west and is equal to, or greater than, 8 m in length by 7 m in width. The postmolds are round-bottomed and, insofar as it is possible to tell at Patale (given the degree of rodent disturbance), are not associated with any iron nails or late pottery.

The questions about Feature 189 are varied. Is this a late prehistoric, premission structure? Is this a native structure that was dismantled before the construction of the church? Is this an earlier mission church or chapel structure? Given its essentially east-west orientation, I would suggest a premission affiliation.

Ceramic/Material Culture Summary

THE 1971 EXCAVATION COLLECTIONS

Jones, Scarry, and Williams (1991:60–61) report a total of 13,285 aboriginal sherds of which 85 percent were classified as Lake Jackson Plain. Grog-tempered sherds dominated this collection. Next most numerous were Fort Walton Incised sherds (2.38 percent). Lamar Complicated Stamped sherds, considered evidence of central Georgia influence, were also present in this collection (1.95 percent). These collections originated in the proposed church/*convento*/*cocina* locations. Jones, Scarry, and Williams considered the majority of the sherds to be uninformative regarding assignment to either a late Mississippian or mission period context. Using 933 rim sherds (7 percent), they studied rim thickness, diameter, profile, and decoration. From this study, Jones, Scarry, and Williams (1991:71) concluded that the Patale site held four successive occupations: Lake Jackson phase (A.D. 1150–1450), Velda phase (A.D. 1450–1633), San Luis phase (A.D. 1633–1704), and a possible postmission ranch (based on the Scarry 1984a:380–394 chronology for Leon County).

The 1984 Surface Collection

Figure 10.3 illustrates recovery of European-derived ceramics from the surface collection. It is clear that on the west side of the site European ceramics cluster around the mission area. Livingston (1984) studied the aboriginal sherds recovered in the surface collection ($n = 8045$) and reported 90 percent plain sherds. Of the 806 decorated sherds, 31 percent were assignable Fort Walton types. A total of 7.5 percent were Lamar Bold Incised–like or complicated stamped (table 10.1).

Several glass beads and a single wrought nail were recovered on the surface. Jones, Scarry, and Williams (1991:89–94) report a total of 862 glass beads from the 1971 excavations. All but one of these beads were associated with burials. The exception, a chevron-type bead, was recovered from the proposed *cocina* excavation area. Jeffrey M. Mitchem (1991) has studied all of the glass beads recovered from Patale. Table 10.2 lists his identifications or descriptions of beads recovered since 1984. Wrought iron nails are not numerous at Patale. Jones, Scarry, and Williams (1991:87) have suggested that this indicates scavenging of the site after abandonment.

The Subsurface Testing Program

The majority of ceramic materials recovered during the subsurface testing program were plain aboriginal sherds (den Breeijen and White 1985). Three sherds of olive jar were recovered in the fields north of the church area. No majolica was recovered. Ceramics from both the Dept-

TABLE 10.1. Ceramic Data from Various Proveniences at the Patale Mission Site

Ceramic type	Surface collection (Livingston 1984)	Northeast yard (Groh 1987)	Feature 136 (Allison et al. 1991)	Feature 138 (Horne and Stanton 1991)	Feature 186 (Horne and Stanton 1991)
Deptford Simple Stamped	3				
Lake Jackson Plain	121		25	11	12
Lake Jackson Incised	126		25	40	5
Fort Walton Incised		19	68	25	
Carabelle Incised	1	1			
Carabelle Punctated	8		16	16	
Wakulla Check Stamped		18			
Lamar-like Incised	12	3			
Lamar Complicated Stamped	49	48			
var. Early		13			
var. Jefferson		20			
var. Curlee		4	1		
var. Pine Tuft		2	1		
Complicated Stamped					

Jefferson Ware	113				
Leon Check Stamped	5	24			
Aucilla Incised	28				
Cool Branch Incised	3				
Pinellas Incised	10				
Folded Rim			1		
Untyped pinched					
Untyped punctated		25			
Untyped incised		46	36	4	
Untyped decorated	326		1263	670	
Untyped plain	7239	470			
Untyped plain paste		491			
Untyped		174		8	
Other		114	3		
Olive jar		1	1		
Colono-ware			1		
Mission Red Filmed	1				
Total	8045	1473	1441	766	25

TABLE 10.2. Data on Glass Beads Recovered since 1984 at the Patale Mission Complex (Compiled from Mitchem 1991)

Bead type	1984 Surface collection	1984–1985 Structure 1 area	1986, 1989 Structure 2 council house	1987–1989 Northeast yard	1989–1991 Church area	Totals
Ichtucknee Plain	2		2	1		5
Drawn: 6.6–10.7 mm dia.						
Barrel, 1 double						
Ichtucknee Inlaid Black	1	1	1			3
Drawn: 11.4–12.0 mm dia.						
Barrel						
Chevron			1			1
Drawn: 9.7–10.1 mm dia.						
Barrel, blue/white/red/blue						
Seven Oaks Gilded		1			1	2
Indet.: 6.2–6.4 mm dia.						
Oblate, 1 molded						
Light blue				1		1
Mold made: 5.7 mm dia.						
Spheriod						

Medium blue					1	2
Drawn: 6.15–7.1 mm dia.						
Olive					1	
Opaque black	1					1
Drawn: 7.7 mm dia.						
Spheroid						
Opaque white			1			1
Drawn: 6.4–6.6 mm dia.						
Spheroid						
Medium green			2			2
Drawn: 6.5–6.8 mm dia.						
Spherical, oblate						
Dark purple				1		1
Drawn: 7.7–7.8 mm. dia.						
Barrel						
Colorless				1		1
Poss. wound: 6.0–6.5 mm dia.						
Tubular						
Totals	4	4	4	5	3	20

ford and Weeden Island periods were present in small numbers. Several large-stemmed projectile points, recovered during the subsurface testing, suggest that Patale was also used during the Archaic period. A small number of iron nail fragments were recovered. No glass beads were recovered.

NORTHEAST YARD

Analysis of ceramics recovered in the Northeast Yard Excavation Area indicates some differences from the South Yard Excavation Area and the Church Excavation Area. In the main, frequencies of Lamar and complicated stamped pottery are higher. In a collection of 1473 sherds from four units, Groh (1987) identified 64 percent plain sherds, 1 percent Fort Walton Incised, and 6 percent Lamar Complicated Stamped varieties (table 10.1).

CHURCH AREA

Several features of the Church Area have been analyzed. The data have been summarized in table 10.1 and are briefly described here.

Feature 136—a ceramic scatter adjacent to the south wall of the church: Allison, Terzis, and Moore (1991) studied a total of 1424 sherds from this feature, which is at least 10 m long and 4–5 m in width. Ceramics came from levels 2 through 4 (1.29–1.50 m below datum). They report 88 percent plain ceramics, 4 percent identifiable Fort Walton sherds, and a single Lamar Complicated Stamped sherd.

Feature 138—a ceramic scatter adjacent to the north wall of the church: Horne and Stanton (1991) studied a total of 755 piece-plotted sherds from this feature. They report 80 percent plain ceramics and 3 percent identifiable Fort Walton varieties. No Lamar ceramics were recovered.

Feature 186—a controlled excavation beneath an extant section of the northeast church floor: Horne and Stanton (1991) recovered a total of 33 sherds. All were either Fort Walton or Lake Jackson types. No Lamar ceramics were recovered. Their analysis supports the contention that the church was built on a substantial late Mississippian midden, and, insofar as it is possible to determine at Patale, it also suggests that the appearance of Lamar ceramics may postdate the early missions.

EUROPEAN CERAMIC DISTRIBUTION

Prior to 1992 two studies (Beers 1990; O'Connell and Jones 1991) examined the distribution of European-derived ceramics across the site. Beers (1990:12) concluded that the highest concentrations of European-derived ceramics occurred in both the South and Northeast Excavation Areas (Resistivity Areas 5 and 6, respectively). Small amounts were recovered in Area 4, none in Area 1. O'Connell and Jones (1991) concluded that small amounts of European-derived ceramics were widely distributed on the site. They also concluded that colono-wares were infrequent in the Patale collections. As a consequence of the 1992 field session, our findings have changed. The European-derived materials from Feature 206/207 exceed, by weight, all materials from previous years. It is interesting to note that the subsurface testing program, while producing only two tests with European-derived ceramics, recovered nothing in the Northeast Yard area.

Summary of Research Questions and Excavation Findings

Evidence to date suggests that the Patale mission is an early expression of Apalachee missionization. The ceramic evidence is supportive of this assertion. The number of individuals buried within the Patale cemetery—67—is small (Jones, Hann, and Scarry 1991:49).

Data indicate that the site represents a nucleated habitation with possible outliers. Several large village sites located nearby may represent Patale's dependencies, but until more extensive testing is undertaken in these sites, both their function and affiliation remain conjectural. Based on preliminary ceramic evidence the Turkey Roost site seems to be later chronologically than Patale. If it is a later location for the Patale congregation, it may represent the next habitation of the Patale congregation or a still later location.

It is clear that site interpretations from excavations conducted during 1989–1991 differ significantly from data recovered in 1971. Recent excavation suggests that the church was rebuilt in the same location at least once and that it was longer than proposed by Jones (Jones, Hann, and Scarry 1991:25–57). I suggest that the former *"convento"* area is a part of the church, perhaps the sanctuary. The church appears to have been built on a late prehistoric Fort Walton Mississippian midden. The stratigraphy of ceramic materials beneath the church suggests that Lamar ceramics may not appear in Apalachee Province until after missionization had begun. Additionally, the presence of structural evidence on the north side of the church suggests activities not previously known. Given these findings, an examination of the Florida mission model is presented here as an assessment of the data generally used in interpretation of mission sites.

An Examination of the Florida Mission Model

The friars regularly observed the current European proprieties in building their churches. First: the church must be consecrated (or sometimes merely blessed), and contain at least one consecrated altar. Second: it must be built to be a church, and never be used for any other purpose, for that would constitute a sacrilege. Third: it should be a permanent structure if possible (clearly not possible in the first missions in new lands). Fourth: it must be arranged with a sanctuary for the altar and celebrants (at the east end if possible), a nave for the congregation, a choir for the singers, a baptismal font with a suitable space around it, and a porch or portal or some suitable space outside the church for use at the beginning of the Baptismal Rite. (McAndrew 1965:133)

Archaeological excavation in Spanish Franciscan mission sites in Florida has been conducted since the late 1940s. Even though these projects have not been as motivated by highway or commercial construction as others have been, they have generally been brief operations. Mission sites have importance to the anthropological archaeologist because they represent primary points of sustained interaction among Europeans and native peoples during the First Spanish period (1565–1764). Data from these projects have been used to formulate a model, or picture, of the Florida Franciscan mission that is currently used by archaeologists, historians, and writers in their efforts to evoke the appearance of these early historic sites and interactions.

The mission model proposes a sacred complex of church, *convento* (or friary), and *cocina* (or kitchen/storage structure). This complex is considered to be the heart of the mission station and is situated among other features of the mission known from historic documents: a plaza, ball field, council house, and village. Structures are believed to have been constructed principally from native materials: wattle, daub, wood, and thatch. To date, architectural evidence has indicated small structures.

Expectations of appearance and composition of Florida mission sites were loosely drawn from mission systems established in other parts of North America, chiefly the American Southwest (Arizona and New Mexico), Alta California, and Texas. In time and plan the missions of Arizona and New Mexico are the most appropriate for comparison because the mission systems of both Alta California and Texas are largely eighteenth-century undertakings. A close examination of the Florida data, however, indicates that the regularity of plan evident in the southwestern mission systems is not present. In fact, the plan of Florida missions, as interpreted from archaeological data, appears to be highly variable. As comparisons have been made between the Florida data and information from elsewhere, this discrepancy has become more problematical.

The Florida mission model is best reflected by the synthesis of findings from Apalachee Province compiled by Jones and Shapiro (1990). This model is predicated on the expectation of European-derived religious buildings and native settlement (fig. 10.12). Of the former, a church and *convento* are basic parts of the mission settlement constituting a church complex. The church is the larger of the two buildings. Currently, reconstructed dimensions from archaeological data indicate a rectangular form with the long axis varying from 17.8 m to 26 m in length (Jones and Shapiro 1990:504). The width ranges from 11 m to 12.6 m. The size and configuration of the detached *convento* are much more variable, and Jones and Shapiro estimate floor space at 30–92 m². Their data indicate separations from the church of 4 m to 30 m in distance. At two sites, they report the position of the *convento* in front of the church (Patale I and II [Turkey Roost]); at two others, the *convento* is situated behind the church (Scott Miller and Pine Tuft or Aspalaga).

A third structure is often associated with the church and convento and is sometimes called a kitchen (*cocina*) or storage structure. This building was squarish in configuration but smaller than the *convento*. In some cases, Jones and Shapiro (1990:504) note that the relationship among all three structures suggests a right triangle. They indicate that an area of 0.25 ha to 0.5 ha was required for placement of the church complex. Orientation of these buildings (that is, the long axis) is generally east-west with the exception of one site (Scott Miller). Jones identified semisubterranean pit houses at two of the mission sites (San Joseph de Ocuya and San Lorenzo de Ivitachuco).

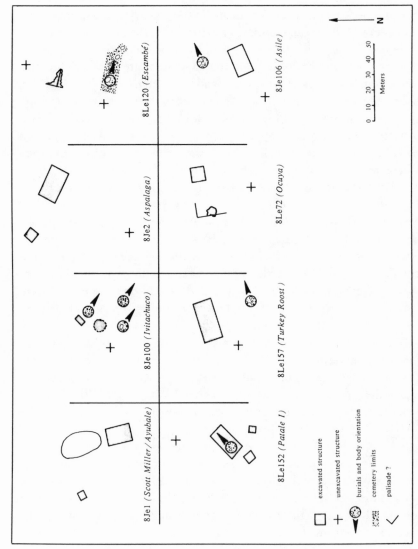

Figure 10.12. A visual summary of data of eight Apalachee missions.

The basic mission model and components must be kept in mind when evaluating the data presented in this chapter. It is appropriate to consider this model here because eight years of work at the Patale mission and personal observations of other mission systems have led me to believe that this model is based on information that is insufficient for the interpretative load that has been attached.

Because the nine Apalachee mission sites have produced much of the data on which this model is based, I will summarize findings from each site. It will then be possible to assess more accurately the strengths and weaknesses of existing interpretations.

Scott Miller site, also known as La Concepción de Ayubale (8JE1). Data from this site are drawn from the work of Mark Boyd in 1940 and Hale Smith in 1947 (see Smith 1951:105–136). Smith exposed the remains of two buildings, the largest of which had internal partitions and was interpreted as the church. Jones and Shapiro (1990:505) define the orientation of the site based on the longest length of the largest structure: north-northwest to south-southeast. It is the only mission orientation that is not on a variation of the east-west lie. No burials were encountered.

San Juan de Aspalaga or Pine Tuft (8JE2). Jones (1970a:3) identified a small church with dimensions of 22.3 m by 12.6 m. This structure had internal partitions, suggesting rooms. Jones (1970a:3) also identified a *convento* of wattle-and-daub construction with large, rectangular-shaped pine logs and wrought iron spikes and nails. The *convento* had dimensions of 5 m by 6 m and lay 19.5 m northwest of the church. The orientation of this site, extrapolated from the long axes of the buildings, was generally northwest to southeast (Jones and Shapiro 1990:499–500). No burials were encountered.

San Lorenzo de Ivitachuco (8JE100). Jones (1972:2) reported the exposure of a *convento*, cemetery, and a semisubterranean structure. The *convento*, a wooden construction, was delineated by the distribution of ash and wrought nails. Its dimensions were 4.7 m by 6.4 m (Jones and Shapiro 1990:501). The cemetery was located immediately east and southeast of the *convento* and was only partially excavated. Jones (1972) found it to be L-shaped and approximately 30 m square. He estimated 300 to 600 burials and noted that children were segregated from the adults in an area near the *convento*. Burial orientation was supine, with the head at the southeast end of the grave pit. The semisubterranean structure was located southwest of the *convento* and was 7.9 m in diameter and 1.12 m in maximum depth.

San Damián de Escambé (8LE120). Jones excavated this site in 1969 and found a probable wooden church structure, fragments of a brass mission bell, and an unusually large quantity of iron and brass tools and artifacts (1970a:3). He also reported the exposure of 143 grave pits in the cemetery, of which he excavated a representative sample of 42 individuals (1970b). Jones (Jones and Shapiro 1990:498) estimated the dimensions of the church as 10 m by 12 m but exposed only two walls of this structure. The cemetery contained supine burials with the heads to the southeast of the grave pits. The cemetery was a "gridded array of about 65 postmolds" that defined the limits (Jones and Shapiro 1990:496). These posts were 10 cm to 30 cm in diameter and spaced about 2.5 m apart. Burials extended a few meters beyond the post pattern to the southeast.

San Luis de Talimali (8LE4). Most of the previous excavations at this site have concerned the fort area (Griffin 1951:137–160). In 1984 a systematic subsurface testing program using mechanical augers provided a view of the distribution of artifacts across the site (Shapiro 1987). Subsequent excavation revealed the presence of an aboriginal-style council house on one side of a plaza. It was assumed that the church complex would lie diagonally opposite the council house on the other side of the plaza, and excavations were opened. The structure revealed was tentatively identified as the church, but subsequent excavation in the cemetery area has suggested that the cemetery lies beneath the church and that the original structure is likely part of the *convento* (McEwan 1991). The cemetery area as originally delimited is 12 m by 22 m. Burial alignment is supine, with the heads to the southeast. There is preliminary evidence to indicate segregation of children at the west end of the cemetery.

San Joseph de Ocuya (8LE72). At this mission Jones (1970a:3) identified a *convento*, a possible wattle-and-daub structure 9.4 m by 10.4 m in dimension. This structure was found to be partitioned into two large rooms (Jones 1972:2) and was associated with wrought iron nails and spikes and a brass candelabra. Some 10 m northwest of the *convento* was a semisubterranean structure 6.7 m in diameter. The maximum depth of this pit was 1.1 m, and Jones found it to be filled with three layers of accumulated cultural debris (1970a:3). No cemetery area was delineated. The church was suspected to be located some 10 m to 30 m southwest of the *convento* (Jones and Shapiro 1990:499).

San Miguel de Asile (8JE106). Jones (1972:2) located a church and cemetery at this mission site. The church structure had a prepared orange clay foundation in which posts had been placed for support. Its dimensions were 10.5 m by 18.5 m. The cemetery was located some 15 m north of the church and was tested by the excavation of one 10-m-square block. This excavation revealed the burials of 10 individuals and the mass interment of at least 5 individuals. Burials were closely spaced, supine, with the heads lying to the northeast. Jones (Jones and Shapiro 1990:501) suspected that the *convento* location lay 18 m southwest of the church, given the concentrations of daub and wrought nails.

San Pedro y San Pablo de Patale or Patale I (8LE152). Jones (1971b:2) identified the remains of two churches, *convento*, kitchen, and cemetery at this site. The earliest church was delineated within the area enclosed by the cemetery, i.e., the burials were located beneath the church floor. The primary church was oriented southwest to northeast and had dimensions of 10.5 m by 26 m. There was a prepared clay floor through which burial pits had been dug. Some 67 individuals were excavated. Burial position was supine, with the head to the northeast. The wattle-and-daub *convento* was located 5.5 m southwest of the church and had dimensions of 6.4 m by 5.6 m. A third structure, a kitchen or storage structure, was located to the southeast of the center of the church and had dimensions of 5.5 m by 4.6 m. This structure was clay-floored, but its orientation was in a more north-south direction.

Turkey Roost or Patale II (8LE157). Jones located the church, cemetery, and *convento* at this site (Jones and Shapiro 1990:499). He excavated approximately one-half of a wattle-and-daub church with dimensions of 12 m by 23.5 m. The orientation of the long length of this structure was southwest to northeast. Jones located but did not excavate the cemetery area. Burials are reported as lying with the heads to the northeast (Jones and Shapiro 1990:497). The cemetery lay 25 m to 35 m southeast of the church. The *convento* is identified as a daub concentration lying 10 m southwest of the church. These structures lie within a 0.4-ha area.

This summary brings together the salient excavation data. I now offer some commonalities among the findings.

Structural orientation. It seems clear that the orientations of all the mission complexes are a variation of an east-west lie, the Scott Miller site notwithstanding. Given the meager data on which Jones and Shapiro based their extrapolation of the orientation, Scott Miller should be reevaluated.

Burial orientation. In sites where burials have been identified, all adhere to the basic east-west orientation. Three sites indicate a southeast orientation for the heads of grave pits (San Luis, Ivitachuco, and Escambé) and three have a northeast orientation (Asile, Patale I, and Patale II). These findings suggest that mortuary alignment conformed to an organizational plan. No burials were encountered in three missions (Scott Miller, San Joseph de Ocuya, and San Juan de Aspalaga).

Church structures. Evidence indicates a variety of church structures: some contain the grave area (Patale I and probably San Luis and Escambé), some contain internal partitions (Aspalaga, Scott Miller), some are only suspected locations (Ivitachuco, Ocuya), and some are simply open, rectangular structures (Asile, Patale II). Dimensions are highly variable.

Convento structures. Convento structures are the most variable. In the main they are small, often almost squarish structures. Their locations relative to the church are inconsistent.

Mission settlement size. Jones and Shapiro (1990:504) figure the spatial requirements of the church/*convento*/*cocina* complex as between 0.25 ha and 0.5 ha, but we know little about the relative size of a mission settlement. At Patale, if the most concentrated distribution of ceramics is used to predict the location of sacred complex and pueblo, the mission lies within an area of about 220,000 square meters (22 ha). At Turkey Roost, however, preliminary subsurface testing indicates that an area in excess of 9 ha represents the settlement.

The Southwestern Mission Model

I would like to explore briefly an alternative mission model drawn largely from the mission systems of Arizona and New Mexico, which chronologically precede and overlap the Florida mission system. These missions were also founded by Franciscan friars and can be expected to express common principles of execution and organization. Because the building stock (adobe and stone in the Southwest, wattle and daub or wood in the Southeast) was not identical, some differences in size and life span of the structure may be expected. Kubler (1972), Bunting (1976), and Kessell (1980) provide excellent architectural overviews for New Mexico.

A typical southwestern mission complex features two components. First, the church and *convento* comprise a single unit, usually joined by a common wall or closely separated by an alleyway. The *convento* is usually located on the same side of the church as the sacristy (a room off the sanctuary where the priest vests for Mass and where altar furnishings are stored). The church is a single-nave structure with trabeated roof. The sanctuary, or altar area, may be raised or level with the floor of the nave. In the Southwest a clerestory may be a feature of the structure. Burials are located beneath the floor of the church. These burials are oriented with the feet toward the sanctuary (or altar). In at least some missions there is evidence that the location of the burial and its proximity to the sanctuary of the church was determined by payment (Kessell 1980:83).

The second mission settlement feature was the pueblo. The settlement of the native population was quantitatively the major feature of the mission. In the Southwest the native building stock is one of square to rectangular rooms, often arranged in a linear fashion, sometimes in several stories. Rows of rooms may also be arranged linearly or clustered.

What we know of native building stock in the Southeast is limited. The LeMoyne drawings (Alexander 1976) and limited archaeological data suggest a preference for round structures. Because there has been no excavation in the pueblos of southeastern mission sites, this feature awaits exposure.

Summary

How, then, should we consider the data that we have? I suggest that these data do not indicate the consistency within the mission complex given the southwestern model. Some assumptions can be tested.

1. *Church structures will have subfloor burials.* Data from Patale I (Jones 1971b) and recent work at San Luis (McEwan 1991) in Apalachee Province support this assumption. In addition, Clark Larsen has excavated 432 individuals from beneath the church floor on St. Catherines Island, Georgia (Larsen 1990:19 and this volume). Jerald T. Milanich, Clark Larsen, and Rebecca Saunders have recovered 118 burials from within the earlier Santa María mission church on Amelia Island, Florida (Saunders 1988:14 and this volume), and Saunders believes that the burial population ascribed to the later Santa Catalina mission also lies within a church (Saunders 1990). Given the presence of burials within a structural area, as indicated by the presence of postmolds, at Escambé, I believe that Jones has excavated a portion of the church in that site. If this

assumption is valid, the identification of structures at Patale II, Scott Miller, Asile, and Aspalaga as churches is called into question.

It is likely that the structures identified as churches at Aspalaga and Scott Miller are *conventos* or some other sort of structure because the presence of internal partitioning defeats the openness of the single-nave church as well as the way in which Catholic liturgy is practiced. As Leone (1977) has shown for Mormon religious structures, we should expect Catholic liturgical practice to be reflected in church architecture. In the Patale I site we have begun to investigate this possibility and have exposed some features that we consider preliminary structural evidence on the north side of the altar end of the church (fig. 10.11).

2. *Convento structures will be closely adjacent or attached to the church structures.* Preliminary data from San Luis indicate that a large, multiroomed structure lies adjacent to the church/cemetery area (McEwan 1991). Preliminary data from Patale suggest structural remains on the north side of the church (fig. 10.11).

3. *Burial pattern will reveal the sanctuary (altar) end of the church.* In the Southwest, burial orientation places the feet toward the altar. In Apalachee Province, this would suggest that the altars of the churches are on the west end. Another feature that would indicate the functional end of the church is the baptismal area, usually located at the end opposite the altar. Jones has identified such a feature at the Patale I mission site but believes that it indicates the altar end. Southwestern mission churches of the period clearly have the baptismal area near the door opposite the altar. Sometimes the area is a separate room off the nave; sometimes it lies beneath the stairs to the bell tower.

4. *Broad-scale exposure of mission sites is necessary to provide the information needed to interpret relationships and functions among struc-tures.* To date, the amount of time and resources available to researchers has been extremely limited. As a consequence, minimal exposure has been effected in most sites. Interpretation has followed a pattern of identifying any exposed structural remains on the basis of expected elements of the mission complex: church, *convento*, kitchen, or storage structure. Long-term projects currently under way—and here I must add researchers outside of Apalachee Province, principally David Thomas (1987) on St. Catherines Island, Georgia, in Guale Province and Jerald Milanich on Amelia Island and other areas within Timucua Province (Milanich and Johnson 1989)—promise to provide the degree of coverage necessary to understand these large and complex sites.

5. *Broad-scale testing serves as a preliminary measure for determining site extent and gaining insight about internal patterning.* We have not been able to use our broad-scale subsurface data at Patale to achieve a predictive advantage such as that at San Luis (Shapiro 1987). Recent findings at Patale convince me that broad-scale subsurface testing must be viewed as a preliminary measure of extracting data about site patterning. Used alone, with little or no "truthing," this technique may have limited utility. In sites where agricultural destruction is extensive, the technique may produce more reliable information about site extent than about structural patterning. In addition, in structural areas a 10-m test interval may be too large to offer fine discrimination among or between structures.

6. *Other features of mission churches must be considered.* It is possible that southeastern Franciscan churches also featured a clerestory. European churches frequently show an east-west orientation with the altar on the east end. When glass or some other transparent or near-transparent material is available for illumination of the altar area, orientation of the altar to capture the earliest light of the day is sensible in view of the way in which the structure is used in the liturgy. However, where such materials are scarce, a clerestory oriented to capture early light is a reasonable accommodation. All of the Apalachee churches for which there are extensive data indicate an orientation off due east-west. In some cases the church is oriented northwest to southeast, in some cases northeast to southwest, but burials indicate that the altars are consistently on the west end. Either orientation would permit illumination of the altar area by southern light through a clerestory. We should be looking for evidence of clerestory construction—for example, greater massing of timbers at the juncture of the nave and sanctuary.

We should also be looking for evidence of choir lofts near the main door (opposite the altar) of the church. Catholic liturgy focuses the attention of the communicant on the altar area. Features of church architecture and spatial arrangement serve to reinforce this directedness. Music often comes from behind the communicant. Other features, attached to or detached from the church, may be bell towers or campaniles. A thesis recently completed by Tina M. Rust (1992) considers many of these features in an attempt to reconstruct the appearance of Franciscan architecture in Apalachee Province.

7. *Attention must be paid to determining mission settlement size.* Little data exist that reflect the real size of mission settlements. From

broad-scale testing at San Luis (Shapiro 1987:37, fig. 20) there is the indication that the settlement size exceeds 13 ha. We would expect San Luis to be larger, given the population data, but its urban setting has probably mitigated against being able to determine its original size. Data from Patale (22 ha) and Turkey Roost (9 ha) indicate a broader range. Weisman's data (1988:36, fig. 5) from the Fig Springs mission in Timucua Province suggest a residential spread in excess of 14 ha.

Even a cursory examination of settlement features and settlement plan in northwest Florida's Apalachee Province indicates the disparity of elemental relationships. In contrast to the precise plans of southwestern missions, these Florida mission data show no coherence of plan. There has been, I believe, a readiness to accept the missions of La Florida as small, rustic settlements. Evidence from other areas indicates that wherever the Franciscans went they demonstrated an organizational concept of mission plan. The ruins of the southwestern missions stand as testimony to their obvious ability to translate, through the labor of the native population, the architectural plan of places of worship in a grand scale. I believe that we will find that the Franciscan missionaries of La Florida were equally capable.

Author's Note

This chapter is largely the same as the one published in *The Florida Anthropologist* 44(2–4):228–254. However, fieldwork in 1992 prompted significant changes in our interpretation of two areas at Patale: Structure 1 and the Northeast Yard. These sections have been revised to include new data. Several figures (10.6, 10.7, and 10.8) have been redrafted. I am indebted to the Florida State University Committee on Faculty Research (COFRs) for a grant enabling these revisions to be made during the summer of 1992.

Acknowledgments

Generous support for this research has been made possible by the Frantisek S. and Eveline B. Bilek Fund for Archaeology (Florida State University Foundation) and the Department of Anthropology, Florida State University. The labor of each field school member, from the 1984 through the 1992 field sessions, has produced the data used herein. This paper is dedicated to the memory of Eveline Bilek (1944–1991).

Bibliography

Alexander, Michael, ed.
1976 *Discovering the New World Based on the Works of Theodore DeBry*. New York: Harper and Row.

Allison, Jeffrey R., Lee A. Terzis, and Barry R. Moore
1991 The Spanish Franciscan Mission of San Pedro y San Pablo de Patale: Analysis of Ceramic Scatter, Feature #136, 1990–1991. Ms. on file, Department of Anthropology, Florida State University, Tallahassee.

Beers, Bridget
1990 Analysis of European-Derived Ceramics at San Pedro y San Pablo de Patale. Ms. on file, Department of Anthropology, Florida State University, Tallahassee.

Bierce-Gedris, Katharine
1981 Apalachee Hill: The Archaeological Investigation of an Indian Site of the Spanish Mission Period in Northwest Florida. Master's thesis, Department of Anthropology, Florida State University, Tallahassee.

Brewer, David M.
1984 A Metal Detector Survey of Selected Portions of the Mission Site of San Pedro y San Pablo de Patale (8LE152). Ms. on file, Department of Anthropology, Florida State University, Tallahassee.

Bryne, Stephen C.
1985 Apalachee Settlement Patterns. Paper presented at the annual meeting of the Florida Academy of Sciences, St. Leo College.

1986 Apalachee Settlement Patterns. Master's thesis, Department of Anthropology, Florida State University, Tallahassee.

1989 Archaeological Investigations at the Spanish Hoe Site (8LE667), Leon County, Florida. Report presented to the Leon County Research and Development Authority. Ms. on file, Department of Anthropology, Florida State University, Tallahassee.

Bryne, Stephen C., and Rochelle A. Marrinan
1984 Excavations at the Mission of Saints Peter and Paul de Patale. Paper presented at the 41st Annual Meeting of the Southeastern Archaeological Conference, Pensacola, Florida.

Bunting, Bainbridge
1976   *Early Architecture in New Mexico*. Albuquerque: University of New Mexico Press.

Carroll, Tom, Glenn Fuller, and Sue Schofield
n.d.   Gran Quivira Guidebook. Southwest Parks and Monuments Association.

DeLong, Leslie, and Sue Schofield
n.d.   Salinas: Abó Trail Guide. Southwest Parks and Monuments Association.

den Breeijen, Cybele, and Susan M. White
1985   An Analysis of Ceramics Recovered during Subsurface Testing at Mission Patale: Map Overlays. Ms. on file, Department of Anthropology, Florida State University, Tallahassee.

Gray, Jonathan, Amanda Kelly, and Kevin McEvoy
1992   Mission San Pedro y San Pablo de Patale: Analysis and Interpretation of Structure 1. Ms. on file, Department of Anthropology, Florida State University, Tallahassee.

Griffin, John W.
1951   Excavations at the Site of San Luis. In *Here They Once Stood: The Tragic End of the Apalachee Missions*, by Mark F. Boyd, Hale G. Smith, and John W. Griffin, 137–160. Gainesville: University of Florida Press.

Groh, Lou
1987   Ceramic Analysis of Aboriginal Pottery of San Pedro y San Pablo de Patale. Ms. on file, Department of Anthropology, Florida State University, Tallahassee.

Harris, Theresa, and Carolyn Sweiderk
1992   European Ceramics at Mission Patale: 1984–1992. Ms. on file, Department of Anthropology, Florida State University, Tallahassee.

Horne, Kenneth A., and William M. Stanton
1991   Analysis of Ceramics from Features #138 and #186: San Pedro y San Pablo de Patale. Ms. on file, Department of Anthropology, Florida State University, Tallahassee.

Jones, B. Calvin
1970a Missions Reveal State's Spanish-Indian Heritage. *Archives and History News* 1(2):1, 3.

1970b Seventeenth-Century Spanish Mission Cemetery Is Discovered near Tallahassee. *Archives and History News* 1(4):1–2.

1971a Field Maps: Excavation of San Pedro y San Pablo de Patale. Ms. on file, Bureau of Archaeological Research, Florida Department of State, Tallahassee.

1971b State Archaeologists Unearth Spanish Mission Ruins. *Archives and History News* 2(4):2.

1972 Spanish Mission Sites Located and Test Excavated. *Archives and History News* 3(6):1–2.

1973 A Semi-Subterranean Structure at Mission San Joseph de Ocuya, Jefferson County, Florida. *Bureau of Historical Sites and Properties Bulletin* 3:1–50.

1990 A Late Mississippian Collector. *The Soto States Anthropologist* 90(2):83–86.

Jones, B. Calvin, and Gary Shapiro
1984 A List of Late Prehistoric and Potential Mission Sites in Eastern Leon County. Ms. on file, San Luis Archaeological and Historic Site, Tallahassee.

1990 Nine Mission Sites in Apalachee. In *Columbian Consequences*. Vol. 2: *Archaeological and Historical Perspectives on the Spanish Borderlands East*, edited by David Hurst Thomas, 491–509. Washington, D.C.: Smithsonian Institution Press.

Jones, B. Calvin, John Hann, and John F. Scarry
1991 *San Pedro y San Pablo de Patale: A Seventeenth-Century Spanish Mission in Leon County, Florida*. Florida Archaeology no. 5. Tallahassee: Florida Bureau of Archaeological Research.

Jones, B. Calvin, John F. Scarry, and Mark Williams
1991 Material Culture at Patale: Assemblage Composition and Distribution. In *San Pedro y San Pablo de Patale: A Seventeenth-Century Spanish Mission in Leon County, Florida*, by B. Calvin Jones, John Hann, and John F. Scarry, 59–108. Florida Archaeology no. 5. Tallahassee: Florida Bureau of Archaeological Research.

Jones, B. Calvin, Rebecca Storey, and Randolph J. Widmer
1991 The Patale Cemetery: Evidence Concerning the Apalachee Mission Mortuary Complex. In *San Pedro y San Pablo de Patale: A Seventeenth-Century Spanish Mission in Leon County, Florida*, by B. Calvin Jones, John Hann, and John F. Scarry, 109–125. Florida Archaeology no. 5. Tallahassee: Florida Bureau of Archaeological Research.

Keel, Frank J., Jr.
1989 8LE152—Mission San Pedro y San Pablo de Patale: Spring 1989 Council House Excavations. Ms. on file, Department of Anthropology, Florida State University, Tallahassee.

Kessell, John L.
1980 *The Missions of New Mexico since 1776*. Albuquerque: University of New Mexico Press.

Kubler, George
1948   *Mexican Architecture of the Sixteenth Century.* 2 vols. New Haven: Yale University Press.

1972   *The Religious Architecture of New Mexico in the Colonial Period and since the American Occupation.* Albuquerque: University of New Mexico Press.

Larsen, Clark Spencer
1990   Biological Interpretation and the Context for Contact. In *The Archaeology of Mission Santa Catalina de Guale: 2. Biocultural Interpretations of a Population in Transition,* edited by Clark Spencer Larsen, 11–25. Anthropological Papers of the American Museum of Natural History, no. 68. New York.

Larsen, Clark Spencer, and Rebecca Saunders
1987   The Two Santa Catalina Cemeteries. Paper presented at the 44th Annual Meeting of the Southeastern Archaeological Conference, Charleston, South Carolina.

Leone, Mark P.
1977   The New Mormon Temple in Washington, D.C. In *Historical Archaeology and the Importance of Material Things,* edited by Leland Ferguson, 43–61. Special Publication no. 2. Society for Historical Archaeology.

Livingston, Cynthia D.
1984   Preliminary Analysis of Aboriginal Ceramics at San Pedro y San Pablo de Patale—Part II. Ms. on file, Department of Anthropology, Florida State University, Tallahassee.

McAndrew, John
1965   *The Open-Air Churches of Sixteenth-Century Mexico: Atrios, Posas, Open Chapels, and Other Studies.* Cambridge: Harvard University Press.

McEwan, Bonnie G.
1990   The Apalachee Council House at San Luis. Paper presented at the 47th Annual Meeting of the Southeastern Archaeological Conference, Mobile, Alabama.

1991   San Luis de Talimali: The Archaeology of Spanish-Indian Relations at a Florida Mission. *Historical Archaeology* 25(3):36–60.

Marrinan, Rochelle A.
1984   Archaeology and the Spanish Mission System. Paper presented at the annual meeting of the Florida Academy of Sciences, Boca Raton.

1985a   The Mission Effort in Spanish Florida. Paper presented at the annual meeting of the Florida Academy of Sciences, St. Leo College.

1985b   The San Pedro de Patale Mission Locations, Leon County, Florida. Paper presented at the 42nd Annual Meeting of the Southeastern Archaeological Conference, Birmingham.

1985c Spanish Mission Research: San Pedro y San Pablo de Patale, 1985. Paper presented at the annual meeting of the Florida Anthropological Society, Daytona Beach.

1986a Acculturation in the Mission Setting: Spanish Florida, 1565–1704. Paper presented at the 43rd Annual Meeting of the Southeastern Archaeological Conference, Nashville, Tennessee.

1986b Community Patterning in Seventeenth-Century Spanish Mission Sites. Paper presented at the annual meeting of the Florida Academy of Sciences, Gainesville.

1986c An Update on Research at the Patale Mission, Leon County, Florida. Paper presented at the annual meeting of the Florida Academy of Sciences, Gainesville.

1987 A Summary of Findings from the Patale Mission. Paper presented at the 44th Annual Meeting of the Southeastern Archaeological Conference, Charleston, South Carolina.

1988 Spanish Mission Archaeology in *La Florida*: The Patale Mission, Leon County, Florida. Paper presented at the 45th Annual Meeting of the Southeastern Archaeological Conference, New Orleans, Louisiana.

1990 An Overview of Settlement Plan in the Missions of *La Florida*. Paper presented at the 47th Annual Meeting of the Southeastern Archaeological Conference, Mobile, Alabama.

1991a Archaeological Investigations at Mission Patale, 1984–1991. *The Florida Anthropologist* 44(2–4):228–254.

1991b The Florida Franciscan Mission Settlement: Questioning the Model. Paper presented at the 1991 Society for Historical Archaeology Conference on Historical and Underwater Archaeology, Richmond, Virginia.

Marrinan, Rochelle A., and Stephen C. Bryne
1986 Apalachee-Mission Archaeological Survey, Vol. 1. Ms. on file, Division of Historical Resources, Florida Department of State, Tallahassee.

1987 San Pedro y San Pablo de Patale: An Outlying Seventeenth-Century Apalachee Mission. Paper presented at the 1987 Society for Historical Archaeology Conference on Historical and Underwater Archaeology, Savannah, Georgia.

Marrinan, Rochelle A., and Tina M. Rust
1992 Franciscan Mission Church Plan in *La Florida*. Paper presented at the 1992 Society for Historical Archaeology Conference on Historical and Underwater Archaeology, Kingston, Jamaica.

Marrinan, Rochelle A., Kenneth Alldredge, and William M. Stanton
1992 A Review of Current Research at the Patale Mission. Paper presented at the annual meeting of the Florida Anthropological Society, St. Augustine.

Milanich, Jerald T., and Kenneth W. Johnson
1989 *Santa Fé: A Name Out of Time.* Miscellaneous Project Report Series, no. 41. Gainesville: Department of Anthropology, Florida Museum of Natural History.

Mitchem, Jeffrey M.
1991 Glass Beads from San Pedro y San Pablo de Patale (8LE152). Ms. on file, Department of Anthropology, Florida State University, Tallahassee.

Morrell, L. Ross, and B. Calvin Jones
1970 San Juan de Aspalaga: A Preliminary Architectural Study. *Bureau of Historical Sites and Properties Bulletin* 1:25–43.

National Park Service
n.d. Salinas National Monument, New Mexico. Pamphlet Guide. U.S. Department of the Interior.

O'Connell, Megan, and Jennifer L. Jones
1991 Analysis of European-Derived Ceramics at Mission San Pedro y San Pablo de Patale. Ms. on file, Department of Anthropology, Florida State University, Tallahassee.

Ruhl, Donna
1987 First Impressions in and on Daub: A Paleoethnobotanical and Ceramic Technological Analysis of Some Burned Clay from Three Mission Sites in *La Florida.* Paper presented at the 44th Annual Meeting of the Southeastern Archaeological Conference, Charleston, South Carolina.

Rust, Tina M.
1992 Franciscan Religious Architecture in Apalachee Province: An Example from Patale (8LE152). Master's thesis, Department of Anthropology, Florida State University.

Saunders, Rebecca
1988 Excavations at 8NA41: Two Mission Period Sites on Amelia Island, Florida. Miscellaneous Project Report Series, no. 35. Gainesville: Department of Anthropology, Florida Museum of Natural History.

1990 Ideal and Innovation: Spanish Mission Architecture in the Southeast. In *Columbian Consequences.* Vol. 2: *Archaeological and Historical Perspectives on the Spanish Borderlands East,* edited by David Hurst Thomas, 527–542. Washington, D.C.: Smithsonian Institution Press.

Scarry, John F.
1984a Fort Walton Development: Mississippian Chiefdoms in the Lower South.

Ph.D. diss., Department of Anthropology, Case Western Reserve University, Cleveland.

1984b A Preliminary Report on Archaeological Investigations of a Late Fort Walton Farmstead at the Velda Site (8LE44), Leon County, Florida. Paper presented at the annual meeting of the Florida Anthropological Society, Palm Beach.

Scarry, John F., and Bonnie G. McEwan
1991 Domestic Architecture in Apalachee Province: Apalachee and Spanish Residential Style in the Late Prehistoric and Early Historic Periods. Paper presented at the 1991 Society for Historical Archaeology Conference on Historical and Underwater Archaeology, Richmond, Virginia.

Shapiro, Gary
1987 *Archaeology at San Luis: Broad-Scale Testing, 1984–1985.* Florida Archaeology no. 3. Tallahassee: Florida Bureau of Archaeological Research.

Shapiro, Gary, and Bonnie G. McEwan
1992 *Archaeology at San Luis: The Apalachee Council House.* Florida Archaeology no. 6, pt. 1. Tallahassee: Florida Bureau of Archaeological Research.

Shapiro, Gary, and Rochelle A. Marrinan
1986 Two Seventeenth-Century Spanish Missions in Florida's Apalachee Province. Paper presented at the 1986 Society for Historical Archaeology Conference on Historical and Underwater Archaeology, Sacramento, California.

Smith, Hale G.
1951 A Spanish Mission Site in Jefferson County, Florida. In *Here They Once Stood: The Tragic End of the Apalachee Missions*, by Mark F. Boyd, Hale G. Smith, and John W. Griffin, 107–136. Gainesville: University of Florida Press.

Storey, Rebecca, and Randolph J. Widmer
1991 Appendix IV: Bioanthropological Data from the Patale Burials. In *San Pedro y San Pablo de Patale: A Seventeenth-Century Spanish Mission in Leon County, Florida*, by B. Calvin Jones, John Hann, and John F. Scarry, 173–201. Florida Archaeology no. 5. Tallahassee: Florida Bureau of Archaeological Research.

Tesar, Louis D.
1980 *The Leon County Bicentennial Survey Report: An Archaeological Survey of Selected Portions of Leon County, Florida.* 2 vols. Miscellaneous Project Report Series, no. 49. Tallahassee, Bureau of Historic Sites and Properties, Florida Department of State.

Thomas, David Hurst
1987   *The Archæology of Mission Santa Catalina de Guale: 1. Search and Discovery.* Anthropological Papers of the American Museum of Natural History, vol. 63, pt. 2. New York.

Weisman, Brent
1988   Archaeological Investigations at the Fig Springs (8C01) Mission: Season 1, January through July 1988. Draft Report for the Division of Recreation and Parks, Florida Department of Natural Resources, Tallahassee.

✿ 11 ✿

Hispanic Life on the Seventeenth-Century Florida Frontier

BONNIE G. McEWAN

Despite intensive research at the primary Spanish enclaves of St. Augustine and Santa Elena, little is known about Hispanic life in the hinterlands of *La Florida*. San Luis de Talimali (fig. 11.1) is unique among most Florida mission settlements in that its Spanish population consisted of more than a resident or visiting friar. As the western capital, the site also housed a garrison along with their families, as well as civilians. Brose (1990) has correctly suggested that for this very reason San Luis was probably different from the "typical" mission and may not be an appropriate model for studying other such settlements. However, the unique demographic makeup of San Luis provides the opportunity to examine a Spanish frontier community that included religious, military, and civilian components.

Historical Setting

Spanish expansion into Apalachee was initially prompted to secure provisions and additional laborers for the garrison at St. Augustine. The first friars arrived in 1633 and reported that after just two years 5000 baptisms had taken place (Hann 1989:17). Despite a brief setback immediately following the 1647 revolt, missionization efforts in the region were considered relatively successful. An account written in the early 1670s by

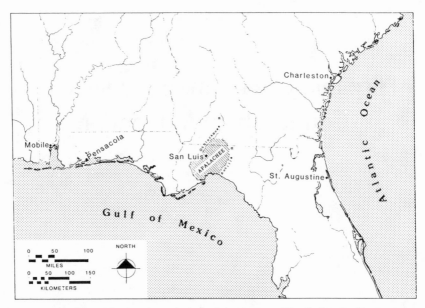

Figure 11.1. The location of Mission San Luis and Apalachee Province.

Domingo de Leturiondo described Apalachee Province as being "thoroughly Christianized" (Hann 1989:24).

The first small group of about 5 soldiers arrived in 1638 and the first deputy governor was appointed to Apalachee in 1645. The garrison was expanded to 12 in the 1650s, when the chief of San Luis offered to "build a capacious and strong house for the soldiers" (Hann 1988:199). Over the decades the size of the garrison fluctuated, expanding to about 45 by the 1680s (Bushnell 1978b:2).

Shortly after the region had been stabilized through the founding of numerous missions and the establishment of a garrison, profitable agricultural endeavors attracted the interest of government officials and civilians. Governor Hita Salazar's wheat farm and cattle ranch at Asile (near the Yustaga-Apalachee border) in the 1640s set a precedent that was to become amplified through time. *Criollos* aspired to a more noble way of life and set in motion the development of a landed aristocracy in Spanish Florida. Tracts across north Florida into the panhandle were gradually parceled off and awarded to influential Spaniards as land grants (Arnade 1965; Bushnell 1978a).

The success of ranches and farms in Apalachee Province rapidly led to surplus commodities, including cowhides, deerskins, tallow, hams, chickens, corn, and beans (Boniface 1971:200–202). Trade was facilitated by the founding of a port at St. Marks, which allowed seagoing vessels to travel from Apalachee to other ports. Markets in Havana were preferred over those of St. Augustine because the voyage was easier and higher prices were generally paid. Furthermore, exotic commodities from throughout the Spanish empire were available for purchase in Havana with the profits from agricultural exports. Government officials in St. Augustine were quick to respond to the diversion of goods from the Florida capital and ordered that the needs of St. Augustine be met before any surpluses could be transported to the Caribbean (Hann 1988:152). It is highly unlikely that this mandate was strictly obeyed.

San Luis was the largest of the Apalachee missions with an estimated population of 1400 by 1675. Although the vast majority of the individuals were Christianized Apalachees, the site became home to several generations of powerful Spanish families who were actively engaged in ranching, shipping, military service, and regional politics. And although the Spanish population at San Luis was predominantly male, in at least one family two generations of Spanish women resided at the site (Chuba 1687). Consequently the Hispanic population of San Luis more closely approximated a cross section of Spanish colonial society than that which typically occupied either missions or military outposts.

Archaeological Investigations in the Spanish Village

RESEARCH GOALS

The location of the Spanish village at San Luis was first proposed in 1984 (Shapiro 1987). A sitewide auger survey revealed evidence of building materials, European hardware, and dense concentrations of Spanish ceramics and colono-wares in the area immediately east of the large central plaza (fig. 11.2). This hypothesis was further substantiated by a test excavation unit (1.5 m × 2 m) located at 188N/520E near the auger test at 190N/520E that had produced relatively large quantities of Hispanic-tradition materials. The auger hole and test unit were later determined to be situated in the middle of a large trash pit (Feature 6).

Two explicit research goals were set forth prior to excavations in the Spanish village (Shapiro 1986). The first was to examine town planning

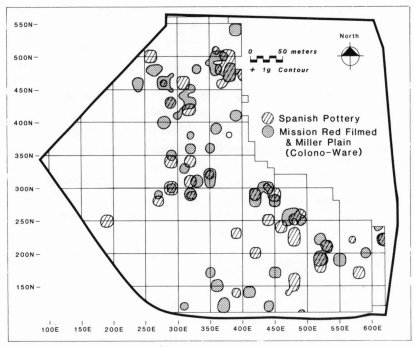

Figure 11.2. The distribution of Spanish ceramics and colono-ware at San Luis based on 1984 auger survey.

traditions at San Luis and test for evidence of a gridded village plan. Royal mandate specified that colonial New World towns were to be arranged in a highly regular and symmetrical pattern radiating out from the central plaza (Crouch, Garr, and Mundigo 1982; Stanislawski 1947; Zéndegui 1977). Although adherence to this basic town plan was often modified to suit local conditions (e.g., Deagan 1985), it has been identified archaeologically in colonial towns throughout the New World (Crouch, Garr, and Mundigo 1982). Shapiro suggested that the configuration of pottery and burned clay concentrations on the northeast side of the plaza in the Spanish village may have been evidence of a gridded town at San Luis (Shapiro 1986:8–9). ,

The second goal was to develop an image of daily life at a Spanish mission (Shapiro 1986). Specifically, it was hoped that architectural remains, artifact assemblages, and spatial patterning at residences would reveal differences in ethnicity, socioeconomic status, and subsistence within the Hispanic settlement and ultimately provide a better understanding of domestic continuity and change among Spaniards and natives living at the site.

Following several years of intensive excavations in the council house (Shapiro and McEwan 1992) and church complex (Shapiro and Vernon 1992), the Spanish village was targeted for large-scale excavations. Investigations focused on two areas within the village: the large trash pit (Feature 6) identified during the broad-scale testing phase and an area approximately 18 m east of the pit where large amounts of daub and hardware were recovered during the auger survey. Because these loci contained evidence of both trash disposal and structural remains, it was anticipated that they would provide baseline information about lot layout, activity areas, grid patterning (if any existed), and evidence for Spanish adaptations to local environmental and social conditions.

ARCHITECTURAL EVIDENCE

Structural evidence was encountered in the area extending from 176N to 196N and from 539E to 551E in the eastern half of the main block excavation (fig. 11.3). The remains of two buildings were identified, one of which intruded into the other. The earlier structure was identified by a series of wall trenches that ranged from 25 cm to 30 cm wide and from 15 cm to 20 cm deep (Vernon and Wilson 1991:22). They represent the remains of a two-room dwelling and associated outbuilding (fig. 11.4; Albert Manucy, personal communication 1989). The residence measured 6 m × 3.75 m and was oriented approximately 30° west of north. The outbuilding was 3 m wide, although its length was indeterminable due to tree disturbance. These buildings are thought to have had split-log foundations (sometimes called "mud sleepers") and were constructed of plank and thatch. Few materials were identified from the portion of the wall trench that was excavated (table 11.1). Given the relatively undiagnostic nature of the artifacts, the structure can only be dated to the mission period. The size, configuration, and construction materials of this building are consistent with pre-eighteenth-century domestic architecture in St. Augustine (Deagan 1985:13; Manucy 1978, 1985).

The later structure was identified by a series of postmolds and daub concentrations. The north and south walls of the structure were each identified by five postmolds spaced at intervals approximately 2.5 m apart (fig. 11.3). The east and west walls were delineated by three posts running north to south at about 3 m apart. There were also two posts

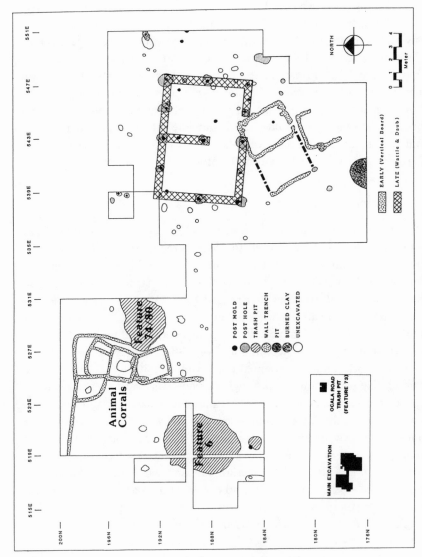

Figure 11.3. Major features revealed during excavations in the Spanish village.

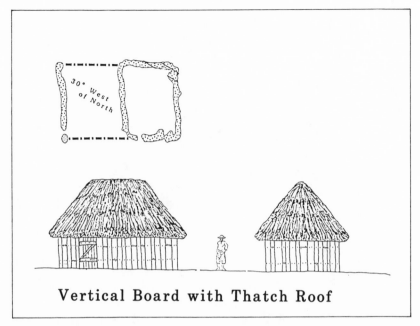

Vertical Board with Thatch Roof

Figure 11.4. Plan view of architectural remains and artist's reconstruction of the earliest house excavated in the Spanish village. (Illustration by Charles B. Poe.)

extending into the center of the structure from the north wall. The average post was 20–25 cm in diameter and extended 60–75 cm below ground surface (Vernon and Wilson 1991:25). This building was determined to be a 6-m-x-9-m wattle-and-daub residence with a central partition that divided the structure into two rooms (fig. 11.5; Albert Manucy, personal communication 1989). Many flat pieces of daub associated with the structure were whitewashed, suggesting that it had a Hispanic appearance.

Although the materials from the postholes were not particularly diagnostic (table 11.1), this residence is thought to have been constructed somewhat late in the 48-year occupation of San Luis because it intrudes into the remains of the earlier structure. Furthermore, a sherd associated with this building cross-mended with a sherd from the nearby large trash pit (Feature 6) whose *terminus post quem* is 1680–1700. The cross-mend also implies that the Feature 6 fill was probably associated with the occupants of this structure.

Unlike the earlier residence which was oriented west of north, the wattle-and-daub residence was situated at an angle 5° east of north (fig.

TABLE 11.1. Materials Associated with Domestic Structures in the Spanish Village[a]

Artifact categories	Plank-and-thatch building (wall trench)				Wattle-and-daub building (postholes)			
	Count	% of cat.	% of totl	weight[b]	Count	% of cat.	% of totl	weight[b]
Aboriginal ceramics								
Colono-ware	0	0	0	—	1	2.50	2.27	—
Lamar Complicated Stamped	0	0	0	—	2	5.00	4.55	—
Lamar Complicated Stamped: var. Early	1	1.79	1.39	—	0	0	0	—
Lamar Complicated Stamped: var. Rectilinear	0	0	0	—	1	2.50	2.27	—
Leon Check Stamped	1	1.79	1.39	—	1	2.50	2.27	—
Plain	47	83.93	65.28	—	27	67.50	61.36	—
Unidentified	6	10.71	8.33	—	6	15.00	13.64	—
Unidentified incised	0	0	0	—	1	2.50	2.27	—
Unidentified stamped	1	1.79	1.39	—	1	2.50	2.27	—
Category total	56	100.00	77.78	—	40	100.00	90.91	—
Glass								
Unidentified glass fragment	3	37.50	4.17	—	0	0	0	—
Unidentified tube bead	5	62.50	6.94	—	0	0	0	—
Category total	8	100.00	11.11	—	0	0	0	—
Lithics								
Chert flake	6	75.00	8.33	—	1	33.33	2.27	—
Chert flake, utilized/retouched	0	0	0	—	1	33.33	2.27	—

Chert fragment/shatter	2	25.00	2.78	—	0	0	0
Chert projectile point	0	0	0	—	1	33.33	2.27
Category total	8	100.00	11.11	—	3	100.00	6.82
Architectural hardware							
Unidentified iron nail fragment	0	0	0	—	1	100.00	2.27
Category total	0	0	0	—	1	100.00	2.27
Construction materials (weights only)							
Burned clay	—	—	—	531.30	—	—	1048.00
Burned clay with flat surface	—	—	—	55.60	—	—	121.90
Whitewash/plaster	—	—	—	2.00	—	—	5.70
Category total	—	—	—	588.90	—	—	1175.60
Miscellaneous							
Iron lump	—	—	—	1.30	—	—	4.40
Iron oxide (concretions and nodules)	—	—	—	255.70	—	—	547.20
Iron slag	—	—	—	0	—	—	4.80
Limestone	—	—	—	0	—	—	6.70
River pebbles	—	—	—	0.40	—	—	0
Sandstone	—	—	—	7.30	—	—	17.90
Unidentified clay	—	—	—	0	—	—	29.90
Category total	—	—	—	264.70	—	—	610.90
Assemblage total	72	100.00	100.00	853.60	44	100.00	1786.50

a. Organic materials such as faunal remains and charcoal are not included in this table.
b. All weights are measured in grams.

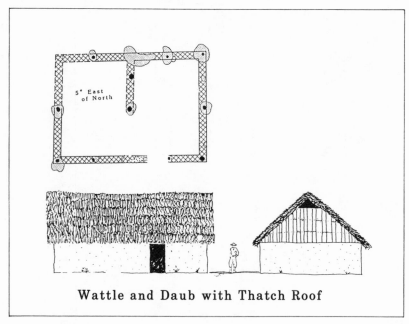

Wattle and Daub with Thatch Roof

Figure 11.5. Plan view and reconstruction of a later residence in the Hispanic village at San Luis. (Illustration by Charles B. Poe.)

11.3). This suggests that if the village had been gridded, houses did not maintain a consistent orientation within their lot boundaries through time.

TRASH PITS

Trash pits in the Spanish village at San Luis have come to be recognized as unusually valuable contexts. Although Charles Fairbanks (1977) articulated the virtues of backyard archaeology more than a decade ago, rarely has this potential been so fully realized as in these particular features.

The first trash pit identified in the Spanish village (Feature 6) measured approximately 6 m north-south and 4 m east-west and was 1.6 m at its deepest point (fig. 11.3). The feature could be characterized as roughly oval with several discrete basins in the bottom (fig. 11.6). Similar features have been identified at other Apalachee missions such as the Scott Miller site (Smith 1951:124–128) and at San Joseph de Ocuya (Jones 1973:1–

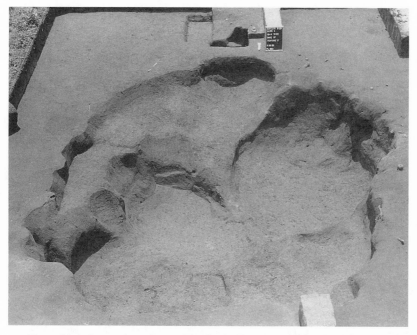

Figure 11.6. Large clay mine and trash pit (Feature 6) in the Spanish village.

50). While Smith interpreted the feature at the Scott Miller site as a borrow pit or clay mine that was filled with refuse, Jones suggested that a similar feature at San Joseph de Ocuya was orginally a semisubterranean pit house that was later used for trash disposal. However, the absence of architectural remains (i.e., postmolds) associated with Feature 6 at San Luis, along with the highly irregular shape of its sides and bottom, leaves little doubt that it was not a pit house but rather a large hole excavated for clay and subsequently used as a refuse pit.

The size and shape of these borrow pits suggest that they were labor-intensive group efforts with individual laborers (presumably native men) mining clay in separate basins. Spaniards readily took advantage of these massive holes for trash disposal. However, similar borrow pits dug to build up the clay platform on which the council house was constructed were left unfilled by the Apalachee and are still evident today as distinct depressions in the landscape (Shapiro and McEwan 1992).

The area north of Feature 6 was also excavated in order to investigate the possibility of nearby butchering activites because large quantities of fauna were found at the north end of the pit. Although there was no direct evidence of slaughtering and/or butchering, a series of corrals was identified (fig. 11.3). It is possible that butchering did occur near the corrals and the remains were carefully disposed of in the trash pit, leaving little evidence in the sheet midden. Additionally, another trash pit was encountered (Feature 74/80) approximately 6 m northeast of Feature 6. The size of the pit is unknown because it was not completely exposed during our excavations. However, like Feature 6, it was characterized by a series of basins rather than a single depression.

During the 1990–1991 field season one other trash pit was partially excavated. Located near Ocala Road on the eastern property boundary, this feature was threatened by city road-widening activities. The Ocala Road trash pit excavation (Feature 73) encompassed 44.5 square meters. It contained several basins, the deepest of which extended 1.94 m below ground surface. Although excavations were suspended before any edges were defined, the pit was more than 8.5 m in diameter, making it the largest trash pit identified to date at San Luis. Analysis of the materials from this massive feature is still in progress, but the assemblage closely mirrors those from the other trash deposits with respect to the quality and abundance of plant, animal, and material remains.

MATERIAL CULTURE

Remains recovered from the Spanish village have provided important material and biological assemblages for understanding Spanish domestic life at this mission outpost. While small amounts of materials were recovered from sheet midden underlying the plow zone (tables 11.2, 11.3), large pits excavated for clay were apparently used as the primary trash receptacles. The significant amounts of daub from the zone deposits and from the upper strata of the trash pits appear to have accumulated from episodes of building disintegration and/or demolition when residue daub was used to cap off trash deposits or left to form part of the ground surface.

Sherds from the largest trash pit analyzed to date (Feature 6) were cross-mended from upper and lower strata, indicating that these features were rapidly filled. The *terminus post quem* of both Feature 6 and Feature 74/80 is estimated at between 1680 and 1700 based on diagnostic majolica types. Despite the occurrence of several later majolica types, Puebla Polychrome was by far the most abundant classifiable type recovered from the village (fig. 11.7).

TABLE 11.2. Ceramics from the Spanish Village

Ceramic group	Main block sheet midden			Feature 6			Feature 74/80		
	Count	% of cat.	% of grp	Count	% of cat.	% of grp	Count	% of cat.	% of grp
Imported ceramics									
Majolica	89	55.28	5.37	636	33.87	3.36	311	66.45	6.22
Coarse earthenware	68	42.24	4.10	1210	64.43	6.40	152	32.48	3.04
Other European/Oriental ceramics	4	2.48	0.24	32	1.70	0.17	5	1.07	0.10
Total imported ceramics	161	100.00	9.72	1878	100.00	9.93	468	100.00	9.36
Aboriginal ceramics									
Traditional aboriginal ceramics	1379	92.18	83.22	15198	89.21	80.35	4041	89.17	80.82
Colono-ware	117	7.82	7.06	1838	10.79	9.72	491	10.83	9.82
Total aboriginal ceramics	1496	100.00	90.28	17036	100.00	90.07	4532	100.00	90.64
Total ceramics	1657	—	100.00	18914	—	100.00	5000	—	100.00

TABLE 11.3. Artifacts from the Spanish Village[a]

Artifact group and class	Main block sheet midden			Feature 6			Feature 74/80		
	Count	% of cat.	% of totl	Count	% of cat.	% of totl	Count	% of cat.	% of totl
Kitchen									
Ceramics	1657	98.05	87.58	18914	98.87	89.23	5000	99.21	89.30
Glass bottles	5	0.30	0.26	14	0.07	0.07	9	0.18	0.16
Other glassware	28	1.66	1.48	200	1.05	0.94	31	0.62	0.55
Utensils	0	0	0	2	0.01	0.01	0	0	0
Category total	1690	100.00	89.32	19130	100.00	90.24	5040	100.00	90.02
Personal									
Beads	18	100.00	0.95	1417	96.92	6.68	361	97.57	6.45
Brass hawk's bells	0	0	0	4	0.27	0.02	0	0	0
Jet *higa* pendants	0	0	0	7	0.48	0.03	0	0	0
Ornamental glass elements	0	0	0	13	0.89	0.06	9	2.43	0.16
Pendants	0	0	0	10	0.68	0.05	0	0	0
Pewter stickpin	0	0	0	1	0.07	0	0	0	0
Rings	0	0	0	3	0.21	0.01	0	0	0
Silver sequins	0	0	0	7	0.48	0.03	0	0	0
Category total	18	100.00	0.95	1462	100.00	6.90	370	100.00	6.61
Arms									
Gunflints	0	0	0	7	21.88	0.03	0	0	0
Lead pellets	0	0	0	13	40.63	0.06	0	0	0
Lead shot	0	0	0	3	9.38	0.01	2	100.00	0.04

Projectile points	9	100.00	0.48	9	28.13	0.04	0	0	0
Category total	9	100.00	0.48	32	100.00	0.15	2	100.00	0.04
Architectural hardware									
Flat glass	1	4.00	0.05	0	0	0	0	0	0
Iron nails	21	84.00	1.11	79	89.77	0.37	31	100.00	0.55
Iron spikes	2	8.00	0.11	5	5.68	0.02	0	0	0
Iron strap hinge	1	4.00	0.05	0	0	0	0	0	0
Iron tacks	0	0	0	4	4.55	0.02	0	0	0
Category total	25	100.00	1.32	88	100.00	0.42	31	100.00	0.55
Sewing and clothing									
Brass aglet	0	0	0	1	5.26	0	0	0	0
Brass button	0	0	0	1	5.26	0	0	0	0
Brass rivet	0	0	0	1	5.26	0	0	0	0
Sewing needles	0	0	0	5	26.32	0.02	0	0	0
Straight pins	0	0	0	11	57.89	0.05	0	0	0
Category total	0	0	0	19	100.00	0.09	0	0	0
Activities									
Aboriginal ceramic pipe	0	0	0	2	5.00	0.01	0	0	0
Brass nested counter weight	0	0	0	1	2.50	0	0	0	0
Iron chain	1	50.00	0.05	1	2.50	0	1	25.00	0.02
Iron hook	0	0	0	0	0	0	1	25.00	0.02
Iron ring	1	50.00	0.05	0	0	0	0	0	0
Iron wire	0	0	0	34	85.00	0.16	0	0	0

a. Material such as faunal remains, charcoal, slag, pebbles, etc., are not included in this table.

(*continued*)

TABLE 11.3. (Continued)

Artifact group and class	Main block sheet midden			Feature 6			Feature 74/80		
	Count	% of cat.	% of totl	Count	% of cat.	% of totl	Count	% of cat.	% of totl
Kaolin pipestems	0	0	0	2	5.00	0.01	2	50.00	0.04
Category total	2	100.00	0.11	40	100.00	0.19	4	100.00	0.07
Lithics									
Chert cores	0	0	0	2	0.59	0.01	1	0.71	0.02
Chert cortex fragments	7	4.83	0.37	2	0.59	0.01	6	4.26	0.11
Chert flakes	116	80.00	6.13	282	83.43	1.33	128	90.78	2.29
Chert fragment/shatter	11	7.59	0.58	25	7.40	0.12	1	0.71	0.02
Chert tools	7	4.83	0.37	11	3.25	0.05	2	1.42	0.04
Coral cores	0	0	0	2	0.59	0.01	0	0	0
Coral flakes	2	1.38	0.11	5	1.48	0.02	0	0	0
Coral fragment/shatter	0	0	0	2	0.59	0.01	0	0	0
Quartz flakes	0	0	0	2	0.59	0.01	0	0	0
Ground greenstone	0	0	0	1	0.30	0	0	0	0
Ground iron concretion	0	0	0	1	0.30	0	0	0	0
Ground sandstone	2	1.38	0.11	3	0.89	0.01	3	2.13	0.05
Category total	145	100.00	7.66	338	100.00	1.59	141	100.00	2.52
Miscellaneous									
Brass straps	0	0	0	0	0	0	2	18.18	0.04
Brass fragments	0	0	0	24	26.97	0.11	0	0	0

	n	% of cat.	% of assem.	n	% of cat.	% of assem.	n	% of cat.	% of assem.
Copper sheet	0	0	0	13	14.61	0.06	1	9.09	0.02
Iron objects	1	33.33	0.05	1	1.12	0	0	0	0
Iron strap fragments	0	0	0	2	2.25	0.01	4	36.36	0.07
Lead fragments	1	33.33	0.05	3	3.37	0.01	4	36.36	0.07
Lead lumps	1	33.33	0.05	33	37.08	0.16	0	0	0
Lead puddle	0	0	0	3	3.37	0.01	0	0	0
Lead splatter	0	0	0	9	10.11	0.04	0	0	0
Pewter fragment	0	0	0	1	1.12	0	0	0	0
Category total	3	100.00	0.16	89	100.00	0.42	11	100.00	0.20
Assemblage total	1892	—	100.00	21198	—	100.00	5599	—	100.00

Weighed construction materials[b]	Weight	% of cat.	Weight	% of cat.	Weight	% of cat.
Burned clay	71958.1	85.83	54860.7	68.35	6218.7	93.81
Burned clay with flat surface	4541.8	5.42	20870.5	26.00	191.8	2.89
Daub with impression	2448.5	2.92	4321.6	5.38	130.1	1.96
Plain lime	4.9	0.01	0	0	0	0
Spanish brick	0	0	12.2	0.02	0	0
Whitewash burned clay with flat surface	4533.6	5.41	197.7	0.25	81.6	1.23
Whitewash/plaster	147.4	0.18	0	0	6.9	0.10
Wood post	200.3	0.24	0	0	0	0
Category total	83834.6	100.00	80262.7	100.00	6629.1	100.00

b. All weights are measured in grams.

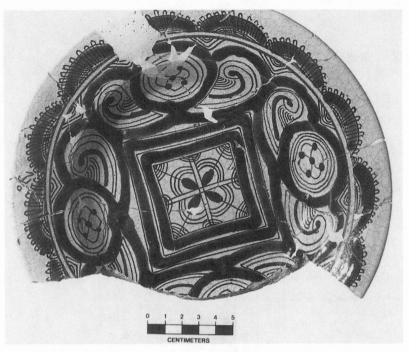

Figure 11.7. Puebla Polychrome plate recovered from one of the trash deposits in the village. (Vessel reconstructed by Ann S. Cordell, Florida Museum of Natural History.)

Collections from three contexts were combined for this study: undisturbed materials from zone or sheet deposits, Feature 6, and Feature 74/80 (tables 11.2, 11.3). Ceramics accounted for approximately 90 percent of all artifacts from each of these contexts and aboriginal ceramics comprised 90 percent of all ceramics. Imported ceramics accounted for 10 percent of each assemblage—considerably less than contemporaneous sites in St. Augustine, where European ceramics make up between 26.9 percent and 35.7 percent of late seventeenth-century deposits (King 1981:69). It appears that the shortage of imported tablewares was compensated for by the availability of colono-wares. These ceramics are thought to be locally made native copies of European vessel forms (Vernon and Cordell, this volume). Colono-wares accounted for 10 percent of the total ceramic assemblage from both trash pits—equal to the quantity of imported ceramics—and 7 percent of the ceramics from zone deposits (table 11.2).

Few weaponry-related artifacts were identified from the Spanish village despite the fact that most of the residents were part of the garrison stationed at San Luis. It appears that most of the arms and munitions were stored in the fort once construction was begun in 1695 rather than in private residences. This interpretation is supported by the large number of weaponry objects recovered from excavations within the fort complex at the site (Griffin 1951; Poe 1991).

The most unexpected materials from the Spanish village were the numerous items of personal adornment. Pendants, rings, and particularly beads accounted for 7 percent of the total artifact assemblage from both trash pits. More than 1400 glass beads were recovered from Feature 6 alone (Mitchem, this volume). This is all the more unusual when compared to contemporaneous proveniences from St. Augustine, where a total of three beads (two glass, one shell) were recovered from the late seventeeth-century components of three domestic sites (King 1981:97).

Although numerically small, objects such as debitage, hardware, sewing items, pipestems, and clay toy figurines illuminate some of the ancillary activities engaged in by Hispanic residents at San Luis and the Apalachee who were undoubtedly integrated into their households.

Another important attribute of the trash pit assemblages was the high concentration of organic materials, which are typically poorly preserved in the highly acidic soils of the region. Plant remains from the village consisted of both Old and New World domesticated and nondomesticated plants including maize, bean, sunflower, chickpea, peach, hickory, acorn, and grape (Scarry, this volume). Although few faunal remains had ever been recovered at San Luis prior to the excavation of the Spanish village, more than 8000 animal bones were recovered from Feature 6 alone. These included deer, horse, pig, cow, turtle, chicken, turkey, and several species of fishes—both freshwater and anadromous (Reitz, this volume).

Discussion

The first objective of the investigations of the Spanish village was to determine whether San Luis had a gridded village plan. Although documentary evidence indicates that the townsite of San Luis had a central plaza as well as subordinate plazas within the village areas, excavations to date have not resolved the extent of adherence to a grid system. The two domestic structures investigated revealed a change in house size, orientation, and location through time. This suggests that if the residential area was gridded, it must have been flexible enough to allow for second-generation buildings to be significantly modified from their earlier counterparts. It also provides evidence that houses probably did not front directly onto streets as they did in St. Augustine, as that arrangement would have dictated a consistent residential orientation and location. A divergence from mandated town planning is also apparent in the central plaza at San Luis, which was probably circular rather than square or rectangular in shape (Ordinance 112 as cited in Crouch, Garr, and Mundigo 1982:13).

With respect to the second research objective of the Spanish village excavations—to investigate daily life—we have been able to develop an image of domestic architecture, diet, and material life at San Luis and explore some of the concomitant implications for social and economic conditions at the site.

Hispanic architectural traditions appear to have been maintained during both phases of development. The earliest residence, constructed from plank and thatch, was similar to those documented in St. Augustine from the sixteenth and seventeenth centuries (Manucy 1978). The later building was larger and demonstrated a shift from plank-and-thatch to wattle-and-daub construction. It is unlikely that the use of wattle and daub can be attributed to native influence since few Apalachee wattle-and-daub structures have been identified archaeologically, and those that have been described are oval or round in shape (Scarry and McEwan 1991). However, rectangular plastered and whitewashed buildings were among the most common forms of architecture in southern Spain and may well have served as the template for colonial architecture in Spanish Florida (Manucy 1985; Morell Peguero 1986:102).

The excavations indicated that residential lots may have been sizable and included a variety of outdoor activity areas (fig. 11.8). Unlike most other Spanish colonial communities in *La Florida*, no wells have been identified anywhere at San Luis, including the Spanish village. It is presumed that water was collected from the several seep springs that flow year-round in the ravine on the northeast edge of the property. Easy access to fresh water and the elevation of the site (ca. 200 ft above sea level) would have made digging wells an arduous and unnecessary task.

Plant and animal remains from the Spanish village suggest that while endemic resources were utilized, introduced species did comparatively

Figure 11.8. Speculative view of daily life in the Spanish village at San Luis. (Illustration by Charles B. Poe.)

well in the area and were consumed by Spaniards in large quantities. This is particularly true of domestic mammals such as cattle and hogs, which, along with maize, formed the economic backbone of Apalachee Province. Reitz (this volume) has noted that the relative abundance of domestic fauna from the Spanish village suggests that the Hispanic residents at San Luis were enjoying many of the preferred foods that were unavailable to residents of other missions and the colonial elite living in the capital at St. Augustine.

The material culture recovered from the village excavations challenges some of the traditional notions of impoverished missions and frontier settlements and offers some insight into daily existence among Spanish colonists in the hinterlands. More than 25,000 artifacts have been analyzed from the limited excavations within the Spanish village, and these do not include the remains from the largest trash pit near Ocala Road. This stands in sharp contrast to the total of 3990 artifacts recovered from the late seventeenth-century components of three sites in St. Augustine (King 1981:98) and may indicate that few material shortages were felt among the Spaniards at San Luis.

The high percentage of local aboriginal ceramics from the Hispanic village at San Luis suggests that, as in St. Augustine (see Deagan, this volume), the demography of the site probably encouraged the incorporation of native women into Spanish households, either as wives or servants. Also, despite readily available local ceramics and some access to imported ceramics, colono-wares were apparently produced on a regular basis for Spanish military personnel and civilians living at San Luis. This may account for the unusually wide variety of vessel forms that occur at the site (Vernon and Cordell, this volume). Thus colono-wares were apparently not made strictly for friars residing at outlying missions (Deagan 1990:308) but supplemented ceramic shortages for other Spaniards as well. The question remains as to why they are abundant in the Hispanic village at San Luis but rare from households in St. Augustine.

The relatively high percentage of personal objects (many of which are luxurious and feminine in nature) recovered from the Spanish village suggests an unanticipated degree of prosperity among the inhabitants. The many beads, pendants, protective amulets (*higas*), rings, and sequins may have belonged to some of the affluent Spanish women who resided at the site and indulged themselves with displays of material wealth. They also may have kept large quantities of such goods (particularly beads) on hand as payment to native domestics.

Because many of these beads are traditionally considered trade items, it could also be that some actually belonged to natives, perhaps servants or wives of soldiers. It is also possible that the beads belonged to elite Apalachee living nearby. Native integration into a predominantly Spanish village would have served to reinforce leadership status among certain Apalachee and to strengthen their ties with the Spaniards. One document suggests that such residential patterning was in existence at San Luis. An account of Lieutenant Antonio Matheos indicates that he admonished one of the Apalachee leaders, who went "to his lodge and plaza crying, and that the Spaniards who lived around the said plaza, had consoled him" (quoted in Hann 1988:206).

Although the image of daily life from the Spanish village suggests a traditional Hispanic life-style, the possibility of highly acculturated Apalachee living among Spaniards cannot be discounted. Irrespective of this possibility, if these objects were readily available to the Apalachee, it is certain that they were even more accessible to the Spaniards.

Perhaps the most perplexing issue regarding these objects is why they were discarded in the first place. Most of the beads, pendants, and sequins are unbroken and were recoverd in perfect condition. It remains unknown why they were intentionally discarded in trash pits along with food remains, building rubble, and other household refuse.

Hispanic Life at San Luis

During its relatively brief existence, San Luis was second in importance only to St. Augustine. It was founded under very different conditions than the capital and its development was shaped by extremely favorable variables. In many ways Apalachee Province provided ideal preconditions for successful missions and colonial enterprises that were not only self-sustaining but even relatively prosperous. This attracted to the area a variety of Spaniards who engaged in both official and entrepreneurial activities.

Previous investigations of various complexes within the San Luis settlement (including the council house, church, and fort) have revealed a strong degree of cultural conservatism, with both native and Spanish areas exhibiting highly traditional building designs, construction materials, and activities (McEwan 1991). This interpretation has been reinforced by excavations in the Spanish village that suggest that the regional aristocracy enjoyed a degree of economic success marked by traditional housing, preferred foodstuffs, and elaborate material goods. The ability to maintain this standard of living and surround themselves in a familiar material world would have reinforced the Spanish community's cultural identity, enhanced social stratification within their enclave, and distinguished it from the native population by whom they were vastly outnumbered. Traditional pottery, colono-wares, clay mines, and perhaps objects of adornment suggest ways by which the local population was integrated into the lives of resident Spaniards as wives, domestics, laborers, and political allies.

There is little evidence to suggest that the Hispanic residents of San Luis were forced to make more profound adaptations than their fellow colonists living in St. Augustine even though San Luis was more isolated. In fact, the relative freedom from the restraints of bureaucracy, in conjunction with the fertile landscape, may have made the lives of Spaniards at San Luis among the most enviable in *La Florida*.

Acknowledgments

Funding for investigations in the Hispanic village at San Luis was provided by the state of Florida's Conservation and Recreation Lands (CARL) Trust Fund and the Florida Legislature. Additional funding was also provided by the National Endowment for the Humanities (RO-21395-87). The Bureau of Archaeological Research, and particularly Jim Miller, were a constant source of support and encouragement to the project.

From the outset, San Luis has been blessed with an unusually gifted and dedicated staff. Gary Shapiro initiated excavations in the Spanish village in 1988 prior to his untimely death. He continues to be with us in many ways. Richard Vernon, Jean Wilson, Elyse White, and Jennifer Lozowski distinguished themselves as superb field supervisors during the four years of village excavations. I also thank our many crew members who put in long hours in one of the most unbearably hot areas on the San Luis property. Charles Poe is responsible for turning dirty field maps and basic descriptions into polished graphics and illustrations. Finally, I would like to thank John Hann, who is a mentor to us all.

This paper benefited from the work of Elizabeth Reitz, Margaret Scarry, and Jeffrey Mitchem, who serve as consultants to the San Luis project, as well as from the comments of four reviewers.

Bibliography

Arnade, Charles W.
1965   *Cattle Ranching in Spanish Florida, 1513–1763*. St. Augustine Historical Society Publication no. 21. St. Augustine.

Boniface, Brian George
1971   A Historical Geography of Spanish Florida, circa 1700. Master's thesis, Department of Geography, University of Georgia, Athens.

Brose, David S.
1990   Apalachee Imposters. Paper presented at the 47th Annual Meeting of the Southeastern Archaeological Conference, Mobile, Alabama.

Bushnell, Amy
1978a The Menéndez Marquéz Cattle Barony at La Chua and the Determinants

of Economic Expansion in Seventeenth-Century Florida. *Florida Historical Quarterly* 56(4):407–431.

1978b "That Demonic Game": The Campaign to Stop Indian *Pelota* Playing in Spanish Florida, 1675–1684. *The Americas* 35:1–19.

Chuba, Matheo
1687 Testimony by, San Luis de Talimali, 29 May 1687.] In Alonso Solana 1687, Autos and Inquiry Made Concerning the Impossibility that Exists for Achieving the Exploration of the Coast of the Bay of Concepción, Which is Called of the Holy Spirit, that Is Planned to be Made from Apalachee. Archivo General de Indias, Escribanía de Cámara, leg. 156, cuaderno E, folio 31, Stetson Collection. P. K. Yonge Library of Florida History, University of Florida, Gainesville.

Crouch, Dora P., Daniel J. Garr, and Axel I. Mundigo
1982 *Spanish City Planning in North America*. Cambridge: MIT Press.

Deagan, Kathleen A.
1985 The Archaeology of Sixteenth-Century St. Augustine. *The Florida Anthropologist* 38(1–2):6–33.

1990 Accommodation and Resistance: The Process and Impact of Spanish Colonization in the Southeast. In *Columbian Consequences*. Vol. 2: *Archaeological and Historical Perspectives on the Spanish Borderlands East*, edited by David Hurst Thomas, 297–314. Washington, D.C.: Smithsonian Institution Press.

Fairbanks, Charles H.
1977 Backyard Archaeology as Research Strategy. *Conference on Historic Site Archaeology Papers* 1976(11):133–139.

Griffin, John W.
1951 Excavations at the Site of San Luis. In *Here They Once Stood: The Tragic End of the Apalachee Missions*, by Mark F. Boyd, Hale G. Smith, and John W. Griffin, 137–160. Gainesville: University of Florida Press.

Hann, John H.
1988 *Apalachee: The Land between the Rivers*. Ripley P. Bullen Monographs in Anthropology and History, no. 7. Gainesville: University of Florida Press.

1989 The Apalachee of the Historic Era. Paper presented at the NEH Summer Institute, Spanish Explorers and Indian Chiefdoms: The Southeastern United States in the Sixteenth and Seventeenth Centuries, at the University of Georgia, Athens.

Jones, B. Calvin
1973 A Semi-Subterranean Structure at Mission San Joseph de Ocuya, Jefferson County, Florida. *Bureau of Historic Sites and Properties Bulletin* 3:1–50.

King, Julia
1981   An Archaeological Investigation of Seventeenth-Century St. Augustine, Florida. Master's thesis, Department of Anthropology, Florida State University, Tallahassee.

McEwan, Bonnie G.
1991   San Luis de Talimali: The Archaeology of Spanish-Indian Relations at a Florida Mission. *Historical Archaeology* 25(3):36–60.

Manucy, Albert C.
1978   *The Houses of St. Augustine, 1565–1821.* St. Augustine: St. Augustine Historical Society.

1985   The Physical Setting of Sixteenth-Century St. Augustine. *The Florida Anthropologist* 38(1–2):34–53.

Morell Peguero, Blanca
1986   *Mercaderos y Artesanos en la Sevilla del Descubrimiento.* Diputación Provincial de Sevilla, Sección Historia, ser. 1a, no. 29. Sevilla: Gráficas del Sur.

Poe, Charles B.
1991   1990 Moat Investigations at San Luis. Project report on file, San Luis Archaeological and Historic Site, Tallahassee.

Scarry, John F., and Bonnie G. McEwan
1991   Domestic Architecture in Apalachee Province: Apalachee and Spanish Residential Styles in the Late Prehistoric and Early Historic Periods. Paper presented at the 1991 Society for Historical Archaeology Conference on Historical and Underwater Archaeology, Richmond, Virginia.

Shapiro, Gary
1986   Town Plan and Town Life at Seventeenth-Century San Luis. Ms. on file, San Luis Archaeological and Historic Site, Tallahassee.

1987   *Archaeology at San Luis: Broad-Scale Testing, 1984–1985.* Florida Archaeology no. 3. Tallahassee: Florida Bureau of Archaeological Research.

Shapiro, Gary, and Bonnie G. McEwan
1992   *Archaeology at San Luis: The Apalachee Council House.* Florida Archaeology no. 6, pt. 1. Tallahassee: Florida Bureau of Archaeological Research.

Shapiro, Gary, and Richard Vernon
1992   *Archaeology at San Luis: The Church Complex.* Florida Archaeology no. 6, pt. 2. Tallahassee: Florida Bureau of Archaeological Research.

Smith, Hale G.
1951   A Spanish Mission Site in Jefferson County, Florida. In *Here They Once Stood: The Tragic End of the Apalachee Missions,* by Mark F. Boyd, Hale

G. Smith, and John W. Griffin, 107–136. Gainesville: University of Florida Press.

Stanislawski, Dan
1947   Early Spanish Town Planning in the New World. *The Geographical Review* 37:94–105.

Vernon, Richard, and Jean S. Wilson
1991   Excavations in the Spanish Village at San Luis, 1988–1991. Project report on file, San Luis Archaeological and Historic Site, Tallahassee.

Zéndegui, Guillermo de
1977   City Planning in the Spanish Colonies. *Americas* 29(2):s1–s12. Special Supplement.

❂ 12 ❂

On the Frontier of Contact: Mission Bioarchaeology in *La Florida*

CLARK SPENCER LARSEN

The establishment of discrete burial areas in missions with exclusive practice of Christian-style modes of interment (versus traditional burial in earth mounds) was undoubtedly high on the list of priorities when missionaries set out to Christianize Native American populations in *La Florida*. Historical sources concur that Indian neophytes were strongly encouraged to follow church guidelines for treatment of the remains of deceased (see Milanich and Sturtevant 1972).

Within a period of less than a century following the establishment of the first missions in Atlantic coastal Florida and Georgia, alterations in native belief systems regarding death and final disposition had been effectively implemented. The archaeological record demonstrates the success of this aspect of the mission effort in Spanish Florida, at least with regard to mortuary behavior and the remarkable uniformity of interment pattern observed in mission sites (Larsen 1990b). Beginning in the 1930s, archaeologists and biological anthropologists working in the region have excavated hundreds of skeletal individuals (summarized in table 12.1), thus offering a wealth of anthropological information relating to mortuary activity. The populations represented by these human remains were among some of the earliest to be contacted by Europeans north of Mexico. Therefore, in addition to information on mortuary behavior, the study of skeletal remains offers an opportunity to understand better the biological ramifications of sustained, long-term contact with Europeans, including responses to introduced diseases, dietary change, undernutrition, labor demands, and a host of other variables that characterize this period of Native American history in the Southeast (see Larsen 1990b).

This chapter will pursue two primary goals: to review and describe the extraordinary mortuary record in the mission sites of *La Florida* and to summarize key developments leading to our present understanding of the biological changes in native populations based on the study of human remains from these sites. Nonmission, historic-era skeletal samples have been recovered from intrusive contexts in prehistoric burial mounds (Cook and Pearson 1973; Larsen and Thomas 1982; Pearson 1977) as well as in other contexts in the region (Hutchinson 1990, 1991; Koch 1983; Storey 1990; Storey and Widmer n.d.). However, this discussion will restrict itself to missions only.

The Mortuary Record

Despite attempts at establishing mission centers among many native groups in the region (Hann 1990; others in this volume), successes were largely restricted to three tribal provinces, Guale, Timucua, and Apalachee. Hence the archaeological record of missions and their cemeteries is associated mostly with these regions. This review begins with the Guale administrative center and primary mission on St. Catherines Island, Georgia, continues southward along the Atlantic coast to St. Augustine, turns westward through Timucua, and terminates with the administrative center of Apalachee at San Luis de Talimali.

GUALE

Santa Catalina de Guale. Except for the presence of several mission efforts north of St. Catherines Island (e.g., Chesapeake Bay), this mission was the northernmost limit of long-term Spanish colonial efforts on the Atlantic coast (G. D. Jones 1978; Thomas 1987). Excavations in the floor of the church under the direction of Clark Spencer Larsen from 1982 through 1986 recovered a minimum of 431 individuals (fig. 12.1; Larsen 1990:19). David Hurst Thomas's excavations of the church walls and

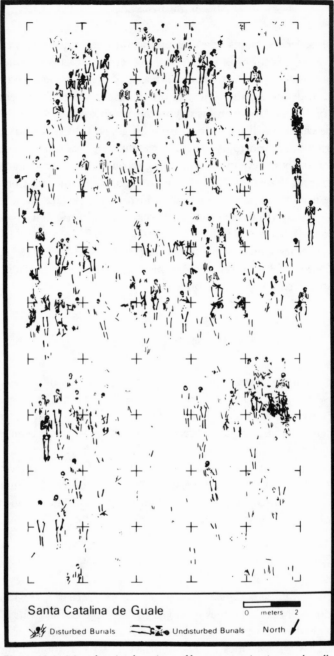

Santa Catalina de Guale

Disturbed Burials   Undisturbed Burials   North

0 meters 2

Figure 12.1. Map showing locations of human remains (except bundle burial) at Santa Catalina de Guale, St. Catherines Island, Georgia. (From Larsen 1990; reproduced with permission from the American Museum of Natural History.)

associated architectural features indicate that most burials are contemporary with a second wattle-and-daub structure erected on the site of an earlier building that had been burned during the 1597 native rebellion (Thomas personal communication 1990). The terminal date of burial activity in the cemetery is 1680, the year the mission was abandoned. Burials were oriented parallel to the long axis of the church (northeast-southwest), which also follows the orientation of the bluffline immediately to the west. Human remains were found in supine, extended positions, with the hands folded on the torso (variously from immediately beneath the chin to the mid-abdominal region). Heads were directed toward the southwest away from the presumed altar. A single instance of coffin burial was found in the immediate vicinity of the altar. All other interments were encountered in oval-shaped pits without coffin associations. Only one grave contained evidence of multiple interment. In this instance, the disarticulated remains of four children were resting on top of the torso and upper legs of an adult female.

Nearly half of the individuals recovered (47.6 percent) were in secondary, disturbed contexts resulting from later burials intruding on earlier burials. This arrangement of human remains reflects the intensive mortuary activity in a limited burial area over the period of use of the cemetery (Larsen 1990b). One additional individual was recovered in 1991 by Larsen on the northwest wall of the church. In contrast to all other burials, this was a bundle burial comprised of completely disarticulated long bones and a skull of a young adult male (16–17 years of age). As far as can be determined, the entire cemetery has been excavated. No other cemeteries dating to the mission period have been encountered elsewhere on St. Catherines Island.

Larsen's excavations at the Santa Catalina cemetery produced an unusual abundance of artifactual grave inclusions or offerings, most of which were European in origin (e.g., religious medallions, crucifixes, copper bells, thousands of glass [and some wood and shell] beads, majolica plates, and vessels). Some native-produced artifacts were also present, including a Mississippian-style shell gorget, chunkey stones, and chipped stone tools. Grave inclusions tended to be associated with burials in the vicinity of the altar.

The human remains from Santa Catalina have been the focus of an ongoing bioarchaeological analysis involving paleopathological and other comparisons with numerous precontact Guale skeletons from this and other localities on the Georgia coast (Larsen 1990; and see Hutchinson and Larsen 1988; Larsen 1992; Larsen, Shavit, and Griffin 1991; Larsen et al. 1990, 1992).

Santa Catalina de Guale de Santa María (Main Cemetery). This mission is also referred to as Santa María de Guale in the historical literature (Hann 1990:498) and as the Harrison Homestead site (Hemmings and Deagan 1973) or, more recently, the Dorion site (Hardin 1986) in the archaeological literature. The predominance of Guale ceramics and the discovery of a brass stamp depicting the patron saint, Santa Catalina, at this site indicate that this locality was the reestablished Santa Catalina de Guale on Amelia Island (Hardin 1986). The mission was occupied mostly in the late seventeenth and early eighteenth centuries (1686–1702) by Guale primarily from St. Catherines Island, but other Guale settlements are also likely represented (Hann 1990:498). Excavations involving the collective efforts of Kenneth Hardin, Rebecca Saunders, Clark Larsen, and Jerald Milanich over a two-year period (1985–1986) produced the remains of 121 well-preserved skeletons from the interior of a simple church (see Saunders, this volume). The long axis of the cemetery and the burial pits contained within were oriented on a southeast-northwest axis. Heads were directed toward the southeast. Few skeletons were recovered in disturbed contexts (7.5 percent). The general lack of disturbance and intrusive burial activity likely reflects the short-term use of the cemetery (Saunders 1988:7). Two double interments were encountered; all other skeletons were single burials.

With the exception of one bundle burial of an adult (50+ years) male, the skeletons were encountered in supine, extended postures. The bundle burial was found on the extreme northwestern margin of the cemetery (Saunders 1988:6). The presence of this unique form of burial treatment may or may not be coincidental with the presence of a single bundle interment in a corresponding location within the cemetery at Santa Catalina on St. Catherines Island. In sharp contrast to the mission cemetery on St. Catherines Island, few grave inclusions were encountered with these burials. The human remains are included in the aforementioned bioarchaeological research program (Larsen et al. 1990).

Santa Catalina de Guale de Santa María (Ossuary). In the northeastern corner of the main cemetery, archaeological crews under the supervision of Saunders and Larsen excavated a large, rectangular pit containing a mass burial comprised of mostly disarticulated human remains representing a minimum of 57 individuals (fig. 12.2). These remains had likely been stored in some type of charnel structure prior to their burial

Figure 12.2 Disarticulated remains contained in the ossuary at Santa Catalina de Guale de Santa María, Amelia Island, Florida.

(Larsen and Saunders 1987:9). Enumeration and analysis of partially articulated skeletal units (e.g., feet, hands, vertebrae) suggest that the accumulation of human remains took place over a period of up to several years and probably did not represent deaths due to an epidemic (Simmons, Larsen, and Russell 1989:7). The sex composition of the series is highly unusual—approximately 80 percent of the adults whose sex could be determined (n = 41) are females (Simmons, Larsen, and Russell 1989:8).

The skeletal remains of two fully articulated adult males in supine, extended positions were encountered immediately beneath the mass interment (fig. 12.3). The presence of a rectangular pattern of iron nails around these two skeletons indicates that they had been placed in a wooden coffin. The two skeletons were oriented southwest to northeast (heads to the southwest), which is perpendicular to the burials in the main cemetery. There is no evidence for passage of time between interment of the primary burials and the disarticulated remains.

The temporal and cultural associations between the ossuary and the main cemetery at Santa Catalina are unclear. However, the orientations of primary burials in the ossuary and main cemetery may provide an impor-

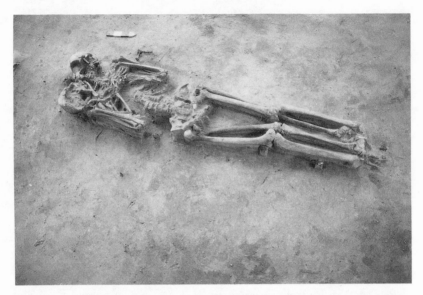

Figure 12.3. The disarticulated remains shown in figure 12.2 have been removed from the Santa Catalina de Guale de Santa María ossuary, revealing two extended, supine adult males. These individuals had been interred inside a wooden coffin prior to the placement of the disarticulated mass burial.

tant clue regarding the temporal relationship of the two skeletal series. That is, the presence of strict uniformity of orientation in the main cemetery suggests that burial of the two primary individuals occurred under a different set of interment rules. In addition, a primary burial with the same orientation as burials in the main cemetery intrudes into the upper pit fill of the ossuary. There is no evidence for intrusion of the ossuary pit into the main cemetery. Had this been the case, human bones originating from the main cemetery would have been scattered throughout the ossuary pit fill. This was not so—the ossuary pit fill was devoid of human remains (excepting the single, intrusive burial). These observations suggest that the ossuary series represents a burial event *predating* the skeletal accumulation in the main cemetery, perhaps by some years.

Although the ossuary is a contact-era death assemblage, the tribal and specific mission affiliations are unknown. It is possible that the ossuary predates the arrival of Guale and establishment of the mission identified with this site. The human remains are under investigation by Larsen and co-workers (Simmons, Larsen, and Russell 1989).

Santa María de los Yamassee. By the 1920s, Amelia Island residents had observed human skeletal remains eroding out of an exposed bank overlooking Harrison Creek at the Dorion site (Saunders 1988). In an area located 30 m to the southeast of the Santa Catalina main cemetery and ossuary, an archaeological survey of Amelia Island revealed several skeletons eroding out of the bank following a hurricane (Bullen and Griffin 1952). Five concentrations of human remains exposed on this bank were explored by Saunders and Larsen in 1986, and a sixth burial was fully excavated in the following year. These remains were in supine, extended positions in a northeast-to-southwest axis with heads to the southwest. The orientations were identical to the two primary interments in the Santa Catalina ossuary.

Virtually complete excavation of the cemetery later in 1987 revealed the presence of an additional 118 burials beneath the floor of a church structure. The long axis of the church/cemetery followed the orientation of the bluff, northeast to southwest (Saunders 1988). Study of the architectural remains of the structure indicates that it was likely a wooden church built on footing constructed out of densely packed marine shells. Grave inclusions were located in only three burials. One double interment (two juveniles) was observed, and all other graves contained one individual each. Erosion caused by the adjacent Harrison Creek has resulted in loss of approximately half of the structure and cemetery since the time of mission occupation. Based on the number of burials excavated, the original cemetery likely contained about 250 individual interments (Saunders 1988:22).

All but four burials at Santa María were extended, supine skeletons aligned along the long axis of the church. Two of the four exceptions were oriented perpendicular to the long axis of the church and intruded into burials aligned in the northeast-southwest axis. Orientations of these two individuals are the same as most of the skeletons in the Santa Catalina main cemetery. The other two exceptions were tightly flexed burials, also lying perpendicular to the long axis of the church.

The temporal position of this cemetery relative to the nearby Santa Catalina main cemetery and ossuary is problematical. However, based on the pattern of burial orientations, this cemetery may be earlier than the Santa Catalina main cemetery. That is, the four later intrusions follow the same orientation as burials in the Santa Catalina main cemetery, while the orientations of most of the burials are similar to the orientations of the two primary individuals in the ossuary. Historical records suggest that this cemetery population is from the earlier mission, Santa María de los Yamassee (Saunders 1988). The first mention of this mission is in 1675, but the actual founding date is unknown. If Santa María and Santa Catalina (Amelia Island) mortality rates were similar, then the presence of a relatively large number of graves indicates that the founding date of the former was likely well before 1675. The refugee Yamassee population inhabiting Santa María abandoned it in 1683 (Bushnell 1986:5). It is possible that the human remains are from a local Timucuan population. However, there is no mention in historical records of a Timucuan mission at this location during the later seventeenth century. Human remains from this cemetery are currently being prepared for detailed study by C. S. Larsen.

TIMUCUA

San Juan del Puerto. When first established on Fort George Island at the mouth of the St. Johns River (probably before 1587), this mission was inhabited by Saturiwa Timucua. However, by the time of abandonment in 1702, it was likely inhabited by Guale and possibly other refugee populations from the Georgia coast and mainland (Hann 1990:436). In a small excavation unit (1 m by 2 m) at the mission site, skeletal elements and teeth representing a minimum of three individuals were recovered from an ossuary. There were no apparent articulations in the skeletal assemblage (Dickinson 1989; Dickinson and Wayne 1985). This may not be the only cemetery for San Juan del Puerto, because partial skeletal remains of one individual were encountered at each of two other localities at the mission site (Dickinson and Wayne 1985). Although the mortuary program is difficult to assess due to the limited extent of the excavation, the presence of disarticulated bones only is reminiscent of the ossuary pattern of burial that has been more fully documented on Amelia Island. Given the strict adherence of mission Indians to Christian burial practices, it is possible that ossuary interment may be representative of death assemblages predating the full development of missionization but certainly postdating initial contact by Europeans. Beyond a listing of bones and teeth recovered from the ossuary at the site (see Dickinson and Wayne 1985), the human remains from this mission have not been subjected to detailed osteological analysis.

Nombre de Dios. Established among Timucua just north of St. Augustine, this was the oldest and most long-lived of the missions in Spanish Florida (Hann 1990:426). The cemetery associated with it was the first to

be excavated by archaeologists. In 1934 J. R. Dickson—in consultation
with M. W. Stirling—exposed 74 skeletons, the majority of which were
extended and supine with heads directed toward the west (Seaberg
1991:220). Three burials were bundles and two were tightly flexed individuals. The cemetery was apparently located outside the church structure.

Seaberg noted that the remains "were in a remarkable state of preservation when found" (Seaburg 1991:221). Unfortunately, many of the
burials were left exposed in situ in a partially protected museum exhibit
at the Fountain of Youth Park (Dickel 1990). The combined effects of
vandalism, theft, and at least two hurricanes resulted in the destruction of
most of the exposed remains. The only biocultural analysis of these remains was completed on site by David N. Dickel (1990) prior to reinter-
ment in 1991. Given the extensive deterioration of the existing materials,
few meaningful data could be collected by him. Of the remains of 12
individuals examined (the other skeletons had completely deteriorated),
10 were adults and 2 were juveniles. Inspection of teeth in the sample
revealed a high prevalence of dental caries, reflecting a dietary focus on
carbohydrates in this population.

Santa Fé de Toloca. This mission was first mentioned by Fray Oré in
his 1616 visitation. Although it experienced dramatic population losses
during the middle of the seventeenth century, the mission survived until
the village was burned in the 1702 raids. The location of the mission was
discovered in the late 1980s in northwestern Alachua County, Florida,
and has since been archaeologically documented by K. Johnson and J. T.
Milanich (Johnson, this volume). Preliminary test excavations in the cemetery area revealed a single skeleton and 18 burial pits. The skeleton was
examined in situ, and the burial pits were not excavated. The skeleton
was supine and extended with the hands folded on the chest. A large
number of spikes and nails in the vicinity of the cemetery suggests that
interments may have been placed within the walls of a church.

San Martín de Timucua. Also called San Martín de Ayaocuto (see
Hann 1990:461), this Utina Timucuan mission is known archaeologically
as the Fig Springs site (Ichetucknee Springs State Park, Columbia County,
Florida). The mission was likely occupied during at least the first half of
the seventeenth century and abandoned in 1656 (Hann 1990:461). Archaeological work completed by Jerald Milanich, Brent Weisman, Rebecca Saunders, and Lisa Hoshower in 1990 and 1991 resulted in the
recovery of 65 skeletons that were in supine, extended positions with

heads to the east. The vast majority of these remains are in a church cemetery, with the remainder possibly from an earlier chapel (Hoshower 1991). About one-third of the remains were from disturbed contexts. No clear pattern of location of burial by age or sex could be discerned. Only four burials contained purposeful artifact inclusions, including three with beads and a single interment with a metal crucifix. The human remains are currently being studied by Lisa Hoshower as part of a doctoral dissertation (see also Hoshower and Milanich, this volume; Weisman, this volume).

San Pedro y San Pablo de Potohiriba. This Timucuan mission and its cemetery were partially excavated by B. Calvin Jones (1972) in Madison County, Florida. More than 50 of an estimated 250 burials were excavated in a nonchurch cemetery representing an occupation spanning most of the seventeenth century. The burials were in extended, supine positions. Only two European-produced grave inclusions were encountered during the course of Jones's excavations. Jones noted a high frequency of burial disturbance and the presence of graves "stacked two and three layers deep" (B. C. Jones 1972:2). It is not clear whether these "stacked" interments represent multiple burials or disturbances arising from later burials intruding into earlier burials. No osteological analysis has been completed on the human remains from this mission.

San Miguel de Asile. This post-1633 mission is considered by most workers as the westernmost Timucuan mission. However, the presence of an Apalachee chief during later occupation as well as its geographic location have added confusion to the process of identifying the tribal affiliation (Jones and Shapiro 1990; and see Hann 1990). The site of the mission, located in Madison County, Florida, was archaeologically tested by B. Calvin Jones (1972). In a 10-ft-by-10-ft test unit, Jones excavated 10 individual skeletons in supine, extended positions. A multiple interment represented by 5 flexed or disarticulated individuals was also exposed. Jones has interpreted the cemetery as being located outside of the church. The human remains exposed in the cemetery were not studied.

APALACHEE

San Lorenzo de Ivitachuco. This mission was among the first founded (1633) and last abandoned (1704) in Apalachee (Hann 1990:476–477). The site of the mission was identified in the early 1970s in Jefferson County, Florida (B. C. Jones 1972). Jones has described the cemetery as being "L-shaped," containing an estimated 300–600 burials (Jones and Shapiro 1990:501). He has suggested that the cemetery is a nonchurch death assemblage. In a limited test excavation in 1972, Jones exposed 15 burial pits, of which only two yielded poorly preserved human bones; no skeletal remains were encountered in the other 13 burial pits (Jones personal communication 1991). The orientation of the burial pits was northwest to southeast. No analysis of human remains from the two burial pits was completed.

San Pedro y San Pablo de Patale. Also known as the Patale I site, this Apalachee mission was located in Leon County, Florida. It was likely the first setting (of two) for a mission going by this name (Hann 1990:498). Historical accounts indicate that it was abandoned by the mid-seventeenth century. During fieldwork in 1971, B. Calvin Jones excavated 65 burial pits containing 67 individuals in the floor of the church (Jones and Shapiro 1990:498; Jones, Storey, and Widmer 1991:109). The cemetery was completely excavated. The burials followed the orientation of the long axis of the church (southwest-northeast), and most individuals were found in supine, extended positions with the heads pointed northeast. Two exceptions to this pattern were observed—one individual with the head to the southwest and another individual with semiflexed legs. The burials were contained within distinct rows and showed little evidence of intrusion. Fourteen of the individuals were found with artifactual grave inclusions.

The human remains (58 individuals were complete enough for study) are part of an ongoing bioanthropological investigation of the skeletal series by Rebecca Storey (1986, personal communication 1991; Jones, Storey, and Widmer 1991).

The post-1647 resettlement of Patale (Patale II: San Pedro de Patale) was discovered and archaeologically tested by B. Calvin Jones in 1969 (Jones and Shapiro 1990). The locality, known as the Turkey Roost site, was found to contain what appeared to Jones as a nonchurch cemetery. To date, this cemetery has not been archaeologically tested.

San Damián de Escambé. This important mission, located in Leon County, Florida, was founded at the Apalachee town of Cupaica in 1639. However, by 1704 the mission population had moved to "within a cannon shot of San Luis" (Hann 1990:484). Archaeological testing of the site in 1969 and 1970 by B. Calvin Jones revealed the presence of a cemetery, the first to be encountered in Apalachee Province (Jones and Shapiro 1990). The cemetery did not appear to be in association with a building. Some 143 burial pits were defined; 42 burial pits were excavated. Three burials were found in association with wooden coffins. Most burials followed the long axis of the church (southeast-northwest) and were in supine, extended positions with heads oriented toward the southeast. Several double interments were encountered, including two adult burials and one juvenile burial (B. C. Jones 1970). Few graves contained artifact inclusions.

Most of the human remains were left in situ, but the fragmentary skeletal and dental remains representing 13 individuals were recovered by Jones for laboratory investigation (Dickel n.d.). Examination of these materials by David Dickel in 1990 shows that the remains observed by him are mostly juveniles. These materials are incomplete, thus precluding detailed analysis (Dickel n.d.).

San Luis de Talimali. Probably one of the first of the missions established among the Apalachee in 1633, this mission was the administrative center for this province (Hann 1990). The San Luis archaeological site, located in Tallahassee, Florida, is the mission, military garrison, and associated village that was first occupied in 1656 and abandoned in 1704 (McEwan 1991; Shapiro 1987). Excavations in a test unit in one area of the cemetery by Gary Shapiro in 1987 revealed the presence of about 20 overlapping burial pits. Disturbed cranial fragments and teeth, representing mostly juvenile individuals, were recovered (Larsen 1990a; McEwan 1991; Vernon and McEwan 1990). Further excavations by Bonnie G. McEwan in the corner of the cemetery demonstrated that it is located beneath the floor of a wooden church building (McEwan 1991). Based on these preliminary excavations, the long axis of the burials and the church is oriented northwest-southeast. In 1991 Larsen and McEwan continued work in the cemetery, locating and excavating 28 additional burials as well as the disturbed remains of perhaps as many as 50 other individuals. A number of burial pits contained no human remains, owing to complete lack of skeletal or dental preservation. Like some of the other mission cemeteries, this investigation revealed a high degree of disturbance of earlier interments by later burial activity. The remains of seven wooden coffins containing adult skeletons were exposed, all in the altar area. The more elaborate mortuary treatment of these individuals suggests the presence of a social hierarchy at San Luis. Three individuals at the extreme west end of the cemetery were buried with their heads to the west, opposite all other skeletons. At least two of these individuals were in coffins. Without exception, skeletons in the San Luis cemetery were supine and extended with hands folded in the chest area. Based on excavations completed thus far, 600 to 700 individuals are likely interred here.

A plethora of artifacts have been recovered in the cemetery, including hundreds of glass beads, glass pendants, and a crystal crucifix (Mitchem 1990, unpublished; Vernon and McEwan 1990). Santa Catalina de Guale (St. Catherines Island) is the only other cemetery in *La Florida* containing this magnitude of grave inclusions. The wealth of material culture recovered from the cemeteries at San Luis and Santa Catalina underscores the importance of these missions within their respective provinces, Apalachee and Guale, and in *La Florida* generally.

SUMMARY OF THE MISSION SKELETAL RECORD

Fourteen mission skeletal samples (from 12 sites) have been excavated in three tribal provinces in *La Florida* (Guale [or Yamassee] = 4; Timucua = 5; Apalachee = 5; see table 12.1). Tribal identification is available for most of the assemblages. Only two of the skeletal series can be characterized as involving predominantly non-Christian interment practices. Mortuary behavior as reflected in these two series—comprised of mostly disarticulated human remains—has been only recently archaeologically documented in *La Florida*. However, this mode of burial is not unexpected, because references to it are provided by early historical accounts of mortuary treatment. Oviedo (1959:328), for example, described a pattern of burial whereby "many bones of the deceased, those of children and infants separated from those of the adults; and these are as ossuaries or burying places of the common people, for those of the principal men are kept apart in a chapel or temple separated from the other community" (quoted in G. D. Jones 1978:199). Therefore, these two localities provide archaeological verification for ossuary interment in these native populations.

Most cemeteries contain interments that are in postures typical of Christian-style burial—bodies were placed in graves in supine, extended postures with hands folded or clasped. Several of these cemeteries contain one or several graves that are different from these burial formats, including several instances of bundle or flexed burials. The graves were mostly oval-shaped and were generally dug to fit the size of the body being interred. No evidence exists for treatment of burial pits—such as the placement of a pit lining—either before or after placement of the bodies.

At least six cemeteries were encountered within walls of churches in these missions; the other cemeteries were not associated with obvious buildings. However, future excavations along the outer margins of some of the latter might reveal the presence of architectural features indicating direct associations with church structures (see McEwan 1991). With the exception of Santa Catalina (St. Catherines Island) and San Luis de Talimali, few graves have associated artifacts.

TABLE 12.1. Missions of *La Florida:* Human Remains

Mission[a]	N[b]	Context	Reference(s)
Santa Catalina de Guale (23)	*432*	church	Larsen 1990; Larsen et al. 1990
Santa Catalina de Guale de Santą María (112)	*121*	church	Hardin 1986; Larsen et al. 1990; Saunders 1988
Santa Catalina de Guale de Santa María (112)	*59*	ossuary	Saunders 1988; Simmons, Larsen, and Russell 1989
Santa María de los Yamassee (111)	124	church	Saunders 1988
San Juan del Puerto (19)	5	ossuary	Dickinson 1989; Dickinson and Wayne 1985
Nombre de Dios (5)	74	cemetery	Dickel 1990; Seaberg 1991
Santa Fé de Toloca (55)	*1*	cemetery	Johnson, this volume
San Martín de Timucua (57)	65	church	Hoshower 1990, 1991
San Pedro de Potohiriba (75)	>50	cemetery	Jones 1972
San Miguel de Asile (78)	15	cemetery	Jones 1972
San Lorenzo de Ivitachuco (79)	2	cemetery	Jones 1972; Jones and Shapiro 1990
San Pedro y San Pablo de Patale (85)	*58*	church	Jones and Shapiro 1990; Jones, Storey, and Widmer 1991; Storey 1986
San Damián de Escambé (89)	13	cemetery	Dickel n.d.; Jones 1970; Jones and Shapiro 1990
San Luis de Talimali (91)	¯75	church	Larsen 1990a; Larsen and McEwan, unpublished; Vernon and McEwan 1990
Total	1094 (771)		

a. Number in parentheses is the index number from Hann's (1990) "Summary Guide to Spanish Florida Missions and *Visitas* with Churches in the Sixteenth and Seventeenth Centuries."

b. N = number of individuals as represented by human skeletal and/or dental remains. This number does not include burial pits lacking preserved human remains (e.g., San Lorenzo). Numbers in italics indicate number of individuals subjected to bioanthropological study.

Biocultural Interpretation

In the remainder of this chapter I will review some of the results of a long-term biocultural investigation of the earlier and later Santa Catalina de Guale mission skeletal series from St. Catherines and Amelia islands, respectively, and from other areas of *La Florida*. Data from these other areas include preliminary analyses completed on the mission skeletal samples recovered from one Timucua mission at San Martín de Timucua (Hoshower 1990, 1991) and from two Apalachee missions—San Pablo y San Pedro de Patale (Jones, Storey, and Widmer 1991; Storey 1986) and San Luis de Talimali (Larsen 1990a).

Stress and Adaptation in Guale

Arguably the most studied biological issue dealing with the contact era is the dramatic decline in native population size following the arrival of Europeans. Although various causes have been suggested for this phenomenon, introduced Old World pathogens have been most frequently implicated. It has become increasingly clear that New World population reductions and demographic alterations resulted from the interaction of a number of factors, including dietary alterations, settlement changes, work demands, harassment by military, out-migration, and overall increase in stress. Only through the investigation of these variables can we expect to understand the biological changes seen in these and other New World native populations (Larsen et al. 1990).

The recovery of human remains from the Santa Catalina mission sites on St. Catherines and Amelia islands has afforded the opportunity to study contact-era human biology. In addition, a greater depth of understanding has been made possible because of the availability of hundreds of precontact-era Guale skeletons from various localities on the Georgia coast (reviewed in Larsen 1982). The comparative analysis of precontact and contact skeletal samples has entailed two broad areas of inquiry regarding biocultural stress and adaptation in mission Indians: quality of life, and physical behavior and life-style. The first area deals mainly with the negative impact of missionization in particular and contact with Europeans in general (dietary change, reduction in resource diversity, population nucleation and increased sedentism, infectious disease). The latter area provides unique insight into work patterns and physical behavior of mission Indians.

QUALITY OF LIFE IN SPANISH MISSIONS

Diet and Nutrition. Several lines of evidence demonstrate that native populations occupying Guale missions underwent a marked reorientation of diet relative to their precontact predecessors. Analysis of stable isotope ratios of carbon and nitrogen from bone collagen shows that there was a reduced dietary intake of marine resources that occurred concurrently with an increase in maize consumption in the mission period (Larsen et al. 1990; Schoeninger et al. 1990). A dramatic change in dental caries prevalence provides corroborative evidence for an increasing focus on maize in these populations (Larsen, Shavit, and Griffin 1991). That is, the prevalence of dental caries in the Santa Catalina de Guale series from Amelia Island is roughly four times greater than prevalence of dental caries at Santa Catalina on St. Catherines Island (32.2 percent versus 8.0 percent of teeth affected). These data argue strongly for a deterioration in nutritional quality, particularly during the late mission period in Guale. It is likely that the increase in dental caries is due to the cariogenic nature of sucrose contained in maize. Microwear patterns on occlusal surfaces of teeth indicate that the Amelia Island population had a softer diet than the St. Catherines Island population (Teaford 1991:349). The consumption of soft foods in the absence of modern oral hygienic practices is known to be a caries-promoting factor. Thus the combination of increase in carbohydrates (maize) and change in food texture may have contributed to a decline in dental health during the later contact period in Guale.

Growth disruption. Comparisons of the Guale mission samples with precontact populations reveal significant increases in growth disruption in the contact-era Indians. This finding is based on comparisons of frequency and morphology of enamel (the outer covering of teeth) defects known as hypoplasias. Hypoplasias are usually characterized as circumferential lines or pits on teeth (fig. 12.4) that are caused by disruption of enamel-producing cells due to environmental insult (Goodman and Rose 1990, 1991). Many factors leading to disruption have been identified, but systemic metabolic stress relating to some interaction of either disease morbidity or dietary stresses (e.g., starvation) is most common. Because of the unknown etiology of hypoplasias, they are considered to be a nonspecific indicator of systemic stress (Kreshover 1960). Hypoplasias

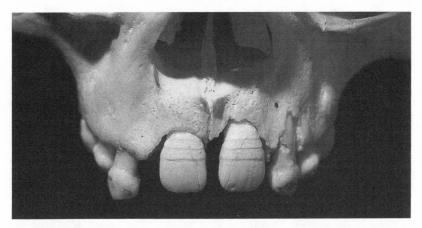

Figure 12.4. Enamel hypoplasias on central incisors (anatomical specimen).

are an ideal chronologic indicator of past stress episodes during the period of tooth development (from birth to about 10 years of age) because enamel does not remodel once formed and teeth have a high survival rate in archaeological contexts.

Comparison of mission populations with precontact populations on the Georgia coast shows that a greater number of individuals were affected by hypoplasias in the mission populations than in the prehistoric populations (Hutchinson and Larsen 1988, 1990; Simpson, Hutchinson, and Larsen 1990). Moreover, hypoplasias in the Santa Catalina (St. Catherines Island) teeth are generally wider than hypoplasias in the precontact teeth (Hutchinson and Larsen 1988, 1990), suggesting that either severity or duration (or both) of stress is greater in the mission period. Because of the nonspecificity of hypoplasias, it is not possible to link specific stressors with this indicator of morbidity. However, these findings are consistent with a model of decaying environmental conditions in general in the region during the contact period. Almost certainly, the combined actions of a variety of stressors—for example, infectious diseases, localized infection, poor diet—operated to produce an increase in growth disruption in these populations.

Additional perspective on the negative impact of missionization on native populations is provided by the comparison of Santa Catalina (St. Catherines Island) hypoplasias with enamel defects in dentitions from the nonmission Pine Harbor site (Hutchinson and Larsen 1988). The sample is represented by dentitions from a burial mound located 15 km to the west of St. Catherines Island on the mainland. Comparisons of hypoplasia widths showed that Pine Harbor hypoplasias are narrower than Santa Catalina hypoplasias (Hutchinson and Larsen 1988). Thus the Santa Catalina population may have experienced relatively more physiological stress than did the Pine Harbor population.

Skeletal infection. Chief among the consequences of resettlement of native populations around mission centers in *La Florida* was the establishment of conditions highly conducive to the spread of infectious diseases, both newly introduced (e.g., influenza, smallpox, and measles) as well as already existing diseases (tuberculosis and treponematosis; Larsen et al. 1990; Powell 1990). This change was likely accompanied by a decline in sanitation, increase in contamination of water sources, and deterioration of health (Larsen et al. 1992:50). Although it is difficult to document precise prevalence of specific infectious diseases based on the study of archaeological human skeletal remains, recent investigation of nonspecific infections—called periosteal reactions—has provided information on infection prevalence in these precontact and contact groups from Guale (fig. 12.5). Comparison of late prehistoric Mississippian populations from the Georgia coast with the Santa Catalina series (Amelia Island) has shown a striking increase in frequency of periosteal reactions (Larsen and Harn 1992).

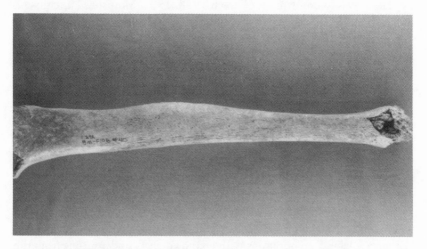

Figure 12.5. Bone infection (periosteal reaction) on a tibia showing characteristic inflammation and swelling in the diaphyseal region (Santa Catalina Guale de Santa María, Amelia Island).

Comparisons of frequency of periosteal reactions for the tibia, the most commonly affected skeletal element in archaeological human remains (Milner 1991), reveal that about 15 percent of precontact bones are affected, whereas 40 percent of Santa Catalina tibiae are affected. The infection prevalence in the mission series is among the highest reported in archaeological settings for the Eastern Woodlands (Goodman et al. 1984; Milner 1991; Milner and Smith 1990). It seems likely that this increase is linked to the deterioration of community health in mission villages. Moreover, the well-known synergy between poor nutrition and infection and other mitigating circumstances, including increased exposure to novel pathogens, decrease in sanitation in mission villages, and reduced host resistance, likely led to increases in infectious pathology during the mission period (Larsen and Harn 1992).

Iron deficiency anemia. The causes of iron deficiency anemia (also called hypoferremia) are numerous, but blood loss due to parasitic infection, dietary and nutritional deficiencies, and inadequacies in iron absorption are the most frequently cited (Stuart-Macadam 1989). Skeletal changes arising from reduced iron bioavailability mostly include the presence of sievelike bone lesions on the outer compact bone of the roof areas of the eye orbits (called cribra orbitalia; fig. 12.6) or on the the cranial vault, especially the frontal, parietal, and occipital bones (called porotic hyperostosis). The skeletal modifications are frequently associated with an expansion of the diploic region between the inner and outer tables of cranial bones, a factor that is related to the increased production of red blood cells. The skeletal changes arising from iron deficiency anemia appear to occur primarily in young children (Stuart-Macadam 1985). Therefore iron deficiency in older children and adults is difficult to assess.

With regard to the Georgia coastal precontact populations and the two mission-era Guale skeletal series, clear patterns of change in prevalence of iron deficiency anemia have been revealed. In the precontact series, prevalence of cribra orbitalia and porotic hyperostosis is low (less than 8 percent). More than 1 in 4 (27 percent) Santa Catalina crania from Amelia Island are affected. Three in 4 (73 percent) juveniles in the mission sample have some skeletal manifestation of anemia.

The shift to a more maize-focused diet in the mission populations may explain the increase in prevalence of iron deficiency. Although maize contains iron, the presence of phytate inhibits its bioavailability. However, experimental studies in humans consuming maize indicate that the addition of fish enhances iron absorption (Layrisse, Martinez-Torres, and

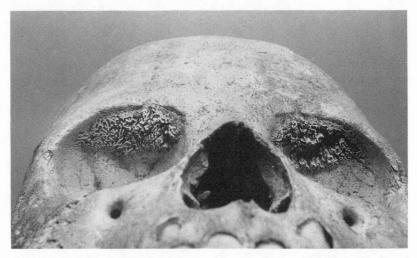

Figure 12.6. Cribra orbitalia shown in roof areas of eye orbits (Santa Catalina de Guale de Santa María, Amelia Island). Similar pathological modifications occur on cranial vault bones in other skeletons.

Roche 1968). Dietary evidence, from both isotopic analysis and study of animal remains from archaeological habitation sites (Reitz 1988), indicates that the majority of protein was derived from marine resources prior to contact. A reduction in availability of marine resources during the mission period may have contributed to the elevation in iron deficiency in mission Indians. The ill effects of this dietary change were likely compounded by increased parasitism, decreased sanitary conditions, and general deterioration of living conditions (Larsen et al. 1992).

Hypoferremia has been implicated as an important defense in restricting access of iron to invading microorganisms, which are completely dependent on the host's iron resources (Kent, Weinberg, and Stuart-Macadam 1990; Weinberg 1991). That is, the reduced availability of iron appears to hinder the ability of pathogens to proliferate. Therefore hypoferremia may be a response to increased infection loads in this population.

THE WORK ENVIRONMENT IN GUALE

Native labor was an essential component of the economic success of the Spanish in the region. Accounts regarding the role of Indians in food production, construction projects, cargo bearing, and other activities attest to the indispensable nature of native laborers. The labor demands on native New World populations have been amply documented in *La Florida*. For instance, with regard to Apalachee, the impact of these demands is illustrated in the account provided by Fray Alonso Moral:

> All of the natives of these provinces suffer great servitude, injuries, and vexations from the fact that the governors, lieutenants, and soldiers oblige them to carry loads on their shoulders to the Province of Apalachee alone more than three hundred are brought to the fort at the time of the planting of corn, carrying their food and the merchandise of the soldiers on their shoulders for more than eighty leagues with the result that some of them die and those who survive do not return to their homes because the governor and the other officials detain them in the fort so they may serve them. . . . This is the reason according to the commonly held opinion that they are being annihilated at such a rate. (quoted in Hann 1988:140–141)

The human skeletal record demonstrates important aspects of changing work loads and physical behavior in the mission period. Two specific areas of inquiry have been pursued with regard to the Spanish Florida skeletal samples—osteoarthritis prevalence and long bone structural morphology.

Osteoarthritis. Also known as degenerative joint disease, this disorder involves the degeneration of articular joints in the skeleton. The most commonly occurring skeletal manifestation of the disorder is the proliferation of bone on joint margins (fig. 12.7), and under extreme circumstances these changes are accompanied by the loss of bone on the joint surfaces due to the disintegration of articular cartilage (Hough and Sokoloff 1989:1576). Various factors can influence the expression of osteoarthritis, but the cumulative effects of mechanical demand figure prominently in its interpretation (DeRousseau 1988; Larsen 1987; Merbs 1983).

Comparisons of late prehistoric skeletal series with the mission sample at Santa Catalina (Amelia Island) reveal a marked increase in prevalence of osteoarthritis (Griffin and Larsen 1989; Larsen, Ruff, and Griffin n.d.). In the thoracic vertebrae, for example, 11.8 percent of precontact males are affected but 65.4 percent of mission males. In females, 1.4 percent of precontact individuals are affected in this joint; 57.5 percent of mission individuals are affected. Virtually all other major articular joints

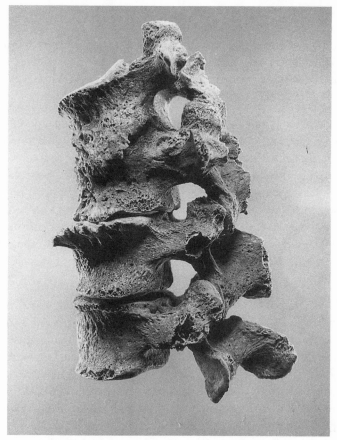

Figure 12.7. Proliferation of bone on joint margins of lumbar vertebrae that is characteristic of osteoarthritis (Santa Catalina de Guale de Santa María, Amelia Island).

show comparable increases in prevalence of osteoarthritis (Larsen, Ruff, and Griffin n.d.). These findings indicate that the establishment of missions in Guale and the resulting changes in the work environment saw a marked increase in mechanical demand. Interestingly, the prevalence of osteoarthritis in mission females and males is more similar than in prehistoric females and males (Larsen, Ruff, and Griffin n.d.). This suggests that activities that lead to osteoarthritis became more similar between sexes during the mission period (see biomechanical evidence presented by Fresia, Ruff, and Larsen 1990).

Cross-sectional geometric properties. The application of biomechanical beam theory developed by civil and mechanical engineers (Timoshenko and Gere 1972) to morphological analysis has facilitated the study of complex cross-sectional shapes of long bones (e.g., femur, humerus). In a beam model, long bone strength (also called rigidity) is determined by two cross-sectional properties: area and second moments of area of bone in a cross section. Area is proportional to strength in compression and tension, while second moments of area are proportional to strength in torsion (twisting) and bending along the long bone shaft (Ruff and Hayes 1983). To put it simply, a decline in these properties represents a decline in bone strength or the ability of bone to resist mechanical loading.

Comparisons of late prehistoric skeletal series from Guale with the two Santa Catalina mission samples reveal a consistent increase in bone strength as determined from cross-sectional geometric properties for both the femur and humerus (Larsen, Ruff, and Griffin n.d.; Ruff and Larsen 1990). These changes reflect an increase in mechanical demand on these contact-era populations, a finding that is fully consistent with the patterns of osteoarthritis prevalence data presented above. Moreover, by comparing a simple ratio of bending strength in the midshaft region of the femur, it is possible to infer degree of mobility, such as that associated with long-distance travel (Ruff 1987). Our comparisons of the precontact and contact populations from Guale reveal that the mission populations became generally less mobile. Study of cross-sectional geometric variation within the mission samples indicates that some of the mission males became more mobile, perhaps reflecting the use of males as draft laborers in projects far from the home missions (Hann 1988:141). However, the overall increase in sedentism—particularly in relation to the concentration of Indians in village areas—likely reflects declining mobility during the mission period.

TIMUCUA AND APALACHEE

Only small skeletal samples from Timucua and Apalachee have been examined by biological anthropologists. Nevertheless, a preliminary survey of osteopathology in the San Martín mission population basically repeats the Guale health patterns—namely, presence of high prevalence of hypoplasias, bone infections, and other nonspecific indicators of stress (Hoshower 1990, 1991). Interestingly, unlike some of the Guale populations, caries prevalence was low, which may reflect minimal importance of maize in their diets (Hoshower 1991).

Aside from details on the mortuary program in Apalachee, little has been learned about the biocultural aspects of native populations in this province based on the study of human remains. The investigation of Apalachee skeletons recovered from San Pedro y San Pablo de Patale (Patale I) has provided some preliminary information, including data on age, sex, and pathology (Jones, Storey, and Widmer 1991; Storey 1986). As with other mission series, high prevalence of dental caries indicates a maize-oriented diet in the Apalachee neophytes. In sharp contrast to findings based on Guale and Timucua skeletal samples, observation of low prevalence of bone infections, hypoplasias, and anemia in Patale remains led the investigators to conclude that the "population appears to have consisted of healthy, well-nourished individuals" (Jones, Storey, and Widmer 1991:115). As they note, however, poor preservation in some individuals recovered from the site may underrepresent the pathology in the series. Moreover, the disproportionately few young juveniles and older adults may contribute to an unrealistic picture of health, especially because some pathologies (e.g., porotic hyperostosis) are most prevalent in juveniles.

The small samples of mission skeletal series from Timucua and Apalachee provinces, coupled with the limited availability of precontact skeletal series, make it especially difficult to assess relative changes in various measures of biocultural adaptation in the same manner as for the Guale populations. Storey (1986) has compared a series from the nearby Lake Jackson site ($n = 24$)—a Mississippian period mound complex— with the Patale sample. In this preliminary study, she reported a decline in prevalence of hypoplasias in the Patale sample relative to the Lake Jackson sample, thus inferring an improvement in health in the mission period Apalachee. However, the study is hampered by the availability of only a limited dental sample.

By the time of the decline of Guale and Timucua in the later seventeenth century, Apalachee had become the principal player in Spanish-Indian interactions. The population of Guale during the last decades of the seventeenth century on the Georgia coast numbered in the several hundreds, whereas in Apalachee there were probably more than 9000 Indians (Hann 1988:165–166). Clearly, one important direction of research to pursue is the study of biological details of success in one region (Apalachee) and failure in others (Guale and Timucua) in *La Florida*. The skeletal and dental samples from future excavations at San Luis will offer valuable insight into this important period of interaction between Spaniards and Indians.

Summary

Archaeological excavations of mission cemeteries in *La Florida* have produced hundreds of skeletons representing Native Americans inhabiting these missions during the sixteenth and seventeenth centuries. The study of their remains offers essential evidence about mortuary behavior and biocultural adaptation and change during this time period. This discussion has demonstrated the importance of the study of human skeletal remains in contributing to the emerging understanding of this complex episode of the colonial Southeast. Based largely on studies of precontact- and contact-era Guale from the Georgia and north Florida Atlantic coasts, four principal findings emerge. First, with few exceptions, the native populations associated with missions adopted mortuary programs that were essentially Spanish in overall character. Second, native groups experienced an overall decline in quality of life and health status generally. These declines, although in part related to the devastation wrought by introduced pathogens, are tied to a variety of other factors (e.g., diet). Third, native populations show evidence for adaptation to new labor demands and related challenges facing them. Finally, although these populations experienced dramatic decline in population size, they nevertheless survived in appreciable numbers until their final removal during the later sixteenth and early seventeenth centuries. The important implication of this last finding is that these populations did not vanish overnight. On the contrary, they existed as stressed, yet viable, populations over a series of generations prior to their dispersal to other regions of the Southeast and the Caribbean following the transfer of *La Florida* from Spanish to British hands in 1763.

Acknowledgments

Numerous individuals have contributed immeasurably to the *La Florida* Bioarchaeology Project. I especially thank David Hurst Thomas, Kenneth W. Hardin, and Jerald T. Milanich, who have been involved in cooperative field programs on St. Catherines and Amelia islands. While directing the excavation of the cemetery on St. Catherines Island, I was fortunate to have Katherine Russell, Dale Hutchinson, and Scott Simpson as my field assistants during the 1982–1986 seasons. The able field supervision given by Rebecca Saunders was instrumental in the success of fieldwork on Amelia Island.

Funding for fieldwork on St. Catherines Island was from the St. Catherines and Edward John Noble foundations. The recovery of human remains from Amelia Island was made possible largely through the generous funding given by Dr. and Mrs. George H. Dorion. Their help in many other ways during the bioarchaeological excavations on Amelia Island is gratefully acknowledged.

Analysis of human remains from the mission cemeteries excavated on St. Catherines and Amelia islands was funded by the National Science Foundation (grant awards BNS-8406773, BNS-8703849, and BNS-8747309). Thanks are extended to my collaborators for their many efforts in this endeavor: Christopher B. Ruff, Margaret J. Schoeninger, Dale L. Hutchinson, Katherine F. Russell, Scott W. Simpson, Anne E. Fresia, Nikolaas J. van der Merwe, Julia Lee-Thorp, Inui Choi, Mark C. Griffin, Katherine Moore, Dawn Harn, Rebecca Shavit, Joanna E. Lambert, Susan Simmons, and Mark F. Teaford. David N. Dickel provided unpublished information on human remains from Nombre de Dios and San Damián de Escambé, which are curated in the collections of the Florida Bureau of Archaeological Research.

I thank the following individuals for preparation of the figures: Lisa Gosciejew (fig. 12.1), Rebecca Saunders (figs. 12.2, 12.3), Barry Stark (fig. 12.4), and Mark Griffin (figs. 12.5–12.7). Permission to reprint figure 12.1 was granted by the American Museum of Natural History.

Thanks are extended to Bonnie McEwan for her invitation to contribute to this volume. Careful reading by Dr. McEwan and three anonymous reviewers contributed to this chapter's accuracy and clarity.

Bibliography

Bullen, Ripley P., and John W. Griffin
1952   An Archaeological Survey of Amelia Island, Florida. *The Florida Anthropologist* 5(3–4):37–64.

Bushnell, Amy T.
1986   *Santa María in the Written Record*. Miscellaneous Project Report Series, no. 21. Gainesville: Department of Anthropology, Florida State Museum.

Cook, Fred C., and Charles E. Pearson
1973   *Three Late Savannah Burial Mounds in Glynn County, Georgia*. Laboratory of Archaeology Research Manuscript no. 276. Athens: University of Georgia.

DeRousseau, C. Jean
1988   *Osteoarthritis in Rhesus Monkeys and Gibbons*. Contributions to Primatology, no. 25. Basel, Switzerland.

Dickel, David N.
1990   Results of Investigations of Twelve Burials at 8-SJ-31, the Fountain of Youth Park, St. Augustine, Florida. Ms. on file, Florida Bureau of Archaeological Research, Tallahassee.

n.d.   Human Remains from 8-LE-120, Leon County, San Cosmos y Damián de Escambé. Ms. on file, Florida Bureau of Archaeological Research, Tallahassee.

Dickinson, Martin F.
1989   Delineating a Site through Limited Research: The Mission of San Juan del Puerto (8DU53), Fort George Island, Florida. *The Florida Anthropologist* 42(4):396–409.

Dickinson, Martin F., and Lucy B. Wayne
1985   Archaeological Testing of the San Juan del Puerto Mission Site (8DU53), Fort George Island, Florida. Ms. on file, Water and Air Research, Gainesville.

Fresia, Anne E., Christopher B. Ruff, and Clark Spencer Larsen
1990   Temporal Decline in Bilateral Asymmetry of the Upper Limb on the Georgia Coast. In *The Archaeology of Mission Santa Catalina de Guale: 2. Biocultural Interpretations of a Population in Transition*, edited by Clark Spencer Larsen, 121–132. Anthropological Papers of the American Museum of Natural History, no. 68. New York.

Goodman, Alan H., and Jerome C. Rose
1990   Assessment of Systemic Physiological Perturbations from Dental Enamel Hypoplasias and Associated Histological Structures. *Yearbook of Physical Anthropology* 33:59–110.

1991   Dental Enamel Hypoplasias as Indicators of Nutritional Stress. In *Advances in Dental Anthropology*, edited by Marc A. Kelley and Clark Spencer Larsen, 279–293. New York: Wiley-Liss.

Goodman, Alan H., John W. Lallo, George J. Armelagos, and Jerome C. Rose
1984   Health Changes at Dickson Mounds, Illinois (A.D. 950–1300). In *Paleopathology at the Origins of Agriculture*, edited by Mark Nathan Cohen and George J. Armelagos, 271–305. New York: Academic Press.

Griffin, Mark C., and Clark Spencer Larsen
1989   Patterns in Osteoarthritis: A Case Study from the Prehistoric and Historic Southeastern U.S. Atlantic Coast. Poster presented at the annual meeting of the American Association of Physical Anthropologists, San Diego, California.

Hann, John H.
1988   *Apalachee: The Land between the Rivers*. Ripley P. Bullen Monographs in Anthropology and History, no. 7. Gainesville: University Presses of Florida.

1990   Summary Guide to Spanish Florida Missions and *Visitas* with Churches in the Sixteenth and Seventeenth Centuries. *The Americas* 46(4):417–513.

Hardin, Kenneth W.
1986   The Santa María Mission Project. *The Florida Anthropologist* 39(1–2):75–83.

Hemmings, E. Thomas, and Kathleen A. Deagan
1973   *Excavations on Amelia Island in Northeast Florida*. Contributions of the Florida State Museum in Anthropology and History, no. 18. Gainesville.

Hoshower, Lisa
1990   *Excavations in the Fig Springs Mission Burial Area, Florida (8CO1)*. Miscellaneous Project Report Series, no. 45. Gainesville: Department of Anthropology, Florida Museum of Natural History.

1991   Excavations in the Fig Springs Mission Burial Area, Florida (8CO1). Ms. on file, Department of Anthropology, Florida Museum of Natural History, Gainesville.

Hough, Aubrey J., and Leon Sokoloff
1989   Pathology of Osteoarthritis. In *Arthritis and Allied Conditions*, 11th ed., edited by Daniel J. McCarty, 1571–1594. Philadelphia: Lea and Febiger.

Hutchinson, Dale L.
1990   Postcontact Biocultural Change: Mortuary Site Evidence. In *Columbian Consequences*. Vol. 2: *Archaeological and Historical Perspectives on the Spanish Borderlands East*, edited by David Hurst Thomas, 61–70. Washington, D.C.: Smithsonian Institution Press.

1991   Postcontact Native American Health and Adaptation: Assessing the Impact of Introduced Diseases in Sixteenth-Century Gulf Coast Florida.

Ph.D. diss., Department of Anthropology, University of Illinois, Urbana.

Hutchinson, Dale L., and Clark Spencer Larsen
1988 Determination of Stress Episode Duration from Linear Enamel Hypoplasias. *Human Biology* 60:93–110.

1990 Stress and Lifeway Change: The Evidence from Enamel Hypoplasias. In *The Archaeology of Mission Santa Catalina de Guale: 2. Biocultural Interpretations of a Population in Transition*, edited by Clark Spencer Larsen, 50–65. Anthropological Papers of the American Museum of Natural History, no. 68. New York.

Jones, B. Calvin
1970 Seventeenth-Century Spanish Mission Cemetery Is Discovered near Tallahassee. *Archives and History News* 1(4):1–2.

1972 Spanish Mission Sites Located and Test Excavated. *Archives and History News* 3(6):1–2.

Jones, B. Calvin, and Gary N. Shapiro
1990 Nine Mission Sites in Apalachee. In *Columbian Consequences*. Vol. 2: *Archaeological and Historical Perspectives on the Spanish Borderlands East*, edited by David Hurst Thomas, 491–509. Washington, D.C.: Smithsonian Institution Press.

Jones, B. Calvin, Rebecca Storey, and Randolph J. Widmer
1991 The Patale Cemetery: Evidence Concerning the Apalachee Mission Mortuary Complex. In *San Pedro y San Pablo de Patale: A Seventeenth-Century Spanish Mission in Leon County, Florida*, by B. Calvin Jones, John Hann, and John F. Scarry, 109–125. Florida Archaeology no. 5. Tallahassee: Florida Bureau of Archaeological Research.

Jones, Grant D.
1978 The Ethnohistory of the Guale Coast through 1684. In *The Anthropology of St. Catherines Island: 1. Natural and Cultural History*, by David Hurst Thomas, Grant D. Jones, Roger S. Durham, and Clark Spencer Larsen, 178–210. Anthropological Papers of the American Museum of Natural History, vol. 55, pt. 2. New York.

Kent, Susan, Eugene D. Weinberg, and Patricia Stuart-Macadam
1990 Dietary and Prophylactic Iron Supplements: Helpful or Harmful? *Human Nature* 1:53–79.

Koch, Joan K.
1983 Mortuary Behavior Patterning and Physical Anthropology in Colonial St. Augustine. In *Spanish St. Augustine: The Archaeology of a Colonial Creole Community*, edited by Kathleen Deagan, 187–227. New York: Academic Press.

Kreshover, Seymour J.
1960   Metabolic Disturbances in Tooth Formation. *Annals of the New York Academy of Sciences* 85:161–167.

Larsen, Clark Spencer
1982   *The Anthropology of St. Catherines Island: 3. Prehistoric Human Biological Adaptation.* Anthropological Papers of the American Museum of Natural History, vol. 57, pt. 3. New York.

1987   Bioarchaeological Interpretations of Subsistence Economy and Behavior from Human Skeletal Remains. In *Advances in Archaeological Method and Theory* no. 10, edited by Michael B. Schiffer, 339–445. San Diego: Academic Press.

1990a   A Bioarchaeological Investigation of San Luis de Talimali. In *Investigations in the Church Complex and Spanish Village at San Luis*, by Richard Vernon and Bonnie McEwan, 86–92. Florida Archaeological Reports, no. 18. Tallahassee: Florida Bureau of Archaeological Research.

1990b   Biocultural Interpretations and the Context for Contact. In *The Archaeology of Mission Santa Catalina de Guale: 2. Biocultural Interpretations of a Population in Transition*, edited by Clark Spencer Larsen, 11–25. Anthropological Papers of the American Museum of Natural History, no. 68. New York.

1992   Telltale Bones. *Archaeology* 45(2):43–46.

Larsen, Clark Spencer, ed.
1990   *The Archaeology of Mission Santa Catalina de Guale: 2. Biocultural Intepretations of a Population in Transition.* Anthropological Papers of the American Museum of Natural History, no. 68. New York.

Larsen, Clark Spencer, and Dawn E. Harn
1992   Nutrition, Infection, and Health Status in the Prehistoric-Historic Transition. Paper presented at conference, Paleonutrition: The Diet and Health of Prehistoric Americans, at Southern Illinois University, Carbondale.

Larsen, Clark Spencer, and Rebecca Saunders
1987   The Two Santa Catalina Cemeteries. Paper presented at the 44th Annual Meeting of the Southeastern Archaeological Conference, Charleston, South Carolina.

Larsen, Clark Spencer, and David Hurst Thomas
1982   *The Anthropology of St. Catherines Island: 4. The St. Catherines Period Mortuary Complex.* Anthropological Papers of the American Museum of Natural History, vol. 57, pt. 4. New York.

Larsen, Clark Spencer, Christopher B. Ruff, and Mark C. Griffin
n.d.   Implications of Changing Biomechanical and Nutritional Environments for Activity and Lifeway in the Eastern Spanish Borderlands. In *Disease*

and Demographic Collapse in the Spanish Borderlands, edited by Brenda J. Baker and Lisa L. Kealhofer. In preparation.

Larsen, Clark Spencer, Rebecca Shavit, and Mark C. Griffin
1991   Dental Caries Evidence for Dietary Change: An Archaeological Context. In *Advances in Dental Anthropology*, edited by Marc A. Kelley and Clark Spencer Larsen, 179–202. New York: Wiley-Liss.

Larsen, Clark Spencer, Christopher B. Ruff, Margaret J. Schoeninger, and Dale L. Hutchinson
1992   Population Decline and Extinction in *La Florida*. In *Disease and Demography in the Americas*, edited by John W. Verano and Douglas H. Uvelaker, 25–39. Washington, D.C.: Smithsonian Institution Press.

Larsen, Clark Spencer, Margaret J. Schoeninger, Dale L. Hutchinson, Katherine F. Russell, and Christopher B. Ruff
1990   Beyond Demographic Collapse: Biological Adaptation and Change in Native Populations of *La Florida*. In *Columbian Consequences*. Vol. 2: *Archaeological and Historical Perspectives on the Spanish Borderlands East*, edited by David Hurst Thomas, 409–428. Washington, D.C.: Smithsonian Institution Press.

Layrisse, M., C. Martinez-Torres, and M. Roche
1968   Effect of Interaction of Various Foods on Iron Absorption. *American Journal of Clinical Nutrition* 21:1175–1183.

McEwan, Bonnie G.
1991   San Luis de Talimali: The Archaeology of Spanish-Indian Relations at a Florida Mission. *Historical Archaeology* 25(3):36–60.

Merbs, Charles F.
1983   *Patterns of Activity-Induced Pathology in a Canadian Inuit Population.* National Museum of Man Mercury Series, Archaeological Survey of Canada Paper no. 119. Ottawa.

Milanich, Jerald T., and William Sturtevant
1972   *Francisco Pareja's 1613 Confessionario: A Documentary Source for Timucuan Ethnography.* Tallahassee: Florida Department of State, Division of Archives, History, and Records Management.

Milner, George R.
1991   Health and Cultural Change in the Late Prehistoric American Bottom, Illinois. In *What Mean These Bones? Studies in Southeastern Bioarchaeology*, edited by Mary Lucas Powell, Patricia S. Bridges, and Ann Marie Wagner Mires, 52–69. Tuscaloosa: University of Alabama Press.

Milner, George R., and Virginia G. Smith
1990   Oneota Human Skeletal Remains. In *Archaeological Investigations at the Morton Village and Norris Farms 36 Cemetery*, by Sharron K. Santure,

Alan D. Harn, and Duane Esarey, 111–148. Illinois State Museum Reports of Investigations, no. 45. Springfield.

Mitchem, Jeffrey M.
1990   Beads and Pendants from the Cemetery and Church. In *Investigations in the Church Complex and Spanish Village at San Luis*, by Richard Vernon and Bonnie McEwan, 93–102. Florida Archaeological Reports, no. 18. Tallahassee: Florida Bureau of Archaeological Research.

Oviedo y Valdés, Gonzalo Fernández de
1959   *Historia general y natural de las Indias*, vol. 4. Biblioteca de Autores Españoles, Tomo 120. Madrid: Ediciones Atlas.

Pearson, Charles E.
1977   Evidence of Early Spanish Contact on the Georgia Coast. *Historical Archaeology* 11:74–83.

Powell, Mary Lucas
1990   On the Eve of the Conquest: Life and Death at Irene Mound, Georgia. In *The Archaeology of Mission Santa Catalina de Guale: 2. Biocultural Interpretations of a Population in Transition*, edited by Clark Spencer Larsen, 26–35. Anthropological Papers of the American Museum of Natural History, no. 68. New York.

Reitz, Elizabeth J.
1988   Evidence for Coastal Adaptations in Georgia and South Carolina. *Archaeology of Eastern North America* 16:137–158.

Ruff, Christopher B.
1987   Sexual Dimorphism in Human Lower Limb Bone Structure: Relationship to Subsistence Strategy and Sexual Division of Labor. *Journal of Human Evolution* 16:391–416.

Ruff, Christopher B., and Wilson C. Hayes
1983   Cross-sectional Geometry of Pecos Pueblo Femora and Tibiae—A Biomechanical Investigation: I. Method and General Patterns of Variation. *American Journal of Physical Anthropology* 60:359–381.

Ruff, Christopher B., and Clark Spencer Larsen
1990   Postcranial Biomechanical Adaptations to Subsistence Strategy Changes on the Georgia Coast. In *The Archaeology of Mission Santa Catalina de Guale: 2. Biocultural Interpretations of a Population in Transition*, edited by Clark Spencer Larsen, 94–120. Anthropological Papers of the American Museum of Natural History, no. 68. New York.

Saunders, Rebecca
1988   *Excavations at 8NA41: Two Mission Period Sites on Amelia Island, Florida*. Miscellaneous Project Report Series, no. 35. Gainesville: Department of Anthropology, Florida Museum of Natural History.

Schoeninger, Margaret J., Nikolaas J. van der Merwe, Katherine Moore, Julia Lee-Thorp, and Clark Spencer Larsen
1990   Decrease in Diet Quality between the Prehistoric and Contact Periods. In *The Archaeology of Mission Santa Catalina de Guale: 2. Biocultural Interpretations of a Population in Transition*, edited by Clark Spencer Larsen, 78–93. Anthropological Papers of the American Museum of Natural History, no. 68. New York.

Seaberg, Lillian M.
1991   Report on the Indian Site at the "Fountain of Youth," St. Augustine. In *America's Ancient City, Spanish St. Augustine, 1565–1763*, edited by Kathleen A. Deagan, 209–274. New York: Garland.

Shapiro, Gary
1987   *Archaeology at San Luis: Broad-Scale Testing, 1984–1985*. Florida Archaeology no. 3. Tallahassee: Florida Bureau of Archaeological Research.

Simmons, Susan, Clark Spencer Larsen, and Katherine F. Russell
1989   Demographic Interpretations from Ossuary Remains during the Late Contact Period in Northern Spanish Florida. Paper presented at the annual meeting of the American Association of Physical Anthropologists, San Diego, California.

Simpson, Scott W., Dale L. Hutchinson, and Clark Spencer Larsen
1990   Coping with Stress: Tooth Size, Dental Defects, and Age-at-Death. In *The Archaeology of Mission Santa Catalina de Guale: 2. Biocultural Interpretations of a Population in Transition*, edited by Clark Spencer Larsen, 66–77. Anthropological Papers of the American Museum of Natural History, no. 68. New York.

Storey, Rebecca
1986   Diet and Health Comparisons between Pre- and Post-Columbian Native Americans in North Florida. Paper presented at the annual meeting of the American Association of Physical Anthropologists, Albuquerque, New Mexico.

1990   A Human Cremation from the De Soto Winter Encampment, Tallahassee, Florida (abstract). *American Journal of Physical Anthropology* 81:302.

Storey, Rebecca, and Randolph J. Widmer
n.d.   Report on Feature 131 of Site 8LE853. Ms. on file, Florida Bureau of Archaeological Research, Tallahassee.

Stuart-Macadam, P. L.
1985   Porotic Hyperostosis: Representative of a Childhood Condition. *American Journal of Physical Anthropology* 66:391–398.

1989   Nutritional Deficiency Diseases: A Survey of Scurvy, Rickets, and Iron-Deficiency Anemia. In *Reconstruction of Life from the Skeleton*, edited by

Mehmet Yasar Iscan and Kenneth A. R. Kennedy, 201–222. New York: Alan R. Liss.

Teaford, Mark F.
1991 Dental Microwear: What Can It Tell Us about Diet and Dental Function? In *Advances in Dental Anthropology*, edited by Marc A. Kelley and Clark Spencer Larsen, 341–356. New York: Wiley-Liss.

Thomas, David Hurst
1987 *The Archaeology of Mission Santa Catalina de Guale: 1. Search and Discovery*. Anthropological Papers of the American Museum of Natural History, vol. 63, pt. 2. New York.

Timoshenko, S. P., and J. M. Gere
1972 *Mechanics of Materials*. New York: Van Nostrand Reinhold.

Vernon, Richard, and Bonnie McEwan
1990 *Investigations in the Church Complex and Spanish Village at San Luis*. Florida Archaeological Reports, no. 18. Tallahassee: Florida Bureau of Archaeological Research.

Weinberg, Eugene D.
1991 Iron Withholding in Prevention of Disease. Paper presented at the annual meeting of the American Association of Physical Anthropologists, Milwaukee, Wisconsin.

❂ 13 ❂

Plant Production and Procurement in Apalachee Province

C. MARGARET SCARRY

In both the late prehistoric and mission periods, the fertile soils of Apalachee Province provided the foundation for highly successful agricultural economies. The chroniclers of the Narváez and de Soto expeditions wrote in glowing terms about both the abundant natural resources of the region and the bountiful harvests of the Apalachee farmers (Hann 1988b:71, 137–139, 1988d:12). Given the known fertility of the province, it is hardly surprising that the later Spanish colonists used the mission system to tap its wealth. In the second half of the seventeenth century, agricultural products were exported from Apalachee Province to St. Augustine and to other New World Spanish colonies (Bushnell 1981:32; Hann 1988a:134, 152).

In this chapter, I combine documentary and archaeological evidence to investigate variability in the use of food plants by the Apalachee and Spanish residents of Apalachee Province. While both late prehistoric and historic data are presented, the focus of the discussion is on the mission period. This is as much a result of necessity as of choice; we have more data for the latter period than we do for the former.

Apalachee Province

Apalachee Province was named for the Native Americans who controlled the region at the time of European contact. In the historic period the province was bounded on the east by the Aucilla River and on the west by the Ochlockonee River. Apalachee Bay and the Gulf of Mexico formed its southern edge. We are less certain about the northern boundary, but it appears to have been somewhere near the present-day Florida-Georgia border. The territory within these boundaries is characterized by rolling hills, numerous lakes and streams, and fertile soils (Hann 1988a:1).

The Apalachee people were agriculturalists whose society was organized as a chiefdom. Based on continuities in artifact types found on late prehistoric and historic sites in the region, the Apalachee have been identified with the late prehistoric Lake Jackson phase chiefdom (A.D. 1000–1500). In the mission period the Apalachee lost their independence and were brought within the jurisdiction of the Spanish colonial authorities. Despite the loss of their political autonomy, however, the missionized Apalachee maintained many aspects of their traditional economic and social relations (J. F. Scarry 1990, 1992).

DOCUMENTARY EVIDENCE

The Apalachee cultivated fields that were as extensive and productive as any the early Spanish explorers saw in eastern North America. In the fall of 1539 de Soto and his men entered Apalachee Province and traveled through vast expanses of fields broken here and there by farmsteads and villages (Hann 1988b:67). Upon reaching Anhaica, the chief's town, the Spaniards commandeered the contents of granaries located within a league and a half of Anhaica (Hann 1988c:21–22, 1988b:129). The maize and other foodstuffs they appropriated fed an army of more than 600 men and 200 horses for the five months they camped in the province. When the expedition left Apalachee, the Spaniards took with them supplies for 60 leagues' travel (Hann 1988c:25).

The plundering of their stores no doubt caused the Apalachee hardship. We do not know, however, whether the Spaniards' actions left the Apalachee without sufficient food for themselves or seed for the next season's planting. Whatever the short-term effects, the appropriation of their food stocks by de Soto and his men does not appear to have had an extended impact on the Apalachee's prosperity.

Less than a century later, the productivity of the Apalachee farmers was a major consideration in the Spaniards' decision to establish missions in the province (Hann 1988a:13). St. Augustine, the capital of Spanish Florida, had chronic supply problems due to unreliable government subsidies, infertile coastal soils, and the dwindling native population, who produced much of the food consumed in the town (Bushnell 1981:11–12). The Spaniards saw the abundant harvests of the Apalachee as a partial solution to their supply problems. Beginning in the early seventeenth century, Franciscan friars made intermittent contacts with the Apalachee and the province became an important source of maize for St. Augustine (Hann 1988a:13). It was not until 1633, however, that permanent missions were established in Apalachee Province (Hann 1988a:11–13, 319–321).

As they had hoped, once the missions were established the Franciscans succeeded in harvesting crops as well as souls. They sent maize and other foodstuffs overland to St. Augustine, and from the port at San Marcos they shipped maize and wheat to Havana, where the grain brought better prices than in St. Augustine (Bushnell 1981:32; Hann 1988a:134, 152).

The priests controlled the disposition of the agricultural commodities, but Apalachee women and men provided the labor that produced them. The missionaries levied tithes on the maize the Apalachee planted for domestic use. They also co-opted the Apalachee practice of planting fields for communal use. The missionized Apalachee planted fields not only for their chiefs and the needy but also for the church (Hann 1988a:144). Once the grain was harvested, Apalachee women processed or prepared it and Apalachee men transported it, often on their backs, to St. Augustine or San Marcos (Hann 1988a:139–144).

Not surprisingly, the Apalachee were dissatisfied with these arrangements. They claimed that the priests sold grain that was intended for communal purposes and used the profits to buy trade goods (Hann 1986b:93, 97). The Apalachee also complained that the priests interfered with their efforts to profit from the grain trade (Hann 1986b:88).

The missionaries were not the only Spaniards who took advantage of the Apalachee's land and labor. Soon after the first missions were built, Governor Salazar Vallecilla established a ranch on the eastern edge of Apalachee Province. There he used native labor to raise cattle and wheat (Bushnell 1981:78; Hann 1988a:20). In 1675 Governor Hita Salazar awarded land grants in Apalachee Province and encouraged Spanish civilians to establish cattle ranches and wheat farms (Hann 1988a:322; McEwan 1991b:38). The ranches rapidly became another source of contention between the Apalachee and the Spaniards. The ranchers made additional demands on the Apalachee's labor, at times using force to get

Apalachee women and men to work in their homes or fields (Hann 1988a:143–144). Besides the forced labor, the Apalachee objected to the ranchers' encroachment on their fields and to the damage done by cattle to their crops and to the grounds where they traditionally foraged for acorns and palm berries (Hann 1986b:131, 143).

There is ample evidence in the records from Apalachee Province that missions and private ventures exported foodstuffs and other commodities to St. Augustine and Havana. Aside from lists of plants that were grown or collected, however, the documents provide little information about patterns of food production and consumption within the province.

ARCHAEOLOGICAL EVIDENCE

In the following pages, I use archaeobotanical data to begin to fill out the picture presented by the sixteenth- and seventeenth-century accounts. The data come from late prehistoric and mission period sites, and for the historic period include plant remains from both Apalachee and Spanish, domestic and public contexts. At present, due to the uneven quality of the data (see below), quantitative analyses are inappropriate. It is possible, however, to make qualitative comparisons between the plant remains found in different contexts and to suggest provisional interpretations of the patterns we see in the assemblages. In the future, I hope we will accumulate systematic plant data appropriate for use in detailed studies of variability in dietary practices within and between the prehistoric and historic communities of Apalachee Province. When this becomes possible the patterns described here and the explanations offered for those patterns will almost certainly have to be revised and may have to be replaced.

For the purposes of this article, plant data from late prehistoric sites are combined with those from postcontact sites that date before the missions were established. The de Soto expedition introduced pigs to the Southeast, but the members of the Narváez and de Soto expeditions were consumers, not propagators, of agricultural products. Their visits to Apalachee Province may have left the native population temporarily short of supplies, but the explorers' impacts on the Apalachee's use of plant foods were probably not long-term.

Most plant data for the premission era come from Alexander's (1984) analysis of flotation samples collected from the Lake Jackson, High Ridge, and Velda sites (fig. 13.1). Lake Jackson (8LE1) was a ceremonial center with seven mounds. From about A.D. 1000 to 1500, the site

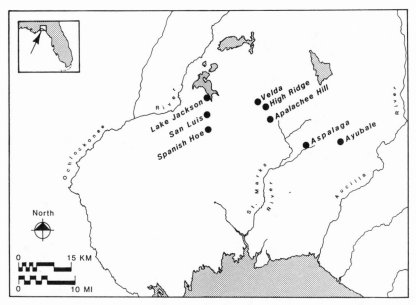

Figure 13.1. Map of Apalachee Province showing locations of sites discussed.

was the capital of the prehistoric Apalachee chiefdom (Payne 1991). The plant remains from Lake Jackson come from salvage excavations in Mound 3, a burial mound that produced a wealth of Southern Cult artifacts (Jones 1982). Besides elaborate grave goods, more than 22,000 maize kernels were found in association with a high-status burial and almost 5000 kernels were recovered from a burned deposit on a floor (Alexander 1984:table 13). The deposits also produced smaller quantities of maize cobs and hickory, acorn, and chinquapin nutshells (see table 13.1 for a list of the common and taxonomic names of the plants discussed in this chapter).

High Ridge (8LE117) was a late prehistoric farmstead with two structures (Fryman 1969). Two pits associated with the structures yielded more than 10,000 maize kernels, beans, a sunflower seed, acorn and hickory nutshells, 120 persimmon seeds, 815 maypop seeds, and a few cabbage palm and saw palmetto seeds (Alexander 1984:table 11).

Velda (8LE44) was a farmstead similar to High Ridge (J. F. Scarry 1984). However, ceramics from the site indicate that its occupation dates to the century between de Soto's visit and the establishment of the Apalachee missions (J. F. Scarry personal communication 1990). Samples

TABLE 13.1. Common and Taxonomic Names of Plant Foods Identified from Archaeological Contexts in Apalachee Province

Common name	Taxonomic name
Domesticated plants	
Indigenous crops	
Maize	*Zea mays*
Bean	*Phaseolus vulgaris*
Squash	*Cucurbita* sp.
Sunflower	*Helianthus annuus*
Old World crops	
Wheat	*Triticum* sp.
Garbanzo	*Cicer arietinum*
Peach	*Prunus persica*
Watermelon	*Citrullus vulgaris*
Fig	*Ficus* sp.
Hazelnut	*Corylus avellana*
Wild plants	
Nuts	
Hickory	*Carya* sp.
Acorn	*Quercus* sp.
Chinquapin	*Castanea pumilla*
Beech	*Fagus grandifolia*
Fruits	
Persimmon	*Diospyros virginiana*
Grape	*Vitis* sp.
Maypop	*Passiflora incarnata*
Saw palmetto	*Serenoa repens*
Cabbage palm	*Sabal palmetto*
Plum/cherry	*Prunus* sp.
Bramble	*Rubus* sp.
Miscellaneous	
Yaupon	*Ilex vomitoria*
Water locust	*Gleditsia aquatica*

of plants taken from pits at Velda yielded maize kernels, beans, and sunflower seeds. Wild plants included hickory, acorn, persimmon, and abundant saw palmetto (Alexander 1984:table 12).

Besides the data from Alexander's (1984) study, there are more limited data from several other premission sites. The only other systematic plant data for the premission Apalachee come from my analysis of four flotation samples collected from late prehistoric deposits encountered below the *convento* (friary) floor at Mission San Luis de Talimali (8LE4) (Shapiro and Vernon 1992; Vernon and McEwan 1990). The samples contain maize, sunflower, hickory, and grape (C. M. Scarry 1992a). Finally, there are several incidental reports of plant remains from sites with late prehistoric components. Maize was recovered from the Winewood site (8LE164; Jones and Penman 1973:84); maize and hickory were recovered from 8LE484 (Tesar 1980:841); and maize, hickory, acorn, and persimmon were recovered from the Bear Grass site (8LE473; Tesar 1980:789).

The plant data from premission Apalachee contexts are in accord with the Spanish accounts of a highly successful agricultural system centered on maize, beans, squash, and sunflowers. The Apalachee seem to have supplemented their bountiful crops with nuts and wild fruits. Overall, the premission Apalachee appear to have had an agricultural economy similar to those of other Mississippian populations of the lower Southeast (see Fritz [1990] and C. M. Scarry [1993] for discussions of variability in Mississippian agricultural regimes). It should be noted that at present there is no evidence that the Apalachee cultivated any of the native seed crops (e.g., chenopod, maygrass, sumpweed) that were part of the farming complexes of contemporaneous groups in the mid-South and Midwest (see Fritz [1990] and B. D. Smith [1989] for good discussions of the native seed crops).

For the mission period, the best data for both Apalachee and Spanish use of plant foods come from recent excavations at Mission San Luis de Talimali (8LE4; fig. 13.1). From the time it was established in 1656 until the destruction of the missions in 1704, San Luis was the capital of the Spanish mission system in Apalachee Province. During its occupation San Luis was home to missionaries, a small population of Spanish soldiers and civilians, and about 1400 Apalachee (Hann 1988a:194–200). Besides the residences of this varied population, the town contained a number of Spanish and Apalachee public buildings. Spanish structures included a church, a *convento*, and a fort; the principal Apalachee structure was a large council house (McEwan 1991b). Archaeological and documentary investigations, begun in 1988 and continuing into the present, have provided us with a wealth of data about this multiethnic, multifunctional community. Among other things, the research at San Luis has greatly enriched our knowledge about plant use in Apalachee Province.

There are few data on the Apalachee's use of plants in domestic settings for the mission period. What little information there is comes from four flotation samples from two sites that I scanned but did not analyze in detail and from a few plant remains recovered in screens from a third site. During the testing phase at San Luis, two flotation samples were collected from the area that is believed to have been the location of the Apalachee village associated with the mission (Shapiro 1987). Two other flotation samples were collected from refuse pits during salvage excavations at the Spanish Hoe site (8LE667), a mission period Apalachee farmstead (fig. 13.1; Bryne 1989). The samples from both sites contain maize, hickory, acorn, and persimmon (C. M. Scarry 1987, unpublished lab notes 1990). Excavations at Apalachee Hill (8LE148; fig. 13.1), another mission period Apalachee farmstead, produced a few fragments of maize and hickory (Bierce-Gedris 1981:234–239). Based on the limited data currently available, it is not possible to determine to what extent the Apalachee changed their production or consumption of plant foods from premission to mission times. Fortunately, excavations currently under way in the Apalachee village at San Luis should help to remedy this situation (McEwan, personal communication 1991).

We are in much better shape when it comes to the Apalachee's use of plants in public settings during the mission period. Excavations of the council house at San Luis (Shapiro and McEwan 1992; Vernon and McEwan 1990) produced plant remains from the structure's floor, its hearth, and 24 smudge pits (C. M. Scarry 1992a). The floor samples contain a diverse but not abundant assemblage of plants; maize, bean, sunflower, wheat, peach, hickory, acorn, and several wild fruits were identified. The hearth contained thousands of hickory shells, much smaller quantities of maize, and a few specimens of bean, sunflower, wheat, and wild fruit seeds. The hearth also produced several yaupon holly (*Ilex vomitoria*) seeds, which are of interest because yaupon is the plant from which the ritual black drink was brewed (Hudson 1979). The 24 smudge pits produced roughly 1000 cob fragments with complete cross sections, untold numbers of cupules, and much smaller quantities of kernels. Other remains were sparse in the smudge pits, but squash, sunflower, wheat, watermelon, hickory, acorn, and several wild fruits were present (C. M. Scarry 1992a).

The assemblage from the council house gives an indication of the plant foods that the Apalachee considered appropriate for use in a public and ceremonial setting. The remains are dominated by indigenous crops and wild plants. If we take away the Old World plants, about which I will say more below, we are left with essentially the plants that occur in premission contexts. With the possible exception of the yaupon used for the black drink, there is no indication that foods prepared or consumed in the council house differed from everyday fare.

For the mission era, there is as much evidence about plant use by the Spaniards as there is for the Apalachee. Recent excavations in the Spanish village area at San Luis (McEwan 1991a and this volume; Vernon and McEwan 1990) produced plant remains from four trash pits (C. M. Scarry 1992b). Plant remains from 30 flotation samples from the four pits have been analyzed in detail, and 24 additional flotation samples have been scanned (C. M. Scarry 1987, 1992b). Maize remains dominate the assemblage from the Spanish village; they are present in moderate quantities in all samples. Bean, wheat, garbanzo, peach, watermelon, and hazelnut occur as isolated specimens in a few samples. Hickory and acorn nutshells are present but not particularly abundant. A few fragments of the spiny, outer husks of beech nuts also are present, but it seems unlikely that they are derived from nuts used for food. Wild fruits recovered from the Spanish village include persimmon, maypop, grape, and cabbage palm (C. M. Scarry 1992b).

Besides the samples from the Spanish village, we have plant remains from the *convento* at San Luis. Excavations of this structure uncovered several concentrations of burned plants on its floor (Shapiro and Vernon 1992; Vernon and McEwan 1990). I analyzed flotation samples collected from these concentrations and identified 101 maize kernels, 426 beans, a few fragments of squash seed, and a sunflower seed. No remains from Old World crops were recovered. Hickory, acorn, grape, and plum or cherry are present but not abundant (C. M. Scarry 1992a).

There are less systematic plant data from the church complexes at two other Apalachee missions (C. M. Scarry 1986). At San Juan de Aspalaga (8JE1) a structure identified as the church was partially excavated by Hale Smith in the early 1950s. Further work at the site in the late 1960s exposed more of the church and revealed a second structure, which is believed to be the *convento* (Jones and Shapiro 1990:499–500; Morrell and Jones 1970). Two Spanish structures, one of which was identified as a church, were also excavated at La Concepción de Ayubale (8JE2; Griffin and Smith 1951; Jones and Shapiro 1990:500; H. G. Smith 1948, 1951). No flotation or fine-screening was done at either site. In each case, however, large concentrations of plant remains were found in what appear to have been storage rooms or bins. The abundant food remains may well be the remnants of provisions that were destroyed when the missions were attacked and burned by Carolinian raiders and their Creek allies in 1704. Unfortunately, it is unclear whether the plant remains were recovered from the structures identified as churches or, as seems more likely, from *conventos*.

I analyzed food plants collected from both Aspalaga and Ayubale (C. M. Scarry 1986). The two assemblages contain more than 4000 maize kernels, about 2000 beans, 196 wheat grains, 4 whole persimmons, 98 persimmon seeds, 95 acorn meats, and 203 acorn nutshells. Hickory nutshells, grape, maypop, cabbage palm, plum or cherry, and bramble seeds are present but not abundant.

PATTERNS IN FOOD PLANT USE IN APALACHEE PROVINCE

In the preceding survey of plant data from Apalachee Province, I divided the assemblages into groups between which differences in the use of plant foods might be anticipated. The major division is between pre-mission and mission period sites. For the mission period, the assemblages are also grouped by ethnic association and by social context: domestic versus council house for the Apalachee, village versus church complex for the Spanish.

To examine what plant foods occur in these different contexts, it is also useful to divide the plants into several categories. The most basic division is between domesticated plants (table 13.2), which are deliberately planted and tended in fields or gardens, and wild plants (table 13.3), which are collected from forests, field edges, or wherever they may happen to grow. For the domesticated plants, it is useful to make a further distinction between those that are native to the New World (Indigenous crops) and those that are of Old World origin (Old World crops).

"Indigenous crops" is used here to refer to domesticated plants that were grown by the Apalachee at contact. In the mission period these crops were the mainstays of both the Apalachee and the Spanish diets (table 13.2). Maize remains are not only ubiquitous but also extremely abundant in some cases. Beans are common, except in mission-era Apalachee domestic settings, where their absence is probably due to inadequate sampling. Sunflower and squash occur in mission-era Apalachee and Spanish assemblages, attesting to their use by both populations.

In the mission era some Old World food plants were also used by both the Spanish and the Apalachee populations (table 13.2). These crops must have been introduced by the Spaniards. But once the seed stock was

TABLE 13.2. Domesticated Plants Identified from Sites in Apalachee Province

	Premission	Mission			
	Apalachee mound and domestic	Apalachee domestic	Apalachee council house	Spanish domestic	Spanish church complex
Indigenous crops					
Maize	x	x	x	x	x
Bean	x		x	x	x
Squash					x
Sunflower	x		x	x	x
Old World crops					
Wheat			x	x	x
Garbanzo				x	
Peach			x	x	
Watermelon			x		
Fig				x	
Hazelnut				x	

Sources: Alexander 1984; C. M. Scarry 1986, 1987, 1992a, 1992b.

TABLE 13.3. Wild Plants Identified from Sites in Apalachee Province

	Premission	Mission			
	Apalachee mound and domestic	Apalachee domestic	Apalachee council house	Spanish domestic	Spanish church complex
Nuts					
Hickory	x	x	x	x	x
Acorn	x	x	x	x	x
Chinquapin	x				
Beech				x	
Fruits					
Persimmon	x	x	x	x	x
Grape	x		x	x	x
Maypop	x		x	x	x
Saw palmetto	x		x		
Cabbage palm	x		x	x	x
Plum/cherry	x	x			x
Bramble			x		x
Miscellaneous					
Yaupon			x		
Water locust	x				x

Sources: Alexander 1984; C. M. Scarry 1986, 1987, 1992a, 1992b.

available, most of the Old World domesticates represented in the samples could have been produced in Apalachee Province. Possible exceptions to this are garbanzos, which grow best in cool, dry climates (Renfrew 1973:119), and hazelnuts, which require two to six months of cold temperatures in order to germinate (Schopmeyer 1974:344). Both of these plants are represented by isolated specimens; their scarcity may be an indication that they were imported.

The greatest variety of Old World plants is found in the Spanish village area at San Luis. In contrast, Old World crops are not well represented in the church complexes. Indeed, despite the fact that large quantities of food plants were recovered from church/*convento* structures, wheat is the only Old World plant that has been recovered from church complexes. Moreover, it is quite possible that the wheat was intended for use in the sacraments rather than for the priests' meals.

Remains from Old World plants also occur in the San Luis council house. The Apalachee held their principal public meetings and ceremonies in the council house, and we might expect food use there to be conservative. The presence of wheat, peach, and watermelon in the council house could be taken as an indication that some Old World plants had been thoroughly incorporated into the Apalachee diet. The problem with this interpretation is that the council house was also used as a guest lodge. The food remains from the structure could be from meals prepared by or served to visitors, some of whom were undoubtedly Spanish. Thus the role of Old World plants in the Apalachee's diet remains ambiguous.

At present, when only qualitative comparisons can be made due to sampling problems, it is difficult to discern any differences in the use of wild plants between contexts (table 13.3). Hickory nuts and acorns are found in all contexts. The assemblages from the premission Apalachee, the council house, and the church complexes each contain six types of wild fruits, while the Spanish village samples produced only four types of wild fruits. This difference is slight, however, and difficult to assess without quantitative data.

Discussion

Taken as a whole, the available evidence suggests a basically similar use of plant foods by all segments of the population during the mission period. Indigenous plants, especially crops, were the staples of everyone's diet.

This conclusion is in accord with the documentary evidence and is not particularly surprising. Foods were exported from Apalachee Province. Consequently, we would not expect to find either the Apalachee or the Spanish population using nonlocal foodstuffs in bulk. High-status Spaniards probably imported some supplies for their own use, but most imported foods were probably high-value, low-volume items (e.g., hazelnuts or olives) that supplemented rather than replaced locally available foods.

Besides the fact that most of the food consumed in Apalachee Province was probably locally produced, there is another reason why similar patterns of food use would exist throughout the multiethnic community. The Apalachee not only grew the crops the Spaniards ate but probably prepared many of the Spaniards' meals as well. We know that Apalachee women worked in several high-status households (Hann 1988a:143–144), and it seems likely that Apalachee women served as domestic labor for soldiers and priests as well.

Research at other Spanish New World sites has shown that the presence of native women in Spanish households is indicated by the presence of aboriginal material culture in those activities that are traditionally the domain of women (Deagan 1983; McEwan 1991a). Spanish material culture is found associated with male activities and in situations where there may be public display. Thus aboriginal pots are used for cooking, but European tablewares are used for serving and eating. If plant foods were both produced and prepared by Apalachee women, then it should not surprise us that such foods were aboriginal in content and flavor.

While everyone relied on indigenous crops for their staple plant foods, within the Spanish community there may have been variations on the basic diet. The assemblage from the Spanish village at San Luis contains a wider range of Old World plants, and possibly a narrower range of wild fruits, than do the assemblages from the church complexes. My research on plant use in St. Augustine has suggested that the townspeople there used fewer wild food plants, especially fruits, as they succeeded in producing Old World fruits and vegetables (Scarry and Reitz 1990). The mainstays of the diet were indigenous crops, but Old World plants grown in kitchen gardens gave the diet a superficially Iberian character. The Spanish secular population in Apalachee Province may have made a similar attempt to maintain old life-styles, including foodways.

In contrast to the residents of the Spanish village at San Luis, the missionaries seem to have eaten a diet that was largely aboriginal in character. The foodstuffs recovered from the church complexes contain an abundance of maize and beans and a varied assemblage of wild plants, but the only Old World plant represented is wheat. The missionaries were Franciscans who would have taken vows of poverty on entering the order. Thus they may have directed their efforts toward enhancing the church rather than maintaining the trappings of Spanish daily life. The missionaries are reported to have sold maize and wheat in Havana (Bushnell 1981:82, 99). If so, judging from the abundance of gold, silver, cloth, and other goods listed in inventories of church furnishings from Apalachee Province (Hann 1986a), the missionaries may have invested their profits in lavish paraphernalia for the church rather than on luxury foods or other goods for themselves.

What I am suggesting is that status markers were different for the various segments of the population in Apalachee Province. Status for the Spanish secular population may have been displayed by maintaining some semblance of Old World life-styles. One element of this would have been a greater consumption of traditional foods. On the other hand, status for the missionaries may have been displayed by the richness of the church they served. Apart from wheat and wine for the sacraments, food would have been inconsequential in this system.

If different ways of measuring status existed, how did the Apalachee fit in the picture? Did the chiefs adopt Iberian material goods and foods to ally themselves with the Spanish authorities? Or did they maintain their traditional status markers and disdain the foreign ones? What about the commoners? Did possession or use of Spanish foods and goods increase their status? Or did they gain respect by contributing to the missionaries' efforts to adorn the churches? Clearly our current data cannot answer these questions. However, as further evidence becomes available we will likely find that in the mission period, foodways were important threads in the social fabric of Apalachee Province.

Acknowledgments

This article draws heavily on my analyses of plant remains from San Luis and other mission sites in Apalachee Province. As is true for most archaeological research, my work could not have been completed without the aid of several agencies and many people. The excavations of the San Luis council house were funded by the state of Florida. Work in the *convento* and in the Spanish village was funded in part by the National Endowment for the Humanities (RO-21395-87). Funds for the analyses of the plant remains were administered through the Florida Bureau of Archaeological Research. Susan Hortenstine and Charles Carpenter, my laboratory assistants, helped sort the plant remains from the council house floor, the *convento*, and the Spanish village. Gary Shapiro, before his death, Bonnie McEwan, and Richard Vernon all provided advice and important information about the archaeological contexts of the samples I analyzed. John Hann's excellent work with the Spanish documents has provided a wealth of information that has complemented and enriched our archaeological investigations. I owe all these individuals a vote of thanks. Any errors in interpretation are, of course, my own.

Bibliography

Alexander, Michelle M.
1984   Paleoethnobotany of the Fort Walton Indians: High Ridge, Velda, and Lake Jackson Sites. Master's thesis, Department of Anthropology, Florida State University, Tallahassee.

Bierce-Gedris, Katherine B.
1981   Apalachee Hill: The Archaeological Investigation of an Indian Site of the Spanish Mission Period in Northwest Florida. Master's thesis, Department of Anthropology, Florida State University, Tallahassee.

Bryne, Stephen C.
1989   Archaeological Investigations at the Spanish Hoe Site (8LE667), Leon County, Florida. Report presented to the Leon County Research and Development Authority. Ms. on file, Department of Anthropology, Florida State University, Tallahassee.

Bushnell, Amy T.
1981   *The King's Coffers: Proprietors of the Spanish Florida Treasury, 1565–1702*. Gainesville: University Presses of Florida.

Deagan, Kathleen A.
1983   The Mestizo Minority: Archaeological Patterns of Intermarriage. In *Spanish St. Augustine: The Archaeology of a Colonial Creole Community*, edited by Kathleen Deagan, 99–107. New York: Academic Press.

Fritz, Gayle J.
1990   Multiple Pathways to Farming in Precontact Eastern North America. *Journal of World Prehistory* 4:387–435.

Fryman, Frank
1969   High Ridge 8LE117. Field notes on file, Florida Bureau of Archaeological
       Research, Tallahassee.

Griffin, John W., and Hale G. Smith
1951   Trait List of Two Spanish Sites of the Mission Period. In *Here They Once
       Stood: The Tragic End of the Apalachee Missions*, edited by Mark Boyd,
       Hale Smith, and John Griffin, 175–177. Gainesville: University of Florida
       Press.

Hann, John H.
1986a Church Furnishings, Sacred Vessels and Vestments Held by the Missions
       of Florida: Translation of Two Inventories. In *Spanish Translations*, 147–
       164. Florida Archaeology no. 2. Tallahassee: Florida Bureau of Archae-
       ological Research.

1986b Translation of Governor Rebolledo's 1657 Visitation of Three Provinces
       and Related Documents. In *Spanish Translations*, 81–146. Florida Ar-
       chaeology no. 2. Tallahassee: Florida Bureau of Archaeological Research.

1988a *Apalachee: The Land between the Rivers*. Ripley P. Bullen Monographs
       in Anthropology and History, no. 7. Gainesville: University of Florida
       Press.

1988b Transcription and Translation of the Apalachee Section of Garcilaso de la
       Vega's Florida of the Inca. Ms. on file, Florida Bureau of Archaeological
       Research, Tallahassee.

1988c Transcription and Translation of the Apalachee Section of the Hidalgo de
       Elvas' True Relation of the Labors that the Governor Don Fernando de
       Souto and Certain Portuguese Gentlemen Experienced in the Exploration
       of the Province of Florida. Now Newly Made by a Gentleman of Elvas.
       Ms. on file, Florida Bureau of Archaeological Research, Tallahassee.

1988d Translation of the Apalachee Section of the Narrative about the de Soto
       Expedition Written by Gonzalo Fernández de Oviedo and Based on the
       Diary of Rodrigo Ranjel, de Soto's Private Secretary. Ms. on file, Florida
       Bureau of Archaeological Research, Tallahassee.

Hudson, Charles M.
1979   *Black Drink: A Native American Tea*. Athens: University of Georgia Press.

Jones, B. Calvin
1982   Southern Cult Manifestations at the Lake Jackson Site, Leon County,
       Florida: Salvage Excavation of Mound 3. *Midcontinental Journal of Ar-
       chaeology* 7(1):3–44.

Jones, B. Calvin, and John T. Penman
1973   Winewood: An Inland Fort Walton Site in Tallahassee, Florida. *Bureau of
       Historic Sites and Properties Bulletin* 3:65–90.

Jones, B. Calvin, and Gary N. Shapiro
1990 Nine Mission Sites in Apalachee. In *Columbian Consequences*. Vol. 2: *Archaeological and Historical Perspectives on the Spanish Borderlands East*, edited by David Hurst Thomas, 491–509. Washington, D.C.: Smithsonian Institution Press.

McEwan, Bonnie G.
1991a The Archaeology of Women in the Spanish New World. *Historical Archaeology* 25(4):33–41.

1991b San Luis de Talimali: The Archaeology of Spanish-Indian Relations at a Florida Mission. *Historical Archaeology* 25(3):36–60.

Morrell, L. Ross, and B. Calvin Jones
1970 San Juan de Aspalaga (a Preliminary Architectural Study). *Bureau of Historic Sites and Properties Bulletin* 1:23–43.

Payne, Claudine
1991 Structure and Development at the Lake Jackson Site. Paper presented at the 48th Annual Meeting of the Southeastern Archaeological Conference, Jackson, Mississippi.

Renfrew, Jane M.
1973 *Paleoethnobotany*. New York: Columbia University Press.

Scarry, C. Margaret
1986 A Descriptive Report of Plant Remains from the Mission Sites 8JE1 and 8JE2. Ms. on file, Florida Bureau of Archaeological Research, Tallahassee.

1987 Appendix 6: A Preliminary Examination of Plant Remains. In *Archaeology at San Luis: Broad-Scale Testing, 1984–1985*, by Gary Shapiro, 249–256. Florida Archaeology no. 3. Tallahassee: Florida Bureau of Archaeological Research.

1992a Appendix 6: Plant Remains from the San Luis Council House and *Convento*. In *Archaeology at San Luis: The Apalachee Council House*, by Gary Shapiro and Bonnie McEwan. Florida Archaeology no. 6, pt. 1. Tallahassee: Florida Bureau of Archaeological Research.

1992b Plant Remains from the Spanish Village at San Luis. Ms. on file, Florida Bureau of Archaeological Research, Tallahassee.

1993 Variability in Mississippian Crop Production Strategies. In *Foraging and Farming in the Eastern Woodlands*, edited by C. Margaret Scarry. Ripley P. Bullen Monographs in Anthropology and History. Gainesville: University Press of Florida.

Scarry, C. Margaret, and Elizabeth J. Reitz
1990 Herbs, Fish, Scum, and Vermin: Subsistence Strategies in Sixteenth-Century Spanish Florida. In *Columbian Consequences*. Vol. 2: *Archae-*

ological and Historical Perspectives on the Spanish Borderlands East, edited by David Hurst Thomas, 343–354. Washington, D.C.: Smithsonian Institution Press.

Scarry, John F.

1984 Preliminary Report of the Mississippian Fort Walton Farmstead at the Velda Site. Paper presented at the annual meeting of the Florida Academy of Sciences, Boca Raton, Florida.

1990 The Rise, Transformation and Fall of Apalachee: Political Centralization and Decentralization in a Chiefly Society. In *Lamar Archaeology: Mississippian Chiefdoms in the Deep South*, edited by J. Mark Williams and Gary Shapiro, 175–186. Tuscaloosa: University of Alabama Press.

1992 Political Offices and Political Structure: Ethnohistoric and Archaeological Perspectives on the Native Lords of Apalachee. In *Native Lords of the Southeast*, edited by Alex W. Barker and Timothy R. Pauketat, 163–183. Archaeological Papers of the American Anthropological Association, no. 3. Washington, D.C.

Schopmeyer, C. S.

1974 *Seeds of Woody Plants*. Agricultural Handbook no. 450. Washington, D.C.: U.S. Department of Agriculture.

Shapiro, Gary

1987 *Archaeology at San Luis: Broad-Scale Testing, 1984–1985*. Florida Archaeology no. 3. Tallahassee: Florida Bureau of Archaeological Research.

Shapiro, Gary, and Bonnie G. McEwan

1992 *Archaeology at San Luis: The Apalachee Council House*. Florida Archaeology no. 6, pt. 1. Tallahassee: Florida Bureau of Archaeological Research.

Shapiro, Gary, and Richard Vernon

1992 *Archaeology at San Luis: The Church Complex*. Florida Archaeology no. 6, pt. 2. Tallahassee: Florida Bureau of Archaeological Research.

Smith, Bruce D.

1989 Origins of Agriculture in Eastern North America. *Science* 246:1566–1571.

Smith, Hale G.

1948 Results of an Archaeological Investigation of a Spanish Mission Site in Jefferson County, Florida. *The Florida Anthropologist* 1:1–10.

1951 A Spanish Mission Site in Jefferson County, Florida. In *Here They Once Stood: The Tragic End of the Apalachee Missions*, edited by Mark Boyd, Hale Smith, and John Griffin, 107–136. Gainesville: University of Florida Press.

Tesar, Louis D.
1980   *The Leon County Bicentennial Survey Report: An Archaeological Survey of Selected Portions of Leon County, Florida.* 2 vols. Miscellaneous Project Report Series, no. 49. Tallahassee: Bureau of Historic Sites and Properties, Florida Department of State.

Vernon, Richard, and Bonnie McEwan
1990   *Investigations of the Church Complex and Spanish Village at San Luis.* Florida Archaeological Reports, no. 18. Tallahassee: Florida Bureau of Archaeological Research.

Evidence for Animal Use at the Missions of Spanish Florida

ELIZABETH J. REITZ

Until recently, most First Spanish period archaeological research focused on Spanish life at two colonial towns, St. Augustine and Santa Elena. Study of faunal remains excavated from these towns has provided a great deal of information about animal use by Spanish colonists on the Atlantic coast (Reitz 1992; Reitz and Cumbaa 1983; Reitz and Scarry 1985). Unfortunately, little comparable zooarchaeological information has been available from missions associated with these towns, but recent archaeological excavations have provided a glimpse into animal use by Spaniards and Native Americans living at some of the missions of Spanish Florida. Excavated faunal materials suggest that there were differences in animal use at missions located in the Apalachee, Timucua, and Guale provinces. They also suggest that Apalachee Province may have been more congenial to Spanish life than were Timucua and Guale provinces.

Spanish Florida

Spanish Florida was founded in 1565 by Pedro Menéndez de Avilés, and this date marks the beginning of the First Spanish period. Originally Spain claimed all of North America south of Newfoundland and west of the Atlantic Ocean indefinitely (Gannon 1967:1); however, the actual occupation was a strip along the Atlantic coast from Santa Elena, on Parris Island, southward to St. Augustine, and west across the north-

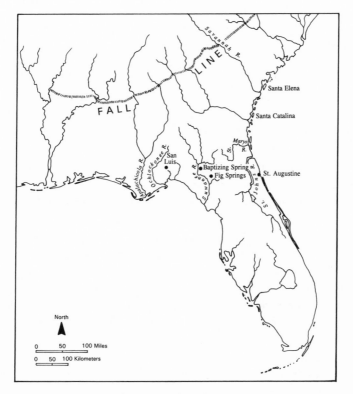

Figure 14.1. Map of region.

central portion of peninsular Florida to the Apalachicola River (fig. 14.1). The real boundaries of Spanish Florida varied considerably throughout the First Spanish period.

Spanish Florida endured for 200 years. Menéndez founded two towns, Santa Elena and St. Augustine (fig. 14.1). He also established a string of fortifications along the Atlantic coast between these towns, south around the tip of peninsular Florida, and along the Gulf Coast (Bolton and Ross 1968:8). Many of the original fortifications, as well as Santa Elena, were abandoned by the end of the sixteenth century in response to a variety of forces, including disease, natural disasters, native resistance to Spanish intrusions, and attacks by competing European nationals. During the seventeenth century new fortifications, missions, and cattle ranches were established. Spanish Floridians continued to endure the assaults experienced in the sixteenth century but managed to reestablish their claims northward along the Atlantic coast and westward throughout the north-central portion of peninsular Florida to the Apalachicola River and perhaps beyond. Like the preceding centuries, the eighteenth century was also a time of turmoil for Spanish Florida (Te-Paske 1964). Raids by Carolina Governor James Moore and his Native American allies succeeded in finally destroying the outlying missions and cattle ranches by 1704, forcing Spaniards as well as missionized Native Americans to retreat to the vicinity of St. Augustine. The First Spanish period ended in 1763 when Spain ceded what remained of Spanish Florida to England. Virtually the entire Spanish and missionized Native American populations evacuated the town at that time (Dunkel 1955). Spain regained Florida in 1783 but ceded it to the United States of America in 1821.

Efforts to convert the native residents of Spanish Florida were initiated early and continued throughout the First Spanish period (Hann 1990). The first missionaries were Jesuits, but they abandoned their efforts in 1572 and were replaced by Franciscans (Gannon 1967:36; Hann 1990:433). Although both Jesuits and Franciscans founded missions in the sixteenth century, the Spanish mission system was most secure and reached its greatest extent during the seventeenth century (Gannon 1967:49). After 1606 a series of missions was established westward from St. Augustine to the Apalachicola River, and the chain of missions north of St. Augustine along the Georgia coast was reestablished (Gannon 1967:49–67; Hann 1988; Lanning 1935:210–235; Tebeau 1971:43–55). Not only were these missions a source of fish, game, and native produce for St. Augustine, but missionized Native Americans also raised European-introduced chickens, cattle, and pigs, as well as a wide variety of Old World plants (Bolton 1917:57; Hann 1988:239). Spaniards in St. Augustine traded with nearby Native Americans and may also have relied heavily on livestock, game, fish, and produce from more distant missions (Boniface 1971:169; Hann 1988:232). St. Augustinians had to compete with French, Dutch, English, and Cuban traders as well as Franciscans for access to the Native American trade (Boyd, Smith, and Griffin 1951:46; Bushnell 1981:92–95, 99).

Also during the seventeenth century, cattle ranches were established between St. Augustine and Apalachee Province and they were particularly productive between 1650 and 1700 (Arnade 1961; Bushnell 1978). Although one might think that this would guarantee an ample supply of beef in St. Augustine, many ranchers preferred to ship their products to the better markets in Havana, using the St. Marks and Suwannee rivers as outlets for hides, dried meat, and tallow (Bushnell 1978).

The missions of Spanish Florida were subdivided into several administrative units roughly defined by the cultural identity of Native Americans living in each province. Precise boundaries for these provinces are not agreed on. According to Lewis Larson (1978), Guale Province extended from St. Catherines Island, location of Mission Santa Catalina de Guale, south along the Atlantic coast to the northern border of Timucua Province. However, John Hann (1990:423, personal communication 1991) notes that in 1655 two missions, San Felipe and Chatuache, were 4 to 10 leagues north of Santa Catalina de Guale. The Guale primarily occupied the sea islands and estuaries that border the Atlantic coast in this area, as well as the adjacent mainland.

Timucua Province included the islands and mainland from the southern border cf Guale extending to the north-central third of peninsular Florida (Hann 1990:423; Milanich 1978). While Lewis Larson (1978) defines the Guale/Timucua border below Jekyll Island, John Hann would extend the boundary above Jekyll Island (Hann, personal communication 1991). The province extended from the Atlantic coast westward to the Aucilla River. The southern boundary is also poorly defined, but it extended southward some distance beyond St. Augustine. This is a region of pine/oak hammocks and sand hills punctuated by numerous lakes and rivers. The Western Timucua occupied that area between the St. Johns and the Aucilla rivers and the Eastern Timucua the area between the St. Johns and the Atlantic Ocean (Milanich 1978).

Apalachee Province is the best-defined province and is associated with the panhandle of peninsular Florida. The eastern boundary is defined by the Aucilla River and the western boundary by the Ochlockonee River (Hann 1988:1). Although the southern edge is formed by Apalachee Bay and the Gulf of Mexico, approximately 30–40 km south of San Luis, the northern boundary is less well defined. The Apalachee mission headquarters, San Luis de Talimali, was located toward the northwest edge of this region. The province is characterized by rolling hills and numerous lakes and streams.

ZOOARCHAEOLOGICAL DATA FROM APALACHEE PROVINCE

Zooarchaeological information for Native Americans and Spaniards associated with the missions of Spanish Florida during the First Spanish period is limited. Some of the best data currently available are from Apalachee Province. Until recently the only archaeological faunal evidence was from three small Apalachee collections. In one of these, from San Joseph de Ocuya, Stanley Olsen reported 5 fragmentary teeth and 16 long bone fragments (Jones 1973:45). Only two specific identifications were made, a pig and a cow. A brief list for San Francisco de Ocone included cow, pig, deer, and oyster (Boyd, Smith, and Griffin 1951:175). The faunal assemblage from Apalachee Hill, a seventeenth-century, non-mission Apalachee domestic site, was somewhat larger (Bierce-Gedris 1981:232). It contained 25 bones, one of which was tentatively identified as a bowfin. Nine of the bones were identified only as turtle and one was identified only as bird. These data provide little information about subsistence at missions during the First Spanish period.

However, recent excavations from the Spanish residential area of San Luis de Talimali (8LE4) have produced quantified evidence for Spanish life at an Apalachee mission (fig. 14.1). San Luis de Talimali was the capital of the Spanish mission chain in western Florida from 1656 to 1704. It was the largest mission village in Apalachee Province and was occupied by Spanish soldiers, civilians, friars, and Native Americans (see McEwan, this volume). The missions in Apalachee played a major role in supplying livestock, tallow, lard, hides, and other agricultural products to St. Augustine and the Caribbean (Boniface 1971:200–201; Boyd, Smith, and Griffin 1951; Hann 1988:136). Presumably Apalachee would not be exporting products such as hams, lard, tallow, and chickens if the local Europeans were unable to satisfy what was probably their own preference for these products. Hence, it seems likely that faunal remains from one of the Apalachee missions, especially those from the capital of the western mission chain, might be dominated by domestic animals.

The San Luis faunal materials were excavated under the direction of Bonnie G. McEwan, Florida Bureau of Archaeological Research. Because these data have not been published elsewhere, they will be described in detail here. Some of the materials were recovered from Feature 6, a large trash pit associated with a domestic area of the Spanish village within the mission complex (see McEwan, this volume). Feature 73/68 was in the Ocala Road area of the Spanish village. Feature 74/80 was in the residential area of the Spanish village, near Feature 6, and was associated with an area that appears to have been corrals. Features 65/66/72 were associated with the fort. The features were probably deposited near the end of the Spanish occupation at San Luis, in the late seventeenth century.

All the materials were fine-screened through 1/16-inch mesh and a 10-liter sample from each level was floated. The 1/16-inch fractions remain to be studied. The faunal materials were studied at the Zooarchaeology Laboratory, Museum of Natural History, University of Georgia (Reitz 1991b; Reitz and Freer 1990; Weinand and Reitz 1992) using methods that have been described elsewhere (Reitz and Scarry 1985).

When the data from these features are combined, the collection contained an estimated 86 individuals (table 14.1). More than 40 percent of these were pigs (*Sus scrofa*) and cows (*Bos taurus*). Chickens (*Gallus gallus*) contributed an additional 3 percent of the individuals (table 14.2). No sheep or goats were identified. Wild mammals contributed 13 percent of the individuals. These included an opossum (*Didelphis virginiana*), rabbits (*Sylvilagus* spp.), a squirrel (*Sciurus* spp.), and deer (*Odocoileus virginianus*). Deer contributed 8 percent of the individuals. Turtles included box turtles (*Terrapene carolina*), gopher tortoises (*Gopherus polyphemus*), and softshell turtle (*Apalone ferox*). Gopher tortoises contributed 5 percent of the individuals. Ten different fish species were identified and included both freshwater (*Amia calva*, *Ictalurus* spp., *Lepomis* spp., and *Micropterus salmoides*) and marine forms (*Arius felis*, *Rhomboplites aurorubens*, *Archosargus probatocephalus*, *Cynoscion* spp., and *Mugil* spp.). Commensal taxa, including dog (*Canis familiaris*), horse or donkey (Equidae), and frog/toad (Anura), contributed 7 percent of the individuals.

The meat contribution of these taxa was calculated for all features except Feature 6. The bones from Feature 6 were in poor condition and could not be weighed. It should be noted that only biomass for those taxa in table 14.1 for which the minimum number of individuals (MNI) was estimated was included when the summary table (table 14.2) was constructed. For example, biomass for sunfish (*Lepomis* spp.) was included in the summary tables, while biomass for Centrarchidae was not. In the following discussion, the percentage of estimated biomass contributed by a specific species or group of species is based on this modified biomass rather than on the total biomass estimated for the site and calculated in the species list.

Domestic mammals contributed almost all of the biomass estimated for San Luis (table 14.2). Beef contributed an estimated 78 percent of the modified biomass and pork 16 percent. Noncommensal wild fauna contributed only 5 percent of the modified biomass. The only major wild fauna were deer (4 percent of the biomass) and gopher tortoises (1 per-

TABLE 14.1. San Luis: Species List

	Count	MNI #	MNI %	Wt (g)	Biomass kg	Biomass %
UID mammal	18874			18612.84	186.0916	53.9
Didelphis virginiana (opossum)	6	1	1.2			
Sylvilagus spp. (rabbit)	5	2	2.3	0.41	0.0118	trace
Sciurus spp. (squirrel)	1	1	1.2	0.09	0.003	trace
Canis familiaris (dog)	2	2	2.3	2.42	0.0583	0.02
Equidae (horse or donkey)	4	2	2.3	5.60	0.1240	0.04
Artiodactyl	44			100.56	1.6679	0.5
Sus scrofa (pig)	652	20	23.3	1974.61	24.5989	7.1
Odocoileus virginianus (deer)	63	7	8.1	437.27	6.2614	1.8
Bos taurus (cow)	476	14	16.3	11590.69	121.9435	35.3
UID bird	40			11.66	0.1909	0.06
Gallus gallus (chicken)	19	3	3.5	6.7	0.1153	0.03
Meleagris gallopavo (turkey)	1	1	1.2			
Corvidae (crows)	1	1	1.2	0.2	0.0047	trace
UID turtle	526			163.87	0.9696	0.3
Emydidae (pond turtle family)	2					
Terrapene carolina (box turtle)	5	2	2.3	0.23	0.0118	trace
Gopherus polyphemus (gopher tortoise)	247	4	4.6	323.64	1.5196	0.4
Apalone ferox (softshell turtle)	19	1	1.2	6.39	0.0758	0.02
Frog/toad	3	2	2.3	0.1		
Elasmobranchiomorphi (sharks)	1	1	1.2	1.20	0.1473	0.04
UID fish	847			57.15	0.7877	0.2
Amia calva (bowfin)	1	1	1.2	0.26	0.0104	trace
Siluriformes (catfishes)	11			2.9	0.0549	0.02
Ictalurus spp. (bullhead catfish)	9	3	3.5	1.89	0.0365	0.01
Arius felis (hardhead catfish)	2	1	1.2	0.99	0.0198	0.01
Morone saxatilis (striped bass)	7	2	2.3	1.00	0.0080	trace
Centrarchidae (sunfishes)	1			0.4	0.0275	0.01
Lepomis spp. (sunfish)	3	3	3.5	0.3	0.0070	trace
Micropterus salmoides (largemouth bass)	40	6	7.0	10.9	0.1293	0.04
Rhomboplites aurorubens (vermilion snapper)	1	1	1.2	0.36	0.0118	trace
Archosargus probatocephalus (sheepshead)	10	2	2.3	7.84	0.1054	0.03
Cynoscion spp. (seatrout)	1	1	1.2	0.8	0.033	0.01
Mugil spp. (mullet)	49	2	2.3	12.42	0.2229	0.06
UID vertebrate				4697.53		
Total	21973	86		38033.22	345.2496	

TABLE 14.2. San Luis de Talimali: Summary

	MNI		Biomass	
	#	%	kg	%
Domestic mammals	34	39.5	146.5424	94.3
Domestic birds	3	3.5	0.1153	0.07
Deer	7	8.1	6.2614	4.0
Other wild mammals	4	4.6	0.0148	0.01
Wild birds	2	2.3	0.0047	trace
Turtles/alligators	7	8.1	1.6072	1.0
Sharks/rays/fishes	23	26.7	0.7314	0.5
Commensal taxa	6	7.0	0.1823	0.1
Total	86		155.4595	

cent of the biomass). Although a wide variety of fishes were identified in the collection, they contributed little meat to the diet.

Not only did domestic mammals provide most of the meat for Spaniards at San Luis de Talimali, but many of these animals were slaughtered young, indicating that they were raised specifically for food rather than for dairy production or traction. One of the pig individuals was less than 18 months of age at death, 3 were less than 42 months of age, 1 was an adult, and the remaining 15 individuals were of indeterminate age, although probably older than 18 months at death. Three of the pig adults were males, as indicated by the presence of larger lower canines typical of adult males of this species, and 2 were females. One of the cattle individuals was less than 18 months of age at death, 8 were subadults that died before 36 months of age, 2 were adults, and the age of 3 individuals was indeterminate.

Zooarchaeological Data from Western Timucua Province

Few data regarding animal use by Spaniards in the western portion of the Timucua Province are available, although recent work has expanded our knowledge of animal use by Native Americans at one of these missions.

Limited Spanish and Native American data are available from excavations conducted by L. Jill Loucks at a seventeenth-century north-central Florida mission site located adjacent to Baptizing Spring (8SU65) near the Suwannee River about 60 km east of Apalachee Province (fig. 14.1; Loucks 1979:226). The identity of the mission is unknown (Hann 1990:470; Loucks 1979:319 and this volume), although Loucks thought that it was probably occupied during the first half of the seventeenth century (Loucks 1979:180, 319–320 and this volume). A 1/4-inch meshed screen was used to recover the materials. Although the sample from Baptizing Spring is small, containing the remains of an estimated 48 individuals, historically it provided the first detailed look at Native American and Spanish animal use at a mission in Spanish Florida.

In the Spanish area at Baptizing Spring pigs and cows were the only domestic animals identified; each contributed 8 percent of the estimated individuals in a sample of 13 individuals (Loucks 1979:226; see also tables 8.6 and 14.3 this volume). Deer accounted for 31 percent of the individuals and the terrestrial gopher tortoise constituted 46 percent. No fish were identified in the Spanish deposits at the mission.

Thirty-five vertebrate individuals were identified from the Native American village associated with Baptizing Spring (Loucks 1979:226 and this volume). European domestic animals, 2 pigs and 1 cow, contributed 9 percent of the individuals, while indigenous wild fauna comprised the rest of the individuals (table 14.3). The most common of these were deer (34 percent of the MNI) and gopher tortoises (23 percent of the MNI). Other reptiles contributed an additional 20 percent of the individuals. A squir-

TABLE 14.3. Mission Period: Western Timucua Faunal Summaries

| | Baptizing Spring | | | | San Martín | |
| | Spanish | | Indian | | Indian | |
	MNI	%	MNI	%	MNI	%
Domestic mammals	2	15.4	3	8.6	1	2.0
Domestic birds						
Deer	4	30.8	12	34.3	6	12.2
Other wild mammals			2	5.7	3	6.1
Wild birds			1	2.9	1	2.0
Turtles/alligators	6	46.2	15	42.9	10	20.4
Sharks/rays/fishes			1	2.9	26	53.1
Commensal taxa	1	7.7	1	2.9	2	4.1
Total	13		35		49	

Sources: Baptizing Spring data from Loucks (1979); Fig Springs data from Newsom and Quitmyer (1992) and Quitmyer (1991).

rel, a raccoon, alligators, pond turtles, box turtles, and a mullet were identified from the village.

More recently another Western Timucua mission collection has been studied. This faunal collection was recovered from the Fig Springs site (8CO1) under the supervision of Brent Weisman and was studied by Irvy Quitmyer (Deagan 1972; Newsom and Quitmyer 1992; Quitmyer 1991; Weisman 1992). Fig Springs was probably the location of San Martín de Ayaocuto, which was established about 1607 and abandoned around 1656 following a Timucuan uprising (Hann 1990:461, 473). The site is on the Ichetucknee River, about 140 km east of Apalachee Province and 30 km east of Baptizing Spring (fig. 14.1). Faunal samples were taken from a Native American structure near the *convento* and church as well as from aboriginal contexts in the village area. A 1/16-inch mesh screen was used to recover the materials.

An estimated 49 vertebrate individuals were identified from San Martín. A single pig contributed 2 percent of the vertebrate individuals, the remainder were indigenous wild fauna (table 14.3). Deer contributed 12 percent of the individuals in the collection and turtles 20 percent. Gopher tortoises alone contributed 10 percent of the individuals. Freshwater fishes contributed most of the individuals (53 percent of the MNI). However, access to marine resources from the site was demonstrated by an earlier faunal study that included 2 species of whelk and 3 species of marine clams (Deagan 1972). Use of fine-meshed screen to collect artifacts during excavation, as in the case of San Martín, usually enhances the recovery of fish remains. Hence, the San Martín data probably provide the most accurate picture currently available for the life of Native Americans at one of the western missions in Spanish Florida.

Summarizing the Western Timucua materials is complicated by several factors. First, Western Timucua samples are limited: there is only 1 Spanish component (Baptizing Spring) and 2 Native American components. All 3 components are extremely small, so the limited range of species may reflect sample size. More important, perhaps, we do not know whether Baptizing Spring was occupied before, during, or after San Martín. The differences in recovery techniques further complicate a synthesis, especially as it pertains to the role of fishing in the subsistence effort.

If allowance is made for these problems, evaluation of the data may suggest that European animals did not replace wild animals in the subsistence strategy at Western Timucuan missions but were incorporated into a pattern that made extensive use of locally available wild foods. Domestic animals may have been rarely used by either Spaniards or Native Americans at Western Timucua missions, although Spaniards may have had somewhat greater access to pigs and cattle than did Native Americans. Chickens may have been uncommonly consumed or else absent in the diet. On the other hand, locally available wild resources were heavily used. Both Spaniards and Native Americans appear to have made extensive use of 2 wild native species: deer and gopher tortoises. The Spanish samples suggest that Spaniards may have limited their diet to deer, gopher tortoise, cow, and pig, while the Native American samples suggest this group made use of a greater variety of wild animals. The contrasts between San Martín and Baptizing Spring in terms of the role of fishes in the diet may be a reflection of the different recovery techniques used or the earlier date of the San Martín deposit.

ZOOARCHAEOLOGICAL DATA FROM EASTERN TIMUCUA PROVINCE

Excavations at the Fountain of Youth Park site (8SJ31) have provided the only zooarchaeological information from a mission in Eastern Timucua. Faunal remains from the mission occupation at the site were recovered during fieldwork conducted under the direction of Kathleen A. Deagan in 1976, 1985, and 1987 (Deagan 1983:48; Luccketti 1977; Merritt 1977, 1983). The site is located about a kilometer north of St. Augustine (fig. 14.1) and is owned by Fountain of Youth Park, Inc. A 1/16-inch mesh was used to recover artifacts. Initially the site interested archaeologists because Pedro Menéndez de Avilés spent his first few months here as he established the Spanish Florida colony. By 1571 St. Augustine was established at its present location about a kilometer south of the original Spanish settlement (Chaney 1987:17).

The Fountain of Youth site is also of interest because of its association with the Nombre de Dios mission, which was separated from the site by a tidal creek (Chaney 1987:17; Gannon 1967:27; Hann 1990:427). The village associated with the Nombre de Dios mission attracted many Native Americans to the area throughout the First Spanish period. Faunal remains were recovered from both late sixteenth-/early seventeenth-century and late seventeenth-/early eighteenth-century mission components (Reitz 1985, 1991a). Timucuans reoccupied their village after Menéndez moved out and were joined by other groups who wanted to be near the mission and the protection of the Spanish town. The early mission animal remains probably represent Timucuan and Guale (Merritt 1983:143) or Mocama (Hann, personal communication 1991) subsistence primarily. The later mission remains may have been deposited by a variety of Native American groups from throughout Spanish Florida as the outlying missionized Native Americans were withdrawn to St. Augustine during the late seventeenth/early eighteenth centuries and settled in nearby mission villages.

The faunal samples from the Fountain of Youth site are probably the best mission samples available for study at this time. They are both large samples and they were recovered using fine-screen recovery techniques. These data are also the most distinctive. They indicate that in spite of the proximity to St. Augustine, the pre-Hispanic focus on marine resources remained intact throughout the First Spanish period (table 14.4; Reitz 1985, 1991a). Only 4 percent of the vertebrate individuals identified in the mission samples were terrestrial mammals. No domestic animals of any species were identified in the Fountain of Youth collection. Considering the prominence that deer and gopher tortoises hold in the species lists from Apalachee and Western Timucua, it is interesting to note that deer contributed less than 2 percent of the vertebrate individuals and no gopher tortoises were identified in the Fountain of Youth collection. Marine vertebrates, including a dolphin and sea turtles, contributed 90 percent of the individuals, and sharks, rays, and fishes contributed 88 percent.

TABLE 14.4. Mission Period: Eastern Timucua Faunal Summaries

	Fountain of Youth		St. Augustine, 17th century	
	MNI	%	MNI	%
Domestic mammals			15	9.0
Domestic birds			11	6.6
Deer	7	1.6	2	1.2
Other wild mammals	12	2.7	5	3.0
Wild birds	4	0.9	7	4.2
Turtles/alligators	13	2.9	14	8.4
Sharks/rays/fishes	398	88.2	105	63.3
Commensal taxa	17	3.8	7	4.2
Total	451		166	

Sources: Fountain of Youth data from Reitz (1991a); seventeenth-century St. Augustine data from Reitz (1992).

This pattern is consistent in both the late sixteenth-/early seventeenth-century and late seventeenth-/early eighteenth-century components and is similar to that available for the pre-Hispanic components at this site (Reitz 1985, 1991a). The emphasis on marine resources even in the late seventeenth-/early eighteenth-century component is surprising given that by the eighteenth century Native Americans from many non-coastal locations throughout Spanish Florida had moved to the missions around St. Augustine. Animal use at Fountain of Youth appears to contrast dramatically with that suggested for Native Americans at the Western Timucua missions. Nonetheless, the basic pattern is the same: limited use of domestic livestock and primary use of locally available wild resources.

ZOOARCHAEOLOGICAL DATA FROM GUALE PROVINCE

Animal use at missions in Guale Province is currently represented by 2 small faunal samples from Santa Catalina de Guale and Fallen Tree, although more data are forthcoming. This mission and the associated Native American village were on St. Catherines Island (fig. 14.1). The mission was founded in the late sixteenth century and was abandoned in the early 1680s (Hann 1990:440–441; Thomas 1987:56–57). The Spanish materials summarized here are from inside the mission compound and were recovered by Joseph R. Caldwell, University of Georgia, in the late 1960s (Reitz 1989, 1990; Thomas 1987:106). The Fallen Tree materials, from a historic Native American village located immediately adjacent to Santa Catalina de Guale, were also recovered by Caldwell. A 11/32-inch screen was used by Caldwell during excavation. This large screen size undoubtedly has biased the recovered materials in favor of large-boned animals such as deer. Work currently in progress on faunal remains recovered by David Hurst Thomas, American Museum of Natural History, should substantially improve our understanding of animal use at this mission. However, an impressionistic evaluation of the materials recovered by Thomas indicates that the Caldwell data are not inaccurate, in spite of the large-gauge mesh.

The Spanish component from Santa Catalina de Guale sample is small, containing the remains of an estimated 26 individuals, and the large-gauge mesh used by Caldwell hampers the interpretive value of the collection. The Spanish sample included the remains of 2 pigs but no other European domestic animals (table 14.5). The majority of the indi-

TABLE 14.5. Mission Period: Guale Faunal Summaries

	Fallen Tree		Santa Catalina de Guale[a]	
	MNI	%	MNI	%
Domestic mammals	1	2.0	2	7.7
Domestic birds	1	2.0		
Deer	27	54.0	9	34.6
Other wild mammals	10	20.0	4	15.4
Wild birds	2	4.0	3	11.5
Turtles/alligators	2	4.0	1	3.8
Sharks/rays/fishes	6	12.0	6	23.1
Commensal taxa	1	2.0	1	3.8
Total	50		26	

a. Santa Catalina de Guale data from Reitz (1989, 1990).

viduals were deer, an estimated 35 percent of the individuals. The only other wild mammal identified was raccoon. Gar, sea catfishes, and drums contributed 23 percent of the individuals.

The Fallen Tree sample recovered by Caldwell is somewhat larger, with an estimated 50 individuals. The sample contained the remains of few European domestic animals (table 14.5). Domestic animals, including a pig and a chicken, contributed 4 percent of the estimated individuals. The majority of the individuals were deer, which contributed 54 percent of the estimated individuals in the Caldwell sample. Other wild mammals, including rabbit, squirrel, and raccoon, were also common in the collection. Fishes were entirely estuarine fishes and constituted an estimated 12 percent of the individuals. Until further work is done with faunal materials recovered using smaller-gauge mesh, it will not be possible to determine whether the percentage of deer in the Fallen Tree collection reflects actual subsistence efforts or recovery technique.

In spite of the sample size and recovery biases, the Santa Catalina de Guale and Fallen Tree materials raise some interesting issues. As in other mission samples, domestic animals are rare, although Spaniards may have had somewhat greater access to domestic livestock than did Native Americans. The bulk of the subsistence effort appears to have emphasized locally available wild resources. Whether the role of fish was in fact as low as these samples suggest cannot be addressed until data recovered with a smaller-gauge mesh are reported. If deer were more heavily used than marine fishes, as the Caldwell data suggest, the contrast in animal use at the coastal Fountain of Youth (table 14.4) and the Fallen Tree (table 14.5) sites is extremely interesting.

Discussion

The faunal data available from Spanish Florida permit only limited discussion of Spanish and Native American animal use during the First Spanish period. The data currently available indicate that animal use at missions in Apalachee, Western Timucua, Eastern Timucua, and Guale was regionally distinctive.

In a recent survey of data from Spanish missions, it was suggested that zooarchaeological evidence for Spanish diets on the Atlantic coast could be interpreted as evidence that Spaniards practiced a subsistence strategy based on the use of a number of terrestrial, riverine, and estuarine animals, with only limited use of domestic animals (Reitz 1990; Scarry and Reitz 1990). Spaniards in St. Augustine, the administrative capital of Florida for most of the First Spanish period, as well as at the mission of Santa Catalina de Guale on St. Catherines Island, Georgia, substantially altered their diets by adopting many wild, locally available foods (tables 14.4 and 14.5). At both places Spaniards made use of few European domestic animals. In the seventeenth-century samples from St. Augustine, cattle may have contributed only 2 percent of the estimated individuals, pigs 5 percent, and chickens 7 percent (table 14.4; Reitz 1992). Noncommensal wild fauna contributed 80 percent of the individuals. More than 60 percent of the individuals and 35 percent of the biomass came from marine fishes. The diet at Santa Catalina de Guale on St. Catherines Island may have been based on the use of far more deer than at St. Augustine, but even lower use of domestic mammals (table 14.5; Reitz 1989, 1990). At the same time, noncommensal wild fauna contributed 89 percent of the individuals in the Santa Catalina materials studied so far. Wild mammals and birds were important resources at Santa Catalina, although marine fishes may have played a less prominent role in the diet at the mission than in St. Augustine.

When the San Luis de Talimali data (table 14.2) are contrasted with the Spanish component from Baptizing Spring (table 14.3; Loucks 1979 and this volume), seventeenth-century St. Augustine (table 14.4; Reitz

1992), and Santa Catalina de Guale (table 14.5; Reitz 1989, 1990), the diversity of Spanish responses to subsistence-related problems is clear. If the information currently available from these locations accurately reflects animal use in these regions of Spanish Florida, it is evident that Spanish subsistence in each province was substantially different. Although St. Augustine was the administrative center of Spanish Florida, its residents had limited access to meat from mammalian sources, especially to pork and beef. Although Spaniards at Santa Catalina also had limited access to pork and beef, they made extensive use of a local wild mammal, deer. Baptizing Spring Spaniards enjoyed similar access to venison and in addition had more beef and pork available to them. They also made extensive use of the gopher tortoise, a resource apparently not mentioned in Spanish records. At San Luis pork and especially beef were even more extensively available, so much so that they dominated the meat-based portion of the diet. This is the only Spanish locality in which domestic animals, particularly cattle, played such a prominent role.

One of the strongest characteristics of Spanish colonial records from St. Augustine is complaints about food shortages. The faunal evidence from St. Augustine cannot demonstrate that food was available in ample quantities for everyone living in the town at all times. It is reasonable to assume that there were periods associated with natural disasters or hostilities when even locally available resources might have been limited. However, when the faunal lists accumulated from St. Augustine are viewed objectively and dispassionately, they do not suggest that any particularly inedible or nonnutritious resources were consumed often enough to become a part of the archaeological record. Species lists from St. Augustine do clearly show that throughout the First Spanish period Spaniards living there consumed a wide range of foods that were not traditional Spanish ones (Reitz 1992; Reitz and Cumbaa 1983; Reitz and Scarry 1985). In fact, the Spanish diet was similar to the pre-Hispanic Native American one, which was presumably enjoyed for centuries before European contact. Given the depth and passion with which most humans identify themselves with their preferred foods, it is understandable that Spaniards at St. Augustine would feel abused, even starving, if forced to alter their diet this substantially. This feeling of poverty and isolation might be exacerbated if Spaniards living at missions such as San Luis had access to resources not enjoyed by administrators in the capital.

Faunal data from the missions and St. Augustine, although limited in scope, suggest that this was the case. By comparison, Spanish meals at St. Augustine may not have been as European, and hence as satisfying, as meals at San Luis. If the Spanish governor in St. Augustine was forced to eat mullet, while a priest at Santa Catalina enjoyed venison and an administrative underling at San Luis enjoyed beef, one would expect the governor to complain to the Spanish Crown as forcefully and repeatedly as possible. This possibility raises interesting questions about norms associated with display of prestige, trade relationships among missions and other administrative centers, and adaptations to specific environmental conditions throughout Spanish Florida. More data are needed before these questions can be well formulated and studied.

Zooarchaeological data for Native American animal use at missions in Spanish Florida permit us to expand on the information available from documentary sources. From written records we know that horses, cattle, swine, and chickens were raised by Native Americans (Boyd, Smith, and Griffin 1951:28, 31, 41; Hann 1986, 1988:239–240), but the zooarchaeological evidence suggests that these animals may have been extremely rare in the Native American diet. No horses have been identified at the missions summarized here and the other domestic animals are extremely rare or absent in Native American contexts. It appears unlikely that cattle, pigs, or chickens replaced wild animals in the diet of missionized Native Americans to any great extent. In this sense, it may be that the animal-based portion of the Native American diet at missions continued to be similar to that practiced prior to missionization or away from missions. We are told that bearskins, bear grease, buffalo skins, and deerskins were prepared and used and that panthers were also hunted (Boyd, Smith, and Griffin 1951:25–26; Hann 1988:248, 1993:152–153, 251–252). However, with the exception of deer none of these animals is known from the archaeological faunal record reviewed here. Opossums, rabbits, squirrels, raccoons, and deer were found in most Native American contexts, although the extent of their use was highly variable. Alligators, turtles, and fishes, resources rarely mentioned in written sources, occupy a prominent place in all of the Native American species lists reviewed here. The percentages range between 16 percent (Fallen Tree) and 45 percent (Baptizing Spring), 74 percent (San Martín), and 91 percent (Fountain of Youth) of the estimated individuals. The extent to which this variability is a function of recovery technique, sample size, cultural affiliation, and environmental variables cannot be assessed at this time.

Summary

Although data from Spanish Florida outside St. Augustine are biased by small sample size and/or recovery techniques, they may contain sufficient information about Spanish and Native American life at missions to formulate some hypotheses for future testing.

Unless both of the Western Timucua mission deposits are too early for cattle raising to have been an important activity, it appears that cattle may have flourished only at Apalachee missions. Further work with Spanish contexts at Apalachee missions may demonstrate a heavy reliance on beef in this province. It seems reasonable that the volume of beef available in Apalachee would have influenced Indian subsistence at missions in the province, although it is anticipated that heavier use of cattle will be found in Spanish deposits than in Native American ones.

At Western Timucua missions, Spanish subsistence and Native American subsistence were probably similar, with both cultural groups complementing limited access to European animals through heavy use of wild resources, including deer, gopher tortoises, and freshwater fishes. Either both Baptizing Spring and San Martín were too early to be influenced by neighboring cattle ranches or these ranches had little impact on mission subsistence in Western Timucua. It will be interesting to see whether there is an increase in cattle in mission refuse deposited in Western Timucua after 1650, when the cattle ranches of Western Timucua were most active.

The Fountain of Youth sample is so large and well recovered that it leaves little room to doubt that Native American subsistence at missions close to St. Augustine depended heavily on marine resources regardless of the ethnic affiliation of the native groups in residence at each mission or time period. Native Americans and Spaniards at more distant missions east of the St. Johns River might have practiced a subsistence strategy similar to that in Western Timucua. It may be found that people at these interior Eastern Timucua missions also made limited use of cattle and other domestic animals during the early part of the seventeenth century but increased consumption of cattle in the later part of the seventeenth century or in the early eighteenth century.

Santa Catalina de Guale has proven to be a rich archaeological site in terms of nonbiological artifacts recovered. It is to be expected that the faunal remains from this mission would also indicate a distinctive life for Spaniards and Native Americans associated with it. It is anticipated that domestic livestock such as cattle and pigs will not be abundant in deposits from here or other Guale missions due to the coastal setting. Instead, it may well be that the wealth of Santa Catalina de Guale is expressed by access to venison, a luxury not enjoyed elsewhere in Guale or St. Augustine. While use of estuarine resources was therefore low at Santa Catalina de Guale, this may be not be the case at other, less affluent Guale missions.

Whether or not these hypotheses are supported as more data become available, it seems likely that we will continue to find that subsistence efforts in Spanish Florida were quite different depending on the province being considered. Based on this survey of the limited archaeological evidence available, it would seem very risky to consider animal use at missions uniform throughout Spanish Florida, but much remains to be learned.

Acknowledgments

I would like to thank Bonnie G. McEwan and the Florida Bureau of Archaeological Research for the opportunity to examine the faunal remains from San Luis de Talimali; Kathleen A. Deagan for the opportunity to study the Fountain of Youth Park site faunal remains; and David Hurst Thomas for the opportunity to work with the Santa Catalina de Guale materials. I am especially grateful to Irvy Quitmyer for permission to make use of his unpublished data from Fig Springs. I also appreciate the assistance of John Hann in preparing this paper. Jennifer Freer, Kevin Roe, Bobby Southerlin, Dan Weinard, and Tracie Jones assisted with identification and analysis of the San Luis faunal materials. Timothy Young, Marc Frank, Carter Vest, and Jim Greenway assisted with the Fountain of Youth faunal materials. Nanny Carder, Gwyneth Duncan, Jennifer Freer, Marc Frank, Kevin Roe, David Varricchio, Timothy Young, and Karen Wood worked on the St. Catherines materials. Funds for the study of faunal remains from San Luis were provided by the state of Florida Conservation and Recreation Lands (CARL) Trust Fund. Excavations in the San Luis village were partially supported by a grant from the National Endowment for the Humanities (RO-21395-87). Work on the Fountain of Youth materials was supported by grant 85030610 from the Florida Bureau of Historic Preservation to the Florida Museum of Natural History under the Historic Preservation Grant-in-Aid Program and the University of Florida, Division of Sponsored Research. Funding for the Santa Catalina de Guale research was provided by the Edward John Noble Foundation. An earlier version of this paper was presented at the 47th Annual Meeting of the Southeastern Archaeological Conference, Mobile, Alabama.

Bibliography

Arnade, Charles W.
1961   Cattle Raising in Spanish Florida. *Agricultural History* 35(3):3–11.

Bierce-Gedris, Katharine
1981   Apalachee Hill: The Archaeological Investigation of an Indian Site of the Spanish Mission Period in Northwest Florida. Master's thesis, Department of Anthropology, Florida State University, Tallahassee.

Bolton, Herbert E.
1917   The Mission as a Frontier Institution in the Spanish American Colonies. *American Historical Review* 23:42–61.

Bolton, Herbert, and Mary Ross
1968   *The Debatable Land*. New York: Russell and Russell.

Boniface, Brian George
1971   A Historical Geography of Spanish Florida, circa 1700. Master's thesis, Department of Geography, University of Georgia, Athens.

Boyd, Mark F., Hale G. Smith, and John W. Griffin
1951   *Here They Once Stood: The Tragic End of the Apalachee Missions*. Gainesville: University of Florida Press.

Bushnell, Amy T.
1978   The Menéndez Marquéz Cattle Barony at La Chua and the Determinants of Economic Expansion in Seventeenth-Century Florida. *Florida Historical Quarterly* 56(4):407–431.

1981   *The King's Coffer: Proprietors of the Spanish Florida Treasury, 1565– 1702*. Gainesville: University Presses of Florida.

Chaney, Edward E.
1987   Report on the 1985 Excavations at the Fountain of Youth Park Site (8-SJ-31), St. Augustine, Florida. Ms. on file, Department of Anthropology, Florida State Museum, University of Florida, Gainesville.

Deagan, Kathleen A.
1972   Fig Springs: The Mid-Seventeenth Century in North-Central Florida. *Historical Archaeology* 6:23–46.

1983   *Spanish St. Augustine: The Archaeology of a Colonial Creole Community.* New York: Academic Press.

Dunkel, John Robert
1955   St. Augustine, Florida: A Study of Historical Geography. Ph.D. diss., Clark University, Worcester, Massachusetts.

Gannon, Michael V.
1967   *The Cross in the Sand: The Early Catholic Church in Florida, 1513–1870.* Gainesville: University Presses of Florida.

Hann, John H.
1986   Translation of Alonso de Leturiondo's Memorial to the King of Spain. In *Spanish Translations,* 165–225. Florida Archaeology no. 2. Tallahassee: Florida Bureau of Archaeological Research.

1988   *Apalachee: The Land between the Rivers.* Ripley P. Bullen Monographs in Anthropology and History, no. 7. Gainesville: University of Florida Press.

1990   Summary Guide to Spanish Florida Missions and *Visitas* with Churches in the Sixteenth and Seventeenth Centuries. *The Americas* 46(4):417–513.

1993   *Visitations and Revolts in Florida, 1657–1695.* Florida Archaeology no. 7. Tallahassee: Florida Bureau of Archaeological Research. Forthcoming.

Jones, B. Calvin
1973   A Semi-Subterranean Structure at Mission San Joseph de Ocuya, Jefferson County, Florida. *Bureau of Historic Sites and Properties Bulletin* 3:1–50.

Lanning, John Tate
1935   *The Spanish Missions of Georgia.* Chapel Hill: University of North Carolina Press.

Larson, Lewis H., Jr.
1978   Historic Guale Indians of the Georgia Coast and the Impact of the Spanish Mission Effort. In *Tacachale: Essays on the Indians of Florida and Southeastern Georgia during the Historic Period,* edited by Jerald T. Milanich and Samuel Proctor, 120–140. Ripley P. Bullen Monographs in Anthropology and History, no. 1. Gainesville: University Presses of Florida.

Loucks, Lana Jill
1979   Political and Economic Interactions between Spaniards and Indians: Archeological and Ethnohistorical Perspectives of the Mission System in Florida. Ph.D. diss., University of Florida. Ann Arbor: University Microfilms.

Luccketti, Nicholas
1977   Archaeological Survey of the Nombre de Dios Mission and the Fountain of Youth Park, St. Augustine. Ms. on file, Historic St. Augustine Preservation Board, St. Augustine.

Merritt, James D.
1977   Excavations of a Coastal Eastern Timucua Village in Northeast Florida. Master's thesis, Department of Anthropology, Florida State University, Tallahassee.

1983   Beyond the Town Walls: The Indian Element in Colonial St. Augustine. In *Spanish St. Augustine: The Archaeology of a Colonial Creole Community*, by Kathleen A. Deagan, 125–147. New York: Academic Press.

Milanich, Jerald T.
1978   The Western Timucua: Patterns of Acculturation and Change. In *Tacachale: Essays on the Indians of Florida and Southeastern Georgia during the Historic Period*, edited by Jerald T. Milanich and Samuel Proctor, 59–88. Ripley P. Bullen Monographs in Anthropology and History, no. 1. Gainesville: University Presses of Florida.

Newsom, Lee, and Irvy R. Quitmyer
1992   Appendix E: Archaeobotanical and Faunal Remains. In *Excavations on the Franciscan Frontier: Archaeology at the Fig Springs Mission*, by Brent Weisman, 206–233. Gainesville: University Press of Florida.

Quitmyer, Irvy R.
1991   Faunal Remains from Fig Springs Mission (8CO1). Ms. on file, Department of Anthropology, Florida Museum of Natural History, University of Florida, Gainesville.

Reitz, Elizabeth J.
1985   A Comparison of Spanish and Aboriginal Subsistence on the Atlantic Coastal Plain. *Southeastern Archaeology* 4(1):41–50.

1989   Faunal Remains from the St. Catherines Island Transect Survey. Ms. on file, Zooarchaeology Laboratory, Museum of Natural History, University of Georgia, Athens.

1990   Zooarchaeological Evidence for Subsistence at *La Florida* Missions. In *Columbian Consequences*. Vol. 2: *Archaeology and History of the Spanish Borderlands East*, edited by David Hurst Thomas, 507–516. Washington, D.C.: Smithsonian Institution Press.

1991a   Animal Use and Culture Change in Spanish Florida. In *Animal Use and Culture Change*, edited by P. Crabtree and K. Ryan, 62–77. MASCA no. 8. Philadelphia.

1991b   Vertebrate Fauna from the Spanish Village and Ocala Road, San Luis de Talimali, Features 73 and 74. Ms. on file, Zooarchaeology Laboratory, Museum of Natural History, University of Georgia, Athens.

1992   Vertebrate Fauna from Seventeenth-Century St. Augustine. *Southeastern Archaeology* 11(2):79–94.

Reitz, Elizabeth J., and Stephen L. Cumbaa

1983 Diet and Foodways of Eighteenth-Century Spanish St. Augustine. In *Spanish St. Augustine: The Archaeology of a Colonial Creole Community*, by Kathleen A. Deagan, 147–181. New York: Academic Press.

Reitz, Elizabeth J., and Jennifer Freer

1990 Vertebrate Fauna from the Spanish Village at San Luis de Talimali, Feature 6. Ms. on file, Zooarchaeology Laboratory, Museum of Natural History, University of Georgia, Athens.

Reitz, Elizabeth J., and C. Margaret Scarry

1985 *Reconstructing Historic Subsistence with an Example from Sixteenth-Century Spanish Florida.* The Society for Historical Archaeology Special Publication no. 3.

Scarry, C. Margaret, and Elizabeth J. Reitz

1990 Herbs, Fish, Scum, and Vermin: Subsistence Strategies in Sixteenth-Century Spanish Florida. In *Columbian Consequences.* Vol. 2: *Archaeological and Historical Perspectives on the Spanish Borderlands East,* edited by D. Hurst Thomas, 343–354. Washington, D.C.: Smithsonian Institution Press.

Tebeau, Charles

1971 *A History of Florida.* Coral Gables: University of Miami Press.

TePaske, John J.

1964 *The Governorship of Spanish Florida, 1700–1763.* Durham, N.C.: Duke University Press.

Thomas, David Hurst

1987 *The Archaeology of Mission Santa Catalina de Guale: 1. Search and Discovery.* Anthropological Papers of the American Museum of Natural History, vol. 63, pt. 2. New York.

Weinand, Daniel C., and Elizabeth J. Reitz

1992 Vertebrate Fauna from San Luis de Talimali, 1992. Ms. on file, Zooarchaeology Laboratory, Museum of Natural History, University of Georgia, Athens.

Weisman, Brent

1992 *Excavations on the Franciscan Frontier: Archaeology at the Fig Springs Mission.* Gainesville: University Press of Florida.

❂ 15 ❂

Beads and Pendants from
San Luis de Talimali:
Inferences from Varying Contexts

JEFFREY M. MITCHEM

Most archaeological studies of trade beads have concentrated on describing the beads and deriving typologies of types and varieties. Accurate descriptions are a necessary first step in any study of beads or other artifacts. While such information is important for using beads as dating tools and for comparative studies, little attention has been devoted to archaeological evidence for different uses or functions of beads among various groups of people.

Beads and other articles of personal adornment often have symbolic meanings beyond their innate attraction as objects of beauty. For example, rosary beads are arranged in groups on the rosary chain, and Catholics use each bead to say specific prayers (Lord 1943). Consequently, rosary beads have specific meanings and serve particular functions for Catholics.

In other situations, beads might have been used to indicate wealth, social status, or group affiliation. If beads and pendants were employed to denote these symbolic meanings, we would expect differences in assemblages to be evident at archaeological sites occupied by both Europeans and Native Americans. European colonists may have worn varieties of beads and pendants distinct from those given or traded to Native Americans. Archaeologists have avoided attempts to address these issues, partly because recognition of such differences is difficult in most archaeological situations, where deposits are mixed or where the cultural affiliation of particular contexts is unclear. Fortunately, the site of San Luis de Talimali (8LE4) in Florida offers a unique situation for addressing questions concerning uses and functions of beads and pendants by different groups in a multicultural situation.

San Luis de Talimali

The mission and town of San Luis de Talimali was the Franciscan capital of Apalachee Province in Florida during the late seventeenth century (fig. 15.1). Established in 1656, the site consisted of a large Apalachee Indian village, a Spanish fort, a settlement of Spanish colonists, and a mission church complex (Hann 1988:194–226). It was destroyed and abandoned in 1704, following raids by British soldiers and Creek Indians (Boyd, Smith, and Griffin 1951:12–19; Hann 1988:264).

The site was acquired by the state of Florida in 1983, and excavations and historical research have been ongoing since 1984. Excavations have demonstrated that many areas of the site are relatively undisturbed, although historic uses have heavily impacted portions of it. The historical documentation of the site is extensive, and many documents have been located and translated by historian John H. Hann (1988). The combination of undisturbed deposits, a segregated intrasite settlement pattern (the Apalachee village, the Spanish colonists' village, the Apalachee council house, the fort, and the church complex were situated in discrete parts of the site), and thorough documentation presents an excellent opportunity for learning about uses of various artifact classes by the different segments of the San Luis population. Studies of colono-ware from the site have provided interesting insights into the use and distribution of aboriginal pottery ostensibly produced for European use (Vernon 1988; Vernon and Cordell, this volume), and similar studies of beads and pendants should result in interpretations that will be useful in understanding the cultural milieu at San Luis and other seventeenth-century mission sites.

Initial archaeological research at the site in the 1940s and 1950s concentrated on the fort area, but excavations since 1984 have led to the identification of various components of the settlement, including the

Figure 15.1. Speculative view of San Luis de Talimali in 1702. (A) Apalachee council house; (B) Spanish village; (C) Franciscan church complex. Illustration courtesy of the Division of Historical Resources, Florida Department of State.

church structure with burials beneath the floor, the *convento* (friary), a probable aboriginal domestic area, a large council house, and the Spanish colonists' village (McEwan 1991; Shapiro and Vernon 1992). A wide variety of artifacts has been recovered from the site, including thousands of glass and lapidary beads and pendants.

Beads and Pendants from San Luis

During the early work in the fort area, only a few beads were recovered. A portion of a rosary, with copper wire links and 39 glass beads, was found in the moat surrounding the fort. These were briefly described and illustrated in the early reports (Boyd, Smith, and Griffin 1951:147–149, pls. V and IX).

The first systematic analysis of beads from San Luis was carried out by Marvin Smith (1992), who classified and described the beads and pendants from the council house excavations. Two glass pendant fragments, 157 glass beads, and a faceted quartz crystal bead were recovered from the council house. Few of them were diagnostic types, but Smith noted that most of the beads and pendants were varieties known from other sites in the Southeast. Most of these types were described in an unpublished manuscript on Spanish beads and pendants written in the 1940s by John Goggin (n.d.).

Three gilded glass beads were similar to Goggin's type Seven Oaks Gilded Molded, which has been recovered from a number of Florida sites dating from the late sixteenth and early seventeenth centuries (Goggin n.d.). Goggin (n.d.) noted that gilded beads had been recovered from two mission sites: San Juan del Puerto (8DU53) in Florida and the Convento site at Casas Grandes in Chihuahua, Mexico.

Another glass bead from the council house was an example of Goggin's type Ichtucknee Inlaid Black. These beads have been found at the Fig Springs mission site (8CO1) in Florida and the Santa Catalina de Guale mission on St. Catherines Island, Georgia (Smith 1992).

Eleven of the council house beads were drawn, opaque turquoise-blue glass necklace beads (fig. 15.2). Smith (1992) notes that these are commonly called Early Blue in the northeastern United States and Ichtucknee Plain in Florida. Deagan (1987:171) dated these beads from the period 1575–1720 and indicated that they are commonly recovered from seventeenth-century missions in Florida. Research by Smith (1983:150) revealed that subspherical beads of this type were most common prior to the mid-seventeenth century, while barrel-shaped specimens were most common from late seventeenth- and early eighteenth-century contexts. Smith (1992) noted that virtually all of the council house Ichtucknee Plain beads were subspherical. One specimen was a double bead.

The Florida Cut Crystal bead from the council house is another type

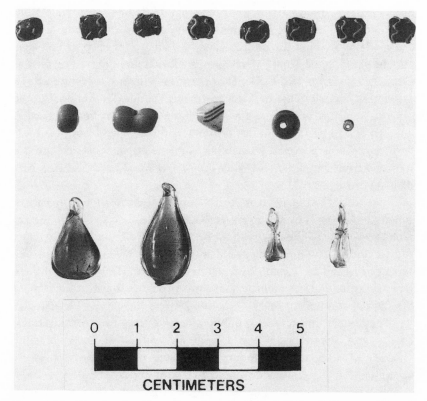

Figure 15.2. Glass beads and pendants from San Luis de Talimali. *Top row:* Wound, burgundy-colored beads with gilding and blue or greenish glass threads applied on the surface (F.S. 3685). *Second row L-R:* Drawn opaque turquoise blue (Ichtucknee Plain; F.S. 1825); double bead, drawn opaque turquoise blue (Ichtucknee Plain; F.S. 3022); olive-shaped, translucent white bead with three sets of triple blue spiral stripes on the exterior (F.S. 3148); Cornaline d'Aleppo necklace bead (F.S. 1820); Cornaline d'Aleppo seed bead (F.S. 3016). *Bottom row L-R:* Two Punta Rassa Teardrop Pendants (F.S. 3685); two San Luis Pendants (F.S. 3600). Photograph courtesy of the Florida Bureau of Archaeological Research.

first described by Goggin. In North America, these have been recovered almost exclusively from sites in Florida dating to the late sixteenth and seventeenth centuries. Outside of Florida, they have been found in Louisiana (Brain 1979:222), Tennessee (Fenstermaker 1978; Polhemus n.d.:48–49), and Virginia (Bushnell 1937).

Smith (1992) classified the two glass pendant fragments from the council house as variants of what Goggin (n.d.) called Punta Rassa Teardrop Pendants. Punta Rassa Pendants (fig. 15.2) are mold-made from ultramarine (blue-green) glass, with an attachment loop at the narrow end made by looping the molten glass into an eye for suspension. They have been recovered from several sites in Florida and the trading post at Ocmulgee, Georgia (Fairbanks 1956:35, 67; Goggin n.d.; Smith 1981). One of the council house pendant fragments fits this description, but the other is smaller, of pale blue glass, and has a triangular cross section. A number of additional examples of these distinctive pendants (fig. 15.2) have since been recovered from other contexts at San Luis and are not recorded from any other site. They are now referred to as San Luis Pendants (Mitchem 1992).

The other glass beads from the council house consisted primarily of simple drawn varieties and many undiagnostic seed beads. Smith (1992) noted that some of these types have been recovered from French contact sites in the Mississippi Valley and in the Great Lakes area from late seventeenth- and early eighteenth-century contexts. The presence of these types suggests that the council house was probably in use at the time of the site's abandonment in 1704 (Smith 1992).

The council house was a public structure used for civic meetings, dances, and ceremonies and as a lodge for visitors. The overwhelming majority of artifacts recovered in the council house excavations were aboriginal (Shapiro and McEwan 1992), so it appears that most of the people who used the building were probably Native Americans. Consequently, the beads and pendants from the council house probably represent an aboriginal sample.

Excavations in 1986, 1987, and 1990 located the church, which had burials beneath the floor, and the *convento* (McEwan 1991; Shapiro and Vernon 1992). The western third of the *convento* had been disturbed prior to excavation. This disturbance, in combination with the fact that the original abandonment and burning of the building by the Spaniards was carried out in a planned fashion, resulted in the recovery of only 35 glass beads there (Shapiro and Vernon 1992; Vernon and McEwan 1990:34). Many of these were partially melted, presumably from the burning of the structure.

A complete description of the assemblage is included in Mitchem (1992). For comparative purposes, only four of the types recovered are discussed here. One bead from the *convento* is an olive-shaped, translucent white bead with three sets of triple blue spiral stripes on the exterior (fig. 15.2). This bead type has been found at many sites in the Mississippi River valley. Smith (1992) noted that four of these were recovered from the council house. Three were also found during initial excavations in the fort area in 1948 (Griffin 1951:149, pl. IX[6]). An identical specimen from the Bayou Goula site in Louisiana (Quimby 1957:87) is on display at the Museum of Geoscience at Louisiana State University. Brain (1979:107) lists seven other sites where this type has been found in and around the Mississippi Valley. His list indicates that the type is commonly recovered from French contact sites.

Two Cornaline d'Aleppo beads were recovered in the *convento*, one a necklace bead and the other a seed (embroidery) bead (fig. 15.2). These beads have an opaque brick-red glass layer over a pale green core. Often these are coated with a thin veneer of colorless glass that gives them a sheen, but the melted condition of the *convento* specimens prevents detection of this layer. Five necklace and one seed Cornaline d'Aleppo beads were found in the council house (Smith 1992). Deagan (1987:168–169) notes that these distinctive beads are most common from sites dating to the late seventeenth and eighteenth centuries, but Smith (1987:fig. 3.3) illustrated specimens from the early seventeenth-century site of Bradford Ferry in Alabama.

Three Ichtucknee Plain beads came from the *convento*. Two of these were barrel-shaped and one was spherical.

Six beads from the *convento* are of special interest. These are barrel-shaped beads of wound construction, made of dark-burgundy-colored glass (fig. 15.2). They have two wavy, medium blue or greenish glass threads applied (overlaid) on the exterior, one at each end. These threads are fragile, and many of them have partially broken off of the beads. On the surface of the beads, most often beneath the area where the threads were located, traces of gilding are present. All of the *convento* specimens showed evidence of melting, as demonstrated by the complete fusion of the applied threads to the bead surfaces. Three of them had an additional inlaid white stripe around the equator.

One specimen of this type was recovered from the council house (Smith 1992). These beads are unknown from other sites, with one exception. In the Pitt-Rivers Museum, Oxford, England, Rochelle Marrinan (personal communication 1989) noted six (one was lacking applied stripes) of these recovered from a burial in an aboriginal mound in Sumter County, Florida. These were excavated in 1864 by H. W. Feilden and were donated to the museum in 1928 by Sir Arthur Evans. Many other glass beads were also in the collection from the mound but are not diagnostic types.

In addition to the *convento* excavations, portions of the church were also excavated. Large wooden posts and chunks of plaster indicated that it was a substantial building, and burials were located beneath the floor. A 4-m-by-4-m unit inside the church revealed about 20 superimposed burial pits (Shapiro and Vernon 1992; Vernon and McEwan 1990:22). Analysis of the poorly preserved skeletal remains indicated that all of the individuals from this portion of the church were children younger than 10 years of age, probably Native Americans (Larsen 1992).

From this 4-m-by-4-m unit, 845 glass beads, fragments of more than 22 glass pendants, an amber bead, and a possible quartzite pendant fragment were recovered. As noted, most of the burial pits were superimposed and disturbed, but one relatively undisturbed burial within the unit was excavated separately. Accompanying this child were 659 drawn and wound glass beads; 23 of the wound, gilded glass beads with applied threads (described above); at least 11 whole or broken glass pendants; the possible quartzite pendant fragment; three *Busycon* shell columella beads; and a fragmentary brass cross.

The beads and pendants from the church excavations are described in detail in Mitchem (1992). The pendants from the burial were both Punta Rassa and San Luis types. It is notable that no Cornaline d'Aleppo or Ichtucknee Plain beads were recovered from the cemetery in these initial test units. A spheroid faceted jet bead, probably a rosary bead, was found in a test unit adjacent to the church structure. According to Deagan (1987:183), round jet beads with facets first came into use on Spanish sites at the beginning of the eighteenth century.

Since 1988, fieldwork has been concentrated in the Spanish village area. Remains uncovered in this part of the site have included various architectural features and associated trash pits. One of these refuse pits (Feature 6) yielded a tremendous number of artifacts, comprising almost one-third of all the artifacts recovered up to that time from the San Luis site (McEwan 1991 and this volume).

Among the more than 25,000 artifacts from this pit were more than 1400 items of personal adornment, primarily beads and pendants. This assemblage is valuable for several reasons. First, diagnostic Spanish ceramics from the feature indicate a secure *terminus post quem* of the late seventeenth century for the trash pit and its contents. Second, the location of the feature in the Spanish village suggests that the refuse includes personal adornment items probably worn by Spaniards. Third, the diversity and nature of artifacts suggest that the feature may have been the trash pit of high-ranking Spaniards. Finally, some of the rings and jewelry indicate that a Spanish woman or *mestiza* may have been one of the nearby residents (McEwan 1991 and this volume).

The majority of the glass beads are seed or embroidery beads, and many of these were probably originally sewn on clothing or other articles. Of these small beads, 163 are Cornaline d'Aleppo types, consisting of a brick-red outer layer over a pale green core.

A wide variety of glass necklace beads was present in the trash pit. A few of these were no doubt rosary beads, but most were probably used on decorative necklaces. Eleven spheroid and seven barrel-shaped Ichtucknee Plain beads were recovered, and one of the wound burgundy-colored beads with applied glass threads was present. Five Cornaline d'Aleppo necklace beads were found in the feature. Most of the bead types have been noted from other parts of the site, but the Spanish village has yielded the greatest variety of beads composed of more than one layer of glass or with striped or faceted surfaces.

Seven thin silver sequins (fig. 15.3), found together in the pit fill, were probably sewn on clothing. These had been carefully hammered from tiny rings of silver wire, as evidenced by the overlapping edges.

In addition to the glass beads, a number of pendants were in the feature. Seven of these were of glass (five were San Luis Pendants and two were Punta Rassa Teardrop Pendants) and probably represent pendants worn as earrings. Earrings of this type were in fashion in Spain during the seventeenth century (P. E. Muller 1972:138). The rest of the pendants were made of lapidary minerals, such as jet and quartz crystal.

The quartz crystal pendants were faceted and teardrop-shaped. The two specimens from Feature 6 are almost identical and may have formed a set of earrings.

At least seven of the jet objects were parts of *higa* (or *figa*) pendants (fig. 15.3). These distinctive clinched fist-shaped amulets were popular among Spaniards during the seventeenth century and are still worn by some Latin peoples today. According to Spanish beliefs, the mineral jet had protective powers against the evil eye, and *higa* amulets were used for this purpose (Hildburgh 1906:460–461; H. Muller 1980:10; P. E. Muller 1972:24).

Two broken jet finger rings were also in the trash pit. All of the jet

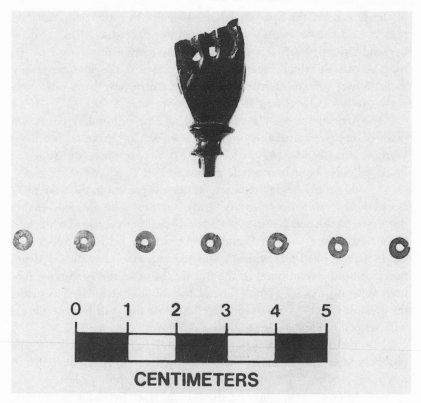

Figure 15.3. Jet pendant and silver sequins from San Luis de Talimali. *Top row:* Carved jet *higa* pendant (F.S. 5043). *Bottom row:* Seven silver sequins (F.S. 4257). Photograph courtesy of the Florida Bureau of Archaeological Research.

and rock crystal items were produced by artisans and were not mass-produced as the glass beads were. These minerals were much sought after in Spain for use in jewelry, both by royalty and by those who wanted to flaunt their wealth or to give the appearance of affluence (P. E. Muller 1972).

Interpretations

When assemblages of beads and pendants from different parts of the San Luis site are compared, some interesting patterns are apparent. From these, we can propose some tentative interpretations that can be tested during future work at San Luis and at other seventeenth-century mission sites in the Southeast.

The wound, dark-burgundy-colored beads with gilded surfaces and applied glass threads were recovered in greatest quantity ($n = 38$) from the church/cemetery. Six were found in the *convento*, one was recovered from the council house, and one from Feature 6 in the Spanish village. It is obvious that these beads were carefully manufactured, and they were probably not mass-produced trade items. Their abundance in the friary and cemetery and their scarcity in both the council house and the Spanish village suggest that they may have had religious significance, possibly functioning as rosary beads. This hypothesis can be tested during future excavations in the cemetery area. If the hypothesis is correct, we would expect to find 53 of the beads in five groups of ten (decades), with a group of three near the crucifix accompanying a burial. In addition, six or seven spacer beads, probably of a different type, should be present. The spacer beads separate the five decades and are also located above and below the single group of three. The rosary would probably either be placed around the neck of the corpse or entwined in the fingers (Lord 1943). The spacers might be jet beads similar to the specimen found near the church. Deagan (1987:170) has suggested that double Ichtucknee Plain beads, such as the specimen recovered from the council house, may have functioned as spacers or joining elements in rosaries.

In contrast, the lack of Ichtucknee Plain beads from the church/ cemetery excavations may be significant. Specimens of this type were recovered from the council house, the *convento*, and the Spanish village. These beads may have been used as everyday decorations, primarily for nonreligious situations. Their apparent absence with the aboriginal burials in the church may be due to the small sample, but it could also mean that this variety either was not given to children or was specifically not buried with the dead. They might also be lacking for temporal reasons (not available or in style at the time of burial) or due to personal preference. Excavations in the church/cemetery and in the aboriginal village should clarify the function and uses of this bead type.

The patterns of distribution of Cornaline d'Aleppo beads from different parts of the site are also of interest. A few of these were recovered from the council house and the *convento*, they were absent in the church/ cemetery, and a great number were present in the Spanish village. This suggests that these distinctive beads were reserved for Spanish use at the site, rather than as trade goods for the native population. Again, excavations in the aboriginal village and additional cemetery excavations should clarify use patterns of this type.

It is not possible to interpret use of the translucent white beads with three sets of spiraling triple blue stripes on the exterior. These have been recovered from the fort, the council house, and the *convento* but not from either the church/cemetery or the Spanish village. Additional excavations and a larger sample size are necessary to develop hypotheses regarding their distribution.

The distribution of glass pendants suggests that they were worn by both Spanish colonists and Apalachee Indians. They were not present in the *convento*, which is not surprising, as we would not expect friars to be wearing earrings.

The Spanish village contains both larger numbers and more varieties of beads of complex construction (multiple glass layers, with stripes or other surface decorations) than do other parts of the site. Items of jet and rock crystal are also more abundant in the Spanish village area. Only one bead of each of these minerals was recovered from areas outside the Spanish village.

The tremendous diversity and sheer number of artifacts from the refuse pit (Feature 6) suggest that the Spanish residents who used the feature had access to a wide variety of imported luxury items. Based on the small size of the finger rings and the fact that the wearing of rings, jewels, and precious stones was generally considered effeminate by Spaniards at this time (P. E. Muller 1972:28), it has been suggested (McEwan, this volume) that these artifacts may have belonged to a Spanish woman or perhaps a *mestiza*.

There is one possible source of bias in the Feature 6 assemblage. There were probably aboriginal servants and workers in the Spanish settlement, and some of the beads and pendants may have been lost or discarded by these individuals.

All of these interpretations must be considered provisional, however, because the differences in assemblages from different parts of San Luis could be due to functional differences, such as assemblages from a domestic area versus a burial area, or a domestic area versus a public building such as the council house. Temporal differences could also be present. However, recent excavation of a second trash pit in the Spanish village area has yielded an even larger assemblage of ornate personal adornment artifacts and does not appear to contradict the interpretations based on the material from Feature 6.

Future Directions

The best opportunity to check our interpretations of ethnicity and gender will come with the results of excavations in the cemetery and in the Apalachee village. The cemetery excavations will provide samples from individuals whose sex and ethnic affiliation can be identified. The Apalachee village research will provide the first domestic aboriginal sample from the site. The results of these analyses can then be compared and combined with data from other southeastern mission sites to develop conclusions about the use and function of items of personal adornment by both Spaniards and American Indians at the missions.

As further excavations are carried out at San Luis and assemblages from varying contexts are analyzed, items of personal adornment should help us understand the complex interactions of Apalachee Indians, friars, soldiers, and Spanish settlers in this seventeenth-century community. The assemblages from the site will also form the basis for developing a comprehensive typology that can be used to classify beads and pendants from other southeastern mission sites, facilitating comparative analyses.

Once these steps are complete, broader anthropological issues can be addressed. Edward Spicer (1961:526) defined a Spanish mission community as "a type involving linkage through ecclesiastical and political interests, intimate face-to-face roles with coercive sanctions, and structural stability." Such situations involved attempts by the Spaniards to reorganize the aboriginal community, not only on the spiritual/belief system level but also on the political level. How did these changes affect the material culture of the Apalachee Indians? For example, did the Apalachees adopt European goods (in this case, beads and pendants) in an attempt to emulate Spanish settlers, or were specific types of personal adornment items assigned symbolic meanings by the Apalachees? Were the European beads and pendants used to replace aboriginal items that had symbolic meaning?

While it will not be easy to answer these questions definitively, the San Luis site provides an opportunity to address them. John White (1975) proposed a model for interpreting the various ways that artifacts are incorporated in such an acculturative situation. The system emphasizes how the specific artifact types were used by the aborigines, including the meanings ascribed to them by the recipients. Ian Brown (1979), in critiquing White's model, noted that it failed to consider values and functions of artifacts changing through time. When Brown's caveats are included, the model provides a useful tool for systematically investigating native acculturation at San Luis.

One aspect of European bead and pendant use by Native Americans that has often been overlooked is the importance of color symbolism. George Hamell has suggested that among northern Iroquoian and central and eastern Algonquian groups, native response to European contact and their acceptance of European goods was affected by their symbolic and mythical beliefs (Hamell 1983, 1987; Miller and Hamell 1986). According to Hamell's model, color symbolism and the ideational and aesthetic values of materials of particular colors may have influenced the desire to obtain specific European beads or other artifact types.

Analysis of beads from the Blackdog Burial site, a nineteenth-century Dakota cemetery in Minnesota, revealed some possible correlations of bead colors with both sex and age (Whelan 1991:26–29). Although the sample size was small, Mary K. Whelan noted that five colors of beads were associated solely with female burials, and two colors were associated exclusively with male burials, suggesting that certain colors were strongly associated with femininity or masculinity (Whelan 1991:27–28, table 4). She noted that color symbolism is especially strong among the Dakota and that study of bead color will be a useful avenue of research in future studies of Dakota gender patterns (Whelan 1991:26–28).

Such factors may also have affected the preferences for certain beads or pendants among the Apalachees. The Apalachees were classified as part of the Muskhogean division of southeastern tribes by Swanton (1979:table 1). It is well documented that color symbolism was significant among Muskhogean groups in the Southeast, and this was intricately tied in with mythology. Blue, white, and red were especially imbued with symbolic significance (Gatschet 1969:38–39; Williams 1927:62–65). Many of the San Luis beads and pendants are composed of one or more of these colors, and assemblages from the Apalachee village and the cemetery should facilitate investigation of color preferences.

Seed beads, presumably often used in embroidery, are abundant at San Luis. While these small beads are often dismissed as useless for interpretive purposes, there may be situations at San Luis where they will provide information about symbolism. At the Quad Block site (8HI998), a Second Seminole War cemetery in Tampa, Florida, seed beads were recovered that had been sewn onto garments (Piper and Piper 1981: fig. 3). These clearly reflected the original decorative patterns. Such remains might also be present in the San Luis cemetery. If so, they may reveal indications of whether traditional designs were employed or whether Christian or other Spanish-introduced designs were used in the embroidery. Mixtures of Christian and aboriginal symbolism were reflected in seed bead embroidery among partially converted Plains Ojibwa groups at the turn of the twentieth century in North Dakota (Phillips 1991:95–96). Similar syncretic changes would be expected among the Apalachees.

The continuing study of beads and pendants from San Luis promises to yield insights into processes of interaction and acculturation at this Franciscan mission community. When combined with other archaeological and historical data, study of personal adornment items may also reveal much about the belief systems operating among the various groups residing in the community.

Acknowledgments

I would like to thank Bonnie G. McEwan and the Florida Bureau of Archaeological Research for the opportunity to study the beads from San Luis. This paper was improved by the comments of three reviewers. Rochelle Marrinan generously shared data on beads from other collections, for which I am grateful. Excavations at San Luis were supported by the state of Florida's Conservation and Recreation Lands (CARL) Trust Fund. Additional funds for research in the church complex and Spanish village were provided by the National Endowment for the Humanities (RO-21395-87). I would like to thank Roy Lett of the Florida Bureau of Archaeological Research for producing the figures accompanying the paper. Equipment and research space was provided by the Department of Geography and Anthropology at Louisiana State University and the Arkansas Archeological Survey. The collections are curated at the San Luis Archaeological and Historic Site, Tallahassee, Florida.

Bibliography

Boyd, Mark F., Hale G. Smith, and John W. Griffin
1951 *Here They Once Stood: The Tragic End of the Apalachee Missions.*
Gainesville: University of Florida Press.

Brain, Jeffrey P.

1979 *Tunica Treasure*. Papers of the Peabody Museum of Archaeology and Ethnology, vol. 71. Cambridge: Harvard University.

Brown, Ian W.

1979 Historic Artifacts and Sociocultural Change: Some Warnings from the Lower Mississippi Valley. *Conference on Historic Site Archaeology Papers* 13:109–121.

Bushnell, David I., Jr.

1937 *Indian Sites below the Falls of the Rappahannock, Virginia*. Smithsonian Miscellaneous Collections, vol. 96, pt. 4. Washington, D.C.

Deagan, Kathleen A.

1987 *Artifacts of the Spanish Colonies of Florida and the Caribbean, 1500–1800. Vol. 1: Ceramics, Glassware, and Beads*. Washington, D.C.: Smithsonian Institution Press.

Fairbanks, Charles H.

1956 *Archeology of the Funeral Mound, Ocmulgee National Monument, Georgia*. Archeological Research Series, no. 3. Washington, D.C.: National Park Service, U.S. Department of the Interior.

Fenstermaker, Gerald B.

1978 *Tennessee Colored Bead Charts*. Archaeological Research Booklets, vol. 13. Lancaster, Pa: G. B. Fenstermaker.

Gatschet, Albert S.

1969 *A Migration Legend of the Creek Indians*. Vol. 2. St. Louis, Missouri: St. Louis Academy of Science, 1888. Reprint. New York: Kraus Reprint.

Goggin, John M.

n.d. An Introduction to Spanish Trade Beads and Pendants, Sixteenth and Seventeenth Centuries. Ms. on file, Bureau of Archaeological Research, Division of Historical Resources, Florida Department of State, Tallahassee.

Griffin, John W.

1951 Excavations at the Site of San Luis. In *Here They Once Stood: The Tragic End of the Apalachee Missions*, by Mark F. Boyd, Hale G. Smith, and John W. Griffin, 137–160. Gainesville: University of Florida Press.

Hamell, George R.

1983 Trading in Metaphors: The Magic of Beads. In *Proceedings of the 1982 Glass Trade Bead Conference*, edited by Charles F. Hayes III, 5–28. Research Records, no. 16. Rochester, N.Y.: Research Division, Rochester Museum and Science Center.

1987 Strawberries, Floating Islands, and Rabbit Captains: Mythical Realities and European Contact in the Northeast during the Sixteenth and Seventeenth Centuries. *Journal of Canadian Studies* 21(4):72–94.

Hann, John H.
1988   *Apalachee: The Land between the Rivers.* Ripley P. Bullen Monographs in Anthropology and History, no. 7. Gainesville: University of Florida Press.

Hildburgh, W. L.
1906   Notes on Spanish Amulets. *Folk-Lore* 17:454–471.

Larsen, Clark Spencer
1992   A Bioarchaeological Investigation of Mission San Luis de Talimali. In *Archaeology at San Luis: The Church Complex*, by Gary Shapiro and Richard Vernon, 233–239. Florida Archaeology no. 6, pt. 2. Tallahassee: Florida Bureau of Archaeological Research.

Lord, Rev. Daniel A., S. J.
1943   *The Rosary: Roses of Prayer for the Queen of Heaven.* New York: William J. Hirten.

McEwan, Bonnie G.
1991   San Luis de Talimali: The Archaeology of Spanish-Indian Relations at a Florida Mission. *Historical Archaeology* 25(3):36–60.

Miller, Christopher L., and George R. Hamell
1986   A New Perspective on Indian-White Contact: Cultural Symbols and Colonial Trade. *Journal of American History* 73:311–328.

Mitchem, Jeffrey M.
1992   Analysis of Beads and Pendants from San Luis de Talimali (8LE4): The *Convento* and Church. In *Archaeology at San Luis: The Church Complex*, by Gary Shapiro and Richard Vernon, 241–259. Florida Archaeology no. 6, pt. 2. Tallahassee: Florida Bureau of Archaeological Research.

Muller, Helen
1980   *Jet Jewellery and Ornaments.* Shire Album no. 52. Buckinghamshire, U.K.: Shire Publications.

Muller, Priscilla E.
1972   *Jewels in Spain, 1500–1800.* New York: Hispanic Society of America.

Phillips, Ruth B.
1991   Comments on Part II "Catching Symbolism": Studying Style and Meaning in Native American Art. *Arctic Anthropology* 28:92–100.

Piper, Harry M., and Jacquelyn G. Piper
1981   Summary Interim Report of Excavations at the Quad Block Site (8HI998), Tampa, Florida. *The Florida Anthropologist* 34:177–179.

Polhemus, Richard R.
n.d.   The Early Historic Period in the East Tennessee Valley. Ms. on file, Frank
        H. McClung Museum, Knoxville, Tennessee.

Quimby, George I.
1957   The Bayou Goula Site, Iberville Parish, Louisiana. Fieldiana: Anthropol-
        ogy, vol. 47, pt. 2. Chicago: Field Museum of Natural History.

Shapiro, Gary, and Bonnie G. McEwan
1992   Archaeology at San Luis: The Apalachee Council House. Florida Archae-
        ology no. 6, pt. 1. Tallahassee: Florida Bureau of Archaeological Re-
        search.

Shapiro, Gary, and Richard Vernon
1992   Archaeology at San Luis: The Church Complex. Florida Archaeology no.
        6, pt. 2. Tallahassee: Florida Bureau of Archaeological Research.

Smith, Marvin T.
1981   European and Aboriginal Glass Pendants in North America. Ornament
        5(2):21–23.

1983   Chronology from Glass Beads: The Spanish Period in the Southeast,
        1513–1670. In Proceedings of the 1982 Glass Trade Bead Conference,
        edited by Charles F. Hayes III, 147–158. Research Records, no. 16.
        Rochester, N.Y.: Research Division, Rochester Museum and Science Cen-
        ter.

1987   Archaeology of Aboriginal Culture Change in the Interior Southeast: De-
        population during the Early Historic Period. Ripley P. Bullen Mono-
        graphs in Anthropology and History, no. 6. Gainesville: University of
        Florida Press.

1992   Glass Beads from the Council House at San Luis. In Archaeology at San
        Luis: The Apalachee Council House, by Gary Shapiro and Bonnie G.
        McEwan, 107–117. Florida Archaeology no. 6, pt. 1. Tallahassee: Florida
        Bureau of Archaeological Research.

Spicer, Edward H.
1961   Types of Contact and Processes of Change. In Perspectives in American
        Indian Culture Change, edited by Edward H. Spicer, 517–544. Chicago:
        University of Chicago Press.

Swanton, John R.
1979   The Indians of the Southeastern United States. Washington, D.C.:
        Smithsonian Institution Press. Reprint. Bureau of American Ethnology
        Bulletin no. 137. Washington, D.C.: Smithsonian Institution, 1946.

Vernon, Richard
1988   Seventeenth-Century Apalachee Colono-ware as a Reflection of Demogra-
        phy, Economics, and Acculturation. Historical Archaeology 22:76–82.

Vernon, Richard, and Bonnie McEwan

1990   *Investigations in the Church Complex and Spanish Village at San Luis.* Florida Archaeological Reports, no. 18. Tallahassee: Florida Bureau of Archaeological Research.

Whelan, Mary K.

1991   Gender and Historical Archaeology: Eastern Dakota Patterns in the Nineteenth Century. *Historical Archaeology* 25(4):17–32.

White, John R.

1975   Historic Contact Sites as Laboratories for the Study of Culture Change. *Conference on Historic Site Archaeology Papers* 9:153–163.

Williams, Samuel Cole, ed.

1927   *Lieutenant Henry Timberlake's Memoirs, 1756–1765.* Johnson City, Tenn.: Watauga Press.

❂ 16 ❂

A Distributional and Technological Study of Apalachee Colono-Ware from San Luis de Talimali

RICHARD VERNON
ANN S. CORDELL

Colono-wares from seventeenth-century mission sites in the Apalachee Province of Spanish Florida have been defined as pottery produced using traditional aboriginal techniques and exhibiting European form characteristics that differ from native vessel forms (Vernon 1988:77). This definition fits into a category of colono-ware ceramics called "mission wares" that are associated with sites throughout the Spanish Borderlands in continental North America (Deagan 1990:239). Deagan (1990:239) characterizes these wares as exhibiting formal European tableware elements and having an association with mission sites as opposed to town sites.

Apalachee colono-wares were originally defined by Hale Smith (1951) as either undecorated or red filmed. The type Mission Red Filmed (Smith 1951:171) was defined on the basis of painted decoration that usually occurs in geometric zones. Mission Red Filmed was also recognized as exhibiting European vessel forms. This type is so rarely encountered in native vessel forms that it can be included in the colono-ware category solely on the basis of painted decoration. Vessel form, however, has been the only reliable criterion for distinguishing between unpainted colono-wares and undecorated traditional Apalachee pottery. This criterion was based on the observation that undecorated colono-wares and at least some traditional Apalachee wares appeared to be similar in terms of paste and manufacturing techniques (Vernon 1988).

This study provides baseline data about the manufacture of Apalachee colono-wares and their distribution across the San Luis site. These data offer insights into how and where these wares were produced and which components of the Indian-Spanish society at the Apalachee missions were making and using them.

Distributional Study

Vernon (1988) presented an initial descriptive study of Apalachee colono-wares and made some inferences about the significance of this pottery in terms of the demography and economics of the missions. A hypothesis was proposed that colono-wares were made by the Apalachee Indians for use by Spaniards in order to supplement imported Hispanic tablewares and serving vessels that were in short supply. An attendant test implication is that colono-wares should be associated almost exclusively with Hispanic contexts on the site, such as the church complex, fort, and Spanish domestic areas. This association would be expressed by relatively high percentages of both imported Hispanic pottery and colono-wares from these contexts. It should be noted that a "Hispanic" context implies that the activities in that portion of the site were controlled or dominated by Spaniards. In a settlement where the vast majority of the population was Apalachee Indian, however, no context is likely to appear as purely Hispanic in terms of material culture.

THE ARCHAEOLOGICAL CONTEXTS

Extensive excavations have been conducted on four culturally distinct areas within the seventeenth-century mission settlement of San Luis: the Apalachee Indian council house, the mission church complex, the Spanish village, and the fort (fig. 16.1). The council house was the center of Apalachee social activities. It served as a lodge for meetings and ceremonies and as a guest house. Analysis of excavated material revealed that the artifacts present were overwhelmingly of aboriginal manufacture (Shapiro and McEwan 1992). Excavations included parts of the outer wall, the

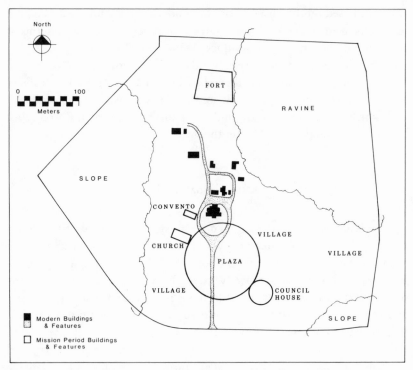

Figure 16.1. San Luis with seventeenth-century features and modern buildings depicted.

central hearth, and a large section of the interior of the building on the northeast side.

The mission church complex was the religious center for Indians and Spaniards alike at San Luis and included a church, *convento* (rectory), and perhaps a separate *cocina* (kitchen). The resident Franciscan friar and perhaps a few Indian assistants lived in the *convento*. Extensive excavations have been conducted on the *convento* and parts of the cemetery and church. Midden areas between and around the buildings have also been tested (Shapiro and Vernon 1992).

Investigations in the Spanish village area northeast of the plaza have included the excavation of three large trash pits. Materials from one of these trash pits, Feature 6, have been completely analyzed. This feature provides an excellent context for what was apparently a high-status Spanish household (McEwan 1991 and this volume; Vernon and McEwan 1990:58).

The fort at San Luis was constructed late in the life of the mission settlement, between 1695 and 1697. It consisted of a blockhouse surrounded by a stockade and moat and housed a minimum garrison of 12 soldiers (Poe 1989). The fort represents a Spanish military context but also served as shelter for the entire population of the village during British-led attacks in 1704. Field investigations have included testing of the moat and central blockhouse by John Griffin in 1948, various portions of the moat and the southeast bastion by Charles Fairbanks in 1956–1957, and the south moat by Charles Poe in 1990 (Griffin 1951; Poe 1989, 1991).

DISCUSSION

Figure 16.2 compares percentages of imported Hispanic ceramics with colono-wares from these four contexts. Traditional aboriginal ceramics, which make up the vast majority of each assemblage, are not

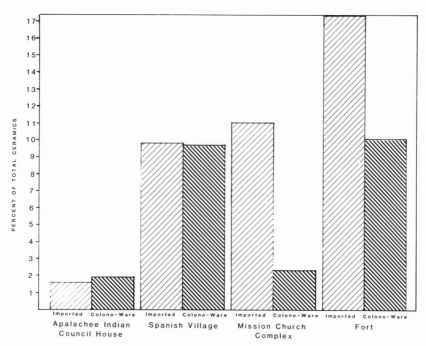

Figure 16.2. Percentages of imported Hispanic ceramics and colono-wares from four different contexts at San Luis.

included in this figure. The hypothesis under consideration suggests that colono-wares were primarily used and discarded in Spanish-dominated areas of the site. Two contexts that support it are the Spanish village trash pit and the fort. Imported Hispanic pottery and colono-wares each make up almost 10 percent of the total ceramics in the Spanish village trash pit. The fort assemblage is the most "Hispanic" of any thus far investigated at San Luis. When all the ceramics are combined from the Griffin, Fairbanks, and Poe excavations, imported Hispanic pottery makes up 17.3 percent of the total, while colono-wares represent another 10.1 percent.[1]

The church complex assemblage represents the one Hispanic context with a relatively high percentage (11 percent) of imported Hispanic pottery and a small proportion of colono-wares (2.3 percent). Clearly, the Franciscan missionaries did not use colono-wares to the same extent as other Spaniards living at San Luis. The paucity of imported ceramics and colono-wares from the Apalachee council house supports both documentary and archaeological evidence that it was a place reserved for mainly traditional Apalachee activities (Shapiro and McEwan 1992).

The church complex is difficult to evaluate in terms of what factors may have caused the low incidence of colono-wares found there (fig. 16.2). Although dominated by a Spanish Franciscan friar, many of his attendants were probably male Apalachees, including a porter, a sacristan, a *fiscal* (steward), and an interpreter (John Hann, personal communication September 1990; Kubler 1940:73). Other servants would likely have been native women who served as food preparers and cooks. Many explanations for the observed ceramic assemblage are possible. For example, a single friar's tableware needs could more easily be supplied with imported ceramics than could the needs of the Hispanic households at the site. If Apalachee women served as cooks, they would likely have used traditional Apalachee cooking vessels (not colono-ware serving vessels) for this task. Whether by choice or for some other reason, it is clear that the Franciscan priests and their Apalachee attendants did not make use of colono-wares to the extent that residents of the Spanish village did.

The results of this preliminary study of the distribution of colono-wares at San Luis are subject to various biases. This is exemplified by spatial data from the fort. Griffin noted that the percentages of Hispanic and aboriginal pottery vary widely from one part of the fort to another (Griffin 1951:153). This is further emphasized by the fact that Griffin's excavations produced much higher percentages of Hispanic ceramics and colono-wares than did the Fairbanks and Poe excavations, which were not located in the blockhouse area. In fact, Griffin's excavations in the vicinity of the blockhouse produced the highest percentage of Hispanic pottery of any San Luis excavation (73 percent; Griffin 1951:153, table 3).

Although the broad context of a given area of the site may be known, such as the church complex or fort, the actual areas excavated do not reflect all the activities that occurred there. In another example, the portion of the Spanish village area included in this study was a domestic trash deposit, while excavations in the church complex concentrated on a structure (the *convento*). Although the *convento* was mainly a domestic structure, only a small sample of the adjacent trash deposits was excavated. This makes the two samples comparable only on a general level. Therefore, the results illustrated in figure 16.2, although broadly reflective of the distribution of imported Hispanic pottery and colono-wares at San Luis, can be refined as data from more comparable contexts in each area of the site become available.

The pattern revealed in the distributional study of colono-ware at San Luis raises as many questions as it answers. While it supports Vernon's original hypothesis that these ceramics were made primarily for use by Spaniards, it is unclear why colono-wares were disproportionately fewer in the church complex than in other Spanish areas of the site.

It is also unclear why colono-wares occur in such abundance in Spanish contexts at San Luis and yet are rarely found in Spanish communities such as St. Augustine. During the seventeenth century, aboriginal pottery was the largest ceramic group from all but one Spanish site tested in the town (King 1981:68). However, despite apparent shortages of Hispanic ceramics and the availability of native potters, colono-wares are rarely recovered in St. Augustine.

As additional data from San Luis and other Spanish colonial settlements become available, it may be possible to develop broader distributional patterns and refine our understanding of the colono-ware phenomenon.

Technological Study

The technological study was undertaken to investigate the presumed continuity in pottery manufacture at San Luis by means of closer scrutiny of

TABLE 16.1. Typological Listing of Pottery Samples

Plain Apalachee	$n = 10$	
Complicated stamped	$n = 9$ Lamar Complicated Stamped:	3 var. curvilinear
		3 var. rectilinear
		2 var. Curlee
		1 var. Jefferson
	$n = 1$ Leon Check Stamped	
Mission period incised	$n = 2$ Marsh Island Incised:	2 var. Marsh Island
	$n = 4$ Point Washington Incised:	2 var. Point Washington
		2 var. unnamed
	$n = 3$ Ocmulgee Fields Incised:	2 var. Ocmulgee
		1 var. Aucilla
Plain colono-ware	$n = 31$	
Mission Red Filmed	$n = 15$ Zoned red painted and incised (interior)	
	$n = 6$ Red painted (both surfaces)	
	$n = 3$ Zoned red painted (interior; no apparent incising)	

physical and mineralogical characteristics and technological aspects of both the traditional Apalachee and colono-ware pottery categories.

DESCRIPTION OF SAMPLES

The sherd samples were selected from trash pit features associated with the Spanish village context at San Luis (fig. 16.1). A control sample of traditional Apalachee pottery included 10 undecorated sherds, 10 complicated stamped sherds, and 9 mission period incised sherds (table 16.1). Most of the plain and complicated stamped sherds consisted of undiagnostic body sherds except for a few collared jar or collared bowl fragments. The mission period incised sherds represent incurving bowl forms. The sample of colono-wares included 31 undecorated sherds and 24 Mission Red Filmed sherds (table 16.1, fig. 16.3–16.5). Footring base fragments representing plate and bowl or cup forms, brimmed plate or dish fragments, and handle fragments were included in this sample. The undecorated colono-ware sherds were so designated solely on the basis of vessel form criteria.

METHODS OF ANALYSIS

Paste was characterized by kind, size, and relative abundance of aplastic and/or temper constituents. A binocular microscope equipped

Figure 16.3. Plain colono-ware rim sherds.

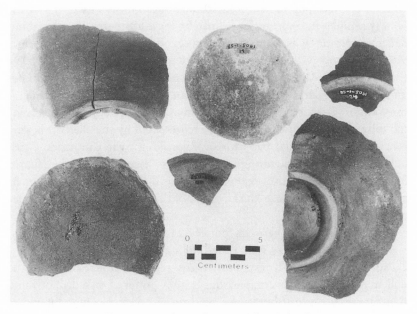

Figure 16.4. Plain colono-ware basal sherds.

Figure 16.5. Mission Red Filmed sherds.

with an eyepiece micrometer and 70 magnification was used to sort the pottery samples into categories defined by these attributes. Relative abundance of aplastics was rated as abundant, common, occasional, and rare. Size of aplastics was estimated with reference to the Wentworth Scale (Rice 1987:38). All observations were made on fresh breaks. In addition, a fragment of each sherd was refired in an electric furnace at a temperature of 800° Celsius for 30 minutes. This was done in order to examine the fully oxidized colors of the clays represented by the sherds, thereby providing an additional basis for distinguishing paste categories. Attributes related to manufacturing technology or processes of forming, finishing, and firing were also examined. These include fracture pattern or shape, methods of surface finishing, vessel thickness, and pottery surface and core color.

Differences noted between pottery samples in terms of paste and manufacturing attributes were tested for statistical significance using the chi-square statistic.[2] All test statistics are recorded in appendix A. The null hypothesis for the comparisons is that pottery types do not differ significantly in the attributes measured or observed; i.e., any differences noted can be attributed to chance or small sample size. The alternative hypothesis is that differences between samples are statistically significant and that chance and/or small sample size can be eliminated as the source of the differences.

RESULTS: PASTE VARIABILITY

Nonmicaceous grog-tempered and micaceous grog-tempered paste groupings were defined from the microscopic examination. Each grouping was further subdivided into "fine" and "coarse" categories on the basis of size variation in quartz constituents. These paste categories are described in table 16.2. The nonmicaceous pottery is assumed to have been locally made. Nonlocal Apalachicola River valley origins have been proposed for micaceous paste pottery found in this area (Bullen 1971). Geologists have suggested, however, that a thorough study of local clays might result in documentation of the local occurrence of micaceous clays and hence the possibility of local manufacture of micaceous paste pottery

TABLE 16.2. Description of Paste Categories

Variability in aplastic and/or temper constituents

Nonmicaceous/fine	Occasional to common medium to very coarse grog
$n = 43$ (51%)	Abundant very fine to fine quartz sand
Nonmicaceous/coarse	Occasional medium to very coarse grog
$n = 31$ (37%)	Common fine to medium quartz sand
Micaceous/fine	Occasional medium to very coarse grog
$n = 5$ (6%)	Common mica
	Abundant very fine to fine quartz sand
Micaceous/coarse	Occasional medium to very coarse grog
$n = 5$ (6%)	Common mica
	Common fine to medium quartz sand

Refired color variability

Paste	Reddish yellow 5YR and 7.5YR hues	Light yellowish brown 10YR hues	White to very pale brown 10YR hues	Total
Nonmica/fine	21 (50%)	17 (40%)	4 (10%)	42
Nonmica/coarse	13 (42%)	7 (23%)	11 (35%)	31
Micaceous/fine	3 (60%)	0	2 (40%)	5
Micaceous/coarse	1 (20%)	0	4 (80%)	5

(John Scarry personal communication May 1991). A study of local clay resources could also provide data for investigating whether the quartz constituents in the pottery can be attributed to naturally occurring aplastics or to tempering practices.

The nonmicaceous categories exhibit a continuum of refired colors in terms of relative iron content of the clays. The refired colors range from white to pale brown (low iron content) to light yellowish brown to reddish yellow (highest iron content). The micaceous categories exhibit only the extremes of this continuum (table 16.2). The relationship between paste (micaceous versus nonmicaceous categories) and refired color was found to be statistically significant (see appendix A).

Comparison of paste variability between the pottery subsamples shows that nonmicaceous grog-tempered pastes are predominant in all subsamples (table 16.3). Plain Apalachee and complicated stamped sherds in the sample are made exclusively of nonmicaceous clays. Micaceous paste categories are restricted primarily to the Mission Red Filmed subsample, but they also occur occasionally in plain colono-ware and mission period incised subsamples. The observed difference between Mis-

TABLE 16.3. Paste and Refired Color Variability by Pottery Type

Paste variability

Pottery type	Nonmicaceous fine	Nonmicaceous coarse	Micaceous fine	Micaceous coarse	Total
Plain Apalachee	7 (70%)	3 (30%)	0	0	10
Complicated stamped	6 (60%)	4 (40%)	0	0	10
Mission period incised	6 (67%)	2 (22%)	0	1 (11%)	9
Plain colono-ware	17 (55%)	12 (39%)	2 (6%)	0	31
Mission Red Filmed	7 (29%)	10 (42%)	3 (12%)	4 (17%)	24

Refired color variability

Paste	Reddish yellow 5YR and 7.5YR hues	Light yellowish brown 10YR hues	White to very pale brown 10YR hues	Total
Plain Apalachee	7 (70%)	3 (30%)	0	10
Complicated stamped	7 (70%)	2 (20%)	1 (10%)	10
Mission period incised	3 (33%)	4 (44%)	2 (22%)	9
Plain colono-ware	16 (51%)	10 (32%)	5 (16%)	31
Mission Red Filmed	6 (26%)	5 (22%)	12 (52%)	23[a]

a. One Mission Red Filmed sherd was not refired.

sion Red Filmed pottery and the other subsamples is statistically significant (see appendix A).

The Mission Red Filmed subsample exhibits primarily white to pale brown refired colors (clays with low iron content), while the traditional undecorated and complicated stamped sherds show reddish-yellow firing colors (clays with higher iron content; see table 16.3). The plain colono-ware and mission period incised samples are intermediate between these categories in terms of range of refired paste colors (clays varying in iron content). The only statistically significant differences observed were for the comparisons between Mission Red Filmed and the other types (except mission period incised; see appendix A).

These observations support the hypothesis of continuity between the traditional Apalachee pottery and much of the colono-ware pottery in terms of the use of clay resources and tempering practices. The micaceous paste pottery, represented primarily by the Mission Red Filmed sample, is the exception to this interpretation.

RESULTS: MANUFACTURING TECHNOLOGY

Construction Method. Coiled construction was evident in virtually all body sherds in the sample. This evidence consisted of obvious coil fractures, parallel fracture pattern, and textural changes in sherd cross section indicative of coil joins. Sometimes coiled construction was revealed when fresh breaks were made for the microscopic examination. Thus the pottery examined, regardless of type, was made by coiling.

Surface Finishing. Comparisons of surface finishing techniques show that plain Apalachee and complicated stamped categories are more variable than the other categories. Mission Red Filmed, plain colono-wares, and mission period incised categories exhibit mostly uniformly burnished, lustrous surfaces (table 16.4). These observations indicate no difference in manufacture between mission period incised and both categories of colono-ware pottery, and this is generally supported by the statistical tests (see appendix A). The differences between plain and stamped Apalachee pottery and the other subsamples are statistically significant.

Vessel Thickness. The comparison of mean body or wall thickness is presented in table 16.5. Plain Apalachee and complicated stamped categories are generally thicker than the other categories, with means of 6.6 mm and 6.4 mm, respectively. Mission Red Filmed sherds are thinnest,

TABLE 16.4. Variability in Surface Finishing Techniques

Surface finishing categories

Burnished = Finished with a nonyielding tool in leather-hard to dry state; luster present; even surfaces were probably scraped to even, uniform level prior to finishing; lumpy surfaces were probably not scraped to uniform level prior to finishing.

Well-finished = Finished with a nonyielding tool in leather-hard to plastic state; no luster; even surfaces were probably scraped to even, uniform level prior to finishing; lumpy surfaces were probably not scraped to uniform level prior to finishing.

Smoothed = Uniformly finished with a yielding tool in plastic to leather-hard state; no luster; even surfaces were probably scraped to even, uniform level prior to finishing; lumpy surfaces were probably not scraped to uniform level prior to finishing.

Partially smoothed = Partially finished with a yielding tool in plastic to leather-hard state; no luster; lumpy surfaces were not scraped prior to finishing.

Exterior surface finish

Pottery type	Burnished even	Burnished lumpy	Well-finished even	Well-finished lumpy	Smoothed even and lumpy	Partially smoothed lumpy	Total
Plain Apalachee	0	3 (30%)	1 (10%)	2 (20%)	3 (30%)	1 (10%)	10
Complicated stamped	N/A	N/A	N/A	N/A	N/A	N/A	10
Mission period incised	6 (67%)	0	3 (33%)	0	0	0	9
Plain colono-ware	23 (74%)	3 (10%)	4 (13%)	0	0	1 (3%)	31
Mission Red Filmed	22 (92%)	1 (4%)	0	0	0	1 (4%)	24

Interior surface finish

Pottery type	Burnished even	Burnished lumpy	Well-finished even	Well-finished lumpy	Smoothed even	Partially smoothed lumpy	Total
Plain Apalachee	0	0	2 (20%)	2 (20%)	2 (20%)	4 (40%)	10
Complicated stamped	3 (30%)	1 (10%)	5 (50%)	0	0	1 (10%)	10
Mission period incised	6 (67%)	0	1 (11%)	0	2 (22%)	0	9
Plain colono-ware	16 (67%)	2 (8%)	1 (4%)	1 (4%)	1 (4%)	3 (12%)	24[a]
Mission Red Filmed	20 (87%)	0	0	1 (4%)	2 (9%)	0	23[a]

a. Most handle fragments are excluded from consideration of interior surface finishing.

TABLE 16.5. Variability in Vessel Wall Thickness

	Mean body/wall thickness	Range	Sample size
Plain Apalachee	6.6 mm	5.5–8.0 mm	$n = 10$
Complicated stamped	6.4 mm	4.8–7.7 mm	$n = 10$
Mission period incised	5.8 mm	4.8–7.5 mm	$n = 9$
Plain colono-ware	5.7 mm	3.8–8.8 mm	$n = 22$[a]
Mission Red Filmed	5.2 mm	3.6–7.4 mm	$n = 23$[a]

a. Handle fragments and unusual forms are excluded.

with a mean of 5.2 mm, and mission period incised and plain colono-wares are intermediate in thickness with means of 5.8 mm and 5.7 mm, respectively. Computed t-test statistics[3] (see appendix A) indicate that the plain Apalachee mean differs significantly from both colono-ware types, and that the stamped Apalachee mean differs significantly from Mission Red Filmed, but that the colono-ware types and mission period incised do not differ significantly from one another. The ranges for these categories show considerable overlap such that thickness by itself may not be a reliable criterion for distinguishing between categories.

Surface and Core Color/Degree of Coring. The presence of fire clouding on most sherds indicates that it is likely that all of the pottery was fired by means of traditional open firing, but considerable variation in pottery colors shows that distinctions in conditions of firing can be made between some of the categories (table 16.6). Plain Apalachee and complicated stamped pottery samples are generally characterized by poorly oxidized exterior surfaces, variable interior surfaces, and heavy dark to medium coring (poorly oxidized core colors). Mission period incised and plain colono-wares are characterized by very poorly and poorly oxidized exterior and interior surface colors and heavy dark coring, while the Mission Red Filmed sherds are characterized by well-oxidized surface colors and variable core colors.

Statistically significant chi-square values were generated for most of the comparisons of surface color between Mission Red Filmed and the other types (see appendix A). These observations do not necessarily mean that red filmed pottery was higher or better fired than the other pottery. Rather, this pattern may indicate that conditions of firing may have been more consistently oxidizing for the red filmed vessels. This may further indicate intentional efforts to control conditions of firing of the Mission Red Filmed pottery.

TABLE 16.6. Variability in Core Color/Coring and Surface Color

Core color/degree of coring

Pottery type	No coring	Light coring	Moderate coring	Heavy medium coring	Heavy dark coring	Total
Plain Apalachee	1 (10.0%)	0	2 (20.0%)	5 (50.0%)	2 (20.0%)	10
Complicated stamped	0	1 (10.0%)	2 (20.0%)	1 (10.0%)	6 (60.0%)	10
Mission period incised	1 (11.0%)	0	0	1 (11.0%)	7 (78.0%)	9
Plain colono-ware	4 (13.0%)	0	1 (3.0%)	7 (23.0%)	19 (61.0%)	31
Mission Red Filmed	3 (12.5%)	2 (8.0%)	3 (12.5%)	7 (29.0%)	9 (38.0%)	24

Exterior surface color

Pottery type	Well-oxidized buff, reddish colors	Moderately oxidized gray to brown colors	Poorly oxidized dark gray to dark brown colors	Very poorly oxidized very dark gray to black colors	Total
Plain Apalachee	2 (20.0%)	2 (20.0%)	5 (50.0%)	1 (10.0%)	10
Complicated stamped	2 (20.0%)	0	5 (50.0%)	3 (30.0%)	10
Mission period incised	3 (33.0%)	0	2 (22.0%)	4 (44.0%)	9
Plain colono-ware	5 (16.0%)	3 (10.0%)	12 (39.0%)	11 (35.0%)	31
Mission Red Filmed	18 (75.0%)	1 (4.0%)	3 (12.5%)	2 (8.0%)	24

Interior surface color

Pottery type	Well-oxidized buff, reddish colors	Moderately oxidized gray to brown colors	Poorly oxidized dark gray to dark brown colors	Very poorly oxidized very dark gray to black colors	Total
Plain Apalachee	6 (60.0%)	1 (10.0%)	3 (30.0%)	0	10
Complicated stamped	3 (30.0%)	1 (10.0%)	1 (10.0%)	5 (50.0%)	10
Mission period incised	2 (22.0%)	0	3 (33.0%)	4 (44.0%)	9
Plain colono-ware	4 (17.0%)	0	7 (29.0%)	13 (54.0%)	24
Mission Red Filmed	16 (70.0%)	1 (4.0%)	5 (22.0%)	1 (4.0%)	24

TABLE 16.7. Summary Description of Grouped Pottery Categories

---

Plain Apalachee and complicated stamped
    Nonmicaceous, reddish yellow firing paste predominant
    Variable surface finishing
    Mean thickness 6.5 mm (range 4.8–8.0 mm)
    Poorly oxidized to variable surface colors
    Poorly oxidized core colors
Plain colono-ware and mission period incised
    Nonmicaceous paste predominant; reddish yellow, light yellowish brown, and
        white to very pale brown firing colors all common
    Burnished, lustrous surface finishing
    Mean thickness 6 mm (range 3.8–8.8 mm)
    Poorly to very poorly oxidized surface colors
    Poorly oxidized core colors
Mission Red Filmed
    Nonmicaceous and micaceous paste; white to very pale brown firing colors pre-
        dominant
    Burnished, lustrous surface finishing
    Mean thickness 5 mm (range 3.6–7.4 mm)
    Well-oxidized surface colors
    Variable core colors

When all of the technological attributes are considered, three groups of pottery are consistently distinguished (table 16.7). The first group includes plain Apalachee and complicated stamped; the second includes mission period incised and plain colono-wares; and the third group consists of only Mission Red Filmed. Plain Apalachee and complicated stamped sherds are generally characterized by variable surface finish, vessel wall thickness of about 6.5 mm, poorly oxidized to variable surface colors, and poorly oxidized core colors. Mission period incised and plain colono-ware samples are characterized by burnished, lustrous surface finish, mean vessel thickness of about 6 mm, and poorly oxidized surface and core colors. Mission Red Filmed pottery is characterized by burnished, lustrous surface finish, mean vessel wall thickness of about 5 mm, well-oxidized surface colors, and variable core colors.

Summary

Studies of the distribution and the technological aspects of Apalachee colono-wares are still in their infancy but important progress has been made. The study of the distribution of colono-wares from different contexts across the San Luis site has progressed as excavations have continued. Ideas about how these ceramics were used and what they can tell us about Spanish-Apalachee relationships continue to be refined as research proceeds. The fact that large quantities of colono-wares were found in contexts associated with the Spanish village at San Luis suggests that these wares were being used either by Spaniards or their Apalachee wives and servants or both. By contrast, the relative scarcity of colono-wares in the *convento*, where only a single Spaniard resided, and in the Apalachee council house suggests that their distribution depends primarily on the presence of Spanish soldiers and settlers. Samples from important contexts such as the Apalachee village have yet to be excavated, and a more complete picture of the function of colono-wares in the Apalachee missions will be revealed as research continues.

The pilot technological study has corroborated that there is indeed considerable technical similarity between traditional Apalachee pottery and colono-wares at San Luis. This supports the interpretation of continuity in resource use and in certain fundamental aspects of vessel manufacture. All of the pottery included in this study was made by coiling and fired in the open, and similar resources (and tempering practices) were used in manufacture. Thus it can also be concluded tentatively that most of the colono-ware pottery at San Luis was locally made, that is, if the assumption of local manufacture of traditional Apalachee pottery is a valid one. This continuity in resource use and methods may also suggest that the makers of most of the colono-wares and traditional Apalachee pottery were one and the same, presumably Apalachee women. The colono-ware types and mission period incised pottery are particularly similar in the additional attributes of thickness and surface finishing. This may have implications for functional differences between mission period incised pottery and other traditional Apalachee pottery.

Despite the fundamental similarities in resources and vessel manufacture, it is clear that closer scrutiny of colono-wares and traditional Apalachee pottery can differentiate the pottery categories in the absence of sherds that exhibit diagnostic vessel forms. Differences in surface color, thickness, and surface finishing can be easily detected and together are useful for distinguishing colono-wares from most traditional Apalachee pottery. More specifically, it should be possible to distinguish undiagnostic body sherds of plain colono-ware from plain Apalachee pottery, but it will be difficult to distinguish undiagnostic body sherds of plain colono-ware sherds from undecorated sherds from mission period incised pots. Although sample sizes were extremely small, the fact that many of the observed differences between categories are found to be statistically significant indicates that chance and small sample size can be virtually eliminated as the source of the observed differences.

The findings of the technological study are fundamental to the formulation of hypotheses concerning the distribution of colono-wares at San Luis as well as other Florida mission sites. Plans are being made to expand the scale and scope of this study by including a larger sample of San Luis materials as well as samples of colono-wares from comparable mission sites. In addition, an investigation of locally and regionally available resources is being considered in order to substantiate the traditional assumptions regarding manufacturing origins of the micaceous and non-micaceous pastes present at San Luis.

Acknowledgments

This paper is a revised version of papers presented at the 47th Annual Meeting of the Southeastern Archaeological Conference, Mobile, Alabama, and the 1991 Society for Historical Archaeology Conference on Historical and Underwater Archaeology, Richmond, Virginia. The present version benefited greatly from the constructive criticisms of William Marquardt, Claudine Payne, Bonnie McEwan, and three anonymous reviewers.

Notes

1. Colono-wares from the Griffin excavation (Griffin 1951:151) were sorted using somewhat different and more liberal criteria than those used on the more recent collections. All sherds classified as Miller Plain (Smith 1951:165–166) were included in the totals derived here from Griffin's report. This included plain sherds not displaying diagnostic European vessel form characteristics.

2. Yate's correction for continuity was incorporated into the calculation of all chi-square statistics to meet the expected cell frequency requirements (Thomas 1976:279–282). All corrected chi-squares were computed using STATISTICS WITH DAISY.

3. All t-test statistics were computed using Statistical Analysis System PROC TTEST procedure (using pooled variance and 1-tailed tests; Ray 1982:217–219).

In Reference to Table 16.2: Refired Color Variability

Evaluation of statistical significance between paste and refired color (micaceous [fine and coarse combined] versus nonmicaceous [fine and coarse combined] paste categories).

Ho = paste categories do not differ significantly in refired color
Ha = paste categories do differ significantly in refired color

Micaceous versus non-micaceous categories:	$X^2 = 6.21$ $df = 2$ $p < .05$ *Ha* supported

In Reference to Table 16.3: Paste and Refired Color Variability by Pottery Type

Evaluation of statistical significance between pottery type and paste (micaceous versus nonmicaceous paste categories) and refired color.

Ho = types do not differ significantly in paste/resources
Ha = types do differ significantly in paste/resources

Paste Variability

Mission Red Filmed versus other types combined	$X^2 = 7.38$ $df = 1$ $p < .01$ *Ha* supported

Refired Color Variability

Plain Apalachee versus complicated stamped:	$X^2 = 0.07$ $df = 2$ $p < .98$ *Ho* cannot be rejected
Plain Apalachee versus mission period incised:	$X^2 = 1.24$ $df = 2$ $p < .70$ *Ho* cannot be rejected
Plain Apalachee versus plain colono-ware:	$X^2 = 0.79$ $df = 2$ $p < .70$ *Ho* cannot be rejected
Plain Apalachee versus Mission Red Filmed:	$X^2 = 6.27$ $df = 2$ $p < .05$ *Ha* supported
Complicated stamped versus mission period incised:	$X^2 = 0.91$ $df = 2$ $p < .70$ *Ho* cannot be rejected
Complicated stamped versus plain colono-ware:	$X^2 = 0.27$ $df = 2$ $p < .90$ *Ho* cannot be rejected
Complicated stamped versus Mission Red Filmed:	$X^2 = 4.65$ $df = 2$ $p < .10$ *Ha* supported
Mission period incised versus plain colono-ware:	$X^2 = 0.24$ $df = 2$ $p < .90$ *Ho* cannot be rejected
Mission period incised versus Mission Red Filmed:	$X^2 = 1.25$ $df = 2$ $p < .70$ *Ho* cannot be rejected
Plain colono-ware versus Mission Red Filmed:	$X^2 = 6.11$ $df = 2$ $p < .05$ *Ha* supported

In Reference to Table 16.4: Variability in Surface Finishing Techniques

Evaluation of statistical significance between pottery type and surface finishing technique (the categories were collapsed into four categories for purposes of computing the X^2 statistics: burnished [even and lumpy combined], well-finished [even and lumpy combined], smoothed [even and lumpy combined], and partially smoothed).

Appendix A. (*Continued*)

Ho = types do not differ significantly in surface finishing technique
Ha = types do differ significantly in surface finishing technique

Exterior Surface Finish

Plain Apalachee versus mission period incised:	$X^2 = 1.90$ $df = 3$ $p < .70$ Ho cannot be rejected
Plain Apalachee versus plain colono-ware:	$X^2 = 8.53$ $df = 3$ $p < .05$ Ha supported
Plain Apalachee versus Mission Red Filmed:	$X^2 = 11.61$ $df = 3$ $p < .01$ Ha supported
Mission period incised versus plain colono-ware:	$X^2 = 1.22$ $df = 2$ $p < .70$ Ho cannot be rejected
Mission period incised versus Mission Red Filmed:	$X^2 = 5.36$ $df = 2$ $p < .10$ Ha supported
Plain colono-ware versus Mission Red Filmed:	$X^2 = 1.96$ $df = 2$ $p < .50$ Ho cannot be rejected

Interior Surface Finish

Plain Apalachee versus complicated stamped:	$X^2 = 3.55$ $df = 3$ $p < .50$ Ho cannot be rejected
Plain Apalachee versus mission period incised:	$X^2 = 7.43$ $df = 3$ $p < .10$ Ha supported
Plain Apalachee versus plain colono-ware:	$X^2 = 10.61$ $df = 3$ $p < .02$ Ha supported
Plain Apalachee versus Mission Red Filmed:	$X^2 = 17.34$ $df = 3$ $p < .001$ Ha supported
Complicated stamped versus mission period incised:	$X^2 = 2.05$ $df = 3$ $p < .70$ Ho cannot be rejected
Complicated stamped versus plain colono-ware:	$X^2 = 5.28$ $df = 3$ $p < .20$ Ho cannot be rejected
Complicated stamped versus Mission Red Filmed:	$X^2 = 7.40$ $df = 3$ $p < .10$ Ha supported
Mission period incised versus plain colono-ware:	$X^2 = 1.12$ $df = 3$ $p < .80$ Ho cannot be rejected
Mission period incised versus Mission Red Filmed:	$X^2 = 0.31$ $df = 2$ $p < .99$ Ho cannot be rejected
Plain colono-ware versus Mission Red Filmed:	$X^2 = 1.34$ $df = 3$ $p < .80$ Ho cannot be rejected

In Reference to Table 16.5: Variability in Vessel Wall Thickness

Evaluation of statistical significance between pottery type and mean vessel wall thickness.

Ho = types do not differ significantly in mean vessel wall thickness
Ha = traditional Apalachee types have greater mean thickness than colono-ware types

(*continued*)

Plain Apalachee versus complicated stamped:	$t = 0.43\ df = 18\ p < .70$ *Ho* cannot be rejected
Plain Apalachee versus mission period incised:	$t = 1.98\ df = 17\ p < .10$ *Ha* supported
Plain Apalachee versus plain colono-ware:	$t = 1.94\ df = 30\ p < .10$ *Ha* supported
Plain Apalachee versus Mission Red Filmed:	$t = 3.25\ df = 31\ p < .01$ *Ha* supported
Complicated stamped versus mission period incised:	$t = 1.61\ df = 17\ p < .15$ *Ho* cannot be rejected
Complicated stamped versus plain colono-ware:	$t = 1.58\ df = 30\ p < .15$ *Ho* cannot be rejected
Complicated stamped versus Mission Red Filmed:	$t = 2.88\ df = 31\ p < .01$ *Ha* supported
Mission period incised versus plain colono-ware:	$t = 0.19\ df = 29\ p < .90$ *Ho* cannot be rejected
Mission period incised versus Mission Red Filmed:	$t = 1.32\ df = 30\ p < .20$ *Ho* cannot be rejected
Plain colono-ware versus Mission Red Filmed:	$t = 1.30\ df = 43\ p < .20$ *Ho* cannot be rejected

In Reference to Table 16.6: Variability in Core Color/Coring and Surface Color

Evaluation of statistical significance between pottery type and original color.

Ho = types do not differ significantly in color
Ha = types do differ significantly in color

Core Color/Degree of Coring

Plain Apalachee versus complicated stamped:	$X^2 = 2.875\ df = 4\ p < .70$ *Ho* cannot be rejected
Plain Apalachee versus mission period incised:	$X^2 = 4.2369\ df = 3\ p < .30$ *Ho* cannot be rejected
Plain Apalachee versus plain colono-ware:	$X^2 = 4.0458\ df = 3\ p < .30$ *Ho* cannot be rejected
Plain Apalachee versus Mission Red Filmed:	$X^2 = 0.7605\ df = 4\ p < .95$ *Ho* cannot be rejected
Complicated stamped versus mission period incised:	$X^2 = 0.8444\ df = 4\ p < .95$ *Ho* cannot be rejected
Complicated stamped versus plain colono-ware:	$X^2 = 1.9024\ df = 4\ p < .80$ *Ho* cannot be rejected
Complicated stamped versus Mission Red Filmed:	$X^2 = 2.2886\ df = 4\ p < .90$ *Ho* cannot be rejected
Mission period incised versus plain colono-ware:	$X^2 = 0.7527\ df = 3\ p < .90$ *Ho* cannot be rejected
Mission period incised versus Mission Red Filmed:	$X^2 = 2.1174\ df = 4\ p < .80$ *Ho* cannot be rejected

Plain colono-ware versus Mission Red Filmed: $X^2 = 2.6111$ $df = 4$ $p < .70$ *Ho* cannot be rejected

Exterior Surface Color

Plain Apalachee versus complicated stamped: $X^2 = 1.1$ $df = 3$ $p < .80$ *Ho* cannot be rejected

Plain Apalachee versus mission period incised: $X^2 = 1.8238$ $df = 3$ $p < .70$ *Ho* cannot be rejected

Plain Apalachee versus plain colono-ware: $X^2 = 1.0785$ $df = 3$ $p < .80$ *Ho* cannot be rejected

Plain Apalachee versus Mission Red Filmed: $X^2 = 6.3779$ $df = 3$ $p < .10$ *Ha* supported

Complicated stamped versus mission period incised: $X^2 = 0.4149$ $df = 2$ $p < .90$ *Ho* cannot be rejected

Complicated stamped versus plain colono-ware: $X^2 = 0.1731$ $df = 3$ $p < .99$ *Ho* cannot be rejected

Complicated stamped versus Mission Red Filmed: $X^2 = 6.7557$ $df = 3$ $p < .10$ *Ha* supported

Mission period incised versus plain colono-ware: $X^2 = 0.5888$ $df = 3$ $p < .90$ *Ho* cannot be rejected

Mission period incised versus Mission Red Filmed: $X^2 = 4.3885$ $df = 3$ $p < .30$ *Ho* cannot be rejected

Plain colono-ware versus Mission Red Filmed: $X^2 = 15.571$ $df = 3$ $p < .01$ *Ha* supported

Interior Surface Color

Plain Apalachee versus complicated stamped: $X^2 = 4.3944$ $df = 3$ $p < .30$ *Ho* cannot be rejected

Plain Apalachee versus mission period incised: $X^2 = 3.4987$ $df = 3$ $p < .30$ *Ho* cannot be rejected

Plain Apalachee versus plain colono-ware: $X^2 = 7.5443$ $df = 3$ $p < .10$ *Ha* supported

Plain Apalachee versus Mission Red Filmed: $X^2 = 0.2197$ $df = 3$ $p < .98$ *Ho* cannot be rejected

Complicated stamped versus mission period incised: $X^2 = 0.4090$ $df = 3$ $p < .95$ *Ho* cannot be rejected

Complicated stamped versus plain colono-ware: $X^2 = 0.7874$ $df = 3$ $p < .90$ *Ho* cannot be rejected

Complicated stamped versus Mission Red Filmed: $X^2 = 7.0521$ $df = 3$ $p < .10$ *Ha* supported

Mission period incised versus plain colono-ware: $X^2 = 0.0472$ $df = 2$ $p < .98$ *Ho* cannot be rejected

Mission period incised versus Mission Red Filmed: $X^2 = 6.4172$ $df = 3$ $p < .10$ *Ha* supported

Plain colono-ware versus Mission Red Filmed: $X^2 = 14.762$ $df = 3$ $p < .01$ *Ha* supported

Bibliography

Bullen, Ripley P.
1971 The Sarasota Mound, Englewood, Florida. *The Florida Anthropologist* 24:1–30.

Deagan, Kathleen A.
1990 Sixteenth-Century Spanish-American Colonization in the Southeastern United States and Caribbean. In *Columbian Consequences*. Vol. 2: *Archaeological and Historical Perspectives on the Spanish Borderlands East*, edited by David Hurst Thomas, 225–250. Washington, D.C.: Smithsonian Institution Press.

Griffin, John W.
1951 Excavations at the Site of San Luis. In *Here They Once Stood: The Tragic End of the Apalachee Missions*, by Mark F. Boyd, Hale G. Smith, and John W. Griffin, 137–160. Gainesville: University of Florida Press.

King, Julia
1981 An Archaeological Investigation of Seventeenth-Century St. Augustine, Florida. Master's thesis, Department of Anthropology, Florida State University, Tallahassee.

Kubler, George
1940 *The Religious Architecture of New Mexico in the Colonial Period and since the American Occupation*. Colorado Springs: Taylor Museum.

McEwan, Bonnie G.
1991 San Luis de Talimali: The Archaeology of Spanish-Indian Relations at a Florida Mission. *Historical Archaeology* 25(3):36–60.

Poe, Charles B.
1989 Preliminary Investigations of Fort San Luis. Paper presented at the 46th Annual Meeting of the Southeastern Archaeological Conference, Tampa, Florida.

1991 Moat Investigations at San Luis. Project report on file, San Luis Archaeological and Historic Site, Tallahassee.

Ray, Alice A.
1982 *Statistical Analysis System User's Guide: Statistics*. Cary, N.C.: SAS Institute.

Rice, Prudence M.
1987 *Pottery Analysis: A Sourcebook*. Chicago: University of Chicago Press.

Shapiro, Gary, and Bonnie G. McEwan
1992 *Archaeology at San Luis: The Apalachee Council House*. Florida Archae-

ology no. 6, pt. 1. Tallahassee: Florida Bureau of Archaeological Research.

Shapiro, Gary, and Richard Vernon
1992   *Archaeology at San Luis: The Church Complex.* Florida Archaeology no. 6, pt. 2. Tallahassee: Florida Bureau of Archaeological Research.

Smith, Hale G.
1951   Leon-Jefferson Ceramic Types. In *Here They Once Stood: The Tragic End of the Apalachee Missions*, by Mark F. Boyd, Hale G. Smith, and John W. Griffin, 163–174. Gainesville: University of Florida Press.

Thomas, David Hurst
1976   *Figuring Anthropology.* New York: Holt, Rinehart and Winston.

Vernon, Richard
1988   Seventeenth-Century Apalachee Colono-ware as a Reflection of Demography, Economics, and Acculturation. *Historical Archaeology* 22(1):76–82.

Vernon, Richard, and Bonnie G. McEwan
1990   *Investigations in the Church Complex and Spanish Village at San Luis.* Florida Archaeological Reports, no. 18. Tallahassee: Florida Bureau of Archaeological Research.

CONTRIBUTORS

❂

Ann S. Cordell, Florida Museum of Natural History, University of Florida, Gainesville, FL 32611

Kathleen Deagan, Florida Museum of Natural History, University of Florida, Gainesville, FL 32611

John H. Hann, Florida Bureau of Archaeological Research, San Luis Archaeological and Historic Site, 2020 Mission Road, Tallahassee, FL 32304

Kathleen Hoffman, Florida Museum of Natural History, University of Florida, Gainesville, FL 32611

Lisa M. Hoshower, Florida Museum of Natural History, University of Florida, Gainesville, FL 32611

Kenneth W. Johnson, Southeastern Archaeological Center, National Park Service, P.O. Box 2416, Tallahassee, FL 32316

Clark Spencer Larsen, Anthropology Research Laboratories and Department of Anthropology, University of North Carolina, Chapel Hill, NC 27599-3115

L. Jill Loucks (deceased), Department of Anthropology, Appalachian State University, Boone, NC 28608

Bonnie G. McEwan, Florida Bureau of Archaeological Research, San Luis Archaeological and Historic Site, 2020 Mission Road, Tallahassee, FL 32304

Rochelle A. Marrinan, Department of Anthropology, Florida State University, Tallahassee, FL 32306

Jerald T. Milanich, Florida Museum of Natural History, University of Florida, Gainesville, FL 32611

Jeffrey M. Mitchem, Arkansas Archaeological Survey, Parkin Archaeological State Park, P.O. Box 241, Parkin, AR 72373

Elizabeth J. Reitz, Museum of Natural History, University of Georgia, Athens, GA 30602

Rebecca Saunders, Museum of Natural Science, Louisiana State University, Baton Rouge, LA 70803-3216

C. Margaret Scarry, Department of Anthropology, University of Kentucky, Lexington, KY 40506–0010

David Hurst Thomas, American Museum of Natural History, Central Park West at 79th Street, New York, NY 10024–5192

Richard Vernon, Southeastern Archaeological Center, National Park Service, P.O. Box 2416, Tallahassee, FL 32316

Brent R. Weisman, Florida Bureau of Archaeological Research, CARL Archaeological Survey, 714 N.E. 7th Avenue, Gainesville, FL 32601

INDEX

❂

Page numbers in italics refer to figures.

Abbott tract, test project at, 101
Acorns (*Quercus* sp.), 120; at Fig Springs
    site, 168, 181, 184; at High Ridge site,
    361; at Lake Jackson site, 361; at San
    Luis de Talimali, 313, 364, 365, 368; at
    Velda site, 362
Africans (slaves), in mission-period
    Florida, 65, 78
Aglet (lacing tip), 79
Agriculture: and health, 233–34, 338,
    346; production for St. Augustine, 358–
    59, 360, 378, 391–92; and site
    destruction, 246. *See also* Diet and
    nutrition; Maize (*Zea mays*)
Agua Dulce province. *See* Freshwater
    Timucua Indians
Ais Indians: of Florida, 111, 116, 118–19,
    120, 132, 133; missions among, 118,
    125, 126; of Texas, 89
Ajamano (*visita*), 248
Alachua Cob Marked pottery, 171
Alachua tradition pottery, 143, 162, 171,
    186, 200, 206–7
"Alachua type" pottery, 202
Alafaya Indians, 131, 132
Alligators, 385, 392
Alta California. *See* California
Altamaha pottery, 77, 95, 98, 100
Altamaha–San Marcos pottery, 95–96, 98
Altamirano, Bishop Juan de las Cabezas
    de, 122
Altars. *See* Sanctuaries and altars
Amacapira Indians, 131, 132
Amelia Island: archaeological
    investigations on, 35; archaeological
    survey of, 37–38; Indian inhabitants of,

36, 57. *See also* Santa Catalina de
    Amelia; Santa María de Yamassee
Anacabile (or Anacabili) (village), 117,
    119
Anhaica (town), 358
Antonico (Agua Dulce Indian chief), 117
Antonico (village), 117, 119, 120
Aotina (Agua Dulce Indian chief), 116
Apalachee Hill site (8LE148), 364, 380
Apalachee Indians: agriculture among,
    357–75; cattle herds belonging to, 90;
    chunkey playing by, 22–23; as laborers
    (*repartimiento* system), 92, 359–60;
    land rights of, 90; mission jurisdiction
    over, 65; pottery of, 91, 100, 418–41;
    at St. Augustine, 78, 94, 98; settlement
    pattern of, 42, 44, 379; trade with, 91
Apalo *visita*/mission, 196
Apios tuberosa, 120
Archaeobotanical remains. *See*
    Paleobotanical remains
Architecture, aboriginal: at Fort King
    George site, 23; of Guale Indians, 23–
    24, 38, 40, 44; at Harrison Homestead
    site, 44; at Patale mission site, 255–59;
    at Santa Catalina de Amelia, 38, 40. *See
    also* Council houses (*buhío*)
Architecture, domestic (Spanish): "mud
    sleeper" construction of, 299; in St.
    Augustine, 81, 299, 314; at San Luis de
    Talimali site, 299–304, 314; at Santa Fé
    site, 145, 156–58, 160–61
Architecture, religious (Spanish): at
    Baptizing Spring site, 152, 202; at
    Convento de San Francisco, 67–74, 80–
    82; coquina construction in, 66, 73, 74,

Mexico—*continued*
  beads from, 402; missionary strategies
    in, 89; population and church size in,
    57
Milanich, Jerald T., 114, 283, 284, 326,
    331
Mill Pond site (8CO43), 188
Mirrors, 13
Mission model, predictive, 244–45, 246,
    276–83
Mission Red Filmed pottery, 418, 424,
    426, 428–29, 431, 433
Mission wares. *See* Pottery, aboriginal:
    colono-wares
Mitchem, Jeffrey M., 269, 404, 406
Mocama Indians, 81, 118, 132, 133
Mocoya (or Macoya). *See* Mayaca (1560s
    Indian chief)
Molona (village), 117
Monasteries. *See* Friaries (*convento*)
Montes, Blas de, 119
Moore, C. B., 26
Moore, Col. James, 37, 65, 73, 80, 93,
    142, 378
Moral, Alonso, 343
Mortuary patterns. *See* Cemeteries (*campo
    santo*); Churches, burials in
Mount Royal. *See* Enacape (later Anacape)
    (village)
Mud turtles, 184
Mullet (*Mugil* spp.), 385
Muskhogean Indians, 412
Myakka, 112. *See also* Mayaca Indians

Native Americans: color symbolism of,
    412; and European diseases, 94, 131,
    133, 141–42, 217, 227, 235, 337, 339,
    340–41, 347, 377; and frontier
    economies, 90–92, 345; influence on
    missionaries, 88–90, 102–3; influence
    on Spanish occupation of St. Augustine,
    94–103; as laborers, 65, 78, 91–92, 93,
    342–45, 359–60, 369; land rights of,
    89–90; and mission food preparation,
    76, 81, 101–2, 369, 422; political
    organization of, 88, 89–90; sex roles of,
    92; shovel-shaped incisors of, 154; and
    tribute system, 77–78, 92, 120. *See also
    names of individual tribes*
Native revitalization movements, 142
Nelumbo lutea, 120
New Mexico: church size in, 267;
    missions in, 245, 266, 277, 282–83
New Smyrna, 114
New Spain: church size in, 267;

jurisdiction of, 63; majolica production
    in, 77; mission plans in, 245
Nocoroco (village), 120, 121
Nombre de Dios Chiquito mission, 93
Nombre de Dios mission (St. Augustine),
    37, 92, 93, 101, 330–31, 388
Nombre de Dios mission at Macaris, 93
North St. Augustine, 101
Nutrition. *See* Diet and nutrition;
    Subsistence strategies
Nyaautina (village), 117

Ocmulgee Fields Incised pottery, 202
Ocmulgee Fields pottery, 77, 202
Olata Ouae Outina (Agua Dulce Indian
    chief), 117
Oldtown site, 37
Opal phytolith studies, 25, 26
Opossum (*Didelphis virginiana*), 184, 381,
    392
Oré, Luís Gerónimo de, 122, 141, 331
Orista (town), 22
Orista Indians, 95
Ornaments. *See* Beads, glass; Clothing;
    Jewelry; Medals and medallions,
    religious
Ossuaries, 52, 326–38. *See also*
    Cemeteries (*campo santo*)
Osteoarthritis, 229, 230, 231, 343–44
Ouae Outina's village, 115
Outina (Agua Dulce Indian chief), 115,
    120
Outina (or Agua Dulce Aotina) (village),
    117, 120, 121
Outina (or Utina) Indians, 170
Oviedo y Valdés, Gonzalo Fernández de,
    335

Paleobotanical remains: at Baptizing
    Spring site, 206, 208; at Fig Springs
    site, 168, 181, 184; at High Ridge site,
    361; and indigenous food use, 360–70;
    at Lake Jackson site, 361; from St.
    Augustine, 90; at San Luis de Talimali,
    313, 314–15, 363–65, 368, 369–70; at
    Santa Catalina de Guale, 12, 21; at
    Velda site, 362
Palisade lines: at Patale mission site, 259,
    265; at Santa Catalina de Amelia, 40,
    49, 51, 53
Palmore site (8AL189), 162
Parejo, Francisco, 118
Patale mission. *See* San Pedro y San Pablo
    de Patale site (8LE152)
Patica (Agua Dulce village), 117

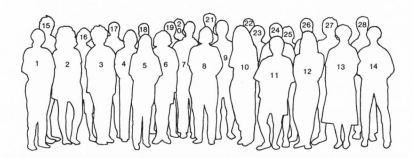

An informal gathering of mission researchers at the home of John and Pat Griffin, St. Augustine, May 1989. Photo courtesy of John W. Griffin.

1. Vicki Rolland. 2. Susan Parker. 3. Mary Herron. 4. Rochelle Marrinan. 5. Bonnie McEwan. 6. Kathy Deagan. 7. Jerry Milanich. 8. Kate Hoffman. 9. Dave Thomas. 10. Becky Saunders. 11. Margie Scarry. 12. Jane Landers. 13. Valerie Bell. 14. Pat Griffin. 15. John Griffin. 16. Dottie Lyon. 17. John Hann. 18. Steve Bryne. 19. Jeff Mitchem. 20. Gene Lyon. 21. Charlie Ewen. 22. Brent Weisman. 23. Donna Ruhl. 24. John Scarry. 25. Chris Newman. 26. Bruce Piatek. 27. Stan Bond. 28. Ken Johnson.